In the Shadow of Selma

In the Shadow of Selma

The Continuing Struggle for
Civil Rights in the Rural South

Cynthia Griggs Fleming

ROWMAN & LITTLEFIELD PUBLISHERS, INC.
Lanham • Boulder • New York • Toronto • Oxford

ROWMAN & LITTLEFIELD PUBLISHERS, INC.

Published in the United States of America
by Rowman & Littlefield Publishers, Inc.
A wholly owned subsidiary of The Rowman & Littlefield Publishing Group, Inc.
4501 Forbes Boulevard, Suite 200, Lanham, Maryland 20706
www.rowmanlittlefield.com

PO Box 317
Oxford
OX2 9RU, UK

British Library Cataloguing in Publication Information Available

Library of Congress Cataloging-in-Publication Data

Fleming, Cynthia Griggs, 1949-
    In the shadow of Selma : the continuing struggle for civil rights in
the rural South / Cynthia Griggs Fleming.
        p. cm.
    ISBN 0-7425-0810-2 (alk. paper) — ISBN 0-7425-0811-0 (pbk. : alk.
paper)
    1. African Americans—Civil rights—Alabama—Selma—History—20th
century. 2. Civil rights movements—Alabama—Selma—History—20th
century. 3. African Americans—Suffrage—Alabama—Selma—History—20th
century. 4. Selma (Ala.)—Race relations. 5. African Americans—Civil
rights—Alabama—Wilcox County—History—20th century. 6. Segregation
in education—Alabama—Wilcox County—History—20th century. 7. Wilcox
County (Ala.)—Race relations. 8. African Americans—Civil
Rights—Southern States. 9. Southern States—Race relations. 10.
Southern States—Rural conditions. I. Title.
    F334.S4F58 2004
    323.1'196073076145—dc22   2003020418

Printed in the United States of America

♾™ The paper used in this publication meets the minimum requirements of American
National Standard for Information Sciences—Permanence of Paper for Printed Library
Materials, ANSI/NISO Z39.48-1992.

To my grandparents Mamie and William Green Wilson,
my uncle William Garrette Wilson,
and to Paul Washington

Contents

Preface: The Forgotten Rural Black Poor ix

Acknowledgments xi

Introduction: You'll Git Dar after While xiii

Chapter 1 Disfranchisement, Despair, and Disillusionment 1

Chapter 2 Onward Christian Soldiers: The Coming of the
Missionaries during the Early Years, 1883–1930 35

Chapter 3 New Negroes in the Cotton Field:
The Great Depression and Gee's Bend 67

Chapter 4 Making the World Safe for Democracy?
What about Wilcox County? 99

Chapter 5 Vote 135

Chapter 6 Ain't Gonna Study War No More: The Struggle to
Desegregate Wilcox County's Schools 187

Chapter 7 After the Movement 235

Chapter 8 The More Things Change, the More They Stay
the Same 283

Notes	315
Index	337
About the Author	349

Preface
The Forgotten Rural Black Poor

In the new millennium the national debate on race continues. Most recently, President George W. Bush's trip to Ile de Goree, a slave trading fort on the west coast of Africa, has served to focus our attention on the African slave trade. Bush has referred to the trade as "one of the greatest crimes in history."[1] The president's advance team carefully constructed the podium from which he was to speak so that the slave trading fort on Goree Island was clearly visible in the background. At the same time, Bush's team made sure that the podium cleverly concealed an air conditioner so that the president would be comfortable while he addressed the crowd of dignitaries gathered in the shadow of the fort in the withering African heat.[2]

Meanwhile, back in the United States, the destination of so many of those kidnapped Africans who passed through the fort on Goree Island, descendants of the victims of the trade are still waiting for public officials to address their plight in this country in a meaningful way. There is a debate on race in this country, but it is sharp, emotional, and, some would argue, ineffective. That debate seems to recognize several categories of African Americans. First, there are the superachievers. This group includes a wide variety of individuals who are as different as night and day—from Colin Powell to Michael Jordan, and from Oprah Winfrey to Snoop Dogg (they both have their own television show). These are the African Americans who have "made it." After all, they have wealth and fame. Then there is the group of African Americans who are the hardworking middle class. They are black folks striving for the American dream: the chance to own their own home, a good education for their children, and financial security. Finally, there is the image of the ghetto youth who epitomize the black underclass. This image, which has been popularized by rap videos, is characterized by young African American men strutting around in sagging pants, heavy gold chains hanging around their necks, and flashing "gold grilles" in their mouths whenever they smile. Of course, no image of the black ghetto underclass would be complete without their "hoopties": big, old domestic cars with twenty-four-inch wheels and loud stereos blasting rap music. These are the most popular images of the descendants of Africa in America.

However, there is another important category of African Americans who are missing from the national debate. They are the huge black rural population, actually a living link to the victims of the slave trade who passed through Ile de Goree and countless other slave trading forts along the West African coastline. Indeed, in some of the most isolated rural areas, these African Americans can trace their ancestry in an unbroken line all the way back to the institution of slavery. They do not have to speculate about the impact of slavery on black life in this country: it is part of their experience every day of their lives. Ironically, back during the era of the civil rights campaigns of the 1960s, many of these people were on the front lines in some of the most historic campaigns of the movement, especially those in the Deep South. These campaigns were instrumental in helping to persuade Congress to pass laws that have changed our society in some fundamental ways. But, after the civil rights workers went home and the federal government withdrew its observers and negotiators, many of these black rural dwellers were once again at the mercy of those who had oppressed them for generations, and in such an atmosphere they were unable to reap the rewards of their activism.

And so now, in the new millennium, despite their historic importance, these black rural dwellers have continued to be ignored in the national debate on race. Until their experience is included, that national debate will be incomplete. A graphic example of the plight of black southern rural dwellers is offered by the example of Wilcox County, Alabama. Wilcox is an extremely isolated and underdeveloped county that is part of the Alabama Black Belt. The experience of the county's residents will add a unique perspective to the national debate on race, if only the rest of the country will pay attention.

~

Acknowledgments

As I worked on this project, there were many people who helped me a great deal. Many of those who helped me immeasurably are the people in Wilcox County who are the real heroes and heroines of this story. In particular, Gwendolyn Bonham was exceedingly generous with her time as she took me around the county and introduced me to many of the people who were kind enough to share their stories. Others who were particularly helpful were Sheryl Threadgill, Reverend Lonnie Brown, Monroe Pettway and his family, and Ralph Ervin Sr., who allowed me to use some of his historic photographs in this book. In addition, the many people who were patient and kind and allowed me to interview them deserve my special thanks, but unfortunately they are too numerous to mention here by name. It is also important for me to mention that Albert Gordon was the first person to tell me that I ought to research the civil rights movement in Wilcox County. I was working on another project at the time, and I was too busy to follow up on his suggestion until later. Unfortunately, by the time I came back to Wilcox County, Gordon had become ill, and I was unable to interview him. But, I owe him my special thanks for giving me the idea.

Here at the University of Tennessee, there are a number of people who also deserve my special thanks. Anne Galloway in the African American Studies Program was particularly helpful in answering my computer questions and solving my computer problems—and there were many. Le'Trice Donaldson, my student research assistant, cheerfully tracked down statistical data, as well as other information I needed. Dr. Nina Elliott, Associate Provost for

Faculty and Student Diversity, and her staff were particularly supportive, especially Sharonne Winston. The library staff also went out of their way for me. In particular, I could always depend on Felicia Felder-Hoehne to find the information I needed—cheerfully and expeditiously. Margaret Casado was also a big help.

At Rowman & Littlefield I would like to thank Assistant Editor Laura Roberts. I would also like to thank Mary Carpenter and Steve Wrinn. While neither of them is at Rowman & Littlefield anymore, each of them provided support and guidance for this project.

Finally, I would like to give special thanks to Charles Thompson, who generously gave of his time and traveled around Wilcox County taking many of the photographs that appear in this book.

~

Introduction
You'll Git Dar after While

Keep on strugglin' when de water gits deep,
Keep on wokin' when you wanter go to sleep
Keep on gwine if you have to creep,
An' you'll git dar after while.

Keep on sowin' by de water side,
Keep on tryin' de things you've tried,
Keep on walkin' bym by youc'n ride,
An you'll git dar after while.

Keep on laughin' when de folks all frown,
Keep on risin' when dey think you's down,
Keep on movin' while de worl' goes roun',
An you'll git dar after while.

Keep on caryin' all yo' troubles to de Lo'd,
Keep on trustin' in de promises of God
Keep on hopin' though you's under de rod,
An' you'll git dar after while.

Keep on marchin' though you don't understan',
Keep on feelin' for de good Lod's han',
Keep on makin for de Promised Lan',
An you'll git dar after while.

These words were written by my grandfather, Reverend William Green Wilson, in 1931. They speak volumes about the ability of the slaves and their descendants in the Alabama Black Belt to continue to hope for a better life. Reverend Wilson was a Presbyterian minister and principal of Camden Academy, a black Presbyterian boarding school in Wilcox County, Alabama, right in the heart of the Black Belt. His daughter, my mother, used to read this and other poems that he wrote in that quaint Negro dialect to my sister and me when we were children. That distinct and magical dialect filled our heads with vivid images of gnarled black hands and weary black faces shaded by the broad brims of straw hats. We did not realize it at the time, but the inspirational message in "You'll Git Dar after While" could have applied to later generations of black Wilcox County residents who would wage a protracted and dangerous struggle in the last half of the twentieth century against the forces of racist oppression that had held them in virtual servitude since the end of the Civil War. Yet, my mother's fond descriptions of her childhood gave us no hint of the sinister forces at work in that county.

Instead, her childhood memories are filled with pleasant gatherings on the Camden Academy campus, the smiling faces of many of her classmates who went on to excel in a variety of pursuits, and a rich family life that made her feel warm and secure. The principal's house on the Camden Academy campus where the Wilson family lived had many large, airy rooms, lots of windows, and high ceilings. A large porch, complete with a swing, graced the front of the house, and it was shaded by a giant chinaberry tree. There were lots of pecan trees too, and my mother and her older brother sometimes made themselves sick by eating too many of the juicy nuts that had ripened in the warm Alabama sunshine. Reverend Wilson was one of the few people, black or white, who had a car in Camden, Alabama, in the early twentieth century. My mother can still remember how the family would often pile into the shiny black Ajax on Saturday morning, and her father would proudly drive the thirty-eight miles to Selma, the nearest sizable town, where they would do their weekly shopping. With the exception of these trips to Selma, the Wilson children rarely left the campus. Their parents insisted that they stay out of the town of Camden and surrounding Wilcox County because they were painfully aware of the many dangers lurking just outside the safe haven of Camden Academy that could damage the spirit or even steal the life of young black children. Indeed, by the 1920s and 1930s when my mother and her brother were growing up, black residents of Wilcox County had been subjected to decades of ruthless oppression. County residents regularly saw hooded Klansmen, burning crosses, and mutilated black bodies. Such horrific sights helped to create an atmosphere of terror that was designed to crush black hopes for change. Ironically, in later years one of the most publicized phases of the civil rights movement, the Selma to Montgomery march, would occur right next door.

The Selma campaign attracted the nation's attention in a very dramatic way on March 7, 1965. That evening the ABC television network interrupted its broadcast of an intense drama depicting the trial of Nazi war criminals, *Judgment at Nuremburg*. The images that replaced Spencer Tracy and Burt Lancaster reenacting the somber Nazi trials held Americans transfixed with horror: stark black-and-white images of fleeing black demonstrators being clubbed by Alabama law officers mounted on horseback were so horrible that they were almost surreal. Clouds of tear gas hung in the air as people gagged, gasped, and fell to the ground. The flickering images of television clearly captured the fear in their faces. The scene was the Edmund Pettus Bridge in Selma, Alabama. The occasion was the beginning of a march from Selma to the state capitol in Montgomery that had been organized by Dr. Martin Luther King's Southern Christian Leadership Conference (SCLC). Organizers had hoped that such a march would publicize the refusal of local officials to allow black residents to register to vote. In time, it became clear that the organizers' instincts were correct. As a result of these dramatic events in Selma, President Lyndon Johnson went on national television that night and gave an impassioned speech to the nation denouncing the brutality and proclaiming, "We shall overcome."

In fact, President Johnson clearly took a hard line and intended to make a point with his handling of the Selma situation. Faced with a determined governor, George Wallace, who refused to cooperate, Johnson federalized 1,900 men of the Alabama National Guard's Dixie Division and authorized the use of 2,000 more regular army troops, 100 FBI agents, and 100 U.S. marshals to protect the marchers. The press in Selma dutifully recorded the beginning of this remarkable march that would eventually succeed in getting to Montgomery. All this press coverage fanned the excitement to a dramatic crescendo. Consequently, by the last night of the march when participants entered Montgomery, it had become a major media event. Everybody who was anybody, from civil rights leaders to Hollywood film stars, was there. Not since the March on Washington had a civil rights march grabbed the nation's attention as this one did. As the jubilant throng reached the steps of the state capitol, Dr. King's eloquent and musical voice addressed the crowd: "Segregation in Alabama is on its deathbed. . . . Confrontation of good and evil compressed in the tiny community of Selma generated the massive power to turn the whole nation to a new course." King's pronouncement combined with all the press coverage to assure Selma's place in the national consciousness and the nation's history books.

However, the dramatic, provocative, and star-studded images recorded by the press that night have forced the quiet and resolute actions of scores of rural black Alabama residents who laid the groundwork for the march into the background. In fact, the voter registration drive in Selma was only part of a much larger voter registration project that targeted several surrounding Black Belt counties. One of those counties is Wilcox County. Although Camden, the Wilcox County seat and the site of my grandfather's school, is only thirty-eight miles from Selma, in terms of press coverage it is light-years away. Equally dramatic and important events that contributed to the success of Selma's voting rights drive occurred in Camden and Wilcox County, but the press was not there to record these developments. In later years scholars writing about the Alabama voting rights campaign have continued to ignore events in Wilcox County. Ironically, there was a much meaner and more repressive atmosphere for black residents in Wilcox and its county seat of Camden than in Selma and Dallas County right next door.

In 1965 when the voter registration drive occurred, the black population of Wilcox County was an incredible 80 percent of the county's total population. Yet, there was not a single registered black voter in the whole county. Moreover, it was one of only two counties in the whole state with no registered black voters. (By contrast, Dallas County was only 57.7 percent black, and it did have a few registered black voters in early 1965 even before the voter registration campaign started.) Wilcox was also one of the poorest counties in the state. It ranked third among the poorest counties in Alabama, and it was number twenty among the poorest counties in the whole country. The average per capita income of black Wilcox County residents on the eve of the voter registration campaign was only $350; the national per capita income was $2,200 at that time. Indeed, one of the most dramatic indicators of black poverty and oppression in the county was the existence of a very large plantation at Miller's Ferry, where six hundred black families worked the land as sharecroppers. These people were paid, when they were paid at all, with octagonal tin coins that could only be used at the plantation commissary. This practice was not discontinued until 1970.

At the same time, neither the state nor the county had taken much responsibility for the education of black Wilcox County residents. Instead, they had abdicated their responsibility to the Presbyterian Church that had been operating mission schools for black Wilcox children since the late nineteenth century. In fact, it was not until 1955 that a black student in Wilcox County finally graduated from a public high school: previously, all the high schools for black residents were church-supported. Furthermore, as late as 1965, more than half of all black students in the county were attending schools owned and maintained by the National Missions Board of the Presbyterian Church.

One of the few bright spots in this dismal picture was Gee's Bend, an all-black community that existed at one end of the county. Most Gee's Bend residents could trace their roots all the way back to slavery, and even after freedom came, they continued to work the same land that their ancestors had worked for generations. By the time of the Great Depression, people in this community found themselves in desperate straits, and only one step away from starvation. At this point, the federal government, through the Farm Security Administration, stepped in and bought land in the area. Then, they extended low interest loans to local black tenants to help them buy the land and build new homes. Consequently, by the time of the civil rights struggles of the 1960s, the people of Gee's Bend lived in an all-black community that enjoyed at least a measure of independence from the county's repressive white power structure. Predictably, many Gee's Bend residents were quite active in local civil rights activities. In fact, there are many who charge that the enthusiastic support of some Bend residents for civil rights activities is the reason why the ferry service that these people had depended on for years was stopped. Gee's Bend is actually a peninsula that juts out into the Alabama River. By ferry, it is only minutes away from Camden. By road, however, it is almost ninety miles away. White county authorities cut off the ferry service when the civil rights demonstrations were at their height, thus limiting the access of Gee's Bend residents to Camden where the demonstrations were taking place. To this day, the ferry service has not been restored, and Gee's Bend residents remain largely isolated from the rest of the county on their peninsula.

When SCLC and the Student Nonviolent Coordinating Committee (SNCC) targeted Wilcox County along with Dallas and other surrounding counties for their voting rights drive in the early 1960s, many in Wilcox did the unthinkable: they volunteered to work with these outside agitators. They knew that their actions placed their livelihoods and their lives at risk, but they would not be dissuaded. They participated in the rallies, they demonstrated at the courthouse, their young people boycotted classes, they participated in the Selma to Montgomery march, and they paid dearly. They carried on their activities out of the glare of the national spotlight. There were no federal troops dispatched to their county to enforce the law and protect their rights. Rather, while the nation's attention was riveted on Selma and Dallas County right next door, Wilcox County's ardent segregationists were free to act. Indeed, they felt compelled to act: they were incensed by the federal government's interference in their state's affairs. They would show the federal government how they handled their *nigras* in Wilcox County, they reasoned. Of course, they also felt that they needed to make sure black residents knew that white people were still in charge.

Retaliation was swift and sure. Many who participated in the movement lost their jobs, sharecroppers were thrown off the land, scores of people were brutalized. Local white officials even went so far as to seize control of the Camden Academy campus from the Presbyterian Church. Camden Academy was the largest of the black Presbyterian schools in the county, and by this time it had been in operation for almost eighty years. However, the school had housed civil rights workers in its dormitories, and it had allowed its chapel to be used for civil rights rallies. As soon as the Wilcox County School Board took control of Camden Academy, its first action was to tear down the chapel. Shortly after this, the board authorized the demolition of the rest of the school's buildings, and Camden Academy ceased to exist. The press never recorded any of these events, and subsequent historians of the civil rights movement have ignored this part of the Alabama voting rights campaign as well.

Despite their best efforts to control things in their county, white Wilcox residents soon realized that they were powerless to stop the passage of the voting rights act, a measure designed to enfranchise their black neighbors. The passage of this act in August of 1965 was hailed by many as one of the major victories of the movement. Many Americans were even convinced that the passage of this act virtually eliminated the need for a civil rights movement. In Wilcox County, however, local segregationists saw the passage of the voting rights act not as the end of the movement, but as the beginning of the war. White defiance intensified exponentially in the years following the passage of this act as black residents pushed to elect black candidates to political office, and integrate the county's public schools. The county's white residents cried NEVER, and the courthouse in Camden became their sacred shrine as they used every legal and extralegal means at their disposal to maintain white supremacy in Wilcox County. However, black residents refused to back down. The result is a remarkable story that is punctuated by cowardice and courage, audacity and timidity, and fear and foolishness.

In the aftermath of the civil rights movement, we as a nation have moved into an era where there is increased dialogue about issues of racial, cultural, and ethnic diversity. Many want to believe that the movement fixed things, and they profess to believe that we are now moving toward a color-blind society. In Wilcox County, however, many residents, both black and white, tenaciously and openly express the view that their sharply divided black and white past is still a defining part of their present. To much of the rest of the country, Wilcox County seems almost like some exotic land that time forgot, a throwback to the years before the civil rights movement when the dialogue on race occupied a central place in the American psyche. Over the years, scholars, journalists, and government officials have been drawn to it. They have studied it, written about it, and experimented with it. Most recently, the CBS news magazine show *60 Minutes II* aired a segment on it. Yet, for all the attention it has received, the critical significance of the continued existence of a place like Wilcox County, Alabama, remains a mystery to most Americans. In fact, the significance of this southern, rural, impoverished, majority-black area is rooted in its isolation. It is both geographically and economically isolated from much of the rest of the South and the country, and it is that isolation that affords even the most casual observer an unobstructed view of the horrific consequences of more than two centuries of brutal racial oppression and economic exploitation on African Americans.

To this day, in this county of contrasts there are white residents who are direct descendants of slave holders living in relative ease alongside black residents living on welfare who are direct descendants of slaves. There are few places where such a direct connection can be made. Instead, all too often the analysis of the plight of African Americans becomes mired down in the ubiquitous imagery of broken black families, urban pathologies, and suspicions of welfare fraud. But in the isolated environment of Wilcox County we can view this damning connection between past sins and present problems with frightening clarity. It was the existence of this atmosphere of black powerlessness and economic deprivation brought on by the exploitation of two centuries that confronted the civil rights workers who entered Wilcox County in the early 1960s. Although those outside activists were determined to help black Wilcox residents become empowered, they quickly recognized that they would be battling the entrenched forces that had been circumscribing black existence in Wilcox County since the antebellum era. Thus, the stage was set for a gargantuan test of wills that would uncover long-simmering conflicts that had been brewing for generations.

In many ways, the struggle of black Wilcox residents during the civil rights movement and beyond to overcome the impact of more than two hundred years of racial and economic exploitation in a country and a world moving toward the global economy of the twenty-first century is a struggle that has been happening in black communities all over the country. The clear and unobstructed view of that struggle in Wilcox County affords us a unique opportunity to assess the complex intersection of race, gender, class, and economic issues from still another perspective in post–civil-rights-era America. This can be an invaluable tool as we seek to understand the nature of black–white relations in this country in the new millennium. However much some might insist that we have now achieved a color-blind society in the wake of the civil rights movement of the 1960s, the continued existence of places like Wilcox County, Alabama, clearly refute that assertion. As we grope toward a new relationship between the races in post–civil-rights-era America, we as a society can ill afford to let this uncomfortable reality remain in the shadow of Selma.

~

CHAPTER ONE

Disfranchisement, Despair, and Disillusionment

Wilcox—The Beginning

Early in the nineteenth century, the western frontier beckoned to many adventurous citizens in the young United States of America. Right after the War of 1812 settled things with Great Britain once and for all, or so Americans hoped, an act of Congress created the Alabama territory on March 3, 1817. Just a little over two years later, on December 14, 1819, Alabama was admitted to the Union.[1] Just before Alabama became a state, however, the territorial legislature passed an act that created Wilcox County on December 13, 1819. This new county consisted of land from the surrounding counties of Clarke, Monroe, and Dallas.[2]

Because its early white inhabitants brought large numbers of slaves with them when they first settled the area, the frontier state of Alabama soon came to be closely associated with the institution of slavery. Just one year after Alabama was granted statehood, the Compromise of 1820 was enacted. This compromise was designed to settle the question of the geographic boundaries of slavery once and for all by establishing the 36-30 line. All the territories south of this line were allowed to practice slavery. Because the white settlers in the new state of Alabama were quite comfortable with the idea of keeping African American slaves, they heartily approved this arrangement. By this time Alabama had a fairly large slave population, but it was not evenly distributed within the state's boundaries. Instead, Alabama slaves tended to be concentrated in the Black Belt counties to the south: Sumpter, Greene, Hale, Marengo, Dallas, Lowndes, Montgomery, Bullock, Perry, and Wilcox. The reason for this distinctive demographic characteristic was rooted in the unique soil and climate conditions of the Black Belt region that made that area particularly suitable for cotton production. Predictably, this region boasted many large plantations with hundreds of slaves toiling away in the hot Alabama sun, producing fluffy white wealth for their owners.

Indeed, the romantic myth of the Old South that has been popularized by countless novels and lavish Hollywood films was born in the Black Belt, and it is in this historical and mythical atmosphere that Wilcox County grew and flourished before the Civil War. In fact, Wilcox County had a reputation for being an "area of centralized wealth during the plantation days. . . . This county was noted for its spacious plantations and for its large slave population."[3] In 1862 the town of Camden became the Wilcox County seat. G. W. Dunn, a settler from Camden, South Carolina, was the first to build a house in the little frontier town in 1832. He donated twelve acres of land for the original town site, and he also donated a plot of land for the town's new cemetery. Ironically, Dunn was the cemetery's first occupant because he died a short time later.[4] Camden, Alabama, is a typical county seat in a rural southern county. In the years before the Civil War the town was dominated by a town square that marked its center. Grouped around the square was a scattering of the usual mercantile establishments, including a carriage factory and a sawmill. The town even boasted three hotels. The first of these, the Wilcox Hotel, was erected in 1848.[5] Outside of the business district, the town's residents could point with pride to the palatial homes of some of the county's leading citizens.

One of Camden's most visible symbols of pride was the Masonic Hall, a magnificent building with fluted columns that rested on a triangular plot of land near the center of town. It was the scene of many fancy balls in the years before the Civil War. On the evenings when the balls were held, high-stepping horses pulling shiny, elaborate carriages lined the street in front of the hall. The sweet strains of orchestra music drifted from inside the ballroom to mingle with the jingle of harness out in the street as the fancy, pure-bred carriage horses stamped their feet and tossed their well-groomed heads in impatience. Slave coachmen attired in fancy livery seemed to be everywhere at once assisting their passengers as they stepped down from their carriages, and calming the fractious horses. Clearly, antebellum Camden was dripping with southern culture, mystique, and charm. The rhythm of life was slow, relaxed, and refined—at least for some. In the years before the Civil War it seemed that life would go on like this forever.

The picture postcard town was surrounded by the natural beauty of Wilcox County. The Alabama River meandered through the county's landscape, tracing a serpentine pattern for over one hundred miles.[6] It periodically over-flowed its banks, further enriching the already fertile black earth. Stands of long- and shortleaf pine gracefully dotted the landscape, and they were joined by a dizzying variety of other trees including oak, hickory, ash, elm, poplar, cedar, cypress, cottonwood, sycamore, beech, and mulberry. In some places these stands of trees looked almost as if they were wearing beards because the high humidity encouraged the growth of Spanish moss that seemed to drip in wisps of gray from their branches. But the one variety of tree that clearly stood out from all the others was the magnificent magnolia. These trees seemed to grow everywhere. Their glossy deep green leaves and huge snow-white blossoms with a distinct cloying fragrance seemed then, as now, so distinctly southern. The county's trees were complemented by a large variety of colorful and fragrant wildflowers. This natural beauty provided a stunning backdrop for the acres of cleared fields, covered by neat rows of cotton plants with fluffy white balls on their tops, that seemed to go on for miles. They were tended by gangs of slaves toiling away in the hot Alabama sun. These men, women, and children scarcely had time to enjoy the natural beauty that was all around. On the contrary, Wilcox County's slaves were more often focused on the stiffness in their backs from bending over to tend those plants hour after hour and day after day. At harvest time their fingers were often raw from the sharp tips on the plants just beneath each fuzzy boll of cotton. Their sight was frequently blurred by the sweat in their eyes, and their senses were dulled by the cramps in their muscles and the aches in their empty bellies.

Every fall as harvest time drew to a close, the county's many hardwoods turned brilliant colors in the warm days and increasingly cool nights. Yet, underlying that brilliant fall landscape and that refreshing nip in the air was an almost palpable sense of decay. Clearly, leaves were falling off the trees, and plants were dying off as the winter months approached, but this natural and seasonal decay was accompanied by a nearly invisible but no less real decay of the human spirit. Wilcox County's slaves knew that they were viewed only as property, and as they worked to bring in the harvest year after year, they were painfully aware that all they could look forward to was another year of the same. Even though they were valuable property, Wilcox County's slaves were often forced to live in primitive conditions, at the same time as they were expected to perform backbreaking labor. Such treatment took a heavy toll. Their work was relentless and unremitting. All slaves, including women and children, were expected to perform the many tasks associated with keeping the plantation running smoothly: "Children began as quarter hands, advanced to half hands, to three-quarter hands, and finally when mature and able-bodied, healthy and strong, to full hands. Many women were rated as full hands."[7] The slaves had little time for anything other than work. The work schedule imposed by prominent Wilcox planter James A. Tait provides a case in point. Tait reported, "They [the slaves] rise at daybreak, eat and start to work half hour by sun; [and] work all day."[8] Tait's demands were hardly exceptional.

Not surprisingly, the slaves' health suffered. Of course, labor took its toll, but this was further exacerbated by an inadequate diet and insufficient shelter. Wilcox County slaves suffered from a variety of illnesses including dysentery, flu, cholera, pleurisy, and pneumonia.[9] Problems with slave health often proved costly to Wilcox planters like James Tait, who lamented, "For the first twenty or twenty-five years my plantations were very sickly and I lost a great many Negroes. I think I have lost about as many Negroes as I now have, say about three hundred."[10] Chief among the health problems suffered by Tait's slaves were pneumonia and "the fever." Clearly, Wilcox County's slaves were trapped in an endless cycle of backbreaking labor that was exacerbated by poor health.

This condition was further complicated by the constant threat of vicious and painful punishment. Whipping was the most common form of punishment. Yet, masters had to be careful about whipping a slave too severely because each slave represented a valuable financial asset that could be damaged by punishment that was too harsh. At the same time, however, masters knew that they had to punish their slaves severely enough to keep them under control. White Wilcox residents were painfully aware of how badly outnumbered they were, and this engendered a vague feeling of unease that never quite went away. In the still of the night masters and mistresses were often haunted by an endless sea of grinning black faces that floated in their imagination, mocking their attempts to feel secure. Even after they awoke in the morning, the feeling of unease never quite left them. Thus, every white man who raised his arm over his head, prepared to swing a lash at a disobedient slave, was silently goaded by that ever-present unease to use all his strength to ensure that this slave, and all slaves, knew who was boss.

Many Alabama Black Belt slaves carried vivid and painful memories of this punishment with them every day of their lives. One recalled that it was common for a master to tie his slave to a tree, "with your face to the tree, an' your arms aroun' it, fastened tight, an' you[r] feet fastened too, so you kain't git away, no way, then a long curlin whip whis'lin aroun' you, cuttin' the blood ever' lick, until folks a mile away hear every lick."[11] Another slave in neighboring Lowndes County recalled that her master would have his overseer whip his slaves "if any-body started to the fiel' on Monday mornin' without bein' clean an' ready to start out the week right."[12] James

Carmichael, a Wilcox County slave, remembered that slaves on his planta-tion were whipped in front of the cotton gin house. "I have seen many Ne-groes whipped within a [sic] inch of his life at these posts. I have seen them whipped so badly that they had to be carried away in wagons. Many never did recover."[13]

Cato Carter, a Wilcox County slave who was born in the little community of Pineapple, recalled the severity of the slave punishment he witnessed: "They whupped the women and they whupped the mens [sic]. I used to work some in the tan'ry and we made the whups. They'd tie them down . . . and give 'em the whuppin'. Some niggers, it taken four men to whup 'em, but they got it."[14] Carter also recalled the white reaction to those slaves who re-fused to be intimidated by a whipping, regardless of the severity: "When they was real 'corrigible, the white folks said they was like mad dogs and didn't mind to kill them so much as killin' a sheep. They'd take 'em to the grave-yard and shoot 'em down and bury 'em face downward with their shoes on." Carter further explained that planters wanted to make sure that the rest of their slaves would learn a lesson from such an episode: "They made some [of] the niggers go for a lesson to them that they could git the same."[15] Still an-other Wilcox County slave, Jennie Bowen, recalled that she and other slaves on the Fisher plantation near Camden were less afraid of their master than they were of his overseer. "We useta [sic] have a mean overseer. . . . An' all de time dere was slaves on our place a runnin' away."[16]

Clearly, slaves were subjected to many harsh reminders of their subordi-nate position, and many burned with resentment. In some instances this smoldering resentment erupted in violent confrontations. For example, in 1834 five Wilcox County slaves were tried for conspiracy and murder in the death of a local white man, Archibald Cawthorn. The two female slaves, Nancy and Ann, were acquitted; but the three male slaves, Tom, John, and Newman, were convicted by a jury of twelve white men.[17] Just the year be-fore that, Jack, a Wilcox County slave belonging to Martha Hobbs, was con-victed of his mistress's murder. Still another Wilcox County slave who lived near Prairie Bluff refused to allow an overseer to whip him. As the overseer raised his hand to whip the slave, the slave startled the overseer by standing up straight, looking him in the eye, and declaring that "he had taken the last whipping he would take from a white man. He wouldn't mind being shot; he had been shot twice already. But he would not be whipped." After making this declaration, the slave turned to run. When a driver attempted to stop him, he stabbed the driver, but then the overseer shot and killed the slave right on the spot.[18] The use of physical violence and intimidation to control the slaves was clearly a well-established practice in Wilcox County. After slavery ended, later generations of the county's white residents would continue to rely on these cruel methods to limit the freedom of the black majority in their midst, and at the same time, members of the county's black majority would continue to draw on their ancestors' tradition of resistance.

As the decade of the 1850s drew to a close, it became increasingly clear to many Americans that civil war was on the horizon. At this time, despite the threat of war, white Wilcox County residents decided to erect a grand new courthouse. They felt secure in their county's preeminence within the Cotton Kingdom, and many were convinced that Wilcox County needed a courthouse that would be more in keeping with their importance. Accordingly, in 1857, the old modest frame courthouse was replaced by an imposing red brick structure with magnificent white columns.[19] The huge new structure dominated Camden's town square. Ironically, a century later, the same courthouse was still standing, and at that time the aging structure would become the backdrop for the voting rights demonstrations by black Wilcox residents. However, in 1859 when the building was brand new, white residents were very proud of their courthouse. Yet, they did not have long to admire it before they became enveloped in the wave of southern patriotism that swept their state out of the Union and into the Confederacy.

During the four years of the Civil War, battles raged all around Wilcox County, but it was not until the war was almost over that federal troops reached this area of the Black Belt. White Camden residents were horrified to see their town overrun by these invaders in their despicable blue uniforms. As the conquering army moved through town helping themselves to whatever they wanted from businesses and even private homes, the resentment of white county residents multiplied exponentially. In the estimation of most white residents the absolute worst act committed by these Yankee invaders was their raid on the grand new courthouse. White Wilcox residents standing in doorways and peering through shuttered windows watched in sullen silence as a group of blue-uniformed soldiers marched right through the front door of the courthouse without even bothering to wipe the mud off their boots. How dare they, those who witnessed the scene fumed. Only the quick action of Judge Jo Cook, the county's probate judge, saved the county's records from destruction. Just before the Union troops arrived, he took the records out of the building and hid them in the woods.

This assault on their town provoked feelings of anger, resentment, and pure loathing on the part of white residents. Of course, all these feelings were dwarfed by a gargantuan fear that white Wilcox residents felt because they were so badly outnumbered by the county's slaves. Clearly, the coming of the Yankees was bound to mean the beginning of black freedom, and it was just too scary to contemplate. On the other hand, Wilcox County's slaves thought that those Union soldiers in their blue uniforms were the most glorious sight they had ever seen. To the slaves, the soldiers seemed to be enveloped in a cloud of excitement that was almost palpable. The air was alive with it; the slaves could feel it; they could almost touch it. They knew that the arrival of these men in blue uniforms with shiny brass buttons meant the end of slavery, and word spread rapidly to outlying areas of the county that the day of Jubilee had finally come.

In some instances the awesome sight of columns of blue-coated Yankee soldiers inspired a kind of fear among some of Alabama's slaves. For example, one reported, "I was powerful scared of de Yankee soldiers. . . . Dey come through Eufala an' all us niggers tried to hide; but dey jist come on by an' laughed at us fer bein' scared."[20] Yet, the fear that Alabama's slaves felt was a delicious kind of fear; born of their overwhelming yearning to be free, and mixed with a suffocating suspicion that real freedom might never come. Regardless of the impending Yankee victory, these slaves understood just how determined their masters were to hang on to the institution that had defined their existence for generations. In fact, some of Wilcox County's slaveholders gathered up a few of their most prized possessions, especially their slaves, and attempted to flee south in advance of the Union troops. One of the favorite destinations of these fugitive slaveholders was the state of Texas. Wilcox County slave Cato Arnold observed, "Near the close of the war I seed folks leavin' for Texas. They said if the Fed'rals win the war they'd have to live in Texas to keep slaves. So plenty started driftin' their slaves west. They'd pass with the womens ridin' in the wagons and the mens on foot." Furthermore, according to Arnold, some of those who did not leave in advance of the Yankees decided to leave later, after Union troops entered the area: "Some took slaves to Texas *after* the Fed'rals done 'creed the breakin' up" [emphasis added].[21]

However, it soon became apparent that slaveholders were running out of options, and the unthinkable was about to occur. Slavery was about to end, and nothing would ever be the same again. Throughout Wilcox County's history, slavery had not only defined who the slaves were, but in a strange and convoluted way, it had defined the place of white residents as well. It had been an economic system, a system of social control, and above all, a way of acting and reacting in a variety of situations for all of the county's residents. As the Civil War ended, rescinding the constitutional blessing on slavery, white Wilcox residents resolved not to let the new legal reality change the racial status quo in their county. They had plenty of company: slaveholders all over the state shared their determination. One Alabama observer reported that in the wake of the Civil War, "The old patriarchal relations were preserved as far as possible." Planters "were inclined to encourage them [slaves] to collect around the big house on the old slavery terms, giving food, clothes, quarters, medical attendance, and *a little pay* [emphasis added]. At that time, no one could understand the freedom of the Negro."[22] Despite their masters' refusal to grasp the concept of black freedom, the ex-slaves seemed to have no problem at all embracing this revolutionary concept.

In the first chaotic days after the war, as Alabama's ex-slaves cautiously sought to make their new freedom meaningful, they were seized by a powerful restlessness. It was a restlessness born of generations of restrictions that had bound them to the plantation; it was a restlessness motivated by a powerful desire to find loved ones who had been sold away from them before the war; it was a restlessness that was fueled by a curiosity about what it would be like to be free to move about as they pleased. The region's roads were clogged with black throngs moving from place to place, testing and trying out their new freedom. However, as the initial excitement waned, the ex-slaves began to settle down and confront the thorny question of how to make a living. In these unsettled months, Wilcox County's black population registered substantial growth as ex-slaves from outside the county settled there, augmenting the already huge number of black county residents.

In fact, Wilcox County's African American population grew at a faster rate during the years right after the Civil War than did the black population of any other county in the state: between 1866 and 1870 the county's black population increased a whopping 26.9 percent.[23] Furthermore, between 1860 and 1880 the county's black population grew from 17,823 to 25,117.[24] Black movement into Wilcox County was part of a larger wave of ex-slave movement into a number of Black Belt counties. In the unsettled years following the war, this movement was largely motivated by white harassment directed at freedmen in various parts of the state. In those counties where they were only a small minority, newly freed slaves felt especially vulnerable to attack. Consequently, many moved to areas where they felt a bit safer because of their superior numbers. Counties that already had large black populations, as well as the state's urban areas, were particularly attractive to the freedmen.[25]

Accompanying the black movement into Wilcox County during this volatile era was a cautious out-migration of the county's white residents: during this same period the county's white population fell from a high of 6,795 in 1860 to 6,711 in 1880.[26] A similar white exodus was occurring all over the Black Belt. The result of this postwar movement was an even more racially polarized state: "Those areas of the state which had been predominantly black in 1860 were even more heavily black in 1870, while the white areas—especially the mountains—were still more white."[27]

In the post-Civil War years as white Alabamans searched for ways to maintain white supremacy at all costs, some planters in the most remote areas of the Black Belt even went so far as to tell their slaves that they were not free.[28] Most did not go this far, but regardless of how they reacted, former slave owners all over the state were convinced that, "if we cannot whip the Negro, they and I cannot live in the same country."[29] Even Alabama's Reconstruction governor, R. M. Patton, made it clear that the state's ex-slaves would occupy a subordinate position in the new regime:

> We shall not only extend to the freedmen all their legitimate rights, but shall throw around them such effectual safeguards as will secure them in their full and complete enjoyment. *At the same time it must be understood that politically and socially ours is a white man's government* [emphasis added].[30]

New Political Reality—Nineteenth-Century Black Power

When the Radical Republican Congress passed the First Reconstruction Act in 1867 over President Andrew Johnson's veto, the worst fears of white Wilcox residents were realized. This act provided for the registration of ex-slaves, and by August 16 of that year, 499 white voters and 2,376 black voters were registered in Wilcox County.[31] For much of the next decade the Radical Republicans, with the help of this huge black majority, controlled the political apparatus of Wilcox County. Indeed, long after the Democrats had managed to seize control of the rest of the state from the Radical Republicans, the efforts of white Wilcox Democrats were frustrated by the overwhelming strength of the county's black majority. During these turbulent years black Wilcox voters, in concert with ex-slave voters all over the South, remained steadfastly loyal to the Republican Party. It was the party of Abraham Lincoln, Charles Sumner, and Thaddeus Stevens. In short, it was the political party that championed black freedom and advocated black voting. Conversely, the Democratic Party was the party of ex-slave holders, ex-Confederates, and all those interested in ensuring the triumph of white supremacy in the postwar South. Ironically, a century later when Wilcox County's ex-slave descendants sought to exercise their right to vote, they would embrace a radically different Democratic Party: the party of John F. Kennedy and Lyndon B. Johnson. By the 1960s this new Democratic Party would be perceived as a close ally of the civil rights movement.

However, back in the nineteenth century, white Wilcox residents, along with white residents all over the state, were looking to the Democratic Party for redemption from the Radical Republican policies that protected black rights. Finally, in November of 1874 white Alabamans were able to elect a Democratic governor and a majority Democratic state legislature amid charges of fraud and intimidation. According to some observers, "ballots were destroyed or stolen or thrown out on bogus technicalities."[32] Radical Republicans carried only six out of sixty-four Alabama counties in that 1874 election, and Wilcox was one of the six.[33] Shortly after the election when Wilcox County's Democrats met to discuss their defeat and plot strategy for the future, they wore their frustration and anger like an ill-fitting, uncomfortable cloak, and they chafed under it. The spectacle of their former slaves voting and holding office was almost more than these powerful men could bear. They were used to exercising the power of life and death over the slaves, and it was against nature and against God, they fumed, for these wretched creatures to possess the right to vote. White Wilcox residents were convinced that the shift in political power in their county was unnatural and unwise. As far as they were concerned, under the new regime their former slaves had become a malevolent force that had to be conquered for the good of their county. Given this state of mind, white Democratic reaction to black Wilcox voters' refusal to support a new constitution that had been proposed by the state's ruling Democrats a short time after that 1874 election is not surprising. The editor of the *Wilcox Vindicator* spoke for most when he commented,

> The fact of the Negro population of Wilcox refusing to vote for the new constitution is prima facie evidence of their bitter and malignant hatred for their old masters. . . . It is the result of the teaching of the Carpetbaggers . . . who have instilled into the minds of these poor, half-witted creatures that nothing good can come from the whites.[34]

White Wilcox residents were particularly offended by the sight of northern white men, derisively labeled carpetbaggers, consorting with former slaves, and encouraging and advising them. What kind of white men were they, the county's white residents wondered uneasily. It is not surprising that in that supercharged atmosphere, the northern white Radical Republicans who moved into Wilcox County were subjected to intense white hostility. One of those carpetbaggers was a man named William Henderson. Born in Scotland, Henderson had left the British Isles with his family and settled in Ohio before the Civil War. Later, as a captain in the Union Army, he got his first view of southwestern Alabama and fell in love. Shortly after the war ended, Henderson purchased his first acreage in Wilcox County, and after subsequent purchases, he and his sons would eventually own a twenty-two-thousand-acre plantation at Miller's Ferry in Wilcox County.[35]

Soon after taking up residence in the county, Henderson, a Republican, was elected to a seat in Alabama's Reconstruction legislature, where he served for three years. A short time later, in 1874, with the overwhelming support of the county's black electorate, Henderson was elected to the office of probate judge.[36] White Wilcox residents were furious at white Northerners like Henderson who settled among them after the war to buy up their land and stir up their former slaves. One local white observer remembered the stories of this enmity that were passed down in her family: "Naturally, the defeated, dispossessed, and despairing Rebels greeted their erstwhile Yankee enemies as they might have greeted the plagues of Pharaoh. . . . Southern ladies lifted their skirts in disdain when passing them." Some went even further than such demonstrative dislike. "Some of the men were threatened with violence; one at least was shot at."[37]

Clearly, white Wilcox residents viewed these northern interlopers with a mixture of alarm and resentment. On the other hand, however, the county's ex-slaves welcomed these outsiders as allies in the struggle to change their society. The ex-slaves knew they faced a long, hard struggle because even a long, bloody civil war had failed to change the racist attitudes of their former masters. However, Wilcox freedmen still remained optimistic about the future because they had just lived through a convincing display of the federal government's power over southern white people. This was the first time that the county's ex-slaves had ever seen anyone successfully challenge local white control of black lives, and in the wake of that success, black expectations soared. African Americans were not naive enough to expect that changes would come easily, but they were convinced that with continued Radical Republican support they would be able to realize their new freedom. All of these critical developments in Wilcox County occurred against the backdrop of vigorous and sometimes acrimonious debate in the United States Congress about the best way to protect the basic citizenship rights of the newly freed slaves.

As early as 1870 Senator Charles Sumner of Massachusetts had sought to sponsor a civil rights bill that would have an extensive impact all over the country. Sumner's bill proposed to safeguard the access of black citizens to every aspect of life from schools to cemeteries, and from railroad cars to churches. In 1874 when the bill began to receive serious consideration in Congress, most white Wilcox residents viewed these deliberations with alarm. Here was more proof, they reasoned, that the Radical Republicans were not just radical, they were deranged. As far as white Wilcox residents were concerned, social equality with the people they had held in bondage just a few years ago was preposterous. Not surprisingly, the county's ex-slaves were elated at the discussion going on in Washington. Their elation was short-lived, however, because the very next year, in 1875, Congress passed only a severely restricted version of the comprehensive measure that Sumner had proposed. It sidestepped some fundamental issues of freedmen's access, and it was altogether silent on the emotional issue of mixed schools.

This was an ominous sign that northern interest in the Negro Question, which was at an all-time high in the first months after the Civil War, was clearly waning. The next few months would offer even more proof that African Americans' northern allies had lost interest in their cause. Finally, just two short years after the passage of the watered-down civil rights act, the Reconstruction process officially came to an end. At that time, southern Democrats officially threw their support to Republican presidential candidate Rutherford B. Hayes in the disputed election of 1876. In exchange for this southern support, Hayes promised to withdraw the remaining federal troops from the South, thus leaving the freedmen totally vulnerable to the intimidation of white Southerners determined to return their region to the prewar status quo. Before Hayes struck the bargain that would ensure his victory, he predicted that if the Democrats captured the White House, "The result will be that the southern people will practically treat the constitutional amendments [designed to protect the rights of the freedmen] as nullities, and then the colored man's fate will be worse than when he was in slavery."[38] Ironically, Hayes's prophecy came true even though the Democrats did not win the White House, because from the end of Reconstruction to the end of the nineteenth century, the political, social, economic, and educational position of African Americans declined precipitously. In fact, things were so bad that one African American historian, Rayford Logan, labeled this period *The Nadir*.[39] He explained why he thought such a label was appropriate: "During the next quarter of the century, the South sought to have the Constitution interpreted, federal laws repealed or rendered innocuous and Northern public opinion made amenable to the end that Negroes should become what were later called second-class citizens."[40]

Near the end of the century the United States Supreme Court placed its stamp of approval on the efforts of white Southerners to render African Americans politically, economically, and socially powerless in the *Plessy v. Ferguson* decision. In that 1896 case plaintiff Homer Plessy challenged the constitutionality of a Louisiana statute that required separate accommodations for black and white passengers on public transportation. The court upheld the constitutionality of that Louisiana law declaring, "If one race be inferior to the other socially, the Constitution of the United States cannot put them upon the same plane. The distinction between the two races, which was founded in the color of the two races, must always exist so long as white men are distinct from the other color."[41] And so, white Southerners could happily continue their practice of segregating their black fellow citizens with the Supreme Court's blessing. While the Supreme Court did insist that when accommodations were separate they must be equal, white Southerners obeyed only one part of this decision: accommodations for black Southerners were always separate, but never equal.

It is against this broad background of adamant intolerance and ruthless repression that black and white residents in Wilcox County struggled to fashion a new relationship to each other. Well after Alabama Democrats *redeemed* their state from the Radical Republicans, and even after President Hayes withdrew the last of the federal troops from the South, signaling the formal end of Reconstruction, Wilcox County's Democrats were still unable to unseat the Radical Republican office holders in their county: in the 1880 election a number of Radical Republican candidates managed to win election to county offices. Wilcox County's white Democrats were incensed. In July of 1880 the all-white Wilcox County Democratic Executive Committee met. The gathering radiated frustration and anger. Before they disbanded, those in attendance adopted a resolution that clearly expressed the depth of their frustration:

> The eyes of the whole Black Belt are turned to Wilcox County. . . . What is the present condition of the people of Wilcox? The prophet Isaiah answers for us: "We have made a covenant with death, and with hell are we at agreement." We permit the Radical party to remain in power. That party is the bitter, vindictive, hereditary enemy of our people.[42]

It was during the early 1880s that white Wilcox residents were finally able to seize control of their county from the remaining white Republicans and their black allies. It had been a long, bitter, acrimonious struggle, a struggle that seared into the collective consciousness of the county's white residents the haunting vision of black voting and office holding. White residents found that vision so repugnant that it fueled their determination to block black access to the county's political process. That determination would last for the next one hundred years.

Back to Business as Usual

Black Wilcox voters stubbornly continued to go to the polls well after their county had been *redeemed*. Even though their numbers steadily dwindled, however, there was a brief glimmer of hope near the end of the nineteenth century. That hope was offered by the Populist movement. Populism grew in response to the agricultural depression that began in the late 1880s and stretched into the 1890s, jeopardizing the livelihood of black and white farmers alike. In the South, the Populists actually tried to build a political coalition that included black voters. In Alabama in particular, Reuben Kolb, a white native of Barbour County, which is located in the Black Belt, led the Populist charge: "In 1892, he embraced open political rebellion against the coalition of planters and emerging Birmingham industrialists that dominated the state Democratic Party." He christened his new political party the "Jeffersonian Democrats."[43] The Jeffersonian Democrats openly courted black support, and predictably, many white Alabamans were alarmed. Newspapers across the state offered the shrill warning that the new party's policies would "raise the niggers to equality with the whites."[44] The state's Democratic machine quickly circled the wagons and vowed to defeat the new party by any means necessary. They "used payoffs, intimidation, and ballot-box stuffing to make certain that most of those black votes were tallied for Kolb's opponent."[45] Shortly after this resounding but fraudulent defeat of Populism in their state, Conservative Alabama Democrats moved to adopt a new state constitution that would end the "problem" of black voting in their state once and for all.[46] Accordingly, in 1901, members of the Alabama legislature held a constitutional convention, and as the all-white convention assembled in Montgomery on May 21, 1901, the issue of black disfranchisement was uppermost in everyone's mind. Even though African Americans were not permitted to attend the convention, four of the state's black organizations decided to send petitions to the gathering to voice their concerns. Realizing their powerlessness, the authors were careful to use a conciliatory tone. One of these petitions was signed by a number of Alabama's leading black educators, including W. H. T. Holtzclaw, who was the principal of Snow Hill Institute in Wilcox County. Holtzclaw tried to appeal to white self-interest:

> And if you of the dominant race will be generous in your dealings with us, generous in the matter of education, you will ever have at your door a people who will not trouble your sleep with dynamite nor your waking hours with strikes. This is the people that appeal to you to make a suffrage law (though the test be the severest that is consistent with reason) *that will operate for all men alike* [emphasis added].[47]

Regardless of such conciliatory appeals, delegates to Alabama's constitutional convention were in no mood to support even limited black enfranchisement. The delegates from the state's Black Belt counties were particularly vigorous in their support for black disfranchisement. Wilcox County's convention delegate, Mr. Jones, unequivocally expressed his county's stand on this issue when he explained that white Wilcox residents "were just as much in favor of the disfranchisement of Negroes as any in the state."[48] In the end, Alabama's new constitution completely disfranchised the state's new African American citizens.

Even after this political victory, white Wilcox residents still felt the need to go further. They predictably wanted to make sure that their ex-slaves understood that total black subordination would continue in Wilcox County despite the end of slavery. Consequently, through the last decades of the nineteenth century and well into the twentieth, white Wilcox residents built a social order on the mirror image assumptions of white superiority and black inferiority. Such a postwar social order was clearly in step with the attitude of many white Southerners throughout the ex-Confederate states. Henry Grady, editor of the *Atlanta Constitution*, clearly articulated the basis of this New South social order in 1887: "The supremacy of the white race of the South must be maintained forever, and the domination of the Negro race resisted at all points and at all hazards—because the white race is the superior race. This is the declaration of no new truth. It has abided forever in the marrow of our bones, and shall run forever with the blood that feeds Anglo-Saxon hearts."[49]

Thus, as the nineteenth century drew to a close, relations between the two races in Wilcox County settled into an unequal but predictable pattern. Black residents knew how risky it was to talk back to a white person, refuse to step aside to let a white person pass, or even look a white person directly in the eye. The restrictions on black lives were endless, and the consequences for challenging them were deadly. Because of their powerlessness, black residents were careful at least to give the appearance of obeying the racial code, and many of Wilcox County's white residents interpreted this apparent acquiescence as a sign of racial harmony. In fact, some of the county's white citizens went so far as to insist that race relations were so good that bonds of real affection routinely developed between black and white. For example, Viola Goode Liddell, a life-long white resident of the county insisted, "If my observations and experience are correct, there is between many individuals and families of black and white real friendship, and between quite a number there is something deeper. It is appreciation and love."[50]

Yet, other white residents thought relations between the races were much more complicated than this. Instead, some insisted, regardless of their closeness, the county's black and white residents have always been separated by an immutable racial divide. For example, Hollis Curl, owner/editor of the county's weekly newspaper, the *Wilcox Progressive Era*, recalls the close relationship he developed with the son of his family's black housekeeper. During the long lazy Alabama summers, Curl and his black buddy played games that delighted little boys. They tested the strength of their developing muscles as they ran and jumped. They gazed in wonder at the magical world around them filled with musical crickets and breathtaking butterflies. Their high-pitched voices, as yet unaffected by male hormones, punctuated their play. After a morning of vigorous play, their young stomachs demanded food. The boys stopped long enough to eat lunch together on Curl's back porch, but they did not linger long. Almost before they swallowed their last bite of sandwich, they were up and running again. Some afternoons, the boys even bathed together in a large metal washtub. Curl's glistening white skin contrasted sharply with the shiny chocolate-colored skin of his pal. The childhood companions were extremely close. As Curl wistfully expresses it, "We were as close [to being] brothers as anybody could be."[51] Despite their closeness, however, Curl also admits, "somehow, though, we perceived that there was a difference."[52]

Clinton McCarty, a white Alabama native, vividly remembers witnessing the impact of the county's racial divide during one of the many summers he spent visiting his Wilcox relatives:

> My mother was the same age as a black woman named Minerva, who had grown up not far from my grandmother's house. They had played together as children. One year when they were around fifty years old, Minerva came to see mother soon after we arrived for the summer. Mother invited her onto the screened porch. They greeted each other with a hug, effusive talk, and laughter. Minerva accustomed as she was to the limits of familiarity with whites, at first politely declined Mother's invitation to sit down. She finally did so after considerable coaxing but rested tentatively and stiffly on the edge of the chair, as if sitting back at ease would have been impertinent.[53]

Shortly after Minerva perched herself on the edge of the chair, a car drove up to the house. Instantly, she jumped up, bid an awkward goodbye, and quickly left the porch. Wilcox county's young people who grew up in this atmosphere of unequal relationships based on race were profoundly affected by it. Historian Melton McLaurin, who grew up in the southeast, succinctly explains the impact on white youngsters. As he put it, "The message I received from hundreds of such signals was always the same. I was white; I was different; I was superior. It was not a message with which an adolescent boy was apt to quarrel."[54]

Conversely, the black subordination demanded by segregation's rules was an important ingredient in defining black self-image as well. Lawrence Parrish, a black Wilcox native, explains, "We had been taught that everything they [white people] did was right."[55] Emmanuel McDuffie, a black Wilcox resident and a graduate of Snow Hill Institute, reported that when he was growing up he had "a very vague idea about life as it pertained to the Negro. In fact, up until that time, I was of the opinion that the Negro had no business being anything."[56] William J. Edwards, founder and principal of Snow Hill Institute, expressed alarm over the impact of the racial atmosphere on the lives of the black people in the vicinity of his school: "The people were thoroughly discouraged and seemingly had lost all hopes."[57] In Edwards's estimation the county's white residents took full advantage of the unequal system they had fashioned. He observed, "Everywhere in their religious services, they [black residents] sang this song: 'You may have all the world, but give me Jesus.'" Edwards concluded, "The white man was taking them at their word and giving them all of Jesus, but none of the world."[58]

Segregation in Wilcox County produced downcast eyes, stooped shoulders, exaggerated politeness, and blank black faces. White residents accepted and expected this constant show of black subordination. However, what they dared not contemplate was the boiling and bubbling rage concealed behind seemingly impassive black faces. That rage was always threatening to erupt, and when it did, it was frightening in its ferocity. Through Grange Copeland, the fictional black sharecropper she created, novelist Alice Walker articulated that dynamic so eloquently when she wrote, "He [Grange] loathed the thought of being dependent on a white person or persons again . . . he would almost rather be blind than have to see, even occasionally, a white face. He had found that wherever he went whites were in control."[59] It seemed that wherever black Wilcox County residents looked in their rural and isolated world, white people controlled everything.

Yet, while their parents were painfully aware of the county's racial realities, it seemed that some black Wilcox children were only dimly aware of the sinister racist forces that controlled everything around them. Families with a degree of economic independence, such as those who owned land or those who taught school, were the ones who were able to provide at least a measure of protection for their children from Wilcox County's ugly racial realities.

Whenever they could, parents and guardians were careful to set strict limits on their children's activities. Worried black parents hoped that such restrictions would keep their children out of harm's way by carefully monitoring and restricting their contacts with white people. For example, Nellie Williams Abner vividly remembers how closely her grandparents supervised her activities. Abner was raised by her grandparents during the 1920s in Camden, and they lived in one of the many small frame houses in the black section of town known as The Bottom. Little Nellie's house had a large yard, and like so many other residents in the neighborhood, her grandparents would loosen the dirt with a hoe and then smooth it over with a broom. They called this cleaning the yard.[60] Young Nellie found that the hard-packed dirt around her house was a perfect place to bounce the rubber ball that she and her neighborhood girlfriends used when they played jacks during the long lazy summers when they were out of school. Nellie also spent much of her time exploring the limits of her grandparents' yard as she played with the dolls that were her constant companions. Yet, the world beyond the immediate vicinity of her neighborhood was a world just out of little Nellie's reach. As she puts it, "We knew we weren't supposed to go out of this little confined area."[61]

When Marguerite Wilson Griggs was growing up in Camden during the 1920s, she and her brothers lived on the campus of Camden Academy, where her father was the principal. Griggs remembers that she was not allowed to leave the campus alone, but she did not mind this restriction too much since she had an unlimited source of playmates: Camden Academy was a black Presbyterian boarding school that enrolled elementary and high school students. There were many places to explore on the campus grounds, and Griggs fondly recalls how the woods just beyond her house often echoed with childish laughter as she and her friends would jump astride one of the many young saplings growing everywhere around them. The children would bounce up and down on their supple saplings, defying gravity for a brief instant. Another favorite activity of the Camden Academy students was their own unique form of sledding. Many pine trees grew on the school's campus, and although snow was extremely rare in southern Alabama, Griggs remembers that the students discovered that a bed of pine needles was just as slippery as a snowy hillside if you had the right sled. Old automobile fenders worked best. The sledder would breathlessly run to the top of one of the gentle inclines nearest the woods where the ground had a thick covering of pine needles, place the fender on the ground, and carefully sit inside. The children took turns pushing each other down the hill in their makeshift sled. For a brief instant, the sledder would see the familiar landscape flash past as the fender gathered speed. The others at the top of the hill watched, eagerly awaiting their turn.

Tennis was another of the students' favorite activities, and many afternoons would find Camden Academy's tennis courts crowded with students running furiously after bouncing tennis balls. The air was alive with the distinctive sounds of balls making contact with tennis racquets, and young voices shouting out scores and good-natured taunts. One activity that the girls in the group were particularly fond of was jumping rope. The woods on campus were filled with thick vines that made perfect jump ropes. As their strong brown limbs propelled them up and over the swinging rope, the girls would giggle, and their braids would bounce up and down. They had a whole repertoire of rhymes that they would call out to the rhythm of the swinging rope: "Mary Mack; dressed in black; silver buttons up and down her back" their girlish voices called out. They continued, "Asked my mother for fifteen cents; to see the elephant jump the fence." They concluded, "he jumped so high; he touched the sky; and he didn't come back 'til the fourth of July." Girlish voices chanted verse after verse of this and many other rhymes as they jumped up and down until they finally got tired. Later, when young Marguerite tired of playing outside, she would go back inside the spacious principal's house and resume working on one of her many embroidery projects.[62] Like many other girls of her generation, Marguerite Griggs learned to embroider at a very young age. This was considered a ladylike activity, and in a world that was almost completely free of electronic distractions, such activities were enormously popular. There were similar oases where black children could feel secure in separate black communities all over the county during this era. In such an idyllic atmosphere, it seemed to some children that Wilcox County's racial troubles were a million miles away.

Yet, as the county's black children attended their segregated schools, engaged in segregated activities, and played their segregated games, their parents continued to fret about the dangerous society just beyond this separate world, and they tried to protect their children as much as they could. For example, Kayte Marsh Fearn remembers the strategy her parents used. Both of Fearn's parents were teachers at Camden Academy in the late 1920s, and the family lived on the edge of the campus. She explains: "My folks tried their best not to talk about things [racism and segregation] like that. . . . Now, my father would not let me take a job for a white person."[63]

Lucy Ephraim, a Camden Academy student, remembers how her family tried to protect her. She explains, "Our father kind of shielded us, kept us away from the city. . . . He really did most of the shopping."[64] Upon graduating from Camden Academy, Ephraim planned to attend Knoxville College in Knoxville, Tennessee, and in preparation for going off to school, she needed a new pair of shoes. But, even then, her father refused to let her go into town. Instead, she declares, "He bought my shoes." Young Lucy was very disappointed because she wanted to do her own shopping at such an exciting time in her life when she was just about to live on her own for the first time. However, despite her disappointment, Lucy Ephraim understood the gravity of the situation. She recalls that her father often said, "I really would like to die a natural death."[65] Her father's quiet voice, and the somber expression on his face instantly stilled her objections. When she looked into his determined dark eyes, the meaning of his grave words practically took her breath away. She knew with sickening certainty that if any white person mistreated any member of his family, her father was fully prepared to confront them. Of course, young Lucy, along with the rest of her family, realized that in the event of such a confrontation, it was quite likely that their father might have to pay with his life. So, they swallowed their frustration and allowed Wilcox County's racial realities to circumscribe their existence.

Far from a Closed Society—Incomplete Subordination

No matter how hard black residents tried, there were still times when racial strife erupted openly, and conflict was unavoidable. It was simply impossible for African Americans in the county to hold all that anger and frustration in check all the time. When those emotions did surface, everyone feared the consequences. Joseph Anderson, a longtime black resident of Wilcox County, remembers that some black people earned the reputation of being rebellious. They made no secret of the anger and hatred they harbored toward white people. The county's racial atmosphere seemed to enrage these angry African Americans to the point where they were willing to sacrifice their personal safety on the altar of racial resistance. Black Wilcox native James Ephraim explains, "See . . . when you get to a certain point, you forget about it [racial etiquette]. That's when you become insane."[66] As far as white residents were concerned, black people like these were simply not normal. Joseph Anderson observes, "Ever since I was a kid, there were certain Negro people . . . If they [white people] knew you didn't take no junk . . . they'd say, 'that's a crazy nigger there. Don't nobody mess with him.'"[67] In short, it made more sense to white Wilcox residents to characterize any black challenge to their authority as aberrant behavior. To admit otherwise would have been tantamount to an acknowledgment that white control of the county was far from complete.

While African Americans with such a *bad* reputation were the exception, the vast majority of black Wilcox residents felt varying degrees of resentment, and their resentment surfaced from time to time. From the era of Reconstruction until well into the twentieth century, black citizens in Wilcox

County disobeyed racial etiquette and resisted segregation in a variety of settings and in a variety of ways. Some of these methods of resistance could be quite creative as Nellie Williams Abner recalls. She gleefully insists, "I would always trick them." She explains that when she went into Liddell's store in the Camden business district,

> You tell the clerk what you want, and she'd invariably ask you fifty times. "You want two yards of blue material?" I'd say, "two yards of blue material. . . ." Then I never did have to say yes [ma'am] or no [ma'am]. I just kept repeating whatever she asked me. I never said yes ma'am or no ma'am to any of them.[68]

When young Nellie came out of that little country store, she walked down the sleepy streets of Camden to her grandparents' house in The Bottom. She felt a little thrill of pride, and she smiled to herself even though her face remained impassive: a mask to conceal her true feelings from white passersby and ensure her survival. It was a small victory, but it was hers alone. Young Nellie's refusal to submit completely to segregation's rules was undoubtedly influenced by the example her grandmother set. On numerous occasions she watched her grandmother challenge one of segregation's most cherished rules: the white prerogative to address black people in a demeaning fashion. Abner vividly recalls, "My grandmother would go down there and they'd say 'Auntie.'" Her grandmother's reaction was quick and unequivocal: "She'd tell them right away, 'I'm not your daddy's sister, and I'm not your mother's sister. So call me by my name.' And they would turn red as a brick."[69]

Another black Wilcox native, Clinton Marsh, watched his father defy the county's racial etiquette in a very dramatic and very public way. The stage was set when a Presbyterian church in Iowa contacted Reverend William Wilson, the principal of Camden Academy, and offered to donate some musical instruments to his school. Wilson gratefully and enthusiastically accepted. A short time later, the Iowa church sent sixteen instruments, and Camden Academy proudly formed a band. Clinton Marsh and his brother, T. P., excitedly joined. Clinton played the trumpet, and his older brother played the clarinet. At that time, in the late 1920s, none of the other schools in the county, not even the white schools, had a band, so most Camden residents had never seen a real band. After the group's members had spent some time practicing with their new instruments, Reverend Wilson asked Camden officials to allow the band the chance to drill and play their instruments on the town square. Permission was granted. On the appointed Saturday, band members excitedly assembled on the Camden Academy campus. The campus sat high on a hill overlooking the sleepy little town, and as the band members left their campus and marched down that hill, the sun glinted off their instruments. Sixteen black young people marching down the hill with glittering musical instruments, straightened backs, and proud expressions on their faces was a sight unlike any that Camden residents had ever seen. As the young people approached the center of town, a small group of spectators watched in awe. The band assembled on the town square and played several songs. After they had performed for a time, band members were given a break, and one of the local merchants provided sodas, Coca-Colas and Nehis, for the thirsty musicians.

Clinton Marsh remembers just how good his Coca-Cola tasted when the sweet liquid slid over his tongue and down his throat, relieving the dry, cottony feeling in his mouth. The young musicians relaxed and joked with each other as they finished drinking their sodas. At this point, Wilcox County's sheriff, Lummie Jenkins, briskly strode into the midst of the group of musicians demanding, "Clear the walk here." Ironically, Marsh remembers that because it was a Saturday, there was virtually no pedestrian traffic on the town square, but the sheriff was clearly determined to assert his authority. As he roughly elbowed his way through the assembly of band members, Jenkins overheard Marsh's older brother say, "uh-huh." Actually, the young man was answering a question posed to him by another band member who was standing right next to him, but Jenkins was convinced that young Marsh was just being insolent. Before the uh-huh had died on the young man's lips, Sheriff Jenkins whirled around, his face crimson with rage, and he screamed, "You say uh-huh to a white man? I'll teach you how to talk to a white man." Before anyone could react, Lummie Jenkins hit the surprised musician in the head so hard that he knocked the young man's glasses off. Jenkins's overreaction to this innocent situation was a clear indication of his discomfort at being around this group of black youngsters who so obviously defied the bowing, scraping, obsequious stereotype that white Wilcox residents wanted so desperately to embrace.

With lightning speed, the Marsh boys' father, who had been in the crowd of spectators, stepped between the sheriff and his son. His gaze locked on Jenkins. The elder Marsh's eyes were blazing, his neck muscles were knotted in fury, and his jaws were clenched. When Sheriff Jenkins felt the fury that emanated from the elder Marsh, he drew his revolver and demanded, "What's it to you, old man?" When Marsh did not respond immediately, Jenkins screamed at him, "I'll blow your brains out." A collective gasp escaped from the throats of black and white onlookers gathered in the Camden town square that afternoon, and then an eerie deep silence settled over the crowd. That silence was filled with the tension of generations of clashes between southern white power and stubborn black resistance. Even the buzzing of insects in the warm humid air was momentarily silenced in the face of this age-old conflict.

The elder Marsh finally broke the silence. His eyes never left the sheriff's face, and in a quiet but steady voice he said, "He's my son, and I want to know why you hit him." Jenkins did not respond. Instead, he stood completely motionless, transfixed by Marsh's bold stare. Then, before Jenkins could react, Marsh grabbed him by the collar, thrust his face just inches from the sheriff's and repeated, "HE'S MY SON. I WANT TO KNOW WHY YOU HIT HIM." Clinton Marsh was standing directly behind the sheriff, and he had a clear view of his father's face. What he saw simultaneously filled him with pride and fear. Young Clinton was still holding his Coca-Cola bottle, and it was very difficult for him to "resist the temptation to try and knock his [Jenkins's] brains out." As Clinton Marsh stood behind the sheriff, clutching his soda bottle in his trembling hand, the elder Marsh and the sheriff stood toe-to-toe with their gazes locked for what seemed like an eternity. Finally, the elder Marsh loosened his grip on Jenkins's collar. The sheriff averted his gaze, holstered his weapon, and walked away, muttering about those uppity niggers up on the hill. Gradually, the town square returned to normal: onlookers began murmuring and insects resumed buzzing.[70]

T. P. Marsh Sr.'s defiant act became a Wilcox legend of epic proportions, and his brashness and courage were greatly admired. Yet, the desire many had to defy their county's racial etiquette in a similar fashion was checked by the ever-present fear of the awful consequences. When he was a youngster, Clinton Marsh recalls, "You lived in a state of subliminal fear. Not that every moment you were afraid, but if my mother sent me . . . to the store, I could never be sure that no racial incident would occur."[71] Nellie Williams Abner agrees. As she puts it, "You never knew what they [white people] might do."[72] This pervasive black fear was rooted in an understanding of the unequal power relationship in Wilcox County. Lucy Ephraim recalls that her father constantly admonished his children about staying out of places where there were white people because they had "the power."[73] As a young black child growing up in Wilcox County, Lawrence Parrish also understood that white people had tremendous power over black lives. However, in order to conduct the practical day-to-day business of life, he insists that African Americans had to try to take control of their fear because, "You got to keep on living."[74] Nellie Abner agrees but insists that living in such an atmosphere created deep scars. She explains, "It does something to you. I have resentment. . . . I think I'll go to my grave with that."[75]

Clearly, conditions were difficult for Wilcox County's African American majority. It is important to note, however, that economic or geographic realities sometimes worked to mitigate the worst effects of the county's racially repressive atmosphere, at least for some. Those who lived in small towns and hamlets generally lived in black neighborhoods where they were at least able to experience a sense of community that was both comforting and reassuring. Some of these people owned their own houses, and that provided them with an additional sense of security and a partial feeling of independence. At the same time, out in the rural areas, those black families who managed to buy their own land also felt a partial sense of independence from the county's white power structure.

Toward a New Kind of Slavery

Wilcox's black landless rural dwellers, who made up a majority of the county's black population, had no such protection. They were always at the mercy of the white landowners who employed them. Clearly, most plantation owners felt a sense of ownership that was based on the reality of their county's slave past. White ownership of black flesh had helped to define the identity of Wilcox County's white residents for generations, and even after Wilcox slaveholders were forced to give up their slaves, this sense of white ownership persisted. The system of sharecropping and tenant farming that took the place of slavery ensnared the county's ex-slaves and their descendants in a debt trap. Landless African Americans farmed year after year only to be told that their share of the crop was not enough to satisfy their indebtedness to the landowner. Thus, at the end of each season, they found themselves obligated to the landowner for still another year. Joseph Anderson saw this happen to countless black families, and he observes, "They [white landowners] always say, 'you like to come out [of] this debt this year; you try it another year, you'll come out of debt.' And they kept them going like that." Anderson goes on to conclude, "It was kind of rough back in those days."[76]

People from outside the region were often shocked and dismayed when they observed the conditions facing Wilcox County's landless black peasants. One of those outside observers, Eliza B. Wallace, expressed frustration about the conditions facing the county's black farm laborers. Wallace, a white Presbyterian missionary and a native of Ohio, was invited to visit the county by her friend, Judge William Henderson. When she arrived at Henderson's plantation in 1893, she was horrified by the scene that confronted her. She explained, "These people [African Americans] do not own the land, that is owned by white men in tracts of a thousand or more acres; each is rented out to the colored people. While the crop is growing, the rich planter provides for the families of the colored men."[77] Wallace was convinced that this assistance from the planters was not intended to help the sharecroppers at all. Instead, she insisted that everything the planters did was designed to keep the ex-slaves enslaved by debt.

Eliza Wallace was particularly troubled by the impact of this system on the children. Because the planters only provided food rations for those members of sharecropping families who were working in the fields, this placed sharecropping parents in the painful position of needing to put even their young children to work to ensure the family's survival. Wallace concluded that whole families were trapped because "when the crop is gathered, each one's work is figured up at a shamefully low rate per day, and when the books are balanced, it generally turns out that the renter is in debt to the planter." In Wallace's estimation, there was no way out: "This happens from year to year, and the man is too poor to get away and better his condition. He can neither read nor write and so cannot keep accounts and has never handled enough money to learn by practice."[78] Black Presbyterian missionary Reverend E. K. Smith corroborated Wallace's account. Smith began working among the freedmen in Wilcox County at the end of the nineteenth century, and he observed, "They [Wilcox County's black sharecroppers and tenants] have nothing and must mortgage their crops before they are planted for food and clothing. . . . They pay a high rate of interest on the food, money, and clothing advanced. When their crops are made, they not only have nothing, but they are often in debt."[79]

Not only did white landowners exert complete control over their black employees' finances, but they also tried to control every other aspect of their workers' existence too. Over a generation later, during the post-World War II period, Morton Rubin, a young white graduate student at the University of North Carolina, wrote his dissertation on Wilcox County. Rubin found that even by this time in the twentieth century white plantation owners were still exerting an enormous amount of influence over the lives of their tenants. He explained that the "power, prestige, and authority of the plantation owner naturally enable him to control the human factor in the situation to a degree far exceeding comparable institutions in a supposedly democratic society. The plantation remains a last vestige of beneficent despotism." Undoubtedly, many of Wilcox County's black farm laborers would not have included the adjective "beneficent" in their description of their dealings with their white landlords. Rubin concluded, "The system makes for potential justice or injustice at the whim of the individual owner."[80] In such an atmosphere, the children of sharecroppers and tenant farmers witnessed many incidents and overheard many conversations that reinforced the reality of black subordination in their young lives. The lesson was inescapable: their lives and the lives of their family members were completely controlled by white people. The plantation owners assumed the role of "protector" in this situation, and they invested their sharecroppers with an identity: a share-cropper became a person in the eyes of white residents only when he became known as somebody's Negro. In a strange way, this provided a kind of pro-tection for some. Joseph Anderson explains, "A lot of times they [law en-forcement officers] run up on you, depending on who[se] place you['re] living on, they wouldn't bother you because they know they have to come in touch with your boss man, the man's place you're living on."[81]

In many instances, landowners demanded that sharecropping parents sac-rifice their children's well-being to improve the landowner's profit margin. The most common casualty of planter ambition was the sharecropping child's education. Landowners routinely insisted that once black children were old enough to work in the fields, they should only be permitted to attend school when all the farm work was finished. Some parents bristled at that *suggestion*. For example, James Ephraim recalls that his mother insisted that all of her children attend school every day, and the planter who owned the land that his family sharecropped complained bitterly. Ephraim's mother was deter-mined: to make up for her children's absence, she hitched up the mule and plowed the fields by herself. Undoubtedly, other black parents would have liked to follow the Ephraims' example, but most were so desperately poor that they felt they had no choice. Ruby Abercrombie, a black Birmingham native who taught in a rural black Wilcox County school during the early twenti-eth century, recalls the endless discussions she had with sharecropping par-ents about their children's poor attendance at school. She explains, "They would say to me . . . 'Us got children to help in these farms. . . . And when it's time for the boys to cut a load of wood . . . they have to be here; you have to excuse them.'"[82] Undaunted, a determined Ruby Abercrombie decided to go straight to the top: she confronted the plantation owners. She recalls that they were amazed at her brashness, and they quickly dismissed her. In a con-descending tone they told the young teacher, "You don't understand our way of life . . . you're from Birmingham."[83] Clearly, black farm laborers in Wilcox County were hemmed in on all sides, from the cradle to the grave. They were victims of a powerful paternalism that suffocated and strangled.

Still another problem that confronted black sharecroppers and tenants was the lack of decent housing. Things were so bad that in many instances their living conditions were reminiscent of the circumstances facing their ancestors during slavery. Eliza Wallace reported, "Their cabins are not homes, but simply places in which to sleep. Often eight or ten occupy the same one-room cabin, a bundle of straw and perhaps an old quilt or two an-swer for a bed. They do not sit at [the] table to eat, but each one takes his cornbread and bacon in his hand and eats sitting on the doorstep or on the ground."[84] Presbyterian missionary Reverend E. K. Smith offered an even more dismal assessment of life among Wilcox County's black farm laborers. From his vantage point as Camden Academy's first principal, he was keenly aware of the misery that was all around him. According to Smith, it was a pathetic sight: "They [black farm laborers] are wretchedly poor. Life with them is a desperate struggle for bread. They actually go hungry and in rags." Smith continued, "Their homes are little one-room huts built of pine poles, with stick and dirt chimneys."[85] In fact, black housing in Wilcox County was so poor that in those rare instances when black rural dwellers were able to afford decent housing, people were awed. William Edwards of Snow Hill Institute reported that "Shortly after the founding of the school [Snow Hill], a Negro built a house and fitted it up with glass windows and people would go for ten miles to see it."[86] At the same time, the problems black people suffered because of inadequate shelter were compounded by their lack of adequate clothing. E. K. Smith lamented, "Most of the children are thinly clad. . . . We do not wonder that they have cold, grippe, and pneumonia. It is painful to hear them cough."[87]

Such appalling physical conditions only served to reinforce the psychological control exerted by landowners. Consequently, some of the early Presbyterian missionaries who were sent to minister to Wilcox County freedmen in the decades after the Civil War were soon convinced that these people desperately needed a way out of this new debt slavery. Accordingly, the Presbyterian Church bought a seven-hundred-acre plantation near their Prairie Mission in Wilcox County, and they employed local black sharecroppers to farm it. Missionaries explained that they were "not doing it as a business venture, but to give employment to ambitious and deserving men under favorable circumstance in the hope that they may purchase their own homes and become independent."[88] The Presbyterians were convinced that their plantation would "encourage self-dependence, obtaining property, morality, and industry."[89] After their plantation had been in operation for a while, the Presbyterians proudly declared, "There are no one room shanties on the place, and no one is allowed to remain on the place whose life is immoral."[90] Yet, while this Presbyterian experiment helped a few black Wilcox families obtain their own land, the vast majority of the county's black rural dwellers remained stuck in an endless cycle of backbreaking labor, poverty, and despair. When these people opened their eyes every morning, their lifeless stares greeted each new day with a kind of indifference. All around them the drab cabin walls reminded them of their confinement. As they stretched out their already sore legs and straightened their aching backs, they could almost feel the biting insects and the burning sun that awaited them just outside the cabin door. They dragged themselves outside and into the fields where the hot Alabama sunshine beat down on their backs, beating the hope out of them, and frying their dreams until they were hard and brittle. The endless days stretched out before them like a seamless shroud, trapping them in a kind of living death.

The despair that the county's black sharecroppers and tenants felt about their situation only deepened when they realized that some of their black neighbors were in a position that was even more lowly: they were peons. In fact, by the early twentieth century peonage had become so widespread in the Black Belt that the United States Justice Department was moved to begin an investigation. Government lawyers realized that there was only a fine line separating the sharecropper or the tenant from the peon, but there was a critical difference nevertheless. According to the Justice Department, peonage "occurred only when the planter forbade the cropper to leave the plantation because of debt. . . . Peonage rested on debt, but the debtor had to be restrained for the legal definition to be fulfilled."[91] During the early twentieth century the Justice Department sent Special Agent A. J. Hoyt to investigate the mounting number of complaints filed by black laborers. Hoyt estimated that in Georgia, Mississippi, and Alabama "Investigations will prove that 33⅓ percent of the planters operating from five to one hundred plows, are holding their negro [sic] employees to a condition of peonage, and arresting and returning those that leave before alleged indebtedness is paid."[92]

"By the dawn of the twentieth century, peonage in the Southern cotton belt was a confusing mass of customs, legalities, and pseudo-legalities. Nearly every southern state legislature had passed a contract-labor measure that in many ways resembled the black codes of Reconstruction."[93] As federal investigation of peonage intensified, countless cases were discovered in a number of Alabama counties, and in 1903 the U.S. Attorney in Mobile, Alabama, M. D. Wickersham, uncovered an estimated fifty cases in Monroe and Wilcox counties.[94] By the time Wickersham filed his report, a legal climate favoring peonage had existed in the state of Alabama for almost two decades. That legal climate was the result of a false pretenses law that had been enacted by the Alabama legislature in 1885. According to the terms of that law, "If a laborer signed a contract, obtained an advance in money intending fraud, and then left the job without repaying the money, he should be punished 'as if he had stolen it.'"[95] Later, in 1903, state lawmakers moved to make this statute even tougher on peons. The amended law stipulated that proving intent to defraud was no longer required to secure a conviction. Instead, any laborer accepting an advance on his salary who either refused to work it off or pay it back would be considered guilty because his mere acceptance of the advance was considered "prima facie evidence of his intent to injure or defraud his employer."[96]

Booker T. Washington was particularly disturbed by this law. Washington, founder and principal of Tuskegee Institute in Tuskegee, Alabama, and the most famous black educator of his day, charged: "Any white man *who cares* to charge that a colored man has promised to work for him, and has not done so, or who has gotten money from him and not paid it back, can have the colored man sent to the chain gang" [emphasis added].[97] These were strong words for a man like Washington, who was considered the quintessential accommodationist of his day. During his long career, he rarely criticized the decisions of southern white policy makers on racial issues, but even Washington thought the provisions of the false pretensions law were morally and legally repugnant. Consequently, Booker T. Washington publicly championed the cause of a black Alabama farm worker, Alonzo Bailey, who was sentenced to a long term on the chain gang under the provisions of this statute.[98] Bailey's case went all the way to the United States Supreme Court, and on January 3, 1911, Justice Charles Evans Hughes delivered the majority opinion in *Bailey v. Alabama*. Hughes declared, "The state may impose involuntary servitude as a punishment for crime . . . but it may not compel one man to labor for another in payment of a debt by punishing him as a criminal if he does not perform the service or pay the debt."[99]

Despite the Bailey decision, peonage continued unabated in Alabama in general, and in Wilcox County in particular well into the twentieth century. Ray Stannard Baker, a leading white journalist who helped raise money for Bailey's defense, was pleased with the Supreme Court's ruling, but distressed by the continuation of peonage. He knew that it would take more than a Supreme Court ruling to end this vicious practice, because in his estimation as long as "so many Negroes are densely ignorant and poverty stricken, and while so many white men are short sighted enough to take advantage of this ignorance and poverty, so long will forms of slavery prevail."[100] His words proved to be prophetic. Long after this period, in the mid-1930s, Wilcox County teacher Ruby Abercrombie heard about two young black men who attempted to leave the plantation where they worked. They wanted to go to Mobile to work on the docks. Mr. Pritchett, the white landowner on whose land they worked, did not discover their absence until they were on a bus heading out of the county. Pritchett jumped in his car and pursued the bus. His fingers drummed the steering wheel as he pressed the accelerator dangerously close to the floor. He was angry, and he was determined.

Finally, he managed to pull even with the bus, and he gestured to the bus driver to pull over to the side of the road. The driver complied.

Pritchett boarded the bus in a rage, and when he looked down the aisle, he spotted the two young men sitting on the rear seat. In a strident voice Pritchett demanded that his two workers return to his plantation at once. The weight of custom and racial etiquette in Wilcox County invested Pritchett's words with an authority that his black workers were powerless to resist. When the two young men saw the commanding figure standing in the middle of the aisle, the last of their resolve crumbled. In one smooth motion, they slumped their shoulders and quickly looked down to avoid eye contact. Wordlessly, they got up from their seats and followed the plantation owner back into the world of debt and subordination that they were so desperate to escape. When Abercrombie heard about the incident, she was outraged. She straightened up to her full five-foot height, marched right up to Pritchett, and demanded to know what gave him the right to such complete control over his sharecroppers' lives. In a succinct summation of black and white relations in Wilcox County Pritchett asserted, "I can't let them go. They owe me."[101]

Clearly, the prospects for advancement for impoverished black Wilcox residents were bleak. In such an atmosphere the county's landless black agricultural laborers desperately needed to find ways to break the monotonous rhythm of their lives. Over the years, one of the few regular breaks in the farm laborers' routine was the Saturday trip into town. Principal Edwards of Snow Hill Institute observed that large numbers of the county's black farm laborers would congregate in Camden every Saturday night without fail. He observed, "Great crowds of Negroes would gather on Saturdays to spend their earnings of the week for a fine breakfast or dinner." Edwards's judgment of this custom was quite harsh. In his estimation, these impoverished African Americans were spending what little money they had on "useless trivialities."[102] Regardless of the principal's assessment, however, black Wilcox County residents really enjoyed this brief break in the monotonous rhythm of their lives. On many afternoons, the little town bulged at the seams with black men in their neatly starched and ironed overalls accompanied by women in gaily colored dresses with their children in tow. The sun glinted off rich ebony skin tones and bright fabric, creating a colorful scene. But a closer look revealed faces bereft of hope and tired bodies covered by ill-fitting clothes made of worn fabric.

The black visitors leisurely strolled around the town square dominated by the imposing sight of Wilcox County's antebellum red brick courthouse. Because it was such a visible symbol of white power, the sight of the courthouse provoked both fascination and fear. Black residents were particularly careful to avert their eyes when they passed a wooden bench that was strategically and comfortably located under a lush pecan tree on one side of the court-house. The bench was the exclusive domain of the town's leading white men who would often enjoy the shade of the pecan tree as they sat on their bench and discussed the issues of the day. Throughout the afternoon as the black crowds strolled past Camden's few shops, they gaily exchanged greetings and wistfully looked at items in store windows. However, every time a white person approached, the emotion automatically drained from their faces, and a mask of subservience snapped into place. During their short outings into town, the county's black sharecroppers knew that their continued survival depended on their unfailing observance of the county's racial etiquette. Even in town there were always reminders of the omnipresence of white authority. Nellie Williams Abner vividly remembers that the presence of Sheriff Lummie Jenkins often provided a forceful reminder. She observes, "I remember the sheriff used to come down . . . big black jack on his hip on Saturday evening, and you better not even breathe hardly."[103]

Going North

Even though Saturday outings in Camden were a welcome respite from their dreary existence, Wilcox County's black farm laborers needed more than temporary relief. Accordingly, by the turn of the century, black Wilcox County residents joined a steady stream of black Southerners leaving their region. Some sought opportunity in the growing cities of the South, while many others left the region altogether to seek their fortunes in the burgeoning industrial centers of the Northeast and Midwest. This vast out-migration reached epidemic proportions: in the first two decades of the twentieth century, hundreds of thousands of black rural Southerners left their homes. In fact, so many left that historians have christened the period 1900–1920 the Great Migration. The largest number of African Americans left the South during the World War I era, between 1916 and 1920.

So many African Americans were leaving that white Southerners who were dependent on this cheap labor source became alarmed. Predictably, the migration had a profound impact on white lives as one white observer explained: "Homes were without servants, farms were without laborers, churches were empty and houses were deserted."[104] When white Wilcox County residents were confronted with a steady stream of black workers leaving their county, they refused to acknowledge the real reason for the migration. Instead, they responded by offering worn-out platitudes: "Other things being equal, the negro

[sic] prefers to remain in the South, his home land where, we feel, it would be better for both races, if he would . . . remain in the country and cultivate the soil."[105] The *Wilcox Progressive Era* even reprinted an article from the *Atlanta Constitution* that warned black migrants about conditions in the North:

> Negroes who left the Southern states for the East or West with the hope of better-ing their condition have not found the welcoming treatment they expected. . . . While wages in some instances are higher in the North than they are in the South, the blacks . . . have found employment irregular and living conditions quite differ-ent from what they were at home. Even members of their own race in the North and East show little or no inclination to associate with the Southern darkie.[106]

Such arguments fell on deaf ears, however, because black Wilcox County residents continued to leave in staggering numbers. Even though the move-ment left white residents wringing their hands, the black press delighted in the migration. Robert Abbot's *Chicago Defender* was a staunch migration ad-vocate, and many black Wilcox residents were regular subscribers of this pa-per. In one issue Abbot declared, "To die from the bite of frost is far more glo-rious than at the hands of a mob."[107] Another black newspaper, the *Christian Recorder*, advised, "If a million Negroes move north and west in the next twelve month[s], it will be one of the greatest things for the Negro since the Emancipation Proclamation."[108] Most black Wilcox residents were in com-plete agreement with such sentiments, but while many could not wait to leave, there were others who remained hesitant. They sensed what their slave ancestors must have felt when they contemplated running away: the heady anticipation of finally having real freedom juxtaposed against the fear of the county's ruthless white repression that would go to any lengths to stop them.

Those who decided to leave were able to lock their fear inside a back cor-ner of their minds because they were invigorated by a delicious sense of ex-citement as they began their journey out of Wilcox County and into their fu-ture. Once they were on their way, however, most were hit by a powerful wave of nostalgia. After all, most of them had been born in Wilcox County, and as they took their last look at the lush vegetation growing all around them, they could smell the moist, humid earth that had a perfume all its own. The trees with gray beards of Spanish moss stood like silent sentinels on the side of the road watching this relentless black exodus out of the county. Be-tween 1910 and 1920 Wilcox County's population declined from 27,600 to 25,010; this represents a loss of 10 percent. Over the next decade the migra-tion continued to accelerate until Wilcox seemed to be hemorrhaging black residents. By 1930, the county's black population had dropped to 19,300.[109]

During the same years that this river of black residents flowed out of the county, Wilcox slowly began to exhibit signs of twentieth-century progress. By 1915, the county had its own telephone company, even though only a handful of residents had telephones. In the same year, $150,000 in county funds was earmarked for road improvement, but given the sorry state of the county's roads, this was only a small portion of the funds needed to make any real difference. In the coming years, as increasing numbers of county residents abandoned their horse-drawn wagons for sleek shiny automobiles, the need for more road improvements would become even more pressing. By 1916, the town of Camden had a new waterworks plant, and officials began to extend sewer lines and install water lines.[110] Clearly, such improvements ensured a more comfortable life for some of the county's residents.

However, in the early years of the twentieth century the lives of the majority of black residents remained unchanged: they continued to be defined by ruthless repression and suffocating subjugation. Indeed, in this new century their lives were disturbingly reminiscent of the lives of their slave ancestors. Like them, black Wilcox County residents in the early twentieth century could not vote, and most were tied to land belonging to a powerful white landowner. Of course, there were exceptions. Some black residents had managed to acquire small farms, while there were others, especially those connected with the county's black Presbyterian schools, who earned a salary from outside sources that allowed them to elude the worst aspects of white repression. Yet, because prospects for the majority of black residents remained bleak and opportunities for black advancement were in short supply, large numbers of black residents continued to leave Wilcox County in the coming decades. At the same time, the county's white residents continued to look to their county's past as they moved toward the future. In their world black people and black interests had always been subject to white control, except for a brief interruption during Reconstruction, and it was inconceivable to them that this relationship would ever change. In view of this white mind-set, it is not surprising that Alabama's first chapter of the United Daughters of the Confederacy (UDC) was established in Wilcox County. In 1913, Camden hosted the state convention of the UDC, and after the organization's president addressed the group, they sang, "Massah's in de Cold, Cold Ground."[111] Clearly, white Wilcox residents had a tenacious grip on the past, and it continued to define their future through the first half of the twentieth century. It was not until the civil rights movement in the second half of the twentieth century that their grip would begin to slip.

Onward Christian Soldiers: The Coming of the Missionaries during the Early Years, 1883–1930

Through the last quarter of the nineteenth century, and into the first decades of the twentieth, as ruthless white repression continued, African Americans who remained in Wilcox County saw few opportunities for advancement. However, there was one ray of hope that seemed to beckon to them. That ray of hope was the prospect of receiving a formal education. Indeed, as far back as the years right after the end of the Civil War, Wilcox freedmen, in concert with freedmen all over the South, focused on education with an enthusiasm that was breathtaking. Historian Vincent Franklin explains what he calls this yearning for learning: "As a result of conditions that masses of Afro-Americans faced during slavery and in the immediate postwar years, there developed within the Afro-American nation a preoccupation with literacy, schooling, and education in general. For thousands of newly emancipated Afro-Americans the acquisition of knowledge became just as important an objective as holding on to their freedom."[1] Noted black educator Booker T. Washington eloquently described the enthusiasm he witnessed: "It was a whole race trying to go to school. Few were too young, and none too old to make the attempt to learn."[2]

In fact, efforts to educate the freedmen began even before the end of the Civil War. As the Union Army advanced into Confederate territory in the last days of the war, it was followed by scores of northern missionaries. Although the missionaries went south intending to educate the ex-slaves, they were unprepared for the overwhelming black enthusiasm that greeted them. Everywhere they went the missionaries were besieged by newly freed slaves

who were begging for schools. Alabama freedmen clearly articulated the reason for their educational desire in no uncertain terms as early as 1865 when
they insisted, "We regard the education of our children and youths as vital to
the preservation of our liberties." They went on to pledge to "use our utmost
endeavors to promote these blessings in our country."[3] V. P. Franklin explains
that these ex-slaves were desperate to become educated "because they saw in
their day-to-day experiences—from one generation to the next—that knowledge and information helped one to survive in a hostile environment." Conversely, Franklin argues, "An important part of the oppression of enslavement was depriving Afro-Americans of knowledge of their condition, and
thus the ways to change it."[4]

All this postwar black enthusiasm was countered by southern white hostility. Clearly, this hostility to black learning stretched all the way back to the
era of slavery when plantation owners recognized that a literate slave was a
dangerous slave: "In 1832 Alabama denied formal education to all blacks to
discourage revolts."[5] Because their notion of the proper place for African
Americans in their society had changed very little from the prewar to the
postwar era, white Southerners in general and white Alabamans in particular continued to disapprove of black education. They were especially critical
of the kind of education dispensed by the northern missionaries. In the estimation of one white Alabaman, these meddling outsiders "taught their
Negroes to give up all habits and customs that would remind him of his former condition. . . . He must not take off his hat when speaking to a white
person. In teaching him not to be servile, they taught him to be insolent."[6]
White Alabama Democratic Congressman Peter Dox exclaimed in dismay
that once his former slaves had received some education, he had to black his
own boots, "because the Negroes would not."[7] All around them, white
Alabamans watched in horror as missionary education began to undermine
the white supremacy they were trying so hard to reestablish.

In the midst of their fears, some white Alabama residents began to argue
that they should preempt missionary efforts as much as possible by taking the
initiative to establish their own schools for their ex-slaves. They reasoned that
they could control the curriculum in these schools, and this would help them
to stop the missionaries from spreading "such *alien* values as equality, brother-
hood, and citizenship for all."[8] A newspaper in Greensboro, Alabama, explained this white motivation in no uncertain terms: "The more interest
whites take in Negro education the better they will be able to control their
former slaves for good."[9] As increasing numbers of Alabama's white citizens
came to embrace this notion, they tentatively began to establish some public
schools for the freedmen in select areas. Added to these local white efforts and

missionary endeavors was the initiative of the Freedmen's Bureau. The bureau provided critical financial support for black education during these early years.

Predictably, these efforts to establish freedmen's education were more than a little chaotic during the immediate postwar years with so many different groups involved. At times, these groups cooperated with each other, but more often than not, white state officials competed against missionaries and federal officials for the hearts, minds, and souls of the freedmen. These over-lapping efforts to educate Alabama freedmen were extremely uneven: missionaries and bureau officials most often flocked to the larger towns and cities, where their teachers and other support personnel felt comparatively safe from local white resentment and aggression. Yet, even though they felt a bit more secure in the cities, these white outsiders realized that they were still vulnerable in the urban areas as well. There are scores of documented attacks against white Northerners who were attempting to educate Alabama freedmen during this volatile period. For example, Alabama Congressman Dox recalled the case of Elijah Fitch, a white Northerner who "had been beaten for teaching Negroes." In another case a Canadian teacher was lynched. Local white Alabama residents justified the murder by insisting that the teacher had "made himself obnoxious to the white people . . . seducing servants from the employ of planters."[10]

Given this hostile atmosphere even in the cities, white missionary societies were extremely reluctant to send their teachers out in the country where the dangers were magnified. This left freedmen in rural areas with few educational options in the immediate postwar years. Thus, the rural nature of their county sealed the educational fate of Wilcox County's ex-slaves in the years immediately following the war. With no missionaries poised to inculcate their former slaves with alien notions, white Wilcox residents saw no need to provide any schooling at all for black residents, even though there were state funds for that purpose that the county could have tapped. In fact, Wilcox plantation owners were even reluctant to provide tax-supported schooling for children of their own race. The white apathy toward public schooling that was so evident in Wilcox County was part of a larger southern reality. All across the region frustrated missionaries and Freedmen's Bureau officials complained about the widespread nature of such apathy and the difficulties it posed. As one bureau official put it, "The whites take little or no interest in educational matters, even for their own race."[11] Thus, even though Alabama's Reconstruction constitution of 1868 set up the machinery for a statewide system of public schools, only the most feeble attempts were made in Wilcox County to provide tax-supported schools for white children; black children were ignored altogether.

This white Wilcox educational reluctance was further complicated by the inefficient structure of the state's educational apparatus. Although Alabama's constitution of 1868 created a state board of education that was empowered to manage the schools and enact relevant legislation, the state legislature had the power to repeal the board's legislation, and the governor could veto it. In practical terms, this unusual division of power led to intergovernmental strife that retarded the growth of public education throughout the state during the era of Reconstruction. And so, for Wilcox freedmen, the die was cast. Local white apathetic attitudes combined with Alabama's postwar poverty and an inefficient state educational system to consign them to a purgatory of ignorance. Furthermore, because of the rural nature of their county, it would be years before any help would come from outside missionary sources.

In the meantime, after the end of Reconstruction there was one last northern Republican effort made to address the educational plight of the southern freedmen. That effort, the Blair Bill, also proposed to provide educational aid for white children, too. The bill was introduced by Senator Henry Blair of New Hampshire in 1881. It provided that the federal government would make ten annual appropriations beginning at $15 million and diminishing by $1 million each year. The funds were to be distributed among the states according to the degree of illiteracy in each. Although appropriations were to have been equally distributed between black and white children, segregation of the races would have been permitted under the terms of the new law.[12] Because of their high rate of illiteracy, Alabama would have received a substantial appropriation had the bill become law. Yet, all across the state, white Alabamans were very vocal in their opposition to the Blair Bill. John Tyler Morgan, a senator from the Alabama Black Belt, explained why so many white residents in his region were unalterably opposed to the bill when he argued that the extra school funds might be used to lengthen the brief term of black schools. He went on to insist that this would never do because it would take black laborers away from their duties on the plantations for too long a time. Yet, at the time when the Blair Bill was under consideration, the few black rural schools that did exist were only in session for two or three months a year. Even this was too long, Senator Morgan complained. As he put it, "Seventy-three days out of a crop is a large item in cotton country." Because the revenue from the Blair Bill would allow many black schools to double their terms, Morgan had no doubt that this would be disastrous for Black Belt planters. He complained, "One hundred and forty-six days would ruin a crop."[13] At the same time, Senator Morgan never expressed any concern for the effect a short school term would have on the lives of black children. Blair's bill passed the Senate three times: The first time was in 1881, and it subsequently passed in 1884 and 1886. But each time it passed the Senate, it went down to defeat in the House of Representatives.[14]

Although Henry Blair's bill would have been particularly beneficial to southern education, it was rooted in a broad and mounting national concern that transcended regional borders. In fact, the last quarter of the nineteenth century witnessed a general decline in the quality and effectiveness of public schooling across the country. Even northern school systems that had expanded during the educational reform movement of the 1830s were suffering under the weight of mounting postwar challenges. One of the most important of those challenges was the influx of large numbers of immigrant children. As these new students flocked into already overcrowded urban schools, class sizes became unmanageable, and recitation by rote became the primary method of instruction. Moreover, these schools also suffered from heating, lighting, and sanitary problems.[15] In the meantime, northern schools in rural areas struggled with equally difficult problems. Many of these institutions had been allowed to fall into disrepair once large numbers of rural residents began migrating to the cities. Teachers in the rural setting were often poorly trained, and many of these schools remained ungraded.[16] Thus, by the end of the nineteenth century, increasing numbers of northerners were becoming concerned about the sorry state of public education in their region as well.

Such late nineteenth-century concern was part of a larger uneasiness about the state of society, which was being transformed by European immigration, rapid industrialization, and urbanization. In the midst of these profound changes, unprecedented prosperity existed alongside abject poverty. Among Northerners who were uncomfortable with these changes in their society, the beginnings of a reform movement became evident by the 1890s. At that time, many Northerners began to view education as the key to the transformation of their society. One reformer succinctly explained, "The one way to bring better times, better civilization, better men, better women, is education."[17] As they sought to use education to improve their society, these reformers expressed a great deal of concern for what they considered the deterioration of America's rural areas. Many were convinced that the farmers must remain the moral mainstay of the nation, and that the new industrial cities would be strong only if they were built on this firm rural foundation. Thus, during the last part of the nineteenth century, schooling for country life became a popular curriculum trend as urban reformers preached the message that more Americans needed to stay on the farm.[18]

Schooling for country life was also a popular curriculum trend among Southerners of this era who were debating curriculum issues, but the southern debate was further complicated by the region's racial realities. While most white Southerners had grudgingly come to accept black schools as a way of life by the end of the nineteenth century, their acceptance was accompanied by the conviction that black youth should only be given a special kind of education: industrial/vocational education. Their endorsement of this kind of education for the ex-slaves and their descendants was clearly motivated by planter self-interest. In his insightful study, *Schooling for the New Slavery*, Donald Spivey insists that there was a direct connection between white planter self-interest and black industrial education. He explains, "Sharecropping, debt peonage, and convict lease were means used to resubjugate black labor." He continues, "Industrial education was [also] a major force in the subjugation of black labor in the New South."[19] Spivey reasons that curriculum content in such education was carefully chosen to produce tractable, obedient, and dependent manual laborers.

The passionate and emotional discussion of black curriculum issues in the late nineteenth century was symbolized by the very public debate between Booker T. Washington and W. E. B. Du Bois. On the one hand, Washington was convinced that industrial education was the only sure means to black advancement. As he put it, "Our greatest danger is that in the great leap from slavery to freedom we may overlook the fact that we shall prosper in proportion as we learn to dignify and glorify common labor. No race can prosper till it learns that there is as much dignity in tilling a field as in writing a poem."[20] On the other hand, W. E. B. Du Bois insisted that the best and brightest black youth should be given a classical liberal arts education. Du Bois reasoned that these young people would become the leaders of the race one day. He argued, "Such educational leaders should be prepared by long and rigorous courses of study similar to those which the world over have been designed to strengthen the intellectual powers, fortify character, and facilitate the transmission from age to age of the stores of the world's knowledge."[21]

After each staked out his position, Du Bois, the quintessential scholar, and Washington, the consummate politician, continued to disagree about the proper direction for black education until well into the twentieth century. However, although contemporary black educators were undoubtedly aware of the Washington–Du Bois debate, their understanding of the possibilities for, and the limitations of African American education in their locale played a much larger role in determining their position on this issue. Black educators in Wilcox County were painfully aware of the harsh racial and economic realities in their county as they formulated their educational policies. The educational philosophy of William Edwards provides a case in point. Edwards, a black native of Wilcox County, and a graduate of Washington's Tuskegee Institute, established a small school in his home county in 1893. In the com-

ing decades, his school, Snow Hill Institute, provided one of the few local opportunities for Wilcox's black residents to receive any education at all.
Edwards's training at Tuskegee combined with his observation of conditions
in Wilcox County to convince him that local black residents desperately
needed industrial training.[22] He painfully described the plight of his people:
"The idea of buying land was foreign to all of them, and there were not
more than twenty acres of land owned by the colored people in this whole
neighborhood. . . . The carrying of men and women to the chain-gang was a
frequent occurrence."[23] Edwards maintained that only the right sort of
industrial training would help alleviate this black suffering and foster black
financial independence in Wilcox County.

Accordingly, Edwards made sure that such industrial education was the
centerpiece of his new school's curriculum. However, to his surprise, he soon
discovered that the black families living near his school did not want any
part of industrial education. Such parental opposition was motivated by their
collective memory of slavery. By the time Edwards established his school, although a generation had passed since slavery had ended, many were still
haunted by the monotonous drudgery of bending over the young cotton
plants under the malevolent stare of an overseer who had his whip coiled and
ready to strike without warning. They could almost hear the awful whistling
of the lash as it snaked out suddenly to bite black flesh. Furthermore, these
memories of slavery were reinforced by the reality of their lives as they struggled to make ends meet under the unfair sharecropping/tenancy/peonage system that had taken slavery's place. Black Wilcox parents desperately wanted
to protect their children from such a dismal, dreary, hopeless existence. Consequently, most simply refused to endorse a type of education that would only
prepare their children to be manual laborers, and bind them even more
tightly to land they would never own. Black parents wanted to be able to give
their children something that would make their lives easier, and because they
had virtually no land and few material possessions, the only thing they could
try to give their children was hope. Most of these black parents were convinced that hope for their children's futures lay not in industrial education,
but in the classical/liberal arts variety.

Parents expressed their sentiments in no uncertain terms, and Edwards knew
that he was fighting an uphill battle. He observed, "They [parents] were much
opposed to industrial education." It seemed that parents were particularly offended by that part of the Snow Hill curriculum that required students to perform actual manual labor on a regular basis. Edwards recalled, "When the school
was started, many of the parents came to school and forbade our working their
children, stating as their objection that their children had been working all

their lives and that they did not mean to send them to school to learn to work." Edwards tried to reason with them, but many parents remained unpersuaded. He lamented, "Not only did they forbid our having their children work, but many took their children out of school rather than allow them to do so."[24]

Not all black parents disapproved of the school's methods, however, and within a short time Snow Hill Institute began to gain support. Some local black residents who lived close to the school began to hold various fund-raising activities on a regular basis to provide the struggling institution with the capital it desperately needed to keep its doors open during the lean early years of its existence. At the same time, the school was even able to gain support from one of the wealthiest white landowners in the area. That landowner, Ransom O. Simpson, donated the dilapidated log cabin where Snow Hill's students first began holding classes. The school's new quarters had originally served as a corncrib, and there were corn shucks still littering the dirt floor when the first excited students crowded into the drafty, rough structure. The former corncrib was soon transformed by the earnest childish voices of black youngsters who were clad in rags reciting their lessons.

Simpson was so impressed by Edwards's determination that he donated seven acres of land to the school at the end of its first year of operation. A short time later, Simpson donated an additional thirty-three acres. Then, right after the turn of the century, Simpson gave the school still another sixty acres.[25] Even though Edwards was grateful for Simpson's gifts, he was determined to acquire still more land for his school. He explained his reasoning this way: "Again, it is a well known fact that many white people in the South, and I presume in many other sections of the country, do not like to have Negro schools and Negro churches near their neighborhood, and to avoid any friction in the future, in this direction, it is very essential that we own this land."[26] William Edwards soon discovered that he would have a very difficult time raising the substantial sum necessary to make such a large land purchase. He refused to give up, however, and by May of 1908 he had raised enough money to buy an additional 240 acres from R. O. Simpson. William Edwards's successful attempt to provide his school with a measure of independence was noticed and appreciated by local black residents, but this was not the only thing they appreciated about the school. Long before Snow Hill expanded its land holdings, black parents in the vicinity of the school had begun to reconsider their condemnation of the school's curriculum. While many still disapproved of the industrial education that was the centerpiece of the Snow Hill program, they soon realized that the school also had an academic department. Parents heartily approved of the courses offered through the academic department, which included mental and moral science, mathematics, bookkeeping, music, reading, literature, grammar, rhetoric, history, geography, hygiene, physics, and civil government. In order to receive a Snow Hill diploma, students were required to complete coursework in both the academic and industrial departments.[27]

Over the years Edwards consistently argued that he thought the national industrial/classical education debate was inimical to black interests. "The fact is," he declared, "there should be no limit placed before the literary qualifications of our people. A race segregated as ours needs its own leaders, teachers, preachers, physicians, lawyers and business and professional men. These should have the highest, deepest, broadest education that is obtainable." But this was only part of what black people needed, Edwards insisted. As he put it, "We need not only a good literary training, but a good industrial training as well. This is a scientific as well as a literary age. . . . Our hand should be as thoroughly taught to work as our minds to think."[28] In addition to providing educational opportunities to thousands of black Wilcox residents over the years, Snow Hill Institute also offered outreach programs designed to improve black community life. At Snow Hill's annual farmers' conferences, local black farmers were given advice on the most modern agricultural methods. The school also established the Black Belt Improvement Society, which aimed to promote black financial independence. According to the group's constitution, "It shall be one of the great objects of this society to stimulate its members to acquire homes." The society also advised, "It shall further be the object of the Black Belt Improvement Society as far as possible, to eliminate the credit system from our social fabric; to stimulate in all members the desire to raise, as far as possible, all their food supplies at home and pay cash for whatever may be purchased at the stores."[29]

As Snow Hill Institute worked hard to provide educational opportunities for black residents, the school's faculty and administration were energized by a sense of urgency. They were determined to reach as many as they could as quickly as possible because they realized how little Wilcox county and the state of Alabama were doing. Edwards lamented,

> I ought to say that the Legislature has grown so hostile towards Negro education in recent years, that we cannot even have a bill introduced now, much less have one passed. You men have read, during the last week the Legislature of Alabama has appropriated $1,673,000 for improvement and maintenance of the white schools of the state, not one dollar is to go toward Negro schools.[30]

Predictably, statistical data for Wilcox school expenditures in the last decades of the nineteenth century and the early decades of the twentieth clearly underscore the gross inequities based on race. During the 1876–1877 school year as Reconstruction was drawing to a close, $2,136 was spent on teachers' salaries for the county's 2,403 white students. During that same school year, the county spent $6,055 on teachers' salaries for the county's 7,357 black students. These expenditures amounted to $0.88 for each white child, and $0.82 for each black child. Clearly, the disparity was small, but it would continue to widen with each passing year. By the 1883–1884 academic year, $2,370 was spent on teachers' salaries to educate the county's 2,057 white students. That same year, $6,574 was spent to educate the county's 6,457 black students. These figures mean that $1.15 was spent for each white child, and $1.01 was spent for each black child. By the 1890–1891 school year, just two years before William Edwards founded Snow Hill, the disparity between expenditures for black and white students had grown considerably. During that academic year, the county spent $4,397 to educate its 2,482 white students. At the same time, Wilcox only spent $6,545 on its 9,931 black students. This means that the county spent $1.77 for each white child, but only $0.65 for each black child.[31]

In 1891 the Alabama State Legislature passed a new apportionment act. This act, which was introduced as House Bill 504, provided that "The Superintendent of Education is relieved of apportioning the school fund between the races." Instead, that responsibility was granted to school officials in each county. Immediately after the passage of this act, the State Education Report discontinued the practice of printing county statistics by race, and expenditure data based on race would not be available again until the 1907–1908 school year. By then, the damage had been done. Particularly in the Black Belt counties, local officials shamelessly diverted most of the state educational dollars they received to the white schools. In fact, within a few months of the passage of the apportionment act, the superintendent of Wilcox County schools gleefully reported, "Wilcox never had such a boom on [white] schools. The new law has stimulated the whites so that neighborhoods where no schools had existed for years are now building houses and organizing schools."[32]

The first set of expenditure statistics based on race that were released after the passage of the1891 apportionment law tell a sorrowful tale of black deprivation in Wilcox County. During the 1907–1908 school year, $28,108 was spent to educate the county's 2,825 white students. On the other hand, the county's 10,745 black students received only $3,940. The disparity was staggering: $12.30 was spent on each white child, but only $0.36 was spent on each black child. A decade later during the 1916–1917 school year, as the county prepared to enter World War I, expenditures for Wilcox County's 1,868 white pupils had risen to $33,289, while the appropriation for the county's 9,872 black students had fallen to $3,462. Clearly, the disparity was continuing to grow unchecked: $17.82 was spent on each white child during the World War I era, while only $0.35 was spent on each black child. Finally, on the eve of the Great Depression, educational expenditures for both black and white pupils increased considerably. But, at the same time, the disparity between appropriations to black and white schools was worse than ever: during the 1928–1929 school year, the county's 1,865 white students received $57,578 while the 8,483 black pupils only received $8,176. Thus, despite the higher appropriations, the gap between black and white expenditures remained huge: only $0.96 was spent on each black child, while $30.87 was spent on each white child.[33]

Thus, as African Americans in Wilcox County passed through the difficult years of the late nineteenth century and into an uncertain future in the twentieth century, they were painfully aware that they could not expect equitable treatment from local school officials. Yet, many still refused to surrender their hopes and dreams for a better life. In the early 1880s an unlikely combination of circumstances occurred that would produce more educational opportunities for black county residents. Those opportunities, which came to occupy a critical place in the lives of black Wilcox residents, all started from a casual visit by white Presbyterian missionary Eliza B. Wallace to Judge William Henderson's plantation in Miller's Ferry. Wallace was a short, stocky, no-nonsense mathematics teacher with curly hair, a square jaw, and a self-assured manner. In August of 1877 she joined the faculty of Knoxville College, a black United Presbyterian college in Knoxville, Tennessee. Wallace's arrival on the East Tennessee campus occurred just two weeks after the school's first president, Dr. J. S. McCulloch, assumed his duties.

From her earliest days on campus, Eliza Wallace did much more than just teach math. In fact, she had grand plans. When she first arrived, the new institution's campus had only one small building in the center of five acres of blackberry and sumac bushes. But, as the young math teacher stood on a hill overlooking this scene, her imagination replaced the wild tangle of vegetation with a neatly trimmed lawn and tidy red brick dormitories arranged around an imposing administration building topped by a large clock tower. Everywhere on her imaginary campus, Eliza Wallace could visualize earnest, soft-spoken, well-dressed black young people. She was determined to make her vision a reality because she was totally committed to the importance of her work among the freedmen. She explained,

Being led by the providence of God to labor among the Freedmen in Knoxville, Tennessee during the last year, my eyes have been opened to the importance of the work. *It is not true that intellectually they are inferior to the white race.* In our school at Knoxville we had about the same proportion of talented and indolent students as in our Northern Academies [emphasis added].[34]

It was obvious to anyone who came in contact with her that Eliza B. Wallace was filled with missionary zeal; she was consecrated to the cause of uplifting the freedmen. Her commitment to this missionary work is not surprising in view of her missionary pedigree. She was born in 1836 in Fairview, Ohio. She had five brothers and four sisters, and her father was a church elder.[35] A number of the other men in her family were intimately involved in the church as well: a grand uncle, two uncles, and one brother all became ministers. After Wallace's father died, the family moved to Monmouth, Illinois, and in 1866 Eliza Wallace graduated from Monmouth College with a BS degree. Armed with her college degree, Wallace taught school and preformed missionary work among the poor for a number of years until the Presbyterian Board of Freedmen's Missions called her to join the faculty of their new freedmen's college in Knoxville.[36]

When Eliza Wallace arrived at her friend Judge Henderson's plantation, he immediately saw the missionary fire in her eyes. Wallace looked out over Henderson's black workers toiling in the fields, and her intense eyes widened in disbelief; her square jaw looked as though it were carved out of granite as she clenched her teeth. All around her Eliza Wallace saw black men in straw hats, and women in gaily colored head rags bending over to tend the young cotton plants in the merciless Alabama sunshine. All the children who were old enough worked right alongside their parents. However, the youngest children, most of whom were scantily clad, scampered about as their elders worked. The resemblance of the scene in front of her to the institution of slavery was shockingly obvious. "Where are their schools?" a missionary voice in Eliza Wallace's head demanded to know. That very afternoon Wallace had a long talk with her friend and fellow Presbyterian William Henderson. Henderson informed her of the county's neglect of the freedmen's educational needs. He explained, "The law grants them three months school but many of the directors give the school to the teacher who promises him the largest per cent of his wages. The director neither knows nor cares whether the teacher spends his time teaching or hunting or fishing."[37] Miss Wallace found Henderson's description very disturbing.

Henderson's assessment of conditions in Wilcox County could easily be applied to counties all over the state. During the earliest days of black state-supported schooling in Alabama just after the Civil War, some of the teachers in these schools were local white residents whose motives were suspect, and whose qualifications were questionable. Of course, many were motivated by the desire to exercise greater control over the curriculum in black schools. Some were convinced that this "was a step towards securing control over the Negro race."[38] Others were motivated more by self-interest, however. They reasoned, "it is easier to sit in the shade [and teach] than to plow."[39] Indeed, some state officials began to encourage this kind of behavior. For example, James H. Clanton, chairman of the Democratic State Executive Committee, "advised white people to teach Negro schools because it would furnish employment to needy white persons."[40]

As Wallace heard more and more about the inadequacy of state and county efforts to educate local freedmen, her brow wrinkled in concentration and an idea began to take shape in her mind. She tactfully suggested to her friend Judge Henderson that he was in a position to help change things because he was one of the wealthiest landowners in Wilcox County. Henderson could not get a word in edgewise as the persuasive Miss Wallace reminded him of his duty as a good Presbyterian. As she pleaded her cause, Wallace watched the judge's face intently. She was not sure that she was getting through to him, so she decided that she needed to appeal to his self-interest. She shrewdly reminded Henderson that establishing a black school close to his plantation would definitely be beneficial because it would keep the more enterprising workers from leaving in search of educational opportunities for their children.

Henderson could not help but smile at his earnest young friend as she talked on and on in an effort to persuade him. In fact, Judge Henderson had already been thinking about the prospect of establishing a black school on his plantation even before Miss Wallace arrived, because all around him a number of other planters had already furnished schools for their sharecroppers in an effort to stabilize their workforce. For example, in 1869, Mr. Saunders, a white landowner in neighboring Perry County, hired a teacher for the "colored" school he set up on his plantation. According to local newspaper reports, "Mr. Saunders bears all the expenses of boarding and paying the teacher, and yet expects to be the gainer for having plenty of good, steady laborers well satisfied with their situation." The newspaper report further explained, "the mere prospect of being able to learn something is regarded as a temptation likely to be more powerful than any other on the minds of the freedmen."[41]

Miss Wallace was still talking when Henderson chuckled and raised his hands in a gesture of surrender. Their conversation then turned to the practical issues involved in actually establishing a freedmen's school. As they began to finalize their plans, Wallace's square jaw finally relaxed, and the corners of her mouth lifted up into a radiant smile. Yet, the determined missionary did not have long to savor the anticipation of opening a new missionary field. Both she and the judge knew from experience that starting a school for freedmen in a rural area was fraught with difficulty and sure to arouse controversy. Regardless of the obstacles, however, the school on Judge Henderson's plantation officially opened in 1884. In the early years it was called the Prairie Bluff Mission. However, by late 1890, after a post office was opened on the east side of the Alabama River not too far from the school, the area was renamed Miller's Ferry.[42]

One of the most remarkable features of this early mission was its isolation and inaccessibility. The eventual extension of a rail line into the area helped make it a bit easier to reach, but for anyone attempting to reach Miller's Ferry, the journey was still long and arduous. Dr. McCulloch, president of Knoxville College, remarked on the mission's isolation after he paid the school a visit. McCulloch was able to ride the train from Knoxville, Tennessee, to Catherine, a Wilcox County town less than forty miles from Selma. But then, according to McCulloch, "from Catherine a private conveyance is taken through Middle Place, four miles distant, and Prairie Bluff, a mile or more farther on, where the river is crossed in a skiff or a ferry-boat propelled by oars." After this long and difficult journey, McCulloch arrived at the school and was immediately struck by its isolation: "The mission is in a strictly country place about two miles from the ferry in the direction of Camden. The road is sandy and level, and liable to be overflowed when the river is high." There were vast stretches of vacant land near the school, and McCulloch observed, "There is no town, not even a village. A store with the Post Office is the rallying point of hundreds of people within three miles."[43]

Despite the school's isolation, word of the Presbyterian mission on Judge Henderson's place spread through Wilcox County like wildfire. Freedmen in the area were wildly enthusiastic, and many excitedly crowded into the school's first building, which was actually "an old log church through any part of which you could throw a cat by the tail."[44] The school day started each morning at 9:00 with singing, recitation of Scripture, and prayer. At 9:30, students began their academic work, and they continued until 3:30 p.m. The school's principal gleefully reported, "The greatest difficulty the parents have is to keep the children at home." In fact, the announcement of the dates for Christmas vacation was greeted by "exclamations of regret instead of gladness; and they [the students] were delighted when it [Christmas vacation] was over."[45] Miss Henrietta Mason was the school's first teacher. She was a graduate of Knoxville College, and Dr. McCulloch expressed his confidence in her in no uncertain terms: "She comes with a strong endorsement. Besides, Henrietta can boss a school better than . . . [most teachers]." McCulloch expressed only one reservation about the mission's new teacher, "She is a miserable singer."[46]

Mason was succeeded in 1887 by Peter Cloud, a Knoxville College graduate from Wytheville, Virginia. Shortly after he assumed leadership of the mission, Cloud began an ambitious expansion program. Initially, he built a three-room box building. Later, a second story was added, making room for additional classrooms and a chapel.[47] Judge Henderson helped facilitate the school's expansion by contributing financial resources and providing the use of his sawmill. Many black residents in the community were convinced that the school was an important force for positive change in their lives. Presbyterian church officials were also convinced that the school was a force for change, and they were especially proud of the efforts of their missionaries. They reported, "Before the opening of our mission schools in this densely populated region the conditions were as deplorable among the colored population as might be expected in the very heart of Africa." As a result of the work of their missionaries in Wilcox County, church officials concluded, "The result is a most wonderful transforming of the communities thus touched."[48] Two particularly important changes resulted from that transformation: "The ability of a large proportion of the young people to read," and "The more stable character of the plantation hands."[49]

Black residents were thrilled; even some white residents were favorably impressed. Not all of the county's white residents were willing to tolerate this alien Presbyterian presence, however, because even though these Presbyterian missionaries were black and southern, they had been educated by the northern white missionaries at Knoxville College. Some white locals feared that alien ideas about black citizenship rights and black equality might have been part of their college training. What was to stop these outsiders from infecting Wilcox County's black workers with their dangerous notions, the planters wondered. The county's white landowners also fretted about the time that the older black children spent in school, which cut into the hours that they could spend working in the fields. Even Judge Henderson, who was obviously an advocate of African American education, expressed reservations about too many of his hands leaving his fields to attend school. Peter Cloud reported, "Judge Henderson grudges a little the loss of the labor of boys & girls in the fields, but he does not say much."[50] Clearly, even white supporters of black education often had trouble maintaining their enthusiasm when they thought the efficient operation of their plantations was threatened.

Unfortunately, the concern of some white county residents soon turned to anger and resentment. For some time, that resentment had simmered among those local white residents who did not want any part of this intrusion into their county. In 1895, this resentment finally boiled over: a local white man set fire to the Miller's Ferry Mission school. At 10:00 on the night of May 4, black residents who lived near the school ran outside in a panic when their darkened homes were suddenly lit up by a fierce red glow. As word spread, neighborhood residents converged on the school, but by the time most people arrived, the pine building was fully engulfed in flames. The dry pine structure crackled and popped as the greedy flames leaped and danced skyward. Students and their parents from all over the area were inexorably drawn to the awesome and awful sight of their school building being consumed by fire. Tears glistened on their faces. Their pain was intense, and their frustration was almost overwhelming because this school represented their only hope for a better life, and all they could do was stand by and watch it burn. After what seemed like an eternity, the fire began to lose its intensity, and the crackling of pine was replaced by the wails and moans of those gathered on the campus, "lamenting as did the Jews of old over the destruction of their beloved Jerusalem." They had lost everything: not even a Bible or a Psalm book survived the fire.[51]

Tillie Johnson, one of the teachers and the wife of the principal, was outraged when she noticed that the arsonist who had set the fire left a can of oil and a bundle of pine kindling in front of the school in plain sight. It seemed to the angry teacher that the arsonist was taunting them. Her outrage quickly spread through the crowd like an epidemic as others began to notice the arsonist's calling card. They were determined to find out who was responsible, and because the perpetrator made no attempt to hide his involvement, he was conclusively identified after only a cursory investigation by Judge Henderson and the missionaries. Clearly, the arsonist was not the least bit worried about suffering any consequences for burning down a black school. He was convinced that his white skin would provide him with immunity. He was right: despite the existence of conclusive evidence, the arsonist was never even charged with the crime. Thus, parents and students of the Miller's Ferry mission were forced to live with the knowledge that the person who had deprived them of their school would never be brought to justice. They knew his identity; they saw him walking around as a free man; and they could not do anything about it. It was maddening.

The arsonist was not satisfied with just burning down the school. When he learned that the black missionaries and their carpetbagger friend had had the audacity to investigate the fire, he was incensed. How dare they, he fumed. As he thought about this violation of Wilcox County's racial etiquette, much of the perpetrator's anger became focused on Judge Henderson. In the arsonist's estimation, Henderson was a carpetbagger, a race traitor, and had it not been for his meddling, there never would have been a black school at Miller's Ferry. The arsonist's anger festered for a few weeks after the fire.

Finally, determined to exact revenge, the outraged perpetrator confronted the judge in broad daylight in front of dozens of black witnesses, pointed a pistol at him, and opened fire. Everybody gasped and braced themselves as they waited for the wounded Henderson to fall. But, amazingly, all they heard was a dull click: the gun misfired, and Judge Henderson was unharmed. The crowd witnessing the scene was stunned. As word of Henderson's miraculous deliverance spread, black people living in the vicinity of the Miller's Ferry mission were more convinced than ever that these missionaries were doing God's work.[52]

After they recovered from this initial trial by fire, local black people, aided by the Presbyterian Church, dedicated themselves to rebuilding their mission school. They were convinced of the importance of their work, and determined to prove that even an arsonist could not stop them. Soon, the area near the burned ruins was humming with activity as eager local black men began the task of rebuilding. Once again, Judge Henderson supplied many of the tools they needed, and he also allowed them to use his sawmill. Ella Earls Cotton, a teacher and principal's wife at a neighboring black Presbyterian school described the scene:

> At a glance, we could see the skeleton of the new building going up in replacement of the one that had been burned. Only it was going to be a much larger building, with added rooms, better equipment, and more departments. In some ways it was to be like the legendary phoenix, which built its own funeral pyre at the end of its five or six hundred years lifespan, inspired it with fire and from the ashes rose to live again and more grandly.[53]

The new Presbyterian school at Miller's Ferry sought to offer a broad curriculum that included both liberal arts and industrial instruction. By the early twentieth century, in response to increasing black demands, Miller's Ferry expanded its curriculum to include courses on the high school level. Furthermore, a short time later, with the blessing of the Presbyterian Board, the school added courses in nurses training, and built Robinson Memorial Hospital. While the hospital was an important training ground for Miller's Ferry nursing students, it also served an equally important function for local black residents: it was one of the few health care facilities in the county that served African Americans.

Miller's Ferry's expanded programs soon began to attract increasing numbers of students from outside the vicinity. School administrators were gratified by this interest in their school from other areas of the county, but they could not accept these students from other places because they did not have anywhere for them to stay. The missionaries were haunted by the earnest pleas of the many black youngsters they had to turn away. There was only one solution: they decided to build dormitories. They excitedly contacted Freedmen's Board officials of the Presbyterian Church at the headquarters in Pittsburgh, Pennsylvania. When those officials expressed their skepticism about the need for boarding facilities at this rural school in the Black Belt, the missionaries were disappointed, but undaunted. Led by the school's principal, local black residents supplied all the labor and materials necessary to construct a boy's dormitory that housed sixteen, and a girl's dormitory that could accommodate thirty-two. Almost before the sound of banging hammers and buzzing saws died away on the construction site, both dormitories were filled to capacity, with many more on the waiting list. When church officials in Pittsburgh realized that the missionaries in Wilcox County had not overestimated student demand, they decided to send funds to the Miller's Ferry mission to enlarge its dormitories.[54]

While the missionaries at Miller's Ferry were thrilled to have all the enthusiastic young students who crowded into their classrooms, they were also convinced that they had a responsibility to others besides the children. They were concerned that older black residents also needed schooling. Consequently, women faculty members decided to create a class for older black women. They called it the mothers meeting, and the class met every Friday from 1:00 to 3:00 P.M. The women were given a heavy dose of religion along with basic instruction in English and arithmetic. Many of these neighborhood women were reluctant to enroll when the class first started because they thought they were too old to learn anything. They had very hard lives: they worked in the fields as hard as their husbands every day, and then they still had to go back to their homes in the evening and take care of all their household chores. Their muscles ached, they had calluses on their hands, and they had lost hope that life would ever be any different for them.

Most of these sharecropping women were thoroughly intimidated by the black female missionaries who were there to instruct them. These teachers wore the kind of clothes that they had only seen white women wear, and their voices and manners seemed so cultured. As the sharecropping women crossed the threshold into the classroom for the first time, most of them felt so awkward that they were seized by a paralyzing self-consciousness that rendered them almost speechless in the presence of these graceful, soft-spoken, unusual black women. But the warm and caring attitude of the black female missionaries at Miller's Ferry soon put their new students at ease. The neighborhood women embraced their lessons with a vengeance, and the missionaries were thrilled. One of them exclaimed, "The enthusiasm some display is of itself sufficient recompense for the effort on our part."[55]

As news of Miller's Ferry's success spread, black residents in other parts of the county became increasingly vocal in their demands for their own neighborhood schools. In response to black demands, through the end of the nineteenth century and on into the twentieth the Presbyterians organized four other black schools in Wilcox County. The next school the missionaries established was the Prairie Mission in 1884, right across the river from Miller's Ferry. The school's enrollment was concentrated in the primary grades, and students were taught basic math and literacy skills laced with a heavy dose of religion. The school's faculty also offered some industrial courses along with instruction in farming. Because they recognized the importance of agriculture in the lives of the black residents in the vicinity of the school, the Women's General Missionary Society of the United Presbyterian Church, which had direct control of the mission, decided to try an experiment. They authorized the purchase of seven hundred acres of land conveniently located near the school, and they employed black residents to work the land. The Presbyterian women had great expectations: "The purpose of the farm is to encourage self-dependence, obtaining property, morality, and industry."[56] The ultimate goal was to allow the families working the land to purchase it. This is just one of the ways that the Presbyterians sought to cultivate an independent spirit in black Wilcox residents.

Four miles from Prairie, the Presbyterians established the Midway Mission in response to unremitting black demands. One church official chuckled, "The plantation owners found no rest when they were among their tenants, for the one inevitable topic was the need of a good school."[57] The two wealthiest landowners in the area offered to donate ten acres of land for the new mission, and their tenants enthusiastically agreed to erect the school building, and deed it to the Presbyterian Church.[58] Like so many of their neighbors, these landowners were alarmed at the prospect of losing their most industrious workers. A school was a small price to pay for a stable labor force, they reasoned.[59]

The next black school the Presbyterians established in Wilcox County, Camden Academy, was the only one of these schools located near a town. It was also the largest of the mission schools, and it sat on a picturesque hill overlooking the sleepy little town of Camden. Ironically, the locals referred to the new school's site as Hangman's Hill because so many lynchings had been carried out there. The board of the Women's General Missionary Society bought a total of forty acres, which included Hangman's Hill, and they financed the erection of four buildings on the land: a combination classroom building and chapel, a teachers' home, and two dormitories.[60] Reverend E. K. Smith, the school's first principal, was pleasantly surprised to discover that a number of the black families living in Camden were property owners. He cheerfully observed, "Several families in and about Camden own their own homes. . . . They are intensely ambitious for the education of their children." Smith was careful to add that such ambition was not limited to property owners. He insisted, "Some others who do not have homes are equally pleasant to visit and ambitious for their children."[61] Yet, Smith realized that even though some black Camden residents had managed to make comfortable lives for themselves, many others continued to live in abject poverty. The minister lamented, "They are wretchedly poor. Life with them is a desperate struggle for bread. They actually go hungry and in rags." Smith found that educating the children of such families proved to be extremely difficult because "Most of the people seem unable to buy their children books or clothes." Despite the difficulties, however, Smith remained hopeful that the mission school would help students realize their full potential because "We have some very promising boys and girls in Camden."[62]

In concert with the other Wilcox mission schools. Camden Academy placed a great deal of emphasis on the religious education of its students. At the same time, however, the school's faculty was determined to provide rigorous academic training as well. Principal E. K. Smith unequivocally expressed his support for a challenging curriculum. As he put it, "The men and schools that make the leaders of the race are more important than those who make the laborers."[63] While Reverend W. G. Wilson, Smith's successor, wholeheartedly agreed with Smith's academic vision, he realized that Presbyterian officials in Pittsburgh were displeased with one aspect of the mission school's work. He explained, "It is true that this work is not doing as much numerically for the Church, and the Church is somewhat disappointed." Clearly, the Presbyterians expected that their schools in Wilcox County would produce a large number of converts to their denomination. They did not. Despite this lack of converts, however, Reverend Wilson was convinced that their work was having a profound impact on the lives of black Wilcox residents. He explained, "we who are on the firing line know that it is being *felt in the lives* of the people among whom we work" [original emphasis].[64]

Camden Academy's students were very grateful for the dedication displayed by their missionary teachers, and they realized the school's importance in their lives. Their pride and gratitude clearly came through in their enthusiastic young voices whenever they sang their school song:

> Camden Academy, may you ever stand,
> A light to guide us by thy mighty hand,
> Be thou our ruler, guardian guide and stay,
> Thy word our law, thy path our chosen way.

So many of these students lived in very difficult circumstances, and the words of encouragement in the second verse of their school song were particularly meaningful for them:

> When on the toilsome battlefield of life,
> We'll turn to thee, for rest, for peace, for life,
> Knowing that thou will grasp us by thy hand,
> And lead us on to victory in the land.

Throughout the twentieth century, Camden Academy continued to provide a rigorous academic program for its students. Finally in 1956, its efforts were rewarded when it received its accreditation from the Southern Association of Colleges and Secondary Schools.[65]

The Canton Bend Mission was the next school established by the Presbyterians in Wilcox County. This school, which was established in 1896, was located halfway between Miller's Ferry and Camden in a very rural area. Ella Earls Cotton, the wife of the school's first principal, described the difficulties she and her husband faced on their first journey to the school's remote location:

> At last we reached the end of our journey by railway. It was seventeen miles inland to our destination. My husband scurried around and soon found the best transportation to be had in a decrepit man with a decrepit mule hitched to a decrepit wagon. After a ten-mile trip we reached the Alabama River, which was a perilous crossing at best on a flatboat.[66]

As the young missionary perched precariously on the seat of that decrepit wagon, she could not help but reflect on the difficult job that she and her husband would face in their new home. The wagon bounced uncomfortably over rutted roads, and worry lines creased Mrs. Cotton's face. But soon the county's spectacular scenery chased the worry lines away. The young missionary could not help but admire the natural beauty all around her: the magnificent trees with their beards of Spanish moss, the vibrant color of the wildflowers dotting the roadside, and the neat endless rows of cotton plants topped by snowy white bolls thriving in the rich Alabama earth. When she looked more closely at the faces of the workers tending the fields, however, she was sickened by what she observed. She explained, "Negroes we saw were habitually forlorn and dejected. And their hopeless faces were abject masks, not as if rebelling at their lot, but as if there had never been nor would there ever be any hope in their hearts for any other future."[67]

Regardless of the difficulties, Ella Cotton's youthful enthusiasm combined with the commitment to racial uplift that was part of her Knoxville College training to convince her that the Canton Bend Mission could make a real difference in the lives of Wilcox County's black residents. Once their school opened and the Cottons became involved in educating the neighborhood children, their students' enthusiasm cancelled out that disturbing first impression they had had of forlorn black faces bereft of hope. Ella Cotton proudly described her students: "Large or small, they were all eager beginners, with little need for discipline. This made it possible for an unbelievable rapid progress."[68] Parents noticed and appreciated their children's progress. In fact, many viewed their children's ability to read and write as nothing short of a miracle, and they were "overwhelmed with joy."[69]

The last of the Presbyterian missions, Arlington, was founded after the turn of the century in 1903 as a result of local black efforts. Several families in the vicinity pooled their money, purchased ten acres, and donated it to the Presbyterian Board of American Missions with the understanding that the church would help them establish a school. In recognition of such overwhelming black interest, the Presbyterian Board purchased an additional three hundred acres and began erecting buildings.[70] Reverend John T. Arter, the school's first principal, was thrilled about the local black commitment to education that greeted him upon his arrival. He proudly exclaimed,

> We found here three white families and three hundred Negro families. The colored people are above average in that they are industrious and ambitious; too proud to allow anybody to do for them what they can do for themselves. We have not received a single garment from the North.

Furthermore, Arter was pleased to point out that his school's sewing department was the only self-supporting sewing department in any of the mission schools.

Arter's appreciation for local black initiative was echoed again and again by black missionaries in the Wilcox County schools, and by the northern white church officials with whom they corresponded. Indeed, white church officials were utterly amazed at the determination to contribute to their own educational institutions exhibited by Wilcox County's African Americans. One church official wrote, "It is really pitiful to see the sacrifices some of these people are making in order to give their children the advantages offered in our schools."[71] Black missionaries who were teaching in these schools agreed that the sacrifices made by black parents were laudable, but unlike white church officials, they did not see such efforts as either pitiful or surprising. On the contrary, the missionaries, like so many of their black contemporaries, firmly believed that African Americans must be responsible for their own destiny. Clearly, the importance of self-help to improve the race's condition had become an important tenet of the value system of African Americans by the late nineteenth century. Members of a national convention of black leaders meeting in Nashville, Tennessee, in 1879 explained, "We are to a great extent the architect of our own fortune, and must rely mainly upon our own exertions for success." They further advised that African American youth should live moral upright lives, acquire land, and make "their way into the various productive channels of literature, art, science, and mechanics."[72]

Because they believed fervently in these principles, the early black missionaries in Wilcox County endured difficult circumstances, and made incredible sacrifices to help improve conditions for local black residents. One of the most difficult problems confronting these missionaries was the chronic shortage of funds that plagued all of their schools. Early letters from Dr. J. S. McCulloch, the president of Knoxville College, to officials of the Presbyterian Church's Board of Missions to the Freedmen frequently mentioned money problems and salary issues at the Wilcox County mission schools. As far as McCulloch was concerned, the salaries of Wilcox missionaries were unacceptably low. He complained, "The colored teachers, such as Mr. Cloud [Miller's Ferry principal], should have a salary equal to the regular teachers in college; because they are doing as hard work, and perhaps doing it better than white teachers could." McCulloch went on to request additional salary funds, and he concluded, "I hope the Board may consider it and if action be favorable, let me know, or let Mr. Cloud know directly."[73] On another occasion McCulloch explained to the board that the Wilcox schools had not received any financial support from the county. Even though the Wilcox County Board of Education had agreed to pay the black share of county school funds to the Presbyterians by the late nineteenth century, there were many times when they refused to surrender even these meager funds. The original motivation to pay the Presbyterians had been rooted in the reluctance of white Wilcox County officials to build schools for African Americans at county expense. Obviously, this white reluctance to educate black children was so strong that it sometimes convinced white officials that they should not supply any support whatsoever for black education. President McCulloch complained, "Mr. Cloud's efforts . . . have failed to get any more money from the county. He thinks he has gone just as far as he can without making a fuss. The only money he has received is $30 whereas in justice the school ought to receive $120."[74] Clearly, the Presbyterians could not depend on county funds to help them provide raises for their teachers.

The problem of low salaries was exacerbated when the missionaries were married with families. In some instances when both husband and wife served as missionaries, only the husband received a salary. Ella Earls Cotton found herself in such a situation when she and her husband began their work at Canton Bend. She recalled that when the school opened that first fall after she and her husband took charge, "I went to work as a full-time teacher. Neither my husband nor I would propose the question of a salary for me to the board." This put the young missionary in a very awkward position. She explained, "Obviously I was under the observation of the other workers during the two years I taught without remuneration."[75] It was very difficult for the Cottons to make ends meet on just one salary. Consequently, the young couple was forced to find ways to supplement Mr. Cotton's small salary. They decided to try their hand at agriculture, so they rented land and hired workers to raise cotton, corn, and hogs for market. However, according to Ella Cotton, "More profitable were the mules he raised and sold. I raised and sold chickens, butter and eggs. I made dresses for women and children while learning to make my own clothes."[76] Clearly, being a missionary was hard work that required dedication in the face of grave difficulty.

Administrators at Knoxville College recognized how frustrating and difficult the job was that faced the young missionaries they sent out from their school. They asserted, "These workers are the thin skirmish line far affront in the enemies' country, far from headquarters, far from home, often far from each other." As they continued to send their graduates into Wilcox County, school officials became increasingly concerned about missionary burnout. Consequently, beginning in 1895, President McCulloch, along with Eliza Wallace, convinced others at the college to sponsor an annual Bible School on the Knoxville College campus, and those in attendance were treated to lectures, singing, Bible study, and plenty of opportunities to reminisce about their carefree days as college students. College officials were convinced that the summer Bible School was necessary for their missionaries' continued well-being because these dedicated young people were, "Educated and refined men and women [and] they miss the things that make for culture, intellectual stimulus, the development of the whole man. . . . The Bible school is their relaxation, their rejuvenation, their re-creation."[77]

The commitment of these young missionaries to racial uplift had been carefully encouraged and nurtured during their student days at Knoxville College, and upon graduation they had been hand picked by Presbyterian Board members. The board explained that, "After the work of the college had begun to show fruit in turning out young men and women qualified to teach others it became necessary to consider where and how these graduates could be most profitably employed."[78] When they looked at the work going on at the Wilcox mission schools, it seemed to board members that this provided the perfect opportunity for Knoxville College graduates. Presbyterian officials asserted, "The graduates from the college found in these mission stations the best field for the exercise of their gifts and acquirements."[79] Over the years, the intimate involvement of scores of Knoxville College graduates in the establishment and administration of the Wilcox mission schools meant that the Knoxville College training these missionaries received would make an indelible imprint on the black Wilcox County residents whose lives they touched.

Throughout this period, Knoxville College students received rigorous academic training, thorough religious instruction, and constant admonitions about character formation. For example, Emma Stokes, a 1926 Knoxville College graduate, vividly remembers that her professors routinely included discussions of moral character as part of their classroom instruction. She particularly remembers the advice of her French professor: "She would sometimes just in the classroom take a few minutes and just talk to us about our conduct and what habits that we should form now would mean to us later on, and the advantages of good moral character." Stokes was convinced that all the advice she received at Knoxville College had a profound impact on her life. She concludes, "It had a lot to do with some shaping of my character."[80]

The Knoxville College campus where Emma Stokes and her classmates lived and studied was a very serene place sitting high atop a hill with a commanding view of the city. The grounds were well maintained, and the red brick classroom buildings and dormitories were shaded by graceful old hardwood trees whose leaves turned brilliant shades of red, orange, and gold every fall. Most of the school's earnest young students treasured the serenity of their campus, and they were especially affected by the dedication of the white Presbyterian missionaries who constantly encouraged them to do their best. At the same time, these missionaries also encouraged their black Knoxville College students to participate actively in racial uplift. In an effort to prepare their students for this mission, college administrators and faculty wanted to make sure that their charges were thoroughly familiar with the history of their own people, so they added a "Negro History" course to the curriculum. Knoxville College students reported that this course had a powerful influence on their lives. As one explained, "There was a lot we learned to be proud of."[81]

Above all, Knoxville College faculty and administrators sought to cultivate a sense of self-worth and self-respect in all of their students. They believed these students were entitled to all the privileges of citizenship, and they were always ready to offer sympathy and encouragement to any of their young charges who were concerned about black citizenship rights. For example, Emma Stokes recalls that white Knoxville College president Dr. J. Kelley Giffen offered encouragement tempered with caution to one of her classmates who was concerned about black voting rights. She explains, "I think one of my classmates particularly had told us of a discussion that he had a time or two with the president." Although the discussion was off the record, "The president was helpful in encouraging him to move forward and look forward to [voting]." But, Giffen issued a stern warning: "He cautioned against some acts of, maybe, that might be aggressive to the extent that it would bring trouble for him."[82]

Thus, armed with their youthful enthusiasm, and the training dispensed by sympathetic white missionaries, many Knoxville College recruits eagerly served in Wilcox County's Presbyterian schools through the last decades of the nineteenth century and on through the middle of the twentieth century. Notwithstanding the serenity of their college campus and the example set by their white professors, these Knoxville College recruits were acutely aware of the reality of racial prejudice in America. However, most were totally unprepared for the ferocity of the racial prejudice that confronted them when they reached the Alabama Black Belt. As soon as they arrived, the ugly racial reality confronting them in Wilcox County quickly banished all thoughts of supportive white professors and carefree college life from their minds. Ella Earls Cotton has vivid and disturbing memories of her first brush with the particular brand of racism afflicting Wilcox County. When she and her husband passed through some of the remote areas of the county on their first trip to Canton Bend, they saw signs that left them speechless and made the blood drain from their faces. On one was printed, "No niggers wanted here." Still another read, "Nigger, read and run. If you can't read, run anyhow." A third advised, "No niggers or dogs allowed here." These signs were symptomatic of a frightening racial hostility all around them, and the intensity of that hostility convinced Ella Cotton that they were about "to engage in the most dangerous profession . . . educating Negroes in the Deep South."[83]

Yet, the danger inherent in that racial hostility only strengthened the resolve of these eager black Presbyterian missionaries. They understood that because the ferocity of the county's racial oppression had had such a devastating impact on local black prospects for improvement, the need for missionary work in the area was critical. Thus, these black teachers were determined to go forward even though they realized how difficult it would be to nurture black initiative and raise black expectations in such an environment. Reverend C. H. Johnson, a later principal of Miller's Ferry, unequivocally explained the restrictive impact of the county's racism: "No one can doubt for a moment that his [the African American's] progress would have been immensely greater but for the ignorance and limitations placed upon him, not because of his ignorance and inefficiency alone, but because of his past condition and the *restraints of race prejudice*" [emphasis added].[84] Clearly, the virulent race prejudice existing in Wilcox County had the power to circumscribe black lives from the cradle to the grave. Ella Cotton was particularly concerned about the negative impact of this prejudice on the lives of the county's children. She explained, "I doubt whether there is ever an antidote for the virus of prejudice upon a young child when he is told that he is hated because his skin is black."[85] Given this grim reality, Wilcox County's black children desperately needed their help, the Presbyterian missionaries reasoned.

These missionaries clearly had their work cut out for them, and as they attempted to help African Americans in Wilcox County, they had to devise their own coping strategies because the county's racial prejudice also had a negative impact on their lives. Because they were bound by the same racial rules that defined the existence of the people they were attempting to serve, these missionaries faced a very complicated situation. In order to serve their black constituency effectively, they had to do three things simultaneously: maintain a certain amount of autonomy in the face of local white control, cultivate black support, and hang on to their own self-respect. At the same time, however, these teachers could not afford to antagonize local white residents who were already suspicious of them. Thus, the missionaries found themselves performing a delicate balancing act: a slip too far in either direction could neutralize their effectiveness, or even endanger their lives.

In such a volatile atmosphere, Wilcox County's black Presbyterian missionaries felt compelled to cultivate friendly relationships with sympathetic and influential local white residents. They realized that in this county where white supremacy was the defining fact of black life, powerful white friends were necessary to ensure their school's survival. Ella Cotton explained, "Needless to say, we chose to continue our policy of diplomacy in relation to white people. For those white people had for years been considerate, cooperative and kind. We couldn't have carried on the school with the same degree of success if they [sympathetic white people] had not been so."[86] Reverend W. G. Wilson of Camden Academy also carefully cultivated relationships with influential white residents in an effort to ensure his school's survival. White Wilcox residents noticed and appreciated his efforts. One remarked, "In his business dealings, which involved many contacts with white people, his integrity was proverbial, and he was held up by white people as the model for Negro youth."[87]

Yet, this same man who was praised by local white residents for his cooperative spirit clearly demonstrated a willingness to speak candidly about issues
of race in certain situations. The poem he wrote in honor of Wilcox County's
black World War I recruits, "A Parting Word," unequivocally demonstrated
that willingness. In the first few verses, Wilson enthusiastically praised earlier
generations of black soldiers, and reassured those going off to war:

> Let not the fact of lowly birth
>   Hold back your arm of might;
> A thousand battles testify
>   How well black soldiers fight.
> The world will recognize a man
>   What e're may be his hue;
> So, as you go, keep this in mind:
>   It's always up to you.

In the poem's later verses, however, Reverend Wilson boldly challenged the state
of Alabama and the nation to treat African Americans as first-class citizens:

> We'll try to make you realize
>   This land is of the free,
> And that her children all may sing,
>   "My Country 'tis of Thee."
> And Alabama, we believe,
>   Will see that each black son
> Shall be regarded as a man
>   For duty nobly done.

Wilson's poem concluded,

> For when a man has done his best,
>   Let him be black or white.
> It's up to those who know the facts
>   To see him treated right.
> And we believe they'll do it too,
>   And so we bid you go
> Across the seas to bleeding France
>   To fight the common foe.[88]

William Edwards, founder and principal of neighboring Snow Hill Institute, expressed equally strong sentiments on the issue of racial justice. At a
public gathering in Camden to honor the county's recruits who were depart-

ing for World War I, Edwards bluntly insisted, "It would be foolish and cow-ardly on my part to stand here in your presence and say that as a race we have no grievances, for we have them." As the audience listened intently, Edwards thundered, "Are we fighting for democracy of all the people, or are we fight-ing for democracy of the white man only?" Edwards went on to insist, "This question has never been answered by the white man," and he warned that this question "must be answered after this great war."[89]

Clearly, Wilson and Edwards, along with all the other black educators in Wilcox County, were in a difficult position: they were trying to maintain cordial relations with white residents in a county where white supremacy cir-cumscribed their options. At the same time, they refused to relinquish their right to speak out against the unequal treatment suffered by black residents. All of this placed these educators in a position that was filled with danger, and fraught with contradictions. For example, Ella Cotton explained how difficult it was for her to cope with the poisonous racial atmosphere in Wilcox County. She explained, "I had to learn about this superiority versus inferiority angle of life and yet keep my own equilibrium."[90] In the final analysis, Cotton concluded, African Americans in Wilcox County were all confronted by a critical question: "How are we as Negroes going to get our bearings and still possess our souls and preserve our individual pride?"[91]

That poignant question reverberated through the minds of scores of black educators in Wilcox County over the years as they sought to prepare their students for an uncertain future. Reverend C. H. Johnson of Miller's Ferry was particularly troubled by the reaction of some black residents to their county's pernicious prejudice. He observed, "In every competitive walk of life he [the African American] hears the mandate 'hitherto shalt thou come, but no further,' which makes, in his way of thinking, voluntary submission prefer-able to forced submission."[92] As Johnson and many of the other Presbyterian teachers observed the submissive behavior exhibited by some of the county's black residents, they could not help but shake their heads in frustration. Yet, in many cases, that frustration served to strengthen the resolve of these mis-sionaries to replace black voluntary submission with creative ways of coping and excelling.

When these earnest black Presbyterian missionaries first came to Wilcox County, they made a profound impression on black residents. One Presby-terian official who made the trip to Wilcox to observe the mission work there described that impression. Everywhere he went, local black residents told him, "You've got white principles in those Negroes. How did you ever get white principles in them? Everybody says they would as soon work for them or deal with them as with white people."[93] Such a reaction is not surprising in view of the striking differences between these black missionaries and the African American population they were attempting to serve. When black Wilcox residents encountered the first black Presbyterian missionaries in their county in the early 1880s, they saw well-dressed, well-educated, soft-spoken black people whose very existence stood in stark contrast to their own lives. These black teachers were truly an inspiration for black Wilcox residents who dreamed of a better life.

Yet, long before these missionaries ever came to their county, local black residents had struggled to fashion their own unique vision of life beyond the cotton fields. That vision had been built on a deep and abiding faith in the power of education to transform their lives and the lives of their children. Thus, with the coming of the missionaries, this local black faith became wedded to black missionary dedication. In such an atmosphere, these missionaries became important and beloved fixtures in the Wilcox communities they served. Ella Cotton fondly recalled the reception she and her husband received in the Canton Bend area. "We had to visit and know the people, and almost always they accepted us in the simple spirit of sincerity if that was the spirit we carried to them." She went on to explain the importance of cultivating good relationships with the black people who lived in the vicinity of the school. "We never isolated ourselves by affecting an ivory-tower attitude toward the people. We listened to them and learned from them while they learned what little we had to offer."[94]

Through the end of the nineteenth century, and on into the twentieth, Wilcox County's black missionary educators were acutely aware of the importance of the example they were setting, and they worked very hard to exert a positive influence in the communities where they served. Black students noticed and appreciated the lessons their teachers taught—both directly by admonition, and indirectly by example. For example, Dr. Kayte Marsh Fearn, who enrolled in Camden Academy in 1929, recalls frequent discussions of the electoral process in her classes. She explains, "We knew we weren't part of it." Yet, young Kayte's teachers made it clear that they were planning for the future, and they told their students, "Our intent [is] to prepare you so that if there's ever a time when we can be a part of that society, we'll be ready. So that's what they did."[95] Lucy Ephraim, another Camden Academy student, had never thought of African Americans voting in Wilcox County until her government teacher, William Garrette Wilson, spoke to his class about the use of the poll tax to disfranchise black county residents. Clearly, in subtle and not-so-subtle ways, the teachers at these schools preached hope for a better life to their students, and they advised their young charges that they must prepare themselves to take advantage of any opportunities that might come their way.[96]

The missionaries insisted that one of the most important ingredients in that preparation was academic excellence. Accordingly, students were treated to a rigorous classical/liberal arts education. At the same time, they were free to join any of the variety of organizations flourishing on their campuses, which included such groups as the Young People's Christian Union and the Junior Missionary Society. In addition, both Miller's Ferry and Camden Academy had football and baseball teams, and their games were always an important social event in the community.[97] At the same time, a very strict code of conduct was a prominent feature of campus life at all these schools. Students were not allowed to play cards or dance, but teachers did allow the boys and girls to march together in the school auditorium. Not surprisingly, school auditoriums regularly reverberated with the lively rhythms of familiar march music as the students took high, lively steps. Yet, even though the youngsters were marching under the stern and watchful eye of their missionary teachers, shy young couples would often exchange short but meaningful glances at each other. Indeed, the missionaries worked hard to supervise contact between members of the opposite sex. Only the high school girls were allowed to have male callers one night a week, and before a young man could call on a young woman, he had to request written permission from the dormitory matron.[98] Over the years, many young men waited with sweaty palms and racing hearts outside the matron's door as she considered their requests.

Predictably, in such an atmosphere, the students' youthful exuberance sometimes collided with the restrictive environment on their campuses. Yet, students rarely complained, and the missionaries had virtually no discipline problems. On the contrary, as far as black Wilcox students were concerned, the strict rules and regulations were a small price to pay for this precious educational opportunity. In fact, as memories of slavery continued to recede further into the county's collective black consciousness, succeeding generations of black Wilcox residents came to accept missionary notions of proper behavior as a normal part of their education and their lives.

Thus, through the end of the nineteenth century when African Americans in Wilcox County had few other options, black Presbyterian missionaries provided one of the few rays of hope that black residents had for a better life. It is important to note that there were a few other black schools established in the county over the years by other denominations, and by county authorities. However, the work of the Presbyterians represents the most concentrated educational effort by any group in Wilcox County during these critical years. Later, as the country moved through the early decades of the twentieth century and to the eve of World War I, Wilcox County's black Presbyterian schools continued to work tirelessly to keep hope for a better life alive in their students' hearts. But after America joined the war effort, and the county's black educators watched some of Wilcox's fine black young men march away to war, some of these educators challenged the county's un-spoken policy of white supremacy—publicly, but politely.

That challenge hung unanswered in the air through the war years, and on through the decade of the 1920s that followed. And still, the county's black Presbyterian schools continued their tireless efforts to educate as many black residents as they could reach. During these difficult years, the black Presbyterian insistence on cultivating an awareness of the racial situation, coupled with their emphasis on strong moral character, a rigorous academic program, and a wide variety of extracurricular activities, ensured the continued production of a cadre of capable, self-assured black young adults. It is hardly surprising, then, that Camden Academy, the crown jewel of the Wilcox County mission schools, would become a major battleground during the county's voting rights drive in 1965. When this later generation of Camden Academy students left their picturesque campus and marched down the hill to the town square, white onlookers were furious, but Camden Academy alumni were overjoyed. Many could even imagine that those early black missionaries who had sacrificed so much were smiling down on these brash and brave young people joyously singing freedom songs as they proudly marched to the courthouse to confront segregation at last.

Yet, before that long awaited confrontation could occur, Wilcox County, along with the rest of the nation, would be dragged down to the depths of economic despair by the Great Depression of the 1930s. On the eve of this unprecedented economic disaster, some 19,300 African Americans remained in Wilcox County. While their numbers would continue to shrink in the coming decades, those who chose to remain became more and more determined to work out their destiny on the land where their ancestors had been slaves. This set the stage for a conflict of epic proportions in the 1960s that would shake race relations and power relationships in Wilcox County to their very core.

~

CHAPTER THREE

New Negroes in the Cotton Field: The Great Depression and Gee's Bend

On October 29, 1929, the New York Stock Exchange experienced the most precipitous downturn in its history. It seemed that almost overnight the rosy vision Americans had of their economy and their futures vanished into a murky sea of economic pessimism filled with failing banks, high unemployment, and dangerous deflation. In Wilcox County, the residents seemed to take the news in stride. After all, they had been wrestling with their own economic demons for well over a decade. For some time before the stock market crash, when much of the rest of the country seemed to be prospering, many of America's farmers, particularly those in the cotton growing regions, were plagued by difficult economic problems. One of the most serious of those problems was the infestation of the boll weevil. In fact, shortly after the beginning of the twentieth century, the destructive little insect crossed the border from its native Mexico into Texas.

From Texas, the boll weevil migrated in a northeastward direction, and by 1907 Alabama farmers began receiving reports that the insect would probably reach their state in the next three years. Farmer's institutes and newspaper editors all over the state sounded an increasingly shrill warning, and many began to claim in frustration that Black Belt cotton growers in particular were not taking the warnings seriously enough.[1] Instead, as they looked out over the endless rows of fluffy white cotton filling their fields, they just could not envision an insect with the power to destroy all of this. Just as their ancestors had trusted in the power of King Cotton to sustain them before the Civil War, twentieth-century Wilcox landowners had always defined their lives by the endless cycle of planting cotton, nurturing it, harvesting it, and selling it. They simply could not accept the possibility that things could ever be any different.

Their faith notwithstanding, however, determined swarms of the little Mexican insects reached the southern edge of the Alabama Black Belt by 1910. Just two years later in 1912, hungry boll weevils were wreaking havoc on cotton fields in some of the state's most fertile counties including Marengo, Greene, Hale, Perry, Dallas, Lowndes, and Wilcox.[2] White landowners and black sharecroppers alike were left shaking their heads in bewilderment when they realized that they had virtually nothing to harvest in their ruined fields. Predictably, the boll weevil infestation accelerated the black out-migration from Wilcox County that had begun some years before. Those who stayed behind began to cast about for solutions, and there was no shortage of suggestions. As early as 1912, the state entomologist advised the "early fall destruction of cotton stalks and general cleaning up of trash and weeds so that the insects will have little chance of hiding over winter." The entomologist further advised "more extensive planting of winter cover crops such as oats, rye, barley . . . [and] clover."[3] The reality of their economic calamity forced the county's farmers to reevaluate the tried and true methods that had served them so well for many years, and finally, as World War I drew to a close, it seemed that things were getting better. The *Camden Journal* gleefully reported in late 1917 that county residents were enjoying "a greater degree of prosperity than [they had] experienced in many years" because they had begun to practice crop diversification and they had also "practiced economy to a degree never equaled before."[4]

Despite their limited success in some years, however, from the late 1910s all the way through the 1920s, white Wilcox farmers still felt as though their way of life was under attack by swarms of hungry little insects. At the same time, black farmers, whether they owned their own land or worked someone else's plantation, were also alarmed. Even before the appearance of the boll weevil, many had been only one step away from starvation as they barely eked out an existence. But once the hungry little insects took up residence in their county, black Wilcox farmers were terrified of the bug's potential impact on their already marginal existence. Fred Bennett, the county's Negro demonstration agent, pleaded with white Wilcox residents to help black farmers. He argued that the economic fate of all county residents was firmly tied to the black farmers' plight. He reasoned, "If the colored farmer of Wilcox fail this year, he will not be the only party hurt; but will retard business of all kinds." Bennett went on to insist, "Cotton is our longtime friend, and it will continue to be our friend if we simply treat it right." But, he warned, "The boll weevil is here to stay, and unless the colored farmer adjusts himself to the conditions[,] we are bound to go under." Bennett pleaded for white citizens to attend a meeting at the courthouse in Camden "for the purpose of discussing general conditions as they affect the social life of our people and the prosperity of our towns, communities, school[s] and churches."[5]

There is no evidence to suggest that white landowners heeded Bennett's warning. In the meantime, the county's black agricultural laborers continued to desert the boll weevil–infested fields throughout this period in search of opportunities outside the region. The alarming proportions of the county's black exodus continued unabated through the 1920s and on into the 1930s, and prompted J. N. Cotton, principal of the Canton Bend Mission school to write a "Letter to the Editor on Keeping the Negro on the Farm." The *Wilcox Progressive Era* thought that Cotton's advice was so important that they printed it on the paper's front page. Cotton began his letter by reminding his readers that "during the last few years, there has been much said and written about the many Negroes who have left the farms and found employment in the north and other industrial centers." The reasons for this exodus were clear, he asserted: "The advent of the boll weevil, the demand for labor in the industrial centers, with the high wages paid, and the restriction of immigrants who usually supply the demand for a certain kind of unskilled labor."[6]

Obviously, this movement had a profound impact on the county's agricultural operations. Cotton explained, "There are more than twenty-five per cent fewer plows now used on the farms in this county than there were ten years ago. That is, we suppose, at least, one-fourth of the tillable land in the county is not being cultivated. Thus, we infer, that the production of cotton and other farm products has been greatly reduced."[7] Cotton was convinced that the most enterprising black laborers were the ones who were leaving: the workers the county could least afford to lose. There was only one way to convince these people to stay, Cotton advised. As he put it, "We are sure that, if the enterprising industrious Negroes were encouraged to become owners of small farms so that they might establish homes of their own, it would be a move in the right direction to relieve the situation."[8]

Cotton's suggestion was clearly problematic. On the one hand, because of the powerful desire of the county's black residents for land ownership, such an inducement would have convinced many to stay. On the other hand, however, the county's white landowners had no desire to help create a class of ambitious black landowners. On the contrary, they wanted to keep their cheap black labor force landless, powerless, and totally dependent. For some time things seemed to be at an impasse, but white landowners blinked first. By the decade of the 1920s, their desperation convinced many white landowners to begin making small concessions in an effort to persuade their black farm laborers to stay. They reduced rents, and they tried to curb some of the worst racial abuse that had characterized their relationships with their workers for generations.[9] But, the planters' refusal to make any fundamental changes in the exploitative relationships they had with their workers ensured the continuation of the black exodus out of their county as the Great Depression approached. Throughout the decade of the 1920s, Wilcox County's white landowners battled the twin problems of hungry insects entering their county and disillusioned black workers leaving it as they sought to reestablish their profitable relationship with King Cotton. Because of their desperation, many white Wilcox residents found an article in their weekly newspaper particularly satisfying. The article, entitled, "Negroes Returning South," claimed, "Now that the Negroes have tasted life in the north, leading agriculturalists here assert, it is safe to say that a great majority of them will remain in the South, where they are known."[10] Regardless of this serious wishful thinking, Wilcox County continued to hemorrhage black laborers, and as the 1920s roared to a close, the county's anemic economy teetered precariously on the brink of disaster.

Within months of the stock market crash, broad segments of the American population began to suffer. Agricultural producers were particularly hard hit as the prices they could expect to get for the crops they produced continued a steep downward slide. By the fall of 1932, Americans everywhere who were seeking a way out of this economic quagmire elected New York's governor, Franklin Delano Roosevelt, to the presidency, thus replacing the hapless Herbert Hoover. In concert with the rest of the white voters in their region, solidly Democratic white Wilcox voters enthusiastically supported the New York Democrat, not just because he was a Democrat, but also because he promised relief from their economic woes.

The new president did not disappoint them. Within days of his inauguration, he instituted a series of measures that collectively became known as the New Deal. One of those early New Deal measures was aimed squarely at the agricultural producers in American society, because Roosevelt and his advisors were sure that the declining income of the American farmer was a major contributing factor to the economic stranglehold that the depression had on the nation's economy. Henry A. Wallace, secretary of agriculture, clearly explained the New Dealers' reasoning: "The Administration accepts as a fundamental principle the view that restoration of the farmers' buying power is an essential part of the program to relieve the present economic emergency."[11] The Roosevelt administration's opening salvo in the war against rural poverty was the passage of the Agricultural Adjustment Act. The act's stated purpose was to "relieve the existing national emergency by increasing agricultural purchasing power."[12] Armed with the authority granted to them by the Agricultural Adjustment Act, New Dealers instituted a series of government programs including marketing agreements, trade treaties, and commodity loans. But, clearly, the centerpiece of the new legislation was the agency it created, the Agricultural Adjustment Administration (AAA).

The first order of business for the new agency was the elimination of agricultural surpluses. New Dealers were convinced that surplus crops were flooding the market and driving down prices. Accordingly, the AAA inaugurated an acreage and production control program that actually distributed benefit payments to farmers who agreed to keep part of their acreage out of production. AAA administrators were particularly concerned about the precarious predicament facing cotton farmers: between 1929 and 1933 the price of cotton dropped from eighteen cents to six cents a pound. At the same time, by late 1932 there were already thirteen million bales of surplus cotton on hand. This was enough to meet the demand for the next year.[13] This dismal outlook for the cotton market spelled disaster for Wilcox County landowners. As the price of the county's primary commodity continued to plummet, Wilcox farmers produced fewer and fewer bales: the county's production fell from 14,645 bales in 1931 to just 5,702 bales in 1933.[14] Agriculture Secretary Wallace recognized that cotton farmers faced special difficulties. He declared, "The crisis in cotton" was "one of the principal reasons for the adoption of the Agricultural Adjustment Act."[15] The cotton crisis was so severe that during the early months of 1933 the Agricultural Adjustment Administration offered benefits ranging from $7.00 to $20.00 an acre to farmers who agreed to plow up between 25 and 50 percent of their cotton crop that was growing in the field.[16] Landowners in the Cotton Belt were overjoyed as their subsidies began to arrive and cotton prices stabilized. Praise for Roosevelt and his New Deal Democrats was on the lips of practically all the Cotton Belt's white landowners. One delegation of Arkansas cotton growers declared, "The tighter the government control the better . . . we never want to see a relaxation of government control. The more inspectors Washington puts on the job, the happier we'll be."[17] Ironically, these same cotton growers who welcomed federal intervention during the Depression would later denounce what they viewed as meddlesome federal interference by the era of the civil rights movement.

For the time being, however, desperate white Wilcox cotton growers were rejoicing along with their counterparts all over the Black Belt. The March 23, 1932, edition of the *Wilcox Progressive Era* crowed, "Nothing in this slow-moving city [Washington, D.C.] ever moved as rapidly as things are moving here now. Within less than a fortnight, a real political revolution has taken place."[18] Clearly, quick government action was saving the day for many of the county's beleaguered landowners. Yet, while white landowners were rejoicing, the outlook for the county's black sharecroppers remained bleak because the AAA's cotton contract provided that benefits should be paid *only* to landowners. Although landowners were *advised* to distribute the subsidy payments among their workers according to the interest each had in the crop, most ignored this advice. Consequently, many of the county's black farm laborers, who had been teetering on the brink of economic catastrophe for some time, tumbled all the way down the steep slope to economic ruin.

As the ranks of penniless and homeless sharecroppers swelled, Roosevelt's New Dealers were horrified. They never intended for government subsidies to result in displacement of landless sharecroppers. Accordingly, AAA officials tacked on Section 7 to the original Agricultural Adjustment Act. The new section required landlords to "endeavor in good faith to bring about the reduction of acreage," but "insofar as possible, maintain on the farm the normal number of tenants and other employees."[19] Such advice inevitably fell on deaf ears. In fact, many scholars argue that New Deal subsidy programs, particularly the cotton allotment, actually set forces in motion that would result in the permanent displacement of scores of landless tenants. That displacement did not end when the Great Depression was over; instead, it continued on through much of the twentieth century. As historian Donald Grubbs explains, "Through the Agricultural Adjustment Administration, Franklin Roosevelt gave Southern planters the means and the incentive to substitute machines and underemployed casual labor for their tenants." Grubbs concedes that Roosevelt tried to help the tenants who had been displaced by New Deal programs, but he also argues that the president did nothing to change the government-sponsored program that had caused the problem in the first place. As he puts it, "he [Roosevelt] allowed the basic pattern of subsidy for landlords and poverty for rural workers to become permanent."[20]

Throughout the 1930s the National Association for the Advancement of Colored People (NAACP) closely monitored conditions in the Black Belt. Publicly, they expressed hope that black farmers would benefit from the AAA's programs. As they put it, "The natural desire of the Negro citizenry of this country is that the New Deal administration shape its course in such a way as to bring relief to those elements of the national population which have suffered most. They hope that the slogans of the new administration will have meaning for black farmers as well as white farmers."[21] However, black farm laborers in Wilcox County knew just how vain the NAACP's hope was. Instead, they realized that every federal dollar the white landowners in their county received made their position a little less secure. Incredibly, in the midst of all this widespread misery in Wilcox County, the plight of one particular black community stood out. That community was Gee's Bend. Conditions facing the residents of the Bend were so pathetic that they soon came to the attention of federal authorities in Washington.

Long before the community's economic plight attracted the attention of federal authorities, however, many observers had taken note of the Bend's unusual character. For example, Renwick Kennedy, a writer for the *Christian Century*, declared,

> There is nothing exactly like Gee's Bend anywhere else in the United States. There are similar bends, of course. Canton across the river from Gee's, is almost identical in shape and size, though its bottle neck is wider. But Gee's Bend represents not merely a geographical configuration drawn by the yellow pencil of the river. Gee's Bend represents another civilization. Gee's Bend is an Alabama Africa. There is no more concentrated and racially exclusive Negro population in any rural community in the south than in Gee's Bend.[22]

One of the crucial factors that facilitated the Bend's exclusive development was the fact of its geographic isolation. Kennedy explained, "The Bend is an isolated community. Few in the United States are more isolated. It is but three and one-half miles from Camden, the county seat of Wilcox, but the river lies between. There is no bridge. An ancient and primitive ferry is available for crossing. . . . The road to the ferry and into the Bend is bad. The steep descents to the ferry are actually terrifying." There was only one other way out of Gee's Bend besides the ferry, and that was by road. However, the road was not always passable. According to Kennedy, "It is a narrow, winding road, none too good in summer and risky in winter." Those who chose to travel by road faced a long journey: almost ninety miles round trip from Gee's Bend to Camden.[23]

Over the years Gee's Bend residents had been content in their relative isolation. A reporter from the *New York Times* who visited the Bend during the Depression insisted, "so quiet, so self-contained are these Negroes, so little inclined to leave their community or to take newcomers into it, that they might have gone on happily lost to civilization if the depression had not come. If cotton hadn't dropped to 5 cents a pound they might have gone on being what the world calls primitive, keeping their Negro blood pure."[24] Indeed, in this relatively isolated environment, far away from most white influence, a unique culture developed and thrived. Over the years, outsiders who have observed the unique belief system of Bend residents, and the distinctive way they express themselves, have been intrigued. For example, John Graves of *The New York Times Magazine* insisted that in the character of the people of Gee's Bend resided "the whole gamut of Southern Negro history from the tribal jungle to antebellum plantation."[25] Some even went so far as to suggest that Gee's Bend residents "can speak a language that outsiders cannot understand—probably an African dialect."[26] Farm Security Administration (FSA) officials in Washington found the behavior of Bend residents so strange that some began a systematic attempt to catalog "superstitions common among the people in the vicinity of Gee's Bend."[27] During this same period, the FSA, in cooperation with officials at Fisk University in Nashville, Tennessee, arranged for a graduate student of noted Fisk sociologist Charles S. Johnson to reside in Gee's Bend for a number of weeks to collect data for a "study of the cultural processes going on."[28]

Bend residents were acutely aware of their uniqueness, and according to some observers, "they feel superior to other Negroes."[29] At the same time, however, even other African Americans in Wilcox County recognized the distinctiveness of Bend residents. In fact, according to some, "other Negroes of the county look down upon the Gee's Bend Negroes socially. They speak of them in disdain as 'Africans.'"[30] This division between African Americans in Wilcox County only added to the difficulties facing activists who would later attempt to organize civil rights activities in the county.

The formation of this unique community has its roots in the early nineteenth century. At that time, Virginia native and confirmed bachelor Joseph Gee bought a huge tract of land that lay in the bend of the Alabama River, directly across from Camden. The prosperous plantation he established on that peninsula, which came to be known as Gee's Bend, was inherited by a succession of Gee relatives after Joseph Gee's death in 1824. Finally, in 1845, Gee's Bend passed out of the hands of the Gee Family once and for all when North Carolina resident Mark Pettway bought the property. After the sale, there would never be another Gee relative living on the plantation, but local people would forever call it Gee's Bend.[31] The plantation's new owner quickly settled his family and his slaves on it, and up through the Civil War, this huge prosperous cotton plantation, complete with a big house with massive white columns and scores of slaves toiling in the fields, epitomized the dream realized by only a few white Southerners. The Pettway family managed to hold on to the plantation through the turbulent years of the Civil War and through the lean years of the late nineteenth century. Finally, as the twentieth century approached, the Pettways decided to sell the plantation. Yet, even after the land passed out of the Pettway family, part of their legacy remained: to this day, many of the Bend's African American residents carry the Pettway surname.[32]

On October 10, 1899, soon after the Pettway family put the plantation up for sale, Tuscaloosa businessman A. S. Vandergraff visited Gee's Bend for the first time, and he was instantly taken by the sight that greeted him. As he looked out over the fertile fields and watched the descendants of Pettway slaves toiling away in the warm sun, he was overcome by a powerful yearning that afflicted so many of his white southern contemporaries as they faced a new century: they yearned to reach back in time and embrace an antebellum South that had been defined by prosperous land holdings and deferential slaves. However, while the scene confronting Vandergraff awakened his nostalgia, it also excited his business instincts. The combination of a fertile plantation and an independent, industrious, and cohesive workforce would surely produce handsome profits, he reasoned. Vandergraff was particularly pleased to know that the Bend's workforce was so independent that they had refused to borrow anything from the previous landowner. Instead, they had brokered their own deals with furnishing agents in Camden and Mobile.[33] Never one to pass up a good deal, Vandergraff decided to buy the plantation. He and the Pettway descendants soon came to an agreement on the price, and Gee's Bend changed hands again. Ironically, the independent spirit of the Bend's laborers that the new owner found so attractive would soon come back to haunt him.

The people in the Bend stoically accepted this latest sale of the land they loved, and they continued to do things the way they always had. Of course, the new owner's decision to continue to live in Tuscaloosa while he allowed others to run his plantation made it easy for the Bend's tenants to continue their independent ways. Through the early years of the twentieth century, the industrious black workforce at Gee's Bend struggled to make a profit, but like so many cotton growers, they seemed to be fighting a losing battle. The forces of nature and fluctuations in the market meant that the bad years far outnumbered the good ones for the Bend's tenants. Soon, things got even worse when the boll weevil invaded their crop.

As the tenants struggled to make ends meet, the Bend's absentee landowner saw his dreams of a prosperous plantation disappear before his very eyes. Vandergraff could scarcely contain his frustration. In fact, the very same independent spirit among his black workers that he had praised earlier now galled him. Because Gee's Bend tenants continued to do business directly with the furnishing merchants, Vandergraff did not receive any income at all from his black workforce during the lean years. Finally, after several successive years of poor harvests, Vandergraff was so fed up that he took the extraordinary step of contacting a Mobile furnishing merchant who did a lot of business with Gee's Bend tenants. Vandergraff demanded that the merchant allow him to deduct the rent these people owed him before the furnishing merchant took the rest of their crop to satisfy their indebtedness.[34] A short time later the angry, embittered Vandergraff died. He never realized his dream of a prosperous orderly plantation reminiscent of antebellum Wilcox County.

Vandergraff's sons inherited the plantation, but they seemed to have little interest in its day-to-day operations. Consequently, the Bend's black residents continued their business dealings with outside furnishing merchants.[35] Despite their best efforts, the poverty of the Bend's black tenants grew exponentially with each passing year. Yet, even in the midst of these bad economic times, Gee's Bend residents still loved the land of their ancestors: The rich dark soil had a perfume all its own, and the mist rising from the river every morning soon dissipated when the sun hit it, revealing the heavy beards of Spanish moss dripping from the trees on the river bank. Most of these descendants of Gee's Bend slaves could not even imagine living anywhere else, but increasingly, the connection they felt to this land was accompanied by a fear that grew larger and larger as their debt grew deeper and deeper. They saw no way out of their situation, and it seemed that they would be unable to pass anything on to their children but their constantly growing debt.

During these lean years, the Vandergraff sons showed no interest in the condition of their plantation or the plight of its tenants. In fact, the only Vandergraff son that Bend residents remember seeing from time to time was Hargrove, and the most vivid memory they have of his visits was his practice of amusing himself at their expense. When Hargrove Vandergraff rode his horse down the dusty path in front of their dilapidated cabins, he would call out, "Here chickie, chickie, chickie."[36] As curious black faces peered from inside their dwellings, young Hargrove would reach in his pocket for some coins, which he would then throw onto the dusty path. As his impoverished, desperate tenants scrambled on the ground to retrieve the coins at his horse's feet, Hargrove roared with laughter. He would then ride on to the next group of cabins and repeat his insulting and offensive game.[37]

By the first years of the Great Depression, things finally spiraled completely out of control. Just prior to this, most of the Bend's tenants had begun doing business with a Camden furnishing merchant. He was the only one around who was willing to carry them year after year when they could not pay their debts because the price of cotton had sunk so low. Unfortunately, the sympathetic Camden merchant died, and his wife and sons, who were not so sympathetic, demanded immediate payment of all their debts from Gee's Bend residents. These impoverished people simply could not pay, and with no hesitation, the furnishing merchant's heirs came into Gee's Bend in horse-drawn wagons and seized everything that was of any value. They took plows, pigs, cows, and they even took the corn out of the crib. They took everything.³⁸ The day that the white men in wagons came into Gee's Bend and foreclosed on everything is seared into the community's collective consciousness. As the white scavengers raided house after house, many Bend residents felt anger, others felt resentment, some even wanted to fight to keep their possessions.³⁹

In the end, they realized that these white men had the power to take whatever they wanted, so most Bend residents watched in angry, numb silence as the precious few possessions they had were led or driven away from their cabins. In one instance, as a white man untied a cow to lead her away, a desperate black woman surrounded by a brood of scantily clad, malnourished children wailed in a high, plaintive voice as she begged the man not to condemn her children to starvation by taking her cow. The white man hesitated for just a split second, and then gruffly muttered something under his breath about too many nigger children as he roughly tossed the rope attached to the cow back into the pleading woman's hands.⁴⁰ Her face dissolved into tears of gratitude as the white man strode briskly to the next cabin. Despite the small show of kindness here and there during the foreclosure, by the end of the day Gee's Bend residents were left with virtually nothing. They no longer had the tools they needed to cultivate the land, and they had no food to eat. On that terrible day, the setting sun provided a dramatic backdrop to the line of wagons loaded down with all their worldly possessions slowly moving out of the Bend. After the sun had set, and the wagons were completely out of sight, residents milled around in small groups, talking in hushed tones, uncertain of what they would do tomorrow; uncertain even of what to do that night.

In a short time, the desperate plight of Gee's Bend residents came to the attention of New Deal policymakers in Washington. They quickly realized that these people were in imminent danger of starving to death, so they decided to dispatch government help to them immediately. As New Dealers looked more closely at conditions in Gee's Bend, they became convinced that the area would be an appropriate place for experimentation with a planned farm community. Accordingly, the federal government bought over ten thousand acres of land in Gee's Bend and subdivided it into one hundred small farms. These farms were to include a garden plot and a house, and area families were offered low interest, forty-year loans to purchase the farms.⁴¹ The government sent agents down to inform the people about their plans, and they quickly called a meeting at a centrally located church to spread the word. For some time, rumors about the government's planned community had been running rampant through the Gee's Bend area, but nobody was re-ally sure of the government's intentions. Consequently, the night of the meeting Bend residents sat on the hard church pews, just brimming with anticipation. Most had donned the best clothes they owned. The men sat stiffly in their best overalls with plaid shirts, although most were frayed and patched here and there, and the women wore their best Sunday dresses, many of which were a bit faded from repeated washing.

Finally, the white men from Washington in their suits and ties stood up before the gathering. Immediately, all the whispering in the audience stopped, and there was dead silence. The spokesman stepped forward, cleared his throat once, and then announced the government's intention to allow Gee's Bend families to buy the land. The church literally erupted in shouts of joy. After the euphoria subsided, Bend residents realized that this govern-ment aid they needed so badly was accompanied by a certain amount of government control. In the planned community government officials envisioned, residents were required to share in a number of cooperative enterprises: a co-op store, a co-op cotton gin, a co-op tractor, and even a co-op bull. Residents were expected to trade exclusively within this cooper-ative system, and the federal government designated a white supervisor, B. N. Ivey, to oversee all of these enterprises along with the rest of the project. Be-cause Washington policy makers were sensitive to local racial etiquette, they were careful to appoint a local white man to this post. In return for the co-operation of Bend residents, the government provided funding to improve roads, construct a school that included instruction through the twelfth grade, and construct a clinic. Up to this time a majority of the Bend's residents had had few educational opportunities and almost no access to health profes-sionals. In fact, few of the Bend's residents had ever seen a doctor.[42]

When they first began preliminary planning for the Gee's Bend project, FSA officials quickly became convinced that one of their first priorities had to be the improvement of educational opportunities for Bend residents because "the facilities for an educational program on the Gee's Bend Project were very unsatisfactory." Officials were appalled when they realized "there were [only] two schools, one having one teacher, and the other having two teachers. One of these schools had for class rooms one building 14'x16', and the other was the old dilapidated church building. The teachers employed in these schools were people with a minimum of preparation for teaching, and were unable, with fa-cilities at hand, to enroll any more than fifty per cent of the children of school age."[43] By the summer of 1938, the FSA moved to upgrade facilities: they con-structed a new building with enough classroom space to accommodate 5 teach-ers and 209 students.[44] Officials admitted that all of the students attending the new school were in the lower grades: "of the two hundred nine enrollment more than one hundred have enrolled in the first grade, the others being scattered through the various grades up to and including the seventh."[45] However, despite this slow start, FSA officials had high hopes for the future, and they gratefully insisted, "The County Board of Education is very sympathetic and cooperative in giving us teaching personnel fitted for the job." They optimistically concluded, "We know that we will strengthen as time passes."[46]

FSA optimism notwithstanding, Robert Pierce, principal of the new school, reported that there were still problems. First and foremost, according to Pierce, the new school building was not nearly large enough. He insisted, "we are [already] overcrowded." The principal also complained that students were not receiving proper instruction in science "due to the lack of a Science Laboratory in which to perform the various experiments. Of course, we are using improvised materials until we are able to do better."[47]

Over the next few months the new school made significant progress, and Principal Pierce was especially pleased to report the addition of a vocational home economics and agriculture teacher. He insisted that the new teacher "adds a great deal to our set up. Our Project Manager, the State Vocational Worker, and our Superintendent were very much interested in our over-age boys and girls taking advantage of the vocational work three hours daily, yet get in their same amount of literary work."[48] Pierce was also happy to report that Bend parents seemed to be quite interested in the education of their children. He explained, "We have a very lively PTA organization. They seem to understand just what this organization means."[49]

The FSA commitment to expanding educational opportunities in the Bend was accompanied by a serious concern about the lack of proper health care in the isolated community. When the project first started, Bend residents rarely saw a doctor or any other health care professional. One observer explained, "There is no doctor in the Bend. People get sick and die or get well as the Lord wills. A doctor is rarely present at childbirth." In those rare instances when Bend residents became desperate enough to seek professional medical attention, they quickly discovered just how difficult it was. "In the desperate emergency someone rides a bareback mule to Camden, crossing the ferry, finds a white man to guarantee the doctor's bill, and then begs a doctor to come."[50] Obviously, if time was of the essence when all of this started, the patient might well be dead before medical help arrived. Even casual observers recognized that Bend residents were deprived of medical care. However, because of their belief in the "primitive, independent, and resourceful" nature of Gee's Bend residents, many of those observers convinced themselves that this did not cause any problems for the people of the Bend.

The description of a casual encounter between a white reporter and a Gee's Bend resident provides a graphic illustration of this attitude. One day the reporter encountered one of the Bend's farmers riding by on a mule. He immediately noticed that the man's big toe on his right foot was badly swollen. When the white reporter questioned the farmer about the condition of his toe, the farmer explained that he had been bitten by a snake. The reporter explained admiringly how the farmer handled the situation. The reporter asked rhetorically, "Did he call for a doctor and a needle of antivenin [sic]? Did he go home and go to bed? Did he appeal to the government in the emergency?" The reporter answered his own questions when he continued, "He did none of these things. Instead, he built a small fire, held his toe in it, tied a string around the toe, and was on his way to plow cotton when we met him."[51] Clearly, the white reporter admired what he thought of as the Bend farmer's self-reliance. Yet, given the conditions facing Gee's Bend residents at the time, what is more likely is that the farmer's actions after the snakebite were motivated by a lack of options: without access to proper medical care and other social services, the snake bite victim simply did the best he could.

By the end of the 1930s the FSA had made progress in attempts to bring professional medical care to the residents of Gee's Bend. In 1938, the government built a clinic in the Bend. This was the first time that any such health care facility had ever been located in the community. The facility was run by Annie Shamburg, a "colored health nurse" supplied by the government. Nurse Shamburg provided "medical care and drugs," including prenatal care and inoculations. FSA officials also contracted with two local white doctors, Dr. J. Paul Jones of Camden, and Dr. R. E. Dixon of Alberta, to provide additional medical services. Families paid a fee at the beginning of the year that guaranteed them the services of one of the government's doctors throughout the year. According to Dr. Jones, the arrangement worked smoothly for the most part. However, he did complain that many of his patients "still make and use teas made of horse hoof, snake grass, tobacco grass, mullein dirt dobber nests," and only call the nurse or doctor when all home remedies have failed."[52]

Dr. Jones went on to explain that some major health problems were already under control even before the government's initiative: "Diphtheria and smallpox had been eradicated by mass inoculations several years ago. Venereal diseases are seldom found." That left "childbirth, malaria and intestinal parasites" for Jones and his colleague to treat.[53] After his experience the first year, Jones concluded that the FSA should begin to provide dental care for Bend residents. He also insisted that there was a serious need for "a thorough malarial control plan." Jones explained that there had been a serious outbreak of malaria after the August floods, and he anticipated a recurrence of the problem if a prevention plan were not implemented.[54]

While social services were improving, the area's economic fortunes also improved. By 1939 crop values had increased dramatically, loan payments were ahead of schedule, and Bend farmers owned over six hundred head of cattle. The FSA was very proud of their model project, and although Bend residents were very grateful for the federal government's aid, many were chafing under government control. Supervisor B. N. Ivey explained, "It took a lot of supervision, and a lot of 'em didn't like that supervision." He added emphatically, "They just didn't like it."[55] As Supervisor Ivey continued to work with the Bend's residents, his negative assessment of their capabilities soon became abundantly clear. Like most other white Wilcox residents, Ivey was convinced that African Americans were a childlike race, incapable of functioning effectively as mature adults. He articulated this view in no uncertain terms as he sought to justify his intervention in their financial affairs. As he put it, "It was what you call a supervised bank account, they didn't like that. But, [since black] people are not able to handle money, what else can you do?" Ivey went on to explain, "I got a little niece, [a] white girl. She can't handle her money either. She gets mad when I handle hers, but, hell, she can't handle it. It's best for her, so I handle it."[56] Clearly, in Ivey's estimation, African Americans in Gee's Bend were not any more capable of handling their financial affairs than his young niece.

Gee's Bend residents often strenuously objected to Ivey's efforts to treat them like children. In some instances, residents acted on their objections. Gee's Bend resident Earl Lee Young vividly recalls his refusal to be treated like a child. One year, Young applied for a government loan to make some improvements on his farm. His application was approved, but when the check came, the government sent it to Supervisor Ivey. Ivey, in turn, sent word to Young that his check had arrived and that they should meet at the co-op store. When Young arrived at the store, Ivey refused to give him the check. Instead, the supervisor said, "The money done come, and I want to tell you how we do." He continued, "You turn the check to me, and I'll put it in the bank . . . whatever you need, you come to me, and I'll write you a check." Ivey's words hit Earl Lee Young like a cold slap in the face. Young took a deep breath, squared his shoulders, looked Ivey directly in the eye and said, "Not me; NOT ME." Young continued in a quiet but determined voice, "I'm borrowing this money to make a crop with, and if me and my wife and kids sit down and eat this money up in . . . sardines and crackers, that ain't your problem." As Earl Lee talked, his voice gathered strength. He concluded emphatically, "If I can't get my check in my hand, you can carry it back."[57]

Ivey was flabbergasted. He could not believe Earl Lee Young's audacity. Supervisor Ivey was particularly angered by the public nature of this show-down: There were a number of Bend residents in the co-op store listening to the exchange between Ivey and Young, and undoubtedly they cheered their neighbor's courage. Ivey tried to calm Young by explaining that he would give Young some of the money whenever Young requested it. But a deter-mined Earl Lee Young refused to be persuaded. In the meantime, all other ac-tivity in the store had ceased. Farmers in their overalls stood motionless; women shopping for household supplies looked up from their task; even chil-dren who had been pleading with their parents to buy candy fell silent. Earl Lee Young declared in an uncompromising tone, "If I break . . . a plow han-dle or something, and I'm standing on the street in Camden looking for you, [and] you['re] somewhere on vacation and I lose a crop . . . I can't go along with that; I ain't got to put up with it." Supervisor Ivey hesitated just a brief moment before handing the check over to Young and leaving the store.[58]

Young's action clearly illustrates the refusal exhibited by many Gee's Bend residents to submit to outside control. While they were grateful to the fed-eral government for rescuing them from certain starvation, that gratitude could not extinguish the independent spirit that had characterized the peo-ple on this peninsula for generations. Predictably, as the fortunes of the Bend's residents continued to improve, they were able to qualify for loans at local banks. Many took advantage of this option because it allowed them to sidestep what they had come to see as suffocating government control. B. N. Ivey criticized the tendency of Gee's Bend residents to secure outside loans. He lamented that there was "no supervision there,"[59] but that is just what the people of Gee's Bend wanted.

Many observers watched developments in Gee's Bend with a great deal of interest. At a time when African Americans were wrestling with the social and economic problems that accompanied their subordinate status, there were some who found the idea of government assistance for a planned rural African American community quite appealing. In fact, despite the sour note of heavy-handed government supervision, many Bend residents expressed enthusiasm for government support of planned communities. They gave the federal government full credit for the dramatic improvement in their for-tunes, and they could scarcely contain their joy when they compared their present situation to the desperation they had felt a short time ago on the day that the white men and their wagons had taken everything out of the Bend. Principal Robert Pierce reminded his friends and neighbors why they should be thankful: "It is quite encouraging to note the progress that we are making here in Gee's Bend. Let us now think of where we were last year this very time and where we are now. We can readily see that we have made rapid progress." He concluded by advising, "If we desire for our community to have success, let us not forget to have faith in ourselves, faith in our leaders, faith in our friends, and above all faith in God."[60] Despite widespread black support, there were some who were less than enthusiastic about the government's administration of the Gee's Bend Project, however. One of those critics, F. D. Tattun, president of Tuskegee Institute, wrote the FSA to express the hope that government officials "were interested beyond the matter of physical comfort and were concerned with the possible and eventual integration of these people . . . into a democratic way of life." President Tattun went on to insist that to ensure success FSA officials should be scrupulously careful about choosing "more and better personnel" to staff the project so that "through their work with the people there would come the desire for a better life." Tattun explained that he was moved to voice his concerns because he had heard rumors "of inefficiency on the part of the leadership chosen [for the Gee's Bend Project] in some instances, as compared with its splendid showing in others."[61] There is no indication that anyone from the FSA ever addressed Tattun's concerns.

As the government focused attention on its Gee's Bend social experiment, other black Wilcox residents worked to cope with the harsh reality of life during the Great Depression as best they could. In fact, by this time, a number of African Americans in other areas of the county had managed to acquire some acreage. A number of those black-owned farms were particularly clustered in the communities of Prairie, Coy, and Annemanie. While these landowners were better off than the county's numerous landless black farm laborers, they still had their share of tough times. Hattie Irene Steele, a black resident of Prairie, has vivid memories of the Depression years. She was born in Prairie in 1920, one of fourteen children, and her family owned their own land. In fact, their land had originally been part of the seven hundred acres acquired by the Presbyterians around the turn of the century in the vicinity of the Prairie Mission. From an early age, Steele remembers, much of her life was centered around the Presbyterian mission. She explains, "We had plenty of hardships, plus we had our regular routine that we really enjoyed . . . which was connected with the church and . . . the Presbyterian school."[62] Her parents valued education, and they insisted that all their children attend school for the whole nine-month term every year. At the same time, the Steele children understood that they still had to do their chores. Steele explains, "we got home in the evening; we had plenty to do. Before we leave in the morning we had plenty. . . . We liked it."[63]

Irene Steele's family grew all their own food, and they often were left with surpluses to sell. The family raised chickens, and young Irene was especially fond of the young birds. It was her job to make sure that they were all locked in the chicken coop at night to keep them safe from nocturnal predators. Every morning, Irene eagerly rose to the sound of the Prairie Mission School's bell that tolled faithfully at 5:00 A.M. She quickly dressed and went outside to feed her beloved birds and free them from their coop. After she finished with the chickens there were many other chores to do before she left for school because her family also grew corn, cotton, peanuts, peas, potatoes, pears, and collard greens. In fact, according to Irene, they grew the best collard greens in the area, and they were able to sell much of their crop to their neighbors. Yet, regardless of how many chores the Steele children had to do, their parents made sure that their schoolwork always came first. After they finished their elementary training at Prairie, they went on to the Presbyterian schools at either Miller's Ferry or Annemanie for their high school studies. During the 1920s, all of Irene's older sisters had lived in the dormitory when they attended high school because both Miller's Ferry and Annemanie were so far from the Steele farm. However, by the time Irene was ready to attend high school, the Steele family was firmly caught in the grip of the Great Depression, and although young Irene and her family still had plenty to eat, they no longer had any extra income. In fact, when the family car broke down in the first months of the Depression, there was no money to repair it, and the broken-down automobile carcass sat in the same spot on the Steele farm for years, a grim reminder of economic hard times. Just after the car broke down Steele finished her course work at Prairie and prepared to start high school at Miller's Ferry. Her mother was forced to tell her young daughter that the family could not afford to pay her board on campus as they had done for all of her older sisters.

A disappointed Irene received the news stoically. She had so looked forward to living in the dormitory with all the other girls, but she knew her family was doing their best. After all, they were still managing to pay her tuition. Over the next three years, a determined young Irene rose long before daybreak, quickly dressed, ate breakfast, did her chores, and began her long trek to Miller's Ferry, seven miles away. Every day in the cold or the heat, whether it was wet or dry, Irene Steele walked seven miles to school, attended classes all day long, and then walked seven miles home. Irene's mother's heart ached for her daughter, and she christened Irene her Depression child.[64]

Edna Bonner Rhodes, who was also born in 1920, remembers what a profound impact the Great Depression had on her life. Rhodes's earliest childhood memories are of Coy. Her mother was a teacher at the Baptist Coy

Academy, and her father, a graduate of Tuskegee Institute, was the academy's principal. Even though the Bonners were both professional educators who were entitled to receive a salary, the family still had to be thrifty in order to make ends meet. In fact, when times were tough, Coy teachers were sometimes paid with molasses and potatoes, but because her father was already farming in his spare time, Rhodes recalls, this did her family little good. Despite the Bonner family's financial condition, however, young Edna's parents were determined to send her to the Presbyterian Camden Academy where they were sure she would receive a superior education. Accordingly, she enrolled in Camden's card class in the fall of 1926. This was the school's equivalent of kindergarten. It was called a card class because the teacher had cards with various words printed on them. Edna and her young classmates would eagerly watch the teacher as she held up a card. Then, the teacher carefully pronounced the word written on the card in an exaggerated fashion so that the children could see how to hold their mouths to make the right sounds. Edna and the other children leaned forward in their seats expectantly. They looked almost like baby birds pursing their lips as they struggled to reproduce the teacher's sounds correctly.[65]

Camden Academy's tuition was only twenty-five cents a month, and Rhodes recalls that even that amount could sometimes be a problem for her family. But somehow they managed to keep her in school. During her early years, young Edna thoroughly enjoyed school, and she particularly enjoyed recess every day. When she and her friends went out on the playground they had to find creative ways to amuse themselves because the majority of the students were from poor families. When they played ball, they often used a stick for a bat, and they made their balls out of string, grass, or whatever was handy. Many of the boys shot marbles while the girls would face each other and pat their hands together in time to one of the many rhymes they knew from memory. "We had a good time," Rhodes declares.[66] As the Depression deepened, Edna's family still continued to scrape together the monthly tuition for her. She remembers that she and many other Camden Academy students picked cotton on neighboring plantations to get money for their books. They always made sure they picked cotton well before school: they never missed class. In 1938 young Edna's hard work paid off: that spring she graduated from Camden Academy. She was eagerly looking forward to attending college in the fall, and she had her heart set on Tuskegee Institute. Ever since Rhodes could remember, she had wanted to attend her father's alma mater, but she soon found that the Great Depression would prevent her from realizing her dream. She explains, "[In] 1938 when I finished [high school], there was no money. Daddy had one one hundred dollar bill that he didn't want to break, and to go to Tuskegee, I would have needed $80, and he said he couldn't afford to spend $80 on me."[67]

Edna was terribly disappointed, but by December of 1938, she learned that she would get the chance to attend college after all. At that time, A. C. Peoples, Camden Academy's principal, escorted Edna and a number of other penniless but proud Camden graduates to Alabama State, the black state-supported school in Montgomery. For some time before this, Peoples had been in touch with the National Youth Administration (NYA), a New Deal agency. The NYA's Bureau of Negro Affairs was headed by renowned black educator Mary McCleod Bethune, and under her leadership the county's black youth were able to share in a variety of NYA-sponsored student work programs.[68] In fact, it was Edna's enrollment in an NYA-sponsored work program that provided her with the opportunity to begin her college training at Alabama State. During her freshman and sophomore years, the NYA paid her school expenses, but by the end of Edna's sophomore year, the NYA was being phased out along with a number of other New Deal agencies as the Depression began to ease. Edna was not worried, however, because she had worked very hard during her first two years of college, and she had consistently been on the honor roll every semester. She confidently expected to receive an academic scholarship to cover the cost of her final two years in college. Alabama State did not disappoint her.

Wilcox native Kayte Marsh Fearn remembers that even before the Depression started in earnest, the stock market crash had a serious impact on her family's finances. Fearn's parents did not own any land. Instead, like the Bonners, they were both professional educators. At the end of the 1928–1929 school year, just previous to the crash, Kayte's father, T. P. Marsh, had taught at Snow Hill Institute. By the spring of 1929, Snow Hill's principal informed the elder Marsh along with the rest of the faculty that Snow Hill had run out of money, and would be unable to pay their salaries. After this devastating announcement, the atmosphere on Snow Hill's campus was very somber: teachers desperately needed their paychecks to make ends meet. Like the others, T. P. Marsh was very concerned because he had a family to support. Never one to dwell on misfortune, Marsh decided to take drastic action. He found a job in one of the growing number of automobile factories in Detroit, Michigan. Thus, in May of 1929, after making sure that his wife and children were safely housed on the Camden Academy campus, Marsh reluctantly left them to go north.[69]

Far from the hustle and bustle of the growing auto industry in Detroit, young Kayte and her three brothers quickly settled into a comfortable routine on the Camden Academy campus. That fall, all the Marsh children enrolled as Camden Academy students, and their mother joined the school's faculty. The three Marsh boys lived in the boys' dormitory, Kayte lived in the girls' dormitory, and their mother lived in a teacher's room in the girls' dormitory. With T. P. Marsh sending money home from his factory job in Detroit, the family's fortunes were definitely improving. Yet, before the Marshes could get too comfortable with their improved economic circumstances, the stock market crashed, and within days Marsh lost his job. Like thousands of others, he was unable to find another job. Thus, six months after he went to Detroit, T. P. Marsh returned to Alabama. When he arrived home late in the fall of 1929, he was overjoyed to see his family, but he was worried about their future.[70]

In the first days after his return to Wilcox County, the elder Marsh moved into his wife's room in the dormitory. By this time, Mrs. Marsh, like all the other teachers in the black Presbyterian schools, had had her salary cut from $50 to $45 a month. In the interest of economy, the church continued to pay its teachers only $45 a month until well into the 1940s. After the elder Marsh finally found local employment, he rented a ramshackle house on Camden Academy's campus, and the Marsh family gratefully moved in. While the Depression tightened its iron grip on the surrounding county, the Marsh children enjoyed their formative years on the Camden Academy campus. One of young Kayte's most vivid memories from these years is of her eighth-grade operetta. At the end of the school year, each of the advanced classes always put on an operetta, and in the spring of 1931, Kayte's class got the chance for the first time. Even though Fearn cannot remember many details, the operetta was still quite memorable because the students were allowed to waltz as part of the performance. Kayte and her classmates were thrilled because at this time, Camden Academy students were still forbidden to dance on campus. The night of the performance, Kayte felt so grown up as she took her place facing her partner, and his arm encircled her waist.[71]

In addition to their year-end performances, Camden Academy students also participated in a series of rallies through the first half of the 1930s. These rallies were the brainchild of Reverend William G. Wilson, Camden Academy's principal at the time. During the rally, each faculty member was expected to find ways to raise money. Teachers and students sold candy, held bake sales, sold peanuts, and held fish fries. Reverend Wilson proudly collected the money raised by his faculty and student body each year and sent it to incredulous Presbyterian Church officials in Pittsburgh, Pennsylvania. Clearly, Wilson was determined to prove to church officials that local black residents were willing and able to contribute to their own advancement. At the same time, Wilson's fund-raising activities reinforced the importance of black self-help that had been part of the county's African American value system since the late nineteenth century.[72]

Mabel Walker Thornton also thrived as a Camden Academy student during the Great Depression. She was born in Camden in 1928, and she was raised by her grandparents, who sacrificed a great deal to keep her enrolled in Camden Academy. By the time young Mabel was in the first grade, it was the middle of the 1930s, and the Depression was raging all around her. On Camden Academy's campus, however, the economic emergency had very little impact on Mabel's daily life. She was too busy attempting to please her teacher, Gertrude Wilson, and Thornton fondly recalls how Mrs. Wilson trained the girls in her class to be prim and proper. Every morning, the girls had to line up for inspection, and their teacher would look down the line of eager young faces, carefully scrutinizing each of her charges. She wanted to make sure they were clean, properly dressed, and carrying the snow-white handkerchiefs that she insisted were part of a proper ladylike appearance. Every time little Mabel took her place in line, there were butterflies in her stomach as her teacher approached. She admired Mrs. Wilson so much, and she wanted to please her. In fact, all the girls wanted to fulfill their teacher's expectations. Thornton explains, "She [Mrs. Wilson] spoke very precisely . . . and of course, we did too. We spoke just like her." In short, Thornton recalls, "We were everything she wanted us to be."[73] It is important to note that Mrs. Wilson not only instructed her pupils, she took care of them, too. She would fix a hot lunch for her young charges every day on a small hot plate she kept in her classroom. Then, after the youngsters had finished their meal, Gertrude Wilson insisted that they should lay their heads down and take a short nap. Thus, despite the economic emergency gripping their country and their county, Thornton recalls that she and her classmates thrived in this Camden Academy atmosphere of high expectations and gentle nurturing.[74]

Throughout this period, black Wilcox residents young and old continued to go about their daily lives as they searched for a sense of normalcy in the midst of this unprecedented economic emergency. As the Great Depression dragged on year after year, it almost seemed as if it would go on forever. However, one of the few bright spots that seemed to excite black Wilcox residents regardless of their age, income level, or educational level was the success of a young African American boxer who managed to win the heavyweight championship of the world during the depths of the Great Depression. In 1936, to the dismay of his many admirers, that young black champion, Joe Louis, was knocked out by Max Schmeling. Yet, by 1938 Louis was able to regain his crown, and many black Wilcox residents remember hearing the radio announcer excitedly describe the action as the young champion avenged his loss. Only a few black Wilcox residents could afford to own radios at that time, so whenever Louis fought, people would gather in tight little knots around the front porches of their neighbors who did own a radio. Their collective cheers and groans provided a perfect accompaniment to the radio announcer's excited voice vividly describing the blow-by-blow action. Edna Bonner Rhodes remembers coming back to her house triumphantly whenever Louis won a fight shouting, "Glad we win."[75]

At the same time that black residents struggled to cope with the emotional and economic emergency of the Great Depression, their white neighbors employed their own methods to break the monotony of their lives. One of the more popular forms of entertainment available to white Wilcox residents at this time was their local movie theater. The Camden Theatre was located right near the town square, and those lucky residents who could scrape up the few cents necessary to purchase a ticket could leave their dreary, desperate lives behind, at least for a while, and escape into the dark fantasy world of a Hollywood movie. During the 1930s Camden Theatre audiences were treated to a variety of Hollywood productions ranging from musicals to murder mysteries. However, the theater's featured program for June 4–6, 1931, is particularly telling: Amos and Andy in *Check and Double Check*.[76] The comic antics of stereotypical black characters were sure to entertain white Wilcox audiences who were struggling to maintain a sense of normalcy amidst all the economic uncertainty that seemed to have ensnared them.

The Camden Theatre's advertisement in the June 4, 1931, issue of the *Wilcox Progressive Era* proudly proclaimed that coming soon after Amos and Andy would be D. W. Griffith's film *Birth of a Nation*. The theater's decision to show this film is quite revealing. The film is riddled with racial stereotypes, and its message is clearly and viciously anti-black. It is set in the South after the Civil War, and it portrays the slaves and ex-slaves as lazy, stupid, crooked, and incapable of governing themselves or anyone else. According to the film's story line, the federal government's insistence on allowing black men to vote is clearly leading to disaster, but in the South's darkest hour, the Ku Klux Klan rides in to save the day and return the ex-slaves to their rightful subordinate place. First released in 1915, it was a silent film, and during the depths of the Great Depression, white Wilcox residents sat in the darkened Camden Theatre with dramatic black-and-white images of black subordination flickering across their faces. Even though this silent film was almost two decades old by this time, its message of black subordination undoubtedly struck a responsive chord in white Camden audiences. As far as many were concerned, it was comforting to know that in the midst of all the economic uncertainty confronting them there was still one aspect of their lives that would remain unchanged, no matter what: black subordination was still a fact of life in Wilcox County, Alabama.

Black residents recall numerous incidents during the 1930s that clearly indicate just how determined their white neighbors were to remind them of their subordinate status. One of those incidents occurred in the small black community of Possum Bend that is located just west of Camden. Jack Bonham, a black Wilcox resident who was born in Possum Bend in 1928, witnessed the incident. Bonham's father was a brick mason and a lay minister, and the family owned a small piece of land. There were nine children in his family, and Bonham remembers having a very happy childhood. Like other black youngsters in the county, he was only dimly aware of the restrictive racism all around him, and it rarely intruded on his young life. He explains, "It's amazing how much our parents shielded us."[77] Despite his parents' best efforts, however, young Bonham came face-to-face with Wilcox County's racial code at the end of his family's driveway one day. It happened in 1938, and it all started when Jack's brother went out to check the mail. Like all the other families in their community, the Bonhams had a rural mailbox that rested on a pole at the end of their driveway. Jack's brother had walked down to get the mail many times, but on this particular day as he looked down the driveway, he could scarcely believe his eyes. The youngster quickly walked toward the mail box so that he could get a better look, but as he got closer, his steps slowed, and then he finally came to a stop just a few feet from the end of the driveway. The little boy felt anger and confusion as he watched a white man from a nearby farm boldly rifle through the contents of his family's mailbox.[78] Just then, the intruder looked up as he sensed young Bonham's presence. He glared at the black youngster with an expression of pure contempt, and then he leisurely turned around and brazenly continued rummaging through the family's mail. After a split second, young Bonham wheeled around and ran back to the house as fast as he could. "Daddy, Daddy," the little boy called. After his son told him about the white mail thief, the elder Bonham was furious. He was also very friendly with two local white ministers, and he wasted no time telling them about the incident. The two ministers immediately went to the sheriff and complained on Bonham's behalf.

Two nights later, Possum Bend was very quiet, but it was prepared. The men in the community had gotten word earlier that day that the white mail thief was furious that the Bonham family had had the temerity to complain. He was determined to teach these uppity black folks a lesson. Shortly after dark, a car with several white men in it rolled slowly into Possum Bend, and it came to a stop in front of the Bonham's driveway. Several white men piled out of the car. Their intentions were never clear, because before they could move away from their vehicle, all the white intruders froze when they heard a distinctive and frightening chorus of clicks as hammers were cocked on guns. The sound seemed to be coming from everywhere at once. Then, as the eyes of the stunned white intruders began to adjust to the inky blackness, they could just make out the barrels of guns pointing at them from everywhere: from behind trees, from tall grass, from behind buildings. Just above the barrel of each gun was the determined face of one of the black men of the community. Each stood poised with his finger on the trigger. With as much dignity as the flustered white intruders could muster, they carefully stepped back into their car and slowly drove out of Possum Bend. Young Jack Bonham remembers feeling a sense of triumph when it was all over, but nobody ever spoke of it again.[79]

Paul Washington, a black Wilcox native who was also born in 1928, has vivid memories of another racial incident that also occurred in the late 1930s. It all started when a local black resident, Jonah Martin, asked a white store owner who lived on the outskirts of Camden to advance him a small amount of money. Macintosh, the white man, refused. Driven by desperation, Martin waited until night fell and broke into Macintosh's store. His palms were sweaty and his heart was hammering as he reached for the cash he needed. After pocketing the money, he quickly left the store and paused for a minute as he contemplated how much trouble he was in and how difficult it would be for him to escape. At this point, convinced that he had nothing to lose, Jonah Martin jumped into Macintosh's car that was parked in front of the store. Without too much difficulty, Martin started the engine, but then the car lurched forward and stalled as he tried unsuccessfully in his haste to balance the clutch and the accelerator. He finally got it started again and drove a short distance out of town, where he ditched the car. Martin was convinced that Macintosh's car would make him too conspicuous a target.

Instead, he made his way to a nearby pickup point where a Trailways bus headed out of the county was scheduled to stop. In the meantime Macintosh discovered the theft and spread the alarm. Within a short time, the local sheriff had raised a posse, and they had started searching for Jonah Martin. Of course, one of the most obvious places to look was on the bus that had just departed. The posse took off after the bus at breakneck speed, and when they spotted it just ahead, the adrenaline started pumping in their veins. The lead car with the sheriff in it drew even with the bus at Miller's Ferry, and the county's chief law enforcement officer motioned to the bus driver to pull off the road. As the bus began slowing down, Jonah Martin began to sweat. He realized that this was an unscheduled stop, and right then and there he vowed not to be taken alive. The bus finally came to a stop, and Jonah Martin unconsciously reached for the reassuring feel of the cold, steel butt of the pistol he had stolen from Macintosh's store. Jonah carefully watched the bus driver, and just as the man opened the bus's front door, Martin bounded by startled passengers, many of whom were almost asleep, and jumped off the bus. He ran past the posse just as they were getting out of their cars, and hid behind a building that sat right by the side of the road.

The first white lawman to get out of his car took off after the black fugitive, and quickly disappeared behind the same building. Almost before anyone could react, two shots pierced the dark night. Members of the posse reacted quickly, running around the corner of the building as fast as they could. They were stunned by the sight that greeted them. Instead of a subdued black fugitive, they saw their fellow lawman lying in a pool of blood. He was mortally wounded. As shock washed over the white lawmen, they heard the unmistakable sound of breaking branches and crackling leaves as Jonah Martin escaped through the woods that were just behind the building.[80]

Obviously, this was a catastrophic breach in Wilcox County's racial etiquette. The call went out immediately for able-bodied white men to help capture the black fugitive. Edna Bonner Rhodes remembers being shocked that even local white preachers armed themselves and joined the search party.[81] In the meantime, after Martin had gotten well beyond the store, he reached the banks of the Alabama River. He knew he was out of options, so he took a deep breath, and jumped in. The icy water quickly soaked his clothes, and he soon felt like he was wrapped in a heavy, wet blanket. But, despite the waterlogged fabric weighing him down, Jonah Martin began to swim with every ounce of strength he had. He knew his life depended on it. Frustrated lawmen could only watch as the solitary black figure in the Alabama River swam farther and farther away from them. The enraged posse pulled out their guns and fired again and again at the rapidly shrinking figure in the river, but he was beyond their range.

The next morning at first light, the sheriff's posse reassembled and hastily drove to Selma in neighboring Dallas County. They had last seen the fugitive swimming in that direction, so they decided to begin their search there. They were right. In a short time, with the aid of bloodhounds, they cornered Jonah Martin in a sugarcane field right outside of Selma. When the cornered fugitive realized that he had finally run out of options, he stoically turned around to face his pursuers. A volley of shots rang out, and Jonah Martin was dead before he hit the ground, but the enraged posse seemed powerless to stop firing their weapons. The rage they felt, which was motivated by generations of white supremacy and black subordination, weighed heavily on the men as they fired their weapons again and again and again at Martin's lifeless form. By the time the group's rage was spent, it seemed that practically every inch of Jonah Martin's corpse was riddled with bullet holes. In short order, the sheriff and his deputies took Martin's body back to Wilcox County. They dragged what was left of him through the streets of Camden, and then they laid the bloody body out on the courthouse lawn.[82]

Some years later a white graduate student at the University of North Carolina who was told about the incident reported that "when the convict was trapped and shot, the mob brought back the body and laid it out on the ground before the courthouse as a warning to others not to tamper with race-caste limits. It is said that many white women also joined in the celebration and gazed upon the body."[83] The sight of a mutilated black corpse on the courthouse lawn was disturbing enough as far as black residents were concerned. However, they were even more distressed when they observed the behavior of the white onlookers who had gathered around Martin's body. It seemed as if the white crowd was mesmerized and energized by the sight of the body decomposing in the sun. Such white behavior in the presence of violent black death threatened to unleash that unspoken fear that was always with black residents, but that they mostly kept confined to a back corner of their minds. Who would be next, some worried. Would one victim be enough?

Because of what they perceived as very real danger, many black residents avoided the courthouse square in Camden for some time. For example, Gwen Bridges Bonham remembers that it was a long time before her family allowed her to come to town after this.[84] On the other hand, however, there were a few brave black souls who were curious enough to take a look. Paul Washington remembers that his brother was one of those who just happened to be in town the afternoon that Jonah Martin was apprehended. While the sight of the bloody body on the courthouse lawn frightened young Washington, he could not help but stare as he walked past. When the youngster looked closely at the corpse, it almost seemed that the dead man's sightless eyes were boring into him. For a split second, he was virtually hypnotized by the lifeless stare, but then as his awareness of the ugly mood of the white onlookers began to register in his consciousness, young Washington quickened his pace, averted his gaze, and walked away. For a long time after this, Washington could not shake the memory of the corpse's sightless eyes piercing into him.[85]

Nellie Williams Abner also remembers witnessing an incident during the 1930s that clearly illustrated the determination of the county's white residents to reinforce the lesson of black subordination with force. The year was

1935. Abner was only a young girl at the time, and she was in the five-and-dime store in Camden. She looked up just in time to see the store owner viciously kick an older black woman who was a customer in the store. The store owner reasoned that the attack was justified "because she said yes to him [instead of yes sir]."[86] Young Nellie recoiled in shock and horror from the scene in front of her. She almost wished that she could make herself invisible as she quietly backed toward the front door, her eyes never leaving the humiliated black customer. Once she was outside, Nellie paused just long enough to take several deep breaths in an effort to steady the violent trembling that had seized her body. She quickly recovered and ran all the way home. Word of the outrage spread rapidly through Camden's black community. While they realized that their options were limited, African Americans in Camden also realized that there was one way they could safely retaliate. Abner explains, "We didn't buy things from him. We knew how to boycott a long time before Martin Luther King came in." She continued, "You can hurt them in their pocketbooks, we learned that early."[87]

Throughout the 1930s, Wilcox County's white population continued to try to enforce the county's racial code. Yet, despite their best efforts, the signs of change were becoming increasingly obvious as the decade wore on. In fact, it was in the 1930s that the Communist Party began focusing a great deal of their attention on disaffected and impoverished Southerners. Party officials reasoned that oppressed black Southerners would be particularly receptive to the Communist message. Accordingly, in late 1929 the Central Committee of the Communist Party in the United States decided to locate the headquarters of its newly established district seventeen in Birmingham, Alabama. By August of 1930, over five hundred Birmingham residents had joined the party's ranks: between 80 and 90 percent of the new recruits were black. Later that fall during the general election campaign the party decided to endorse Walter Lewis, a black candidate, for governor. White Birmingham residents were alarmed, but a short time later they were able to breathe a sigh of relief, because U.S. congressman Hamilton Fish's committee to investigate Communist propaganda decided to hold hearings in Birmingham. Predictably, the hearings whipped anti-Communist hysteria into a frenzy. Yet, despite all this negative publicity and the hysteria it engendered, the party continued to attract an increasing number of recruits in the Birmingham area. The party's popularity was clearly an indication of just how desperate impoverished Alabamans had become by this time, and in 1930, in light of their increasing popularity in Birmingham, party officials made the fateful decision to expand into the rural areas.[88]

Party officials were acutely aware of the misery in southern rural areas. In fact, by January 1931, sharecroppers in England, Arkansas, became so desperate that they staged a public protest. This spontaneous grassroots movement spurred party leaders in other parts of the South, including Birmingham, to action. Birmingham leaders advised Alabama farmers to "Call mass meetings in each township and on each large plantation. Set up Farmers' Relief Councils at these meetings. Organize hunger marches on towns to demand food and clothing from the supply merchants and bankers who have sucked you dry year after year."[89] Hopeful black sharecroppers from all over the state responded enthusiastically to the Communist plea. Party officials were delighted with the response, and this convinced them that the next logical place for them to go to extend their movement was the Black Belt. At this point, party officials naively believed that circumstances in these Black Belt counties were so desperate that economic concerns would unite the people across racial lines. They would soon find, however, that despite the existence of a catastrophic emergency, the stubbornly entrenched white supremacy in counties like Wilcox militated against any kind of interracial grassroots action.

In February of 1932, party officials dispatched Angelo Herndon, a black Communist, to Wilcox County to meet with the county's newly formed sharecroppers' organization.[90] In his moving autobiography, *Let Me Live*, Herndon described the difficulties he encountered trying to organize Wilcox County's black sharecroppers. When he first entered the county, the young Communist was particularly struck by the condition of many of the black youngsters he encountered:

> I spoke to the children. My heart went out to them. Despite all the sweetness of childhood on their faces, they looked so pinched, so stunted and sickly from neglect and undernourishment, that I felt there was little I could say to them for their young ears to hear. For I was choked with bitterness and anger at the society which deprived them of their right to health and happiness and to the joys of childhood.[91]

Herndon carefully scrutinized the faces of his young audience as he tried to find the right words to say. Suddenly, it seemed that the faces that were staring back at him were not the faces of children after all: they had experienced too much misery too soon. Herndon observed, "I was startled for I found myself talking to a group of little old men of six and seven and eight."[92]

After this emotional session with the county's children, Angelo Herndon was eager to speak to their parents. He was confident that conditions facing impoverished Wilcox County residents were so miserable that his pleas to organize would be favorably received. Along with his optimism, however, the young Communist was also gripped by a feeling of dread that became his constant companion the whole time he was in Wilcox County: he was convinced that

his every move was being watched by county authorities. His fears notwithstanding, when Herndon finally got the chance to speak to an audience of
adults, he decided he must speak candidly. He explained, "As I addressed myself
to my audience of Negro and white sharecroppers and peered into their faces,
and read in them such deep suffering and helplessness, I flung all caution to the
winds and spoke to them what was on my mind." The young Communist tried
to find encouraging words to say to his audience. As he put it, "I assured them
that the only possible solution to their problem was complete unity between
black and white sharecroppers, in short, a militant union which would fight for
the improvement of their lot."[93] Herndon's suggestion of cooperation across
racial lines in Wilcox County, Alabama, in the 1930s was truly revolutionary.

The audience politely applauded Herndon's words, but immediately after
he finished speaking, the men in the audience crowded around the young organizer, asking about the availability of jobs in Birmingham. When Herndon
asked them why they wanted to leave so badly, they began to tell him their
heartrending accounts of the misery they were suffering. Some even tried to
get federal help. One man explained, "A lot of us have borrowed money from
the government to help us along with our work, but we never see any of it.
When the mail brings the checks, the postman delivers them directly to the
landlords."[94] Herndon quickly informed them that the streets of Birmingham
were already clogged with men who had left the farms hoping to find industrial jobs in the city. The audience of sharecroppers stoically listened to
Herndon's advice, quietly turned around, and with stooped shoulders and
downcast eyes, they filed out of the meeting.

The young Communist was undaunted, however, and over the next few
days as he traveled around Wilcox County, he continued to preach the virtues
of a sharecroppers union. He was convinced that "I was planting my seed in
the right kind of soil."[95] Despite the young organizer's optimism, Wilcox
sharecroppers had serious doubts that unionization would work in their
county. Out of desperation, however, many were still willing to try it. One
sharecropper asked pointedly, "What have we got to lose?" He continued, "It
is far better to be dead than to continue living the way we do."[96] It soon became apparent, however, that Angelo Herndon did not have long to spread
his message in Wilcox County because, just as he had suspected, white Wilcox
landlords had been monitoring his activities. One morning, as the young
organizer was walking on the side of the road on his way to a sharecroppers
meeting, he received a frightening warning. A white sharecropper who had
attended one of Herndon's earlier meetings was driving down the road, and he
recognized the solitary black pedestrian. Herndon turned around to face the
man just as his ancient battered automobile wheezed to a stop.

Herndon recognized the sharecropper immediately, and greeted him warmly, but before he could say anything else, the sharecropper warned in a shrill voice, "For God's sake, get out of here as soon as you can! The landlords are organizing a lynch mob over there, ten miles yonder." Herndon was not surprised by this news, and he was about to question the sharecropper further so that he could get more details, but the sharecropper would not let the young Communist get a word in edgewise. The sharecropper continued breathlessly, "Here's some money. Take the next train out. It's the only one that stops at this station today."[97] A grateful Herndon accepted the money, and as the sharecropper's old car rattled off down the road, the man called out over his shoulder, "Here's hoping that your train will come faster than the lynch mob."[98] The young activist spent the next anxious moments at the train station pacing nervously, and looking down the track for the approaching train. After what seemed like an eternity, the train came and Herndon boarded it gratefully. The young Communist never saw any sign of the lynch mob, but he did not doubt its existence.

Even though powerful white Wilcox landowners were successful in running this young reformer out of their county, many were afraid that it was just a matter of time before they would face others, because clearly, the winds of change were sweeping the South. Much of the impetus for those winds was centered squarely in Washington, D.C., in Franklin Roosevelt's new Democratic Party. In fact, by 1936, many political analysts began to insist that the Democratic Party was a new party that had "emerged as a national party, incorporating new constituencies that had been drawn to the programs and party of Franklin Roosevelt."[99] In his 1936 inaugural address, Roosevelt clearly articulated this new Democratic Party's concern for the plight of individual citizens. He asserted, "I see one-third of a nation ill-housed, ill-clad, and ill-nourished." The president went on to pledge his commitment "to speed the time when there would be for all the people that security and peace essential to the pursuit of happiness."[100] It is important to note that Roosevelt's concern for America's poor included African Americans. Furthermore, by the 1936 election the president had come to identify the South as "the nation's number one economic problem."[101] After the election, members of the Roosevelt administration continued to extend their New Deal initiative in the South, but they soon began to encounter mounting opposition from the region's lawmakers who had eagerly embraced earlier federal initiatives that had benefited white landowners. These same Southern legislators bitterly resented the later New Deal policies aimed at America's poor. That growing resentment would fester over the next three decades until it formed the basis for a major shift in white southern political party affiliation.

However, their elected officials' reservations notwithstanding, poor Southerners, both black and white, embraced the Roosevelt administration with open arms.

In this atmosphere of federal sympathy, the NAACP was poised to strike. Under the guidance of Charles Hamilton Houston, NAACP lawyers began to mount a relentless campaign against discrimination in education and voting. Houston adamantly insisted that NAACP-sponsored litigation must be accompanied by community organizing designed to cultivate mass support and educate local African Americans about their rights. As he put it, "The social and public factors must be developed at least along with and if possible before the actual litigation commences."[102] In cooperation with that NAACP initiative, Arthur Shores, the only black practicing attorney in Alabama at that time, filed suit on behalf of eight black school teachers in Bessemer who had been prevented from registering to vote. Shores was successful, and the Bessemer board was forced to issue registration certificates to the eight black plaintiffs.[103] This marked the beginning of the long struggle to break down discriminatory barriers blocking black voter registration in Alabama.

Even though these initial skirmishes had begun elsewhere in their state, the leisurely rhythm of life for Wilcox County's residents seemed to continue uninterrupted. Yet, just beneath the surface was a growing anxiety: Residents knew that the emergency of the Great Depression had ushered in fundamental changes in their relationship with the federal government, and those changes would forever alter their lives.

CHAPTER FOUR

~

Making the World Safe
for Democracy?
What about Wilcox County?

As the difficult decade of the 1930s drew to a close, the profound social consequences of the New Deal's focus on southern poverty became abundantly, and for
many white Southerners, painfully, clear. One of those consequences that some
white Southerners would find particularly distasteful was the birth of a group
calling itself the Southern Conference for Human Welfare (SCHW). The organization grew out of a *Report on the Economic Conditions of the South* that was
written by President Franklin Roosevelt's advisors. The report was intended to
be a campaign document supporting the president's advocacy of continued federal aid to the South because it was "the nation's number one economic problem."[1] This campaign document quickly galvanized the forces for change in the
South, and accordingly, with the president and the first lady's blessing, a number
of southern liberals began planning a convention that was designed to address
the issues raised in the *Report on the Economic Conditions of the South*. The president was quick to indicate that one of the most important issues the group should
address was the issue of black disfranchisement in the South.

The convention met in Birmingham, Alabama, during the Thanksgiving
weekend in 1938. There were approximately twelve hundred in attendance,
including people from a wide variety of backgrounds and occupations: "business executives, labor organizers, WPA workers, state and federal government officials, members of Congress, sharecroppers, newspaper editors, college professors, and students." Because 20 percent of the delegates were
black, the conferees would soon be forced to face the issue of racial segregation.[2] This thorny issue was not originally on the delegates' agenda, but by

the second day of the conference, Eugene "Bull" Connor, Birmingham's soon-to-be notorious commissioner of public safety, informed the gathering that the municipal auditorium where they were meeting was subject to an ordinance requiring segregated seating. Because they were anxious to continue their meeting, the group reluctantly acquiesced, and African American delegates moved to one side of the auditorium, while white delegates sat on the other.

Birmingham city officials considered the matter closed until First Lady Eleanor Roosevelt arrived for a late afternoon session, and promptly seated herself among the black delegates. A Birmingham police officer immediately informed her that she would have to move to the white side. Mrs. Roosevelt refused to defy the policeman's order outright, but she also refused to comply. Instead, she took a chair and carefully placed it atop the line in the middle of the auditorium separating the black and white sides. Many in the group could scarcely contain their glee as they watched Birmingham policemen shake their heads in frustration. Officers felt that they could not arrest the first lady even though she was not exactly complying with their city's segregation ordinance; but she was not exactly defying it either. One delegate remarked about Mrs. Roosevelt's standoff with the police: "That was a glorious moment."[3] After spirited discussion and debate, delegates passed a resolution stipulating that they would never again hold a meeting in a segregated facility.[4] With that behind them, conferees went on to adopt a number of proposals that addressed the South's economic woes, and they also endorsed anti-lynching legislation and equal salaries for black and white teachers. They also decided to continue as a permanent organization, and thus, the Southern Conference for Human Welfare was born.

Conference participants were convinced that their interracial cooperation was a harbinger of things to come. One conferee described the gathering as "one of the most exaggerated expressions of change in the South . . . here was a revival, a bush-shaking, something that just jumped up."[5] Another insisted, "[It was] a wonderful sort of love feast because it was the first time that all of these various elements from the South had gotten together. And we were not segregated."[6] Still another was optimistic about possibilities for change, but his optimism was tinged with a note of caution. He agreed that the formation of the SCHW clearly indicated that the South was "on the move," but, he continued, "The hind wheel may be off and the axle dragging, but the old cart is hovering along."[7] The birth of the SCHW occurred against the backdrop of other dramatic and hopeful changes. One of those was the establishment of the Congress of Industrial Organizations (CIO) in the fall of 1935. The CIO brought thousands of semiskilled workers into the organized labor movement who had previously been excluded by the craft-oriented American Federation of Labor (AFL). These workers "represented a newer, more fluid, and ethnically diverse segment of the laboring class."[8] Furthermore, the CIO's first southern organizing drive, which occurred in 1937 and 1938, exposed serious cracks in the "Solid South" and dramatized the "police repression, violence, and political disfranchisement that pervaded southern society."[9]

In the midst of these first efforts aimed at interracial cooperation, the National Association for the Advancement of Colored People (NAACP) began to rack up an impressive string of courtroom victories that were clearly striking at the very heart of the "legal" justifications for the de jure segregation governing southern society. The organization's most impressive victories would not come until the 1940s and the 1950s. However, one of the first of these successful legal challenges came as early as 1938 in the Supreme Court decision in *Missouri ex rel Gaines v. Canada*. In that case the NAACP represented Lloyd Gaines, a black Missouri resident, who was refused admittance to the University of Missouri's law school. The high court ruled in Gaines's favor, clearly signaling a shift in the position of some segments of the federal judiciary. At the same time, in this case and in subsequent cases, part of the legal strategy employed by NAACP attorneys mandated the use of local black lawyers whenever possible to assist in trying the case. That strategy, which was the brainchild of premier civil rights attorney Charles Hamilton Houston, had a powerful psychological impact on the black community. Local African Americans were often awed by the sight of one of their own in court boldly facing down white judges and other public officials who had oppressed them for years. Indeed, many reveled in these interactions, and "scenes were reenacted in pool halls, and barbershops."[10] Houston had no doubt that such local involvement would stoke the fires of resistance in black communities across the South.[11]

Against this background of impending social change, as war clouds began to gather on the horizon in Europe, many white Southerners began to feel the first stirrings of an ill-defined uneasiness. Yet down in Wilcox County white residents appeared to be either unaware, or unwilling to acknowledge the currents of change that were swirling all around them. Instead, local planters continued to revel in their myths of the Old South. Like the mules they had used to plow their fields before they had tractors, white Wilcox residents seemed to be wearing blinders. Many black residents, on the other hand, began to feel the first stirrings of a very cautious optimism. Things came to a head when the Japanese bombed Pearl Harbor on December 7, 1941. In the months before the Japanese attack, some 2,716 Wilcox County men of both races had been registered for the draft.[12] As the country prepared to enter the war, the airwaves were bombarded with slogans intended to fuel the fires of patriotism by explaining that this was a war that would make the world safe for democracy. The irony of that pronouncement was not lost on African Americans in Wilcox County, and this wartime atmosphere only served to heighten black expectations for change.

In such an atmosphere, black residents were acutely aware of the sacrifices they were being asked to make. Black Wilcox resident Gwendolyn Bonham vividly recalls the fear she lived with every day because two of her brothers were serving in the military. One was in the Pacific, and the other was in the European theater. She also remembers the long lines at the office near the courthouse where they got their ration coupons.[13] African American resident Ruth Bonner Collins particularly remembers that the oleomargarine they got during the war was an unappetizing white lump that came with a little package of yellow food coloring.[14] Black Wilcox native S. C. Collier, who was destined to become the county's first black male school superintendent, recalls the serious difficulties his mother faced when she tried to get the ration coupons she needed for shoes for her six children. It was winter. Collier's mother, Essie Mae Kimbro, was determined to get the shoes her children needed, so she went to the nearby town of Pine Hill, the closest location where ration coupons were available. Kimbro positioned herself at the end of the long line, and over the next few hours she waited patiently as the line inched forward. Then, just as she was about to reach the office window, the clerk dispensing the coupons informed those in line in a loud, tired voice that the office was closing and they would have to come back the next day.

Essie Mae Kimbro blinked in anger and frustration, but she swallowed her disappointment, and came back the next day to stand in line. Again, just as she reached the office, it closed for the day. After the same thing happened to Kimbro the following day, her growing frustration finally bubbled over. Consequently, the next day when a cold and tired Essie Mae Kimbro assumed her place at the back of the line once again, she vowed under her breath that she would get her ration coupons this time. Once again, just as Kimbro's turn came, the clerk made his familiar announcement while he was reaching out to close the door. In response, an angry Kimbro yelled, "NO," and placed herself right in the doorway. In a voice shaking with frustration and fatigue, Kimbro told the clerk, "I'm going in this door. My children need shoes, and this is the time I'm coming in here." Without a word, the hapless clerk ushered the determined black woman into the office and issued her ration coupons.[15] Of course, white residents also made sacrifices, but white Wilcox resident Viola Goode Liddell recalled that the sacrifices were not too difficult, and "we never went hungry." She further insisted that "If our food-ration stamps gave out, there were always large Negro families who could spare us some."[16]

Despite their common sacrifices, many of Wilcox County's white residents still expected their black neighbors to observe the same racial etiquette that had governed their county's race relations since before the Civil War. Viola Liddell came face-to-face with the expectations of her white neighbors in a very dramatic way during the war years. It all started when Liddell boarded a bus bound for nearby Selma. Ironically, the only reason she was forced to ride a bus to Selma that day was because of wartime gas shortages. As soon as she boarded the bus, Viola Liddell, a white woman who rarely traveled by bus, was struck by the absurdity of segregation's rules. She immediately noticed that the back of the bus was crowded with black riders while there was an abundance of vacant seats in the white section up front. Liddell gingerly took a seat, and once she was settled, she looked up and noticed in dismay that a young and very pregnant black woman was hanging onto the luggage rack up above her head. Every time the bus rounded a curve or lurched over a bump, the expectant mother's heavy body swayed precariously as she fought to keep her balance. Liddell could not stand to watch the woman's discomfort, and she explained, "Being alone on a double seat, I leaned over and told her I'd be glad to have her sit down beside me." The woman gratefully accepted. Viola Liddell had not counted on the vehemence with which many of her white neighbors were prepared to defend segregation's rules, but she quickly became aware when the bus driver, who had heard her comment to the young black woman, expressed his opinion in no uncertain terms. A sur-prised Liddell described the exchange that followed: "You'll have to move," he said to the black passenger. Liddell protested, "But it's all right with me." The driver was adamant: "Maybe it is [all right] with you, lady, but I drive this bus and the rule is, she ain't to sit there."[17]

As Viola Liddell reflected on the inflexibility of Wilcox County's racial etiquette, she was struck by a disturbing awareness of the impact of this at-mosphere on African American attitudes. She concluded, "The blacks . . . largely marked time in their deprived state until the 1930s. Then their dis-content became a flickering flame of anger, which grew slowly at first but soon began to spread like a prairie fire." That black anger was terrible in its intensity with unimaginable consequences. In Liddell's estimation, "It was destined to endure longer than most of us would live, and it would require more active attention than well-meaning people and old-line politicians could imagine."[18] While Viola Liddell was at least willing to try to under-stand the impact of segregation on black Wilcox County residents, many of her white neighbors were far less sympathetic. They were convinced that black people were innately inferior, and a segregated society was the only way to manage them. As the manager of the Wilcox Hotel put it in 1941, "in other words, a nigra is a nigra. You can try to fix 'em up and make . . . something out of them and try and treat 'em decently. [But] you don't do anything but make a mean nigger out of 'em that somebody eventually will have to kill."[19]

In the midst of such white intransigence, black county residents reported that racial violence continued unabated during the war years. Black Wilcox resident Paul Washington remembers one racial incident involving an African American resident who made moonshine. The man, William Martin, and his wife were driving home one Saturday evening when Martin anxiously looked up in his rearview mirror and saw the flashing lights of a police car. His hands clutched the steering wheel tightly, and his palms became slick with sweat as he carefully slowed the car to a stop. A nameless, formless fear overtook him as he remembered that there was one little quart jar of moonshine in the trunk of his car. With sickening certainty, Martin knew that even that small amount of illegal whiskey in his trunk was enough to get him in big trouble. All of his neighbors knew that he sold homemade whiskey, but frustrated white policemen had been trying for months to catch him in the act, and they had failed—until tonight. After Martin's car stopped, he and his wife sat in tense silence as they heard the door of the police car open. Before they could react, a big, burly white officer seemed to materialize right next to their car. The outlines of the officer's body seemed fuzzy, almost indistinct in the gathering dusk, but the hard edges of the shiny badge pinned to his chest glittered menacingly.

Almost unconsciously, Martin began to raise his hands in a gesture of supplication. But, before he could get them all the way up, the policeman jerked open the car door and dragged William Martin out of his car. Martin quickly insisted, "I'm not resisting." "Shut up," the officer retorted as he roughly dragged Martin back to the patrol car. The officer growled, "Nigger, we['re] gonna take you to jail, and we['re] gonna kill you tonight." As Martin was pushed into the waiting police car, he briefly savored the irony of his predicament: They had been trying for months to catch him with something incriminating, and they had finally stopped him when he had moonshine in his trunk, but they had not even bothered to search his car. Martin's wife had sat rigidly staring straight ahead throughout the whole ordeal. But the receding brake lights of the patrol car holding her husband prisoner finally broke her trance. She knew that there was only one way to save her husband's life. She quickly slid under the steering wheel, put the car in gear, and took off down the little dirt road toward Camden with a thick cloud of dust billowing out behind her. Once she reached the Camden city limits, Mrs. Martin barely slowed her speed as she drove straight to Mathis Hardware Store where her husband worked. She knew that her husband's only hope lay in the intervention of a powerful white man.

She pounded on the door screaming, crying, and beseeching the owner to do something. When the store's owner was finally able to make some sense of what Martin's hysterical wife was saying, he took a minute to calm her down and reassure her that he would take care of everything. He sent the woman home with a comforting pat on her shoulder. When she got back to her car, William Martin's wife felt somewhat better, and she slowly backed her car from in front of the store and turned it around for the drive back to the Martin home. As she drove through Camden's quiet streets, Mrs. Martin's breathing finally began to slow, and her heart stopped hammering against the walls of her chest. But in order to get home, Martin's wife had to pass right by the city jail. As she drew near to the jail, she saw a large crowd. With a sinking feeling, Martin's wife slowed down, and because her windows were open, snatches of conversation from the crowd drifted into the car. The words hit her like lead weights, and she wished that she had rolled the windows up before those awful words had ever reached her ears. But it was too late. Some were bragging about it: they had already killed her husband.[20]

For the most part, however, despite the occasional violent interlude, life during the war years continued at the same leisurely pace that had characterized life in Wilcox County for generations. Black Wilcox native Ruth Bonner Collins was only a child at that time, and she vividly remembers walking to school with her older brother. Young Ruth's family lived all the way on the other side of town from Camden Academy, and she has vivid memories of pumping her little, short legs as fast as they would go as she tried to keep up with her brother's longer stride. Despite the outwardly calm atmosphere in her county, young Ruth realized that her color made her vulnerable. As she puts it, "You had a place, and you stayed in your place because you heard the horror stories." On those occasions when she had to walk by herself, Collins remembers, "I always ran through town . . . it was an instilled fear." Young Ruth's fear stayed with her for some time. She explains, "I ran until I was ten years old."[21] Once Ruth and her schoolmates arrived at Camden Academy during these years of uncertainty, their teachers were careful to provide a nurturing and challenging environment that made the war in Europe and the Pacific recede into the background of their lives. Collins was particularly fond of the Negro history courses, but she is quick to explain that all the courses she took at Camden Academy were demanding, rigorous, and engaging. In fact, she learned so much from these courses that she insists, "college courses, many of them, were easy because of what we had in the tenth, eleventh, and twelfth grade."[22]

In addition to their rich academic experience, Ruth Bonner Collins and her classmates were also treated to a variety of extracurricular activities, sports contests, and the relaxation of recess. Everyday when the bell rang for recess, the younger children could barely contain their enthusiasm as they waited for the teacher to dismiss the class so they could go outside and play. Once they were on the playground, the children jumped and ran, glad to have a break from classroom discipline. Often, a group would form a ring around one of their classmates who had been designated as "it." The war overseas seemed a million miles away as the group chanted,

> Little Sally Walker,
> Sittin' in a saucer,
> Cryin' and weepin' over all she's got.
> Rise Sally rise,
> Wipe your weepin' eyes.

Some of the children were seized by a fit of giggles as they placed their hands on their hips and swayed in time to the rhyme they were chanting. They continued,

> You're gonna shake it to the east,
> You're gonna shake it to the west,
> You're gonna shake it to the one that you like the best.

As the rhyme ended, the child in the center who had been "it" darted toward the circle of classmates and tagged one of them. The newly designated "it" reluctantly walked to the center of the circle, and the chanting began again.[23]

Camden Academy student Mabel Walker Thornton also remembers her playground activities during the war years. She particularly recalls how disappointed many Camden students were because schools around them had begun to schedule regular May Day celebrations, but their school did not sponsor one. In a rural area like Wilcox County this rite of spring was an important milestone in the rhythm of life. During the early 1940s, motivated by their disappointment, a number of Camden Academy students began convincing their parents to write letters to Mr. Peoples, Camden Academy's principal, requesting permission for their children to miss school so that they could attend the nearby celebration in Pine Apple. As increasing numbers of students began to attend the neighboring celebration every year, Camden Academy's young gym teacher, Nora Smith, watched in dismay. Finally, during the last months of the war, Smith decided that Camden students should have their own celebration. With the principal's blessing, the enthusiastic gym teacher set about planning their very first May Day celebration.[24]

Because track and field events were usually part of most May Day celebrations, Nora Smith decided that this was the perfect opportunity to organize a girls' track team. For some time, Smith had restlessly watched while the school's male students had the chance to compete in organized team sports, but it seemed that nobody realized the value of female athletic competition. However, Nora Smith was undaunted by the apparent lack of support for organized women's athletics, and she quickly called a meeting of interested girls from various grades after school. Thornton remembers that they all met on the playground that day, and she and her excited schoolmates gathered around their young gym teacher waiting for instructions. Smith asked each of the girls what sports she played as she tried to assess each girl's athletic talents. Finally, she asked the question, "Who can run?" A number of girls in the group timidly raised their hands. Mabel Walker looked around at her schoolmates who had raised their hands. They were all quite a bit bigger than she was, but she could not resist raising her hand too.[25]

Nora Smith ushered the track hopefuls out onto the football field. The group radiated excitement as their teacher instructed them to walk to the other end of the football field, wait until she gave the signal, and then run back as fast as they could. As the girls rushed off in the opposite direction, Smith turned and limped to the other end of the field: she had been born with one leg that was slightly shorter then the other, but despite her disability, or maybe even because of it, Nora Smith loved athletic competition, and she was thrilled about the prospect of coaching a girls' track team. "All right, is everyone in position?" she yelled to the girls at the other end of the field. She hesitated for just the briefest second, and then she screamed, "GO." Camden Academy's girl track hopefuls took off in a tangle of arms and legs pumping and pushing as each girl tried to beat the others to the far end of the field. Except for the young athletes' heavy breathing, and the sound of their feet striking the ground as they ran, Camden Academy's football field was deadly quiet that day.

From her vantage point at the far end of the field, Smith noticed that within a few strides of the start of the race, a short, dark girl had begun to pull away from the others. With every stride, she lengthened her lead over the rest of the runners. An amazed Nora Smith stood at the other end of the field intently watching this remarkable display of athletic ability that quickly made her think of the possibility of athletic competition far beyond the sleepy little town of Camden and the rural environment of Wilcox County. The small, fast girl in the lead was Mabel Walker. Her lean, strong legs propelled her faster and faster, and the wind whizzed past her ears as she neared the end of the football field. Young Mabel was not even aware of the growing distance separating her from the girls running behind her. Instead, if she really concentrated, she could almost hear her grandfather urging, "Run big baby, run; run big baby, run." Both Ruth Collins and Mabel Thornton remember that when they were younger, Mabel's grandfather used to have his afternoon coffee every day at 4:00 P.M. sharp. Usually Mabel and Ruth were out in the fields playing around that time, and they would come in and fix the old man's coffee. Then, he would take a seat on the porch, and the girls would go out in the yard and race. The old man would watch in delight as his small, fast granddaughter pumped her legs faster and faster; her body almost appeared to get lower to the ground as she picked up speed. Young Mabel's playmate Ruth was always so far behind that the old man liked to give her encouragement, and so he would yell to Ruth, "run big baby, run." His granddaughter Mabel never needed that kind of encouragement.[26]

But that day on Camden Academy's football field, an excited Nora Smith exclaimed in delight as little Mabel Walker stopped short in front of her, far ahead of the rest of the girls in her wake. After the other girls reached her, Coach Smith began organizing her girls' track team. Thus, in the spring of 1945 as the war was winding down in Europe, Camden Academy was gearing up to host its first May Day celebration, and thanks to the determined efforts of Nora Smith, women's track and field events were a prominent part of the festivities. In order to get ready for their first competition, the girls trained every morning on the football field before school started. In fact, members of Camden Academy's girls' track team were already out on the field jogging every morning even before the cooks who prepared breakfast for the boarding students reported to work. Nora Smith's runners were so excited that they trained with a vengeance. Yet, despite their enthusiasm and commitment, their inexperience did create problems. In fact, Thornton recalls, "We did everything wrong." She remembers that they trained in tennis shoes because they did not even know what track shoes were. They ran clockwise when they should have run counterclockwise.[27] When the day of the competition finally arrived, the girls were beside themselves with anxiety. Many of Wilcox County's black communities sent teams including Pine Apple, Snow Hill, and Miller's Ferry, but the day belonged to Nora Smith's new team.

Energized by her squad's convincing success, a confident Nora Smith traveled to nearby Tuskegee University to ask the coach for an invitation for her girls to compete in an upcoming meet. Tuskegee's coach, Major Cleve Albert, ushered the young, inexperienced coach with a limp into his office. After they were both seated, Coach Smith explained the purpose of her visit. As Tuskegee's coach listened to Nora Smith's request, he could not help but notice the deadly serious expression on her face, and his own facial expression registered mild shock initially, but that soon turned to amusement. By the mid 1940s, Coach Albert's school, along with Tennessee State University in Nashville, had produced some of the finest female track stars in the nation. Yet, this woman from some little high school in the Black Belt had the audacity to think that her squad could successfully compete with his. Who does she think she is, Coach Albert wondered. Regardless of how ridiculous he thought the request was, Tuskegee's coach simply could not refuse because of the intensity of Smith's expression as her eyes bored into his. As Nora Smith left Coach Albert's office, she tried to hide a small, self-satisfied smile that threatened to split her face into a wide grin. She was thrilled that her girls would get the opportunity to show off their athletic talent at a big track meet, but at the same time she realized that Tuskegee's coach did not take her or her squad seriously. "We'll just see about that," Nora Smith promised herself as she drove back to Camden.

Whoops and screams of delight greeted the news that they had been invited to compete at Tuskegee when Coach Smith told her team about her meeting with Coach Albert. As Nora Smith looked at the circle of eager young faces surrounding her, she explained as gently as she could that the odds were stacked against them: they would be like David confronting Goliath. Yet, Smith and her runners were undaunted. They trained harder than they ever had before, pushing their young bodies to the limits of physical endurance and beyond. Finally, the day arrived that they had been simultaneously dreading and anticipating. The morning of the track meet, members of Camden Academy's girls' track team all donned uniforms representing their school's colors: black trimmed in orange. The girls were all fiercely proud of their uniforms, even if they were not actually proper track uniforms. In fact, they were actually the uniforms for the girls' basketball team. When the Camden Academy squad arrived out on the track in Tuskegee, they were greeted by the sight of a well-conditioned, powerful group of female athletes sporting gold and maroon track uniforms and the finest track shoes available. Members of the Tuskegee team could scarcely believe their eyes: they were being challenged by this group of younger girls in basketball uniforms and tennis shoes. But Nora Smith refused to show how nervous she was. Instead, in a quiet, steady voice, she offered her runners a few brief words of encouragement, and then the meet began. Her runners' performance exceeded even their coach's wildest expectations that day. In many events, the Camden runners captured first, second, third, and fourth place. The Tuskegee runners were baffled. Some exclaimed, "Camden, where is that? New Jersey?"[28]

Nora Smith and her squad were jubilant, and Mabel Walker Thornton remembers hearing her coach say, "I'm going to send somebody to the Olympics." After their convincing win over one of the finest teams in the country, nobody doubted their coach's prediction.[29] Before the Camden team left his campus, Tuskegee's coach expressed his desire to explore the possibility of having some members of their team compete with his squad. Coach Albert was particularly interested in the small, brown-skinned girl with the blinding speed: Mabel Walker. But all this would come later. In the meantime, the spring semester came to an end, and all over Wilcox County students proudly participated in closing exercises. Ruth Bonner Collins remembers that her Camden Academy class put on a production of Little Red Riding Hood. The night of the production, county residents were awed by the magnificent sight of a meteor shower. Nature's fireworks that spring would soon pale in comparison to manmade fireworks later that summer: in August, American planes dropped the first two atomic bombs the world had ever seen on the Japanese cities of Hiroshima and Nagasaki. With this final and convincing display of American military might, World War II officially came to an end.

Although many did not realize it at the time, the end of the war marked the beginning of remarkable changes that would forever alter the pattern of life in Wilcox County along with the rest of the segregated South. At the forefront of those changes were black veterans of World War II. These men had risked their lives in this war that was supposed to make the world safe for democracy. Many returned to this country, determined to become full participants in democracy at home. One black veteran, Private Herbert Seward, expressed the determination shared by so many others:

> Our people are not coming back with the idea of just taking up where they left off. We are going to have the things rightfully due us or else, which is a very large order, but we have proven beyond all things that we are people and not just the servants of the white man.[30]

Monroe Pettway, Gee's Bend resident, World War II veteran, and a man destined to play a pivotal role in civil rights campaigns in his county, also came back from the war in Europe determined to become a full participant in the political process in his homeland. He explains, "I put up my life for this country." As far as he was concerned, that fact alone gave him the right to vote irrespective of poll taxes and literacy tests.[31]

In this atmosphere of heightened black expectations, the same groups that had been active before the war, particularly the SCHW and the NAACP, resumed their activities just as the war ended. In fact, just one year before the war ended, on April 3, 1944, the NAACP won a crucial victory in a Supreme Court case, *Smith v. Allwright*. This decision, which outlawed the all-white democratic primary in Texas, affirmed the right of African Americans to the protection of the Fifteenth Amendment to the Constitution, which "sheltered their right to vote from racial discrimination."[32] In the wake of this landmark decision, many southern white lawmakers vowed to block any attempts made by the Roosevelt administration to implement the *Smith v. Allwright* decision. Indeed, when Alabama's senator, John Sparkman, discovered that federal officials were planning to punish white election officials in his state who were clearly violating this decision by blocking black participation in Democratic primaries, he warned the president that this would "be a very dangerous mistake."[33] The president was troubled by this intransigence, but he reluctantly concluded that he was obliged to heed the warnings of southern white politicians who were part of an increasingly unstable Democratic coalition. The cold reality was that with the majority of black Southerners still disfranchised, Roosevelt and the Democratic Party were dependent on southern white support. Consequently, members of Roosevelt's Justice Department displayed increasing timidity and reluctance when they were called upon to punish southern white election officials who violated the dictates of the Smith case.[34]

Despite Washington's refusal to provide vigorous support for the Supreme Court's decision in *Smith v. Allwright*, the black community was still hopeful and energized. In fact, in the wake of this decision, pressure to organize black registration drives increased exponentially. One such drive occurred in Birmingham in January 1946, and it was led by black World War II veterans. Some one hundred men wearing their uniforms and carrying their discharge papers marched to the courthouse in Birmingham, and demanded the right to vote. It was a sight unlike any other that had ever been seen in that city's history. Flustered white election officials quickly turned the men away. Undoubtedly, those who witnessed this remarkable event that day recognized that this was only the beginning, and these men would be back. In fact, shortly after they left the courthouse, the African American veterans filed an appeal in Circuit Court.[35]

In Wilcox County, just a few miles to the south, the embers of discontent were smoldering, but they would not ignite and become an open flame of protest until later. Meanwhile, however, the smoldering black discontent in the county did lead some to organize a Wilcox County chapter of the

NAACP. Nancie Thomas, the wife of the *Mobile Beacon's* editor, clearly re-calls that her husband accompanied those who went to Wilcox County to or-ganize the chapter. Among the local African Americans involved in that organizing effort was T. P. Marsh, the same T. P. Marsh who had confronted Sheriff Lummie Jenkins when the Camden Academy band played on the town square in front of the courthouse almost twenty years earlier. Those few brave souls who were involved in this organizing effort knew to keep their participation a secret. They were convinced that if the white power structure got wind of their activities, the consequences facing them and their families could be deadly. Prairie resident Hattie Irene Steele observes, "They stuck their neck out a long way."[36]

The organization of a Wilcox County branch of the NAACP was part of a broad organizing effort in the postwar years that was spearheaded by the SCHW and endorsed by the NAACP.[37] Membership in the SCHW's affili-ates and the NAACP's new chapters was drawn primarily from the ranks of the middle class, indicating the prominent role that many from this class would play in the voting rights struggles of the coming decades. The primary goal of these early organizing efforts continued to be the extension of the elective franchise to black Southerners. One black Georgia veteran elo-quently observed, "the most difficult job ahead of us is to win the peace at home. 'Peace is not the absence of war, but the presence of justice.'"[38]

The latter part of the 1940s witnessed a flurry of activity on the civil rights front. One of the most visible of those activities was the establishment by Harry Truman of the President's Committee on Civil Rights. Truman had been prompted to form the committee by a series of brutal attacks on black veterans returning to the South. After learning of one particularly vicious attack on a black serviceman named Isaac Woodward, who was passing through South Carolina on his way home, the president exclaimed, "My God! I had no idea that it was as terrible as that!"[39] A short time later, President Truman formed the committee and charged its members with the responsibility of reporting on the racial situation in this country. The committee's report, *To Secure These Rights*, was issued in October of 1947, and it made many white Southerners, in-cluding those in Wilcox County, distinctly uncomfortable. The report insisted, "The national government should assume leadership in our American civil rights program because there is much in the field of civil rights that it is squarely responsible for in its own direct dealings with millions of persons." The report further insisted that the states must share responsibility with the federal government. In short, "In certain areas the states must do far more than parallel federal action. Either for constitutional or administrative reasons, *they must remain the primary protectors of civil rights*" [emphasis added].[40]

In the meantime, the NAACP was attempting to keep the pressure on Washington politicians by petitioning the United Nations to review black grievances against American racial policies.[41] Then, in early 1948, black activist A. Philip Randolph threatened to recommend that young black men "resist a [Selective Service] law, the inevitable consequences of which would be to expose them to un-American brutality so familiar during the last war."[42] Randolph informed President Truman that unless he issued an executive order outlawing discrimination in America's armed services, he would carry out his threat to dissuade young black men from registering for the draft.[43] Truman capitulated by issuing an executive order desegregating America's military in 1948. In the late summer of that year, President Truman's sympathy for civil rights issues would set the stage for an acrimonious Democratic convention.

As the convention approached, increasing numbers of white southern Democrats vowed to oppose Truman's nomination. One particularly acerbic critic of the Truman administration's record on civil rights was Camden's own Miller Bonner. Bonner had been born in Wilcox County in 1878, and his father was a planter and a major in the Confederate Army during the Civil War. After he finished the University of Alabama's law school in 1900, Bonner established his law practice in Camden, and he was quickly elected chairman of the Wilcox County Democratic Executive Committee. He was later elected to the Alabama State Senate, where he served for many years. Miller Bonner was a rabid segregationist, and when he became a candidate for delegate-at-large to the 1948 Democratic Convention, he unequivocally stated his intention: "I will never vote for the nomination of Truman for president." Bonner was convinced that Truman did not deserve the nomination because he "has recommended to congress a 'civil rights' program which proves him to be the arch enemy of the white man of the South."[44]

Despite Bonner's best efforts, and those of other southern Democrats, Harry S. Truman did receive his party's nomination for president in 1948. Many southern Democrats were so incensed that they walked out of the convention. Miller Bonner "bears the distinction of having led the walkout."[45] The southern renegades formed their own party, the States' Rights Party, popularly known as the Dixiecrats, and they quickly nominated Strom Thurmond of South Carolina for president. Over a million angry white Southerners deserted the Democratic Party in 1948 to vote for the Dixiecrat candidates. In Wilcox County all but 14 of the 1,176 white registered voters who cast their ballots in the 1948 election voted against the national Democratic ticket, and for the States' Rights Party candidates. The year after the election Miller Bonner expressed the frustration that many of his friends and neighbors felt, and he vowed that regardless of official Washington policy, "The South belongs to the white man. He's going to govern it, and he's going to enforce its code of segregation. *It doesn't matter what happens—anywhere, ever*" [emphasis added].[46] Clearly, by the late 1940s, white Wilcox residents were on a collision course with a federal government that was becoming increasingly sympathetic to black demands for change.

As black Wilcox residents observed these signs of federal sympathy, some became cautiously optimistic. In the meantime, they witnessed an event that many thought was utterly miraculous. The year 1948 was not only a presidential election year, but it was also the year when the first Olympic games of the post–World War II period were scheduled to be held in England. Many people all over the world were anxious to put their war experiences behind them. They were haunted by the piercing sound of sirens signaling bombing raids that seemed to hang in the air long after the bombers were grounded; they were horrified by the tragic image of the shriveled limbs and hollow eyes of concentration camp survivors; and they were depressed by the sad rubble of once magnificent buildings in Europe and Asia. People all over the world were hungry for a happy occasion, and so they embraced the 1948 games with gusto. Although the 1948 Olympic Games were light-years away from Camden and Wilcox County, for the first time in the area's history, one of their own would represent the United States of America in the world's most prestigious athletic competition.

Wilcox County's Olympian would come from none other than the black Presbyterian school on the hill: Camden Academy. Indeed, after Nora Smith's runners had done so well in their first track meet at Tuskegee, the team and their coach had returned to their campus fired with enthusiasm and determination. Everyone was so excited that Coach Smith did not have to push her girls to train hard. On the contrary, the runners eagerly embraced the blistering training regime that Smith devised. Although everyone worked hard, one member of the squad continued to stand out: Mabel Walker. Walker was the short, fast runner who had so impressed Coach Smith that day on the school's football field when the first tryouts were held for the school's new girls' track team. Coach Smith's tutelage combined with Walker's natural talent to mold her into a world-class athlete, and by 1946, Tuskegee's coach, Major Cleve Albert, recognized and appreciated the Camden star's potential. Consequently, he eagerly invited Mabel and her cousin Juanita Walker, who had also demonstrated amazing speed, to run with the Tuskegee women's squad. Always the mother hen, Nora Smith was not about to let her girls go to Tuskegee alone: She made it clear to Albert that she would be accompanying her athletes, and both Mabel and Juanita welcomed their coach's familiar nurturing presence.

When the trio arrived in Tuskegee in the summer of 1946, Coach Albert's track team was already hard at work preparing for the national Amateur Athletic Union (AAU) track meet scheduled for later that summer. Albert quickly and unceremoniously assigned the Camden runners to the same blistering training regime as his Tuskegee AAU hopefuls. He also made sure that the newcomers were issued maroon and gold Tuskegee track uniforms, and their very own track shoes. Thornton recalls that her new shoes were quite uncomfortable because Major Albert insisted that all his runners wear shoes that were one size too small so that they would not be the least bit loose on any of the runners' feet.

The whole summer seemed like a dream to the Camden Academy athletes. They had been told that they were being groomed for the AAU meet, but it seemed much too good to be true. Of course, right by their side every step of the way was their dedicated coach, Nora Smith. Mabel Walker Thornton fondly recalls that Coach Smith was always there to nurture them, encourage them, and make sure they had everything they needed, even when she had to use her own money to provide for them. At the AAU track meet that summer, Mabel and Juanita racked up a string of impressive victories, and their winning streak continued through subsequent track meets. Finally, in the spring of 1948, after competing with the Tuskegee squad for almost two years, the girls found themselves in Providence, Rhode Island, competing in the Olympic trials. She was just a little black girl from rural Alabama, Mabel thought, and it simply did not seem possible that she was here competing in the Olympic trials. But it was true, and Thornton clearly remembers that her nervousness threatened to overwhelm her. After she arrived in Rhode Island, the young runner was dismayed to realize that her main strength, the fifty-yard dash, was not offered in the Olympics, and she would be forced to compete in the one hundred-yard dash instead. This last-minute switch shook Mabel's already fragile confidence. Then, just before the competition, Mabel's anxiety was ratcheted up another notch when Camden Academy principal A. C. Peoples came to watch his athletes' final workouts. As he watched approvingly, Peoples offered words of encouragement and guidance to each of the girls. But then, he paused for a brief moment, fixed the anxious Mabel with a stern stare, and declared in a gruff voice, "Walker, you can win if you want to."[47]

Mabel was stunned. She had never heard the kindly principal speak so harshly. Initially, the young runner's feelings were hurt, but then the hurt turned to angry determination. Meanwhile, Peoples took a seat in the stands. Safely out of sight of his athletes, the stern mask on his face slipped away, and A. C. Peoples beamed with pride. The principal was surrounded in the stands by friends and family from Camden who were there to wish the girls well. Of course, standing in front of the group was the girls' track coach, Nora Smith. Smith was much too excited to sit down with the others, and she alternately paced, screamed encouragement, and jumped up and down.

The day of the competition dawned bright and clear. Mabel and Juanita were up early, but by the time they reached the athletic field, members of their Camden cheering section were already seated. Much of the day is a blur to Mabel Walker Thornton, but she does remember looking up in the stands as she prepared to start her first race, and seeing friends and relatives from Camden. The sight of all those hopeful black faces banished young Mabel's anxiety and gave her strength.[48] She slowly shook out her compact, powerful legs, took a deep breath, and prepared to run. With the shot of the starter's gun echoing in her ears, Mabel Walker's strong brown legs propelled her forward faster and faster, her calf muscles bulged, her thigh muscles were strained to the breaking point, and she could not even feel the too-short track shoe pinching the blister on her left toe. As her young body gathered speed, the faces of the onlookers in the stands began to blur until they finally disappeared altogether. The only thing the young runner was conscious of was the sound of the wind rushing by her ears and the tightness in her chest as her lungs strained to take in more and more air. Then, suddenly, the cyclone fence at the end of Mabel's lane rushed up to meet her, and snapped her back to full consciousness of her surroundings. Two more times Mabel Walker repeated her performance, and at the end of her third heat, the young runner from Camden, Alabama, realized with a start that her times were fast enough to earn her a spot on the 1948 Olympic women's track team representing the United States of America.

The scene down on the track confronting the stunned Mabel Walker seemed almost surreal. All around her, Mabel's Camden supporters had rushed out of the stands to hug her and hug each other. As they jumped up and down, the soft Alabama accent of these black Wilcox residents was transformed into shrill screams of excitement. Slowly, the reality of her achievement began to sink into the young runner's consciousness, and her face split into a wide grin. She spotted her principal and her coach among all the well-wishers, and the emotion of this remarkable day threatened to overwhelm her as her eyes misted over for just a brief instant. But, as Mabel Walker basked in the congratulations of her hometown supporters, she was shocked when she looked behind her to see that some of the other competitors who had not qualified for the team were standing on the track sobbing. Walker was shocked at their reaction because these girls were white. The fact of their race was very important to Mabel, because even though she was now an Olympic athlete, Mabel Walker was still first and foremost a black girl from Camden, Alabama, whose race had always had a powerful impact on her existence. Thornton remembers the significance of the scene:

> And I noticed these white girls, and I said, "crying, because of something I did?" Cause, you know, we were basically taught that they were better, and we were just inferior, PERIOD. And they are crying for something I have done?[49]

The scene that young Mabel witnessed was a turning point in her life: she realized that white people were not all-powerful after all. That realization convinced her that "I can do anything I want to do if I set my mind to it."[50]

Mabel Walker did not have long to savor her new-found empowerment, however, because she soon found herself involved in frantic preparations for the upcoming trip to England for the Olympics. When she told her grandmother that she had earned a spot on the U.S. women's track team, but she would have to travel to England to compete, Walker's grandmother expressed concern. She questioned her granddaughter: "You're going to go over there over all that water?" Mabel answered simply, "Yes, mama." When the old woman saw the eager excitement in her granddaughter's face, she smiled, and nodded her assent. During much of her boat trip to England Mabel Walker felt like she was living in a dream: her bed was turned down every night at 6:00 P.M., and a fruit basket was left outside her door. As she looked around at her luxurious surroundings the young athlete thought, "I could get used to this."[51]

Despite the special treatment she received on the trip, Mabel Walker was soon forced to confront the harsh reality of inequality. This time the inequality was not based on race, but rather on gender. Walker was dismayed to discover that the U.S. women's track team was virtually impoverished while their male counterparts traveled with a huge entourage that included their own doctors, cooks, and trainers. The men's team often shared some of their resources with the women, but Walker was still very sensitive to the unequal treatment. After the athletes arrived in England, most found that the conditions under which they had to compete were not up to American standards. In particular, the tracks where the runners were scheduled to compete were not as well maintained as American tracks, and they were often quite muddy, a condition that put American runners at a distinct disadvantage. Such unfavorable conditions combined with a number of factors to spell disaster for the U.S. women's track team in the 1948 Olympics. Not surprisingly, Walker and her teammates were terribly disappointed, but the young runner from Camden still savored the return trip on the luxurious ocean liner. The experience of traveling abroad to represent her country in the 1948 Olympic

Games broadened Mabel's outlook. She would never be the same again, and after arriving back in Tuskegee, Mabel Walker contemplated the challenge of stepping back into the life she had led previously as a black girl living in the Alabama Black Belt. She had not been in Tuskegee long when Mr. Peoples, her principal, offered to drive up and bring Mabel and her cousin Juanita home. Although Walker was grateful for the offer of a ride, she was a little worried, because she had always thought Peoples drove too fast. It seemed that she and Juanita had barely settled themselves in Mr. Peoples's Oldsmobile before the principal turned the big car around and accelerated rapidly toward Camden and Wilcox County. As the big, heavy car gathered speed on the unpaved county roads leading deep into the Black Belt, a huge cloud of dust billowed out behind it. Lost in thought, Walker gazed out the window, but she soon realized that the Oldsmobile was gaining speed. Cars, trees, barns, and fences flew by. Peoples held on tight to the steering wheel as they bounced over the ruts and ridges in the road while the car's suspension efficiently absorbed the worst of the bumps, leaving its passengers unjostled.

Without realizing it, Walker had gripped the armrest so hard that her hand hurt. She was flooded with anxiety because her principal was driving so fast, but she was also nervous about seeing her family and friends for the first time since her Olympic experience. Finally, when they reached the outskirts of Camden, Mr. Peoples began braking sharply to slow the big car down. While Mabel was relieved that the car was no longer traveling at breakneck speeds over the county's unpaved roads, her relief soon turned to impatience as Peoples continued to apply the brakes until he had slowed the car to a crawl. Just then, they came within sight of a store. Without a word, the principal steered the big car onto the shoulder of the road, and they finally came to a stop right in front of the store. He quickly got out and closed the door with a resounding thump. As the principal walked toward the store, Mabel and Juanita looked at each other with impatience and confusion.

Finally, just when it seemed that their impatience would cause them to explode, the girls spotted an amazing sight coming their way. It was a beautifully decorated float. Mabel could not believe her eyes and she thought, "I must be dreaming." No sooner had this thought entered her mind than the float stopped right in front of the Oldsmobile. Returning Olympian Mabel Walker felt like Cinderella getting into her coach as she climbed high atop the elaborate float for the triumphant ride into town. All along the parade route white Wilcox residents came out of stores and offices to watch their returning Olympian ride by. They clapped enthusiastically. Camden Academy had excused students from class for the day, and the school's students and teachers lined the route leading up to the campus. They were joined by scores of other well-wishers, including parents, family members, and friends. Their cheers followed the float onto the campus, and rang in the young Olympian's ears as she pinched herself to make sure she was not dreaming. Standing right there to welcome her home was Mabel's coach, Nora Smith. Coach Smith had tears in her eyes when she embraced her young athlete.[52]

That summer of 1948 black and white Wilcox residents could easily agree on the pride they felt in their returning Olympian, but they could agree on little else. Instead, in the wake of the acrimonious Democratic National Convention that summer, and the election of President Harry S. Truman that fall, black Wilcox residents were cautiously optimistic while white residents were furious. Indeed, as the critical decade of the 1940s drew to a close, white Wilcox residents stubbornly and publicly continued to cling to their old ways, and their old ideas. When *New York Times* reporter Cabell Phillips visited Camden in 1949, he was amazed at the tenacity of the old beliefs of the white residents he encountered. One of those he interviewed succinctly insisted, "whether you like it or not . . . you have to start from the premise that the Lord made the world for the white man to enjoy and the nigger to work." He concluded, "That philosophy is basic to our way of life here."[53] Still another advised, "We've got a good bunch of niggers here. . . . Long as they don't go mixing it up with labor unions and outside agitators, or try to vote in our elections."[54] According to another, the county's black residents were practically indispensable as a cheap labor force. All the while white residents insisted that they really did appreciate their black neighbors. However, the kind of appreciation they expressed left black Wilcox residents barely able to contain their fury. The words of one white resident made that conclusion inescapable. He insisted, "I'd sooner have a sorry nigger on my place any day than a sorry white man."[55]

Despite this stubborn white commitment to a way of life based on black subordination, Phillips was convinced that change was inevitable. In part, Phillips's conclusion was based on his realization that black county residents were clearly unhappy with the status quo. One black resident who was a deacon in his church confirmed this dissatisfaction when he told Phillips that in the face of local white intransigence, "Cullud [sic] folks don't want to stay here any longer than they can help. . . . They [sic] ain't no way for them to get ahead or help themselves." The deacon went on to explain that local African Americans were determined to break their county's cycle of black subordination, "But they [black Wilcox residents] can send their children to school so's maybe *they* can get away. And that's what we're doin', nearly every one of us."[56] In Phillips's estimation, this black resistance to the status quo was accompanied by a barely perceptible but nonetheless real white insecurity about the wisdom of clinging to the old ways in the midst of the sweeping changes all around them. As the reporter put it, "Most important of all, a slow ferment of discontent, a virus of doubt and introspection is spreading ever so gradually through some of the 'best families' themselves." Phillips concluded prophetically, "Doubt is the shadow of truth. . . . It is also the seed of change."[57]

Clearly, the closing years of the 1940s witnessed the beginning of many unsettling changes. However, the 1950s would mark the beginning of the most effective challenge to the Black Belt's racial status quo since the era of Reconstruction following the Civil War. In 1952 the Republicans captured the White House for the first time since Franklin Roosevelt's election to the presidency twenty years earlier in 1932. Although the new president, Dwight D. Eisenhower, was initially reluctant to use the power of the federal government to address the problem of racism, he eventually came to believe that some limited federal action was necessary. In fact, by the end of Eisenhower's first term in 1956, his attorney general, Herbert Brownell, drafted a civil rights proposal that was aimed at addressing the problems of black disfranchisement and public school segregation. After Eisenhower's reelection to a second term in the fall of that year, he became determined to introduce Brownell's civil rights bill to Congress—but only if the section that was aimed at facilitating school desegregation was omitted. It was.[58] The result was the passage of the Civil Rights Act of 1957. This law, the first national civil rights legislation enacted since Reconstruction, created a separate civil rights division in the Justice Department, and an independent civil rights commission.[59] Yet, because of the way the new law was written, it was only minimally effective: registration of southern black voters increased only slightly in the first few years after the bill's passage. Indeed, as late as 1960, some 70 percent of southern African Americans were still unable to register to vote. Despite its shortcomings, however, the new law pushed the fact of southern black disfranchisement squarely onto the center stage of the nation's consciousness.[60]

In the meantime, despite the changes all around them, many white Wilcox County residents continued to demand absolute deference from their black neighbors as they desperately tried to cling to a way of life that was clearly doomed. Morton Rubin, a young researcher from the University of North Carolina at Chapel Hill, began to spend a great deal of time in Wilcox County at this time, and he quickly detected that white desperation. Rubin wanted to study conditions in the southern Black Belt, and he decided to make Wilcox County a case study. When he examined the county's race relations, the young scholar found that the desperation he observed was born of a profound white insecurity. He explained,

The whites . . . have gone through a succession of crises that have rocked their world. There was the military and economic defeat during the Civil War, a hated Yankee occupation . . . cycles of prosperity and poverty with the cotton market, the boll weevil, and recently the economic depression of the thirties. Civil Rights legislation and the general pressure of worldwide public opinion for democratic equality of opportunity reach the white man daily through his radio, newspapers, and magazines.[61]

Rubin found that the white residents he questioned were particularly concerned about black behavior. They longed for the return of the old-fashioned "good Negro" from their past. A "good Negro" was defined as one who "behaves strictly in accordance with the race-caste code when dealing with white people. He 'gets along'"; he "isn't looking for trouble"; and "he is humble above all." Rubin went on to explain that the "good Negro" "waits until a white person is disengaged before approaching for conversation," and he says "sir or ma'am at all times, punctuating his conversation frequently with these titles of courtesy." Finally, Rubin concluded, "he [the good Negro] will go out of his way to do favors for white people, even if it inconveniences him."[62]

Despite white longing for the mythical "good Negro" of the past, however, it seemed that a new Negro had come to Wilcox County. Morton Rubin clearly recognized the change in black behavior. As he put it, "A new type of Negro is emerging in the plantation area who is at the same time a product of the mass culture. This kind of Negro appears 'uppity' to white people, for he appears to seek status beyond that which the local whites are willing to grant."[63] One characteristic of the "new Negro" behavior that particularly irritated white Wilcox residents was the increase in black automobile ownership. White Wilcox resident Viola Liddell observed, "For Southern whites, first seeing blacks driving their own cars . . . surprised some whites, shocked some, and irritated others. In the Deep South, driving cars . . . had long been reserved for whites." According to Liddell, white residents "swore that Negroes were hogging the road and driving like crazy." She concluded, "maybe some were. Having this new power at their fingertips—this new right to make whites wait for them, to obey their signals, and to give them half the road—had to be heady stuff for some blacks."[64]

Black Camden native Horace Young vividly recalls the white reaction he unwittingly caused when he drove through Camden one day. On this particular day in 1952 he was driving his 1949 Ford sedan through the town's business district. He was quite proud of his car; he had bought it right after he returned home from the service. Just as he reached the center of town, Young slowed the big car down, and then he braked sharply, coming to a complete stop when he realized that the car in front of him was completely stationary even though its engine was still running. When Young craned his neck to see why the car in front of him was not moving, he noticed that the white woman who was driving it had stopped to talk to a pedestrian. Horace Young waited patiently, but he soon realized that the white woman in front of him was deeply engrossed in her conversation. Without a second thought, Young steered his Ford around the woman's car and proceeded to the stop sign directly in front of him. After bringing his car to a complete stop, Young proceeded on through the intersection and went on his way. He did not notice the white woman driver peering intently at him when he drove around her. In fact, the woman had abruptly stopped talking when she looked up just in time to see that there was a "Negro" driving the car that had just pulled around her. She became positively apoplectic. How dare this Negro pull around her car, she raged. She was white; she was in front of him, and that is the way that things were supposed to stay. She vowed that he would pay for this. The pedestrian who had been chatting pleasantly with the white woman driver just moments before watched in sympathetic silence as her friend quickly got out of the car, went into a nearby business, and called the highway patrol. Fortunately for Young, neither of the women got his license number, and by the time the Alabama State Troopers arrived on the scene, he was long gone.[65]

Young's experience is completely consistent with the observations of eminent black sociologist Charles S. Johnson. According to Johnson, "the automobile is a technological innovation which has disturbed many of the traditional patterns of association, caused some modification of the established mores, and presented new problems of interracial etiquette."[66] Johnson explained that when African Americans were employed by white residents as chauffeurs, "they were identified with the whites and accorded the rights of the road."[67] The real trouble started, however, when black people began driving their own cars: "they were expected to maintain their [subordinate] role as Negroes and in all cases to give whites the right-of-way. Obviously, this made for much uncertainty and confusion."[68] Johnson further insisted that the behavior of white women drivers was especially problematic. In fact, the observations offered by one of the African Americans Johnson interviewed during the course of his research are especially telling: "These white women act like they think these brakes is colored too and just naturally stop dead still when they sees a white woman busting into a [sic] open highway without stopping. They look up and sees you colored and keep going like it's a disgrace to stop at a stop sign to let a nigger pass."[69]

The county's roads were not the only places where postwar challenges to local racial etiquette occurred, and other African American Wilcox residents have vivid memories of these challenges. For example, black Camden native Matthew Wilmer, who was a teenager during the 1950s, recalls that many of his peers began to test the limits of the county's racial etiquette. One of the places where Wilmer observed such behavior on numerous occasions was in the balcony of Camden's movie theater. Of course, the theater was segregated, and African Americans were forced to sit in the balcony. Motivated by their frustration at this unfair treatment, some black patrons began to express their anger by throwing popcorn and various other food items on the heads of white theatergoers sitting on the main floor. Members of the white audience howled in protest as they peered up into the darkened balcony in a vain effort to identify the perpetrators. Wilmer remembers that amid a chorus of white complaints, the theater's manager rushed up the stairs to demand that the black patrons behave themselves. On more than one occasion, the black reaction to his demand hit the theater manager like a cold slap in the face. Wilmer explains, "it got to the point, up to a certain degree, where people almost ignored him. The kids were beginning to . . . become a little bit more aware [of civil rights activities around them], and they weren't afraid as much."[70]

Matthew Wilmer also remembers that by this time he began devising his own methods for sidestepping Wilcox County's restrictive deference patterns. "I always felt, that I was going to handle myself with respect too, and if I carried myself a certain way, they might see this, and they just might stay away from me a little bit more."[71] Wilmer's older sister, Gertrude, remembers how she questioned the continuation of the county's restrictive atmosphere during the 1950s. Gertrude Wilmer graduated from high school in the spring of 1955, and as she was thinking about what to do next, she happened to see a Help Wanted sign in the window of Camden's telephone company. Secure in the skills she had learned during her Camden Academy experience, young Gertrude was sorely tempted to go into the telephone company and apply. She explains, "I wanted to go in so bad and ask if I could get hired." Gertrude Wilmer was confident she could do the job, but she recalls sadly, "Something kept saying, 'no, don't do that, cause you're going to get embarrassed,' so I didn't go in." Later, Gertrude learned, the telephone company filled the position with a young white woman. Also, some of the offices in the courthouse hired young white female workers that summer. Gertrude Wilmer was furious. She explains, "It made you feel like they didn't care." Her fury ignited her determination to "get what [I] can, and get out." She did.[72]

Camden native Geraldine Pettway White remembers that local white reaction to even a perceived change in deference patterns during this era was swift and sure. White unwittingly became the focus of such a reaction when she went to the bank in Camden one day to cash her paycheck. The year was 1957, and White was a young teacher at Camden Academy. At the time, she had recently gotten married, but her husband did not live in Camden. Instead, he was working out of state in Knoxville, Tennessee. During this period, the young husband regularly sent his bride money, and because of that, White lived in reasonably comfortable economic circumstances. Those circumstances set the stage for a revealing encounter at the bank one day. White explains,

> I recall going into one of the banks, and . . . the lady [teller] said to me, "Why is it that you can wait so long and come in and cash your check? You're not like the other girls," and I said to her, "What is it to you when I cash my check?" And so one thing led to another. . . . I finally said to her, "Don't just cash this check, give me all my money."

At this point, the flustered teller left her window and went in the back to get the bank president. White remembers that the president swaggered out. He was a big, heavyset man with a scowl on his face, and a blackjack on his hip. He fixed the young teacher with a stern stare and demanded to know what the problem was. White refused to be intimidated, and she replied, "Oh nothing's the matter. I'm just getting what's mine." After staring at her a few more seconds, the president directed the teller to comply. Geraldine White took her money, and walked down the street to the next corner where there was a competing bank. She quickly opened a new account there. Word spread rapidly in the black community about the young teacher's defiance. By the time White had finished transacting her business in her new bank, her father had arrived there, concerned about his daughter's welfare.[73]

Geraldine White also remembers that by the end of the decade the accelerating pace of civil rights activities all around them promoted continued growth in local white insecurity. This, in turn, produced an increasingly tense atmosphere in the town of Camden. In such an atmosphere, White recalls, Camden Academy faculty warned students to be especially careful. She explains, "They would tell the students don't wear shorts to town, and don't do different things because it seemed like they were picking on them more then." She insists that the male students seemed to be the preferred targets of white harassment. At one point, the harassment even came to the Camden Academy campus. She explains, "We started getting buildings being burned on campus, and things like that."[74]

While many of the county's African American residents were clearly aware of and affected by the winds of change that began to blow in the 1950s, others were so mired down in poverty that the desperate economic circum-stances of their lives left them little time to think about much else. One of those black county residents was Bessye Ramsey Neal. Neal was one of ten children, and her mother, who was a single parent, worked very hard to pro-vide for her family by doing domestic work for local white residents. Even though her family received some public assistance, Neal remembers that she was often hungry. At the same time, Neal was painfully aware of the disre-spect that her mother suffered at the hands of her white employers. By the late 1950s when Bessye entered the seventh grade at Camden Academy, her mother was working for a white family that lived right down the hill from the school. One day, when she was on her way home, young Bessye happened to see the white woman for whom her mother worked come out of the house with a plate full of food. A puzzled Bessye paused to watch as the woman walked into the chicken coop, and left the plate on the ground. The little girl's eyes filled with tears as she stood there looking at the plate of food her mother had cooked surrounded by chickens and chicken excrement. As Bessye stood there transfixed by the sight in front of her, the image of the chickens pecking at the plate disappeared, and it was replaced in her mind by the sad faces of her hungry brothers and sisters at home. "How could she?" a voice in the little girl's head demanded to know. She recalls, "I was so up-set; I begged my mother to quit that day."[75] Her mother refused. Even though it broke her heart to see her child in such pain, the elder Ramsey simply could not afford to quit.

Larry Nettles, another black Wilcox native, who was just four years younger than Neal, recalls that the late 1950s were a difficult time for his family too. Nettles, one of nine children, was also being raised by a single parent mother. When he was a very young child, he recalls how hard his fam-ily's poverty forced him to work:

> Our day started at daybreak . . . especially at cotton picking time, we would get up at daybreak, 5:00. [We would] pick cotton for a couple of hours and come back, clean up, and go to school. And after school [we would] come home and go [back out] in the fields, and then we would stop a little bit so we could get our lessons.[76]

Larry was only five years old when he started doing field work. He was too little to carry his own sack, so he walked along behind his mother, putting the cotton he picked in her sack. In the evenings when he returned home, young Larry often reflected on how hard he had to work in the fields, and he knew he did not want to spend the rest of his life picking cotton. Although

Larry's mother knew that her children were dissatisfied with their lives, she had no time for sympathy or sentimentality. Instead, she would fix each of them with her stern gaze and advise, "Education is the way out." This message resonated with young Larry, and consequently he worked very hard in school. His farm chores and his schoolwork left Larry Nettles little time to think about the beginnings of the black freedom struggle that were all around him. Ironically, in later years, Nettles was destined to become the only black student to successfully integrate all-white Wilcox County High School.

Throughout the 1950s the attempts of black Wilcox residents to cope with the problems of grinding poverty, racial restrictions, and growing white insecurity were played out against the broad backdrop of dramatic national events that were destined to have a crucial and lasting impact on black lives all over the country. One of those events, the U.S. Supreme Court's decision in *Brown v. the Board of Education*, unleashed a storm of protest all over the South, particularly in the Black Belt. The high court's majority opinion in that decision declared that segregating students on the basis of race was unconstitutional. Viola Liddell, long-time white resident of Wilcox County, succinctly explained the depth of the emotion unleashed by the Supreme Court's pronouncement:

> Wherever white people got together, one could be fairly certain that the talk was about this shocking ruling and how it could be evaded, avoided, or nullified. The very idea of white children going to school with black children, playing together, growing up together, dancing together, and inevitably marrying each other! *Never, never, never!* [emphasis added][77]

Southern white lawmakers were just as disturbed as their constituents, and reaction in the United States Congress was swift and sure. On March 12, 1956, southern white lawmakers banded together to issue a document they titled "A Declaration of Constitutional Principles: The Southern Manifesto." Both of Alabama's senators signed the manifesto, which unashamedly advocated resistance in no uncertain terms: "We commend the motives of those States which have declared the intention to resist forced integration by any lawful means." The document goes on to make it clear that its supporters were not content just to advocate resistance; they forcefully declared their intention to practice what they preached. As they put it, "We pledge ourselves to use all lawful means to bring about a reversal of this decision which is contrary to the Constitution and to prevent the use of force in its implementation."[78]

Of course, white residents who were worried about the new decision were able to derive at least a small measure of comfort from knowing that it would probably be a long time before this decision which had been made in far away Washington, D.C., would have any impact on conditions in their community. African Americans also realized that implementation of the decision was years away. At the same time, however, most were painfully aware that the very existence of such a decision, whether it were enforced or not, inflamed the passions of their white neighbors, prompting some black residents to lament, "Lord help us all."[79] As black and white Wilcox residents waited to see who would make the first move in this post-*Brown* atmosphere, their state capital, Montgomery, became one of the first battlegrounds of the modern civil rights movement when black citizens there began a bus boycott. Montgomery was only seventy-eight miles from Camden, and the boycott soon began receiving a great deal of national attention and sympathy. The last thing white Wilcox residents wanted was to have racial practices in their state's capital become the focus of national attention: that was just too close for comfort.

It was against this background that many of the county's white residents boldly and publicly began to organize for resistance. They were not alone. In fact, even before the historic *Brown* decision, rabid segregationists in the Deep South had been poised to act. In November of 1953 as word spread of the school cases that the Supreme Court had agreed to hear in early 1954, white supremacists all over the South began meeting to discuss their options. At one of those meetings Robert Patterson of Leflore County, Mississippi, urged those in attendance to "stand together forever firm against communism and mongrelization."[80] Just months later, when the Supreme Court confirmed segregationists' worst fears with their decision in the *Brown* case, chapters of a new organization, the White Citizens' Council, began to spring up all over the Mississippi Delta. Members of this new organization were steadfastly committed to combating the implementation of *Brown*. In a short time, the Citizens' Council movement spread like wildfire in all of the southern states facing court-ordered desegregation. During its heyday the movement was not only wildly popular with white Southerners, but enormously powerful as well. Historian Numan Bartley notes,

> At their height the Citizens' Councils and associated groups had perhaps 250,000 members, although a considerably larger number of white southerners probably enrolled at one time or another. But organized segregationists exercised an influence far more pervading than membership roles implied. . . . Effective leadership and organization exploited the movement's position on the popular side of the racial controversy, often allowing Council spokesmen to usurp the voice of the white community.[81]

Citizens' Council chapters quickly sprang up all over Alabama, and even though the council movement received a warm welcome from white citizens all over the state, its most enthusiastic reception came from white residents in the Black Belt. Numan Bartley explains, "the basic thrust of organized resistance and its most solid foundation of support came from whites of the black-belt South."[82] Obviously, because they were so badly outnumbered by their black neighbors, they had the most to lose. It was against this background that segregation proponents in Wilcox quickly organized a Citizens' Council chapter. As far as local white county residents were concerned, their Citizens' Council chapter was an important part of their community. In light of this widespread white acceptance, it is not surprising that the organization's annual election of officers was held at the Camden School athletic field, right in the middle of town. At that meeting, Fred Henderson, a resident of Miller's Ferry, was unanimously reelected president. Ironically, Henderson was a direct descendant of William Henderson, the Union Army officer who settled at Miller's Ferry right after the Civil War and established a black Presbyterian school on his plantation.[83]

Notwithstanding their Yankee ancestors, it seems that some twentieth-century members of the Henderson clan were staunch segregationists. Indeed, that same summer of 1956, Fred Henderson's brother, J. Bruce Henderson, fired off a letter to all of the state's delegates to the upcoming Democratic National Convention urging them to "vote segregation with every vote." Henderson, a former state senator and gubernatorial candidate, argued that "our politically created Supreme Court is wrong and could and should be repudiated before the American people and the world." He went on to advise the delegates that their position on the issue of segregation should "conform to both the desire of the people and to the policies of the White Citizens Council" [emphasis added]. "Finally," he concluded, "let us always remember that to win, we must believe segregation, practice segregation and vote segregation. It is our duty under the law, under the constitution, under the court, and under God who set the pattern."[84]

The fervor with which J. Bruce Henderson advocated the continuation of segregation at all costs was clearly in concert with white sentiment all over the state. In fact, the depth of that white sentiment was clearly illustrated by a bill introduced in the state legislature in 1957. During the legislative session in 1957 with the Brown decision already a fact of life and President Eisenhower's Civil Rights Bill looming on the horizon, Macon County's state senator Sam Englehardt introduced legislation that was designed to abolish his county. The senator was convinced that if increasing numbers of African American Alabamans were allowed to register to vote, the inevitable result would be catastrophic in those counties with large black populations. As he put it, "in those counties where the Negroes outnumber the whites there will be but two alternatives—face an almost certain integrated courthouse and legislature, or abolish the counties."[85] Clearly, Englehardt believed that having no counties at all was preferable to having counties under black control. Englehardt's neighbors to the south in Wilcox County listened to his reasoning with great interest, and had actually invited him to speak at one of their Citizens' Council meetings just before he introduced his bill.[86]

It is against this background of white intransigence that James Foster Reese, a black Presbyterian minister, attempted to register to vote in Wilcox County in 1958. At that time, Reese was the pastor of three Presbyterian churches in the county, Canton Bend, Camden Academy, and Miller's Ferry; and he had lived in the county for over a decade. Reese, a native of Kentucky, had first come to Wilcox County in the summer of 1947. He was a seminary student then, and his school had assigned him to do fieldwork in Wilcox for six weeks. Within a few minutes of his arrival, Reese was treated to a rude awakening. He was standing in front of a store in the town's business district, and he was both excited and anxious at the same time, wondering what the next six weeks would bring. In particular, the dapper young student noticed the slow pace of the pedestrians and the intense heat of the sun as he stood looking out over the sleepy little town. Suddenly, the calm of the quiet afternoon was shattered when a white proprietor rushed out of his store just a few doors from where Reese was standing. The store owner ran out into the middle of the street and bellowed to nobody in particular, "Alright, I want three or four of you big nigger bucks to come here and move this lady's car." As the man's words hung in the hot, humid air, Reese was shocked by such a crude intrusion into the quiet afternoon, and he noticed for the first time that there was a stalled car sitting in front of the man's shop. The young ministerial student stood there trying to make sense of the scene, and a mighty shiver traveled down his spine, accompanying his dawning realization that the shopkeeper's demand was aimed at all of the black men within shouting distance, including him. Over the next six weeks as Reese worked with local black Presbyterians, he was haunted by the memory of the red-faced shopkeeper demanding the help of "nigger bucks."[87]

The next summer, Reese was again sent to Wilcox County to do fieldwork. Finally, after his graduation from the seminary, Reese was assigned to pastor the three black Presbyterian churches in the county where he had been doing field work for the past two summers. Accordingly, the Reese family moved to Camden in September of 1949. Because the churches he was pastoring were all affiliated with schools, Reese had a great deal of contact with students. The rude introduction to oppression he had received during his initial visit to Wilcox County in the summer of 1947 remained fixed in his consciousness, and the new pastor spent a lot of his time counseling and encouraging black youngsters. He hoped that his guidance would help these young people to see that they were much more than "nigger bucks." Many students noticed and appreciated the young pastor's efforts. One former student explains that the dapper young minister was a wonderful role model. He concludes that Reverend Reese showed him "the way" to succeed.[88] As Reverend Reese continued to work with his parishioners through the decade of the 1950s, he became increasingly convinced that somebody was going to have to stand up for change in the county, and he also knew it would not be easy, and it might very well be dangerous. Finally, as the end of the decade approached, James Foster Reese made a fateful decision: he would be the one to stand up for change. Reese's decision was fraught with uncertainty. He explains, "I didn't know what anybody would try to do." Yet, despite the potential for violence, he insists, "I didn't have any fear about it at all." He just knew that whatever the consequences, he simply could not wait any longer. He explains, "I was thirty-four years old and I just felt that was long enough to hang around without registering [to vote]."[89]

After deciding to register, Reverend Reese inquired about the registration process, and he was informed that at least two registrars had to be present before he could be registered. The determined pastor spent the next eighteen months dropping into various offices in the courthouse trying to locate two members of the Wilcox County Board of Registrars. It was a frustrating and fruitless search. Every time he climbed the courthouse steps and walked between the structure's massive white columns, the dapper but determined minister could feel the hostile stares of countless pairs of eyes as they watched him continue his seemingly never-ending search for the county's registrars. The answer the minister received was always the same. In clipped, impatient tones bordering on hostility, one white county official after another insisted that they did not know the registrars' whereabouts. Finally, a fellow minister told Reese where and when the Board of Registrars convened each month. At last, the young minister thought, he would finally get his chance.

On the appointed day, Reese arrived at the courthouse bright and early. Without hesitation, he marched past the customary hostile stares of white onlookers. But this time he did not look left or right as he made his way to a large room in the back of the building. Reese confidently marched right up to the two registrars on duty and said, "I'd like to get an application for voting." The startled women exchanged a quick glance, and one replied, "I don't know what you're talking about." He had come too far to turn back now, so

Reverend James Foster Reese continued to stand in front of the registrars. For a few brief moments, nobody moved, and nobody uttered a word. Finally, one of the women broke the impasse. In a slow, deliberate voice laced with a southern Alabama drawl and tinged with barely concealed anger, the woman advised, "You'll have to talk to the Judge of Probate." Careful to keep his frustration in check, the dapper minister thanked the woman for the information, and then calmly and deliberately made his way to the probate judge's office. He paused at the door for just a brief instant, and then he carefully turned the knob. As soon as Reese walked in, a secretary sitting right inside the door demanded to know, "Can I help you?" Once again, Reese patiently repeated his request for a voter registration application. At that precise moment, the probate judge walked into the office just in time to hear the black minister's request. Acting as if the minister was not even there, the judge asked his secretary, "What did he say?" The secretary replied, "He wants an application for voting." Without ever acknowledging the minister's presence the judge declared, "Well I don't have any." With that, the judge turned on his heel, went into his inner office, and closed the door. Through this whole exchange, Reese had stood motionless in front of the secretary's desk watching in amazement, with his brow knitted in concentration. Finally, without uttering another word, Reese turned and left the office, closing the door softly behind him. The secretary, who had returned to her duties as soon as the judge had closed the door to his inner office, did not even acknowledge the minister's departure.[90]

As he left the courthouse that day, Reverend Reese's mind was racing. He was sure that the last eighteen months would have tried the patience of Job, but he still could not let it go. As he walked along, a small smile of satisfaction suddenly replaced his look of consternation: Reverend Reese had just devised another plan. All this time, he had tried to register alone, and they had stalled him and ignored him. But if a whole group went, he reasoned, it would be impossible to ignore all of them. Over the next few days, the young, determined minister began asking around for volunteers to accompany him to the courthouse. To his dismay, however, not a single black Wilcox resident who he approached expressed any interest at all. While Reese was terribly disappointed, he was not surprised because so many of the people he had approached were public school teachers who were afraid for their jobs.

By this time it was late November of 1958, and while Reese was trying to decide what to do next, the Civil Rights Commission began holding hearings right up the road in Montgomery. The commission had decided to take testimony in Montgomery because of the large number of complaints they had received from African Americans in the area when they tried to register to vote after the passage of the Civil Rights Act of 1957. The first Sunday in December Reese was teaching a Sunday school class when one of his church members breathlessly rushed into the room. Everyone, including Reese, looked at the intruder quizzically while he explained in a voice that actually squeaked with excitement that a member of the U.S. Civil Rights Commission was on the phone asking to speak to Reverend Reese. All thoughts of the Sunday school lesson were banished momentarily from his consciousness as the excited pastor rushed into the church office to take the call. Reese listened to the voice on the other end of the line informing him that the commissioners were aware that he had been attempting to register to vote in Wilcox County. Would Reese be willing to testify before the committee, the official-sounding voice asked. The stunned minister mumbled his assent, and then the caller apologetically explained that Reese would have to drive to Montgomery that afternoon. The commissioner on the other end of the phone explained that Reese would have to come to them because they could not come to Camden. He went on to say that the commission had recently visited the courthouse to investigate the voting situation, and local officials were so hostile to them that they felt threatened. He concluded, "I'll be damned if we [are] coming back to Wilcox County anymore."[91]

Reese drove to Montgomery that afternoon to meet with members of the U.S. Civil Rights Commission. After discussing the difficulties he had faced while trying to register to vote in the last eighteen months, the commissioners asked Reese if he would be willing to give sworn testimony. He eagerly agreed. Commissioners then asked if the young minister could return very early the next morning to testify before the hearings were open to the public. They explained that because opposition to black voting was so deeply ingrained in Wilcox County, they were afraid for Reese's safety. They explained, "We cannot give you any protection." Therefore, they concluded, "It would [not] be good for you to testify in public."[92] Meanwhile, back in Camden, Reese's family was busily packing up all their household goods in preparation for a move to Knoxville, Tennessee. The Reese family had known for weeks that the Presbyterian board had transferred Reverend Reese to Knoxville. When Reese returned to Camden from Montgomery later that day, he stopped by the courthouse to transact some business before returning to his house. As soon as he entered the front door, he sensed something sinister in the atmosphere. He was used to hostile stares after eighteen months of attempting to register to vote, but this trip to the courthouse was different. The hostility on the faces of the onlookers was mixed with something else this time: Their glances had a menacing quality that was more than a little unsettling, and in that instant Reese was sure that these people knew that he had been talking to members of the U.S. Civil Rights Commission. For the first time during his long voter registration ordeal, James Foster Reese began to feel unsafe. As he thought about his predicament, Reese became convinced that he should get out of town immediately. He quickly made his way to a pay phone, called his wife, and asked her if she could move the family to Selma, where he would meet them after testifying in Montgomery. As Mrs. Reese listened to her husband, she heard an edge to his voice that she found very unnerving. She was afraid for him, and she was afraid for her whole family, but she knew she must conquer her fear. She took a deep breath, trying to compose herself, and then, in a carefully controlled voice she asked her husband to come home so that they could all move together. Reese complied. They packed all their belongings as quickly as they could, and after discussing the dangers they faced, the Reeses decided to leave the state together as quickly as possible. Reverend Reese never testified.[93]

Clearly, at the end of the 1950s, the forces favoring black subordination continued to control Wilcox County. But, even in that repressive atmosphere, there were a few white citizens who thought their county should make at least some tentative efforts to prepare for a new era in race relations. One of those was the owner of a grocery store in the Camden business district. In the late 1950s, the owner of this store, the Yellow Front Store, decided that the time was right to hire his first black employees. Clifford Crowder was one of the two black youngsters hired by the Yellow Front management to bag groceries. Crowder recalls that the presence of black employees made black customers feel more comfortable. Crowder also remembers that both he and the other black employee were treated well, and the tips were good. The whole experience left young Clifford Crowder feeling that perhaps his county could resolve its racial dilemma after all. Likewise, there were other black youngsters Crowder's age who began to notice just the slightest thaw in racial attitudes by the late 1950s, but black Wilcox native Gertrude Wilmer is convinced that this apparent softening of white attitudes was motivated largely by self-interest. She explains that at that time, many black youngsters were intent on leaving the county just as soon as they graduated from high school, and in response some white county residents began to try to "be nice" to black residents. She continues, "People like that made you know that some of them were concerned about some of us leaving." However, there were limits to this white concern. Wilmer concludes, "They might turn against you if they knew you were leaving [anyway]."[94]

Thus, as the 1950s drew to a close, Wilcox County, along with the rest of the South, was poised on the brink of a steep precipice that edged the region's great racial divide. For generations, black and white Southerners had existed on opposite sides of that divide, but the 1950s witnessed a number of serious breaches of this racial divide that most had thought was impregnable. Still, many residents in the Black Belt in general, and in Wilcox County in particular, refused to believe that any of these changes would ever reach their area. Long-time Wilcox resident Viola Liddell remembers the refrain that was repeated so often by many of her white neighbors: "It just can't happen here." Yet, as the pace of change accelerated all around them, there was an enforced bravado in the chorus of voices repeating the familiar mantra, indicating a worrisome insecurity. At the same time, the mantra was joined by a warning: "Never let the Negro get his toe in the door, for if he does, he'll take over."[95] As the country faced a new decade and an uncertain future, few white residents were willing to admit, even to themselves, that their now familiar warning was probably already too late.

CHAPTER FIVE

~

Vote

After Reverend James Reese's aborted attempt to register to vote in the late 1950s, there were others. For example, Camden Academy teacher Geraldine Pettway White remembers that she made several unsuccessful trips to the courthouse in the late 1950s. She also recalls that there were a few other members of the Camden Academy faculty who did likewise. None was successful.[1] Tydie D. Pettway remembers that her father, Eddie Pettway, also made trips to the courthouse to register on more than one occasion in the late fifties and early sixties. She accompanied him on those trips, and she remembers that her father was also turned away.[2] Finally, in the early years of the 1960s, many realized that individual attempts to register were doomed to failure, and with increasing frequency, little knots of black residents began to gather after church or at each others' houses to plot strategy. These people were Wilcox natives, and they were fully aware of the commitment of their white neighbors to continued black disfranchisement. At the same time, however, most felt that they had reached a turning point. It was time for a change, and they had to be the agents of that change. Many of the most vocal black citizens in those early strategy sessions were landowners, many were veterans, and all of them had long chafed under the unfairness of a system that demanded that they serve their country, but would not allow them the right to register to vote.

One of those particularly disturbed by his county's refusal to let him vote was Reverend Lonnie Brown. Brown, a landowner, an insurance salesman, and a Korean War veteran, was born in Alberta in the northern part of

Wilcox County in 1931. As a boy, Brown was only dimly aware of segregation's rules because his all-black community effectively sheltered him. But, finally, when he was thirteen years old, Lonnie Brown had an unforgettable introduction to the meaning of racial segregation. That was the year when his father made the fateful decision to send him to a school in nearby Linden, Alabama, for his seventh-grade year. Up to this point, young Lonnie had attended the tax-supported elementary school at Pine Grove, but this school only offered six grades. Lonnie felt so grown-up that morning when he was about to board the bus for Linden all by himself. After paying his fare to the driver, the lanky teenager eagerly took a seat right behind the driver where he could see everything clearly. He ruefully remembers that his father had failed to warn him about segregated seating on buses. What happened next would teach Lonnie Brown a lesson he would never forget. Brown explains, "This bus driver had a fit. . . . If I didn't move back, he was going to slap me." The teenaged Brown was stunned. He observes, "That's when I first was introduced to segregation."[3] Just a few years later, at the tender age of nineteen, Lonnie Brown got married, and he took his new bride to Ohio to escape segregation. He quickly landed a job in a steel mill, and the newlyweds soon settled into a comfortable routine.

One evening, the Browns decided to go see a movie. After deciding where to sit, they made themselves comfortable, the lights dimmed, and the movie began. Shortly after the show started, a young white couple took seats right next to the Browns. Because their eyes had not yet adjusted to the dark, the white couple was unaware that the people sitting next to them were African American. Brown remembers the precise moment when the white man who had taken the seat next to him realized that he was sitting next to a black man. Brown sensed rather than saw the man's upper body jerk, almost like he was having a spasm. The sudden motion prompted Brown to turn around in his seat to get a good look, but before he could turn all the way around, the white man sitting next to him had twisted his body all the way around in his seat so that his back was to Lonnie Brown and his wife. For the rest of the movie, the white man sat sideways and looked over his shoulder at the movie: Obviously, he was determined not to move, but he was equally determined not to sit side by side with a black man. The absurdity of the white man's actions angered Brown, and it also made him think. Shortly after that time when Lonnie Brown was inducted into the service, he made himself a promise: "I vowed then . . . there's no need of going any further . . . to run away from racism. I'm going back home when I get out of the service, and we're going to fight it."[4]

After he returned to Wilcox County, Lonnie Brown began to work for an insurance company selling policies to local black families, and that meant that he had close contact with a lot of black Wilcox residents. On many occasions, Brown voiced his frustration to clients, family, and friends about the restrictive racial atmosphere in their county. Most agreed as they nodded their heads in sympathy. Finally, Brown and some of the others at those early strategy sessions decided to start their own organization: in early 1961 a small group met at Lonnie Brown's house and established the Wilcox County Civic and Progressive League (WCCPL).[5] Brown remembers how determined they were to demand change. He explains, "All of us had some of the same aspirations and the same goals." He continued, "We needed to make progress in [many] areas: the economic area, law enforcement, so we named it the Progressive Civic League."[6] But one goal took precedence over all the other goals in the minds of all of those present at this founding meeting. Brown says simply, "we wanted to be registered to vote. . . . I'm a veteran, and . . . some of the others [are also veterans]. We just thought that if we're going to fight for our country, we ought to have a right to vote."[7] Clearly, voting was on everybody's mind that night, but Lonnie Brown was particularly focused on the franchise because just prior to this inaugural meeting, he had seen a reference to "Negro Voting" in the local *Wilcox Progressive Era*. Brown remembers the article as clearly as if he had seen it just yesterday. He explains that "it [the article] stated that . . . the Negroes did not want to vote, and that disturbed me tremendously."[8]

Monroe Pettway, who was also in attendance at that inaugural meeting, found the *Progressive Era* assertion utterly ridiculous. Pettway was a veteran of World War II, and regardless of what the newspaper said, he knew he had the right to vote because, as he stated, "I put up my life [for this country]."[9] In fact, Monroe Pettway's path to the gathering in Lonnie Brown's living room had been long and difficult. The short, wiry farmer had been born in Gee's Bend in 1914. He has vivid memories of working in the fields alongside his father and older brothers. By the time Pettway reached his teenage years, the Great Depression held the country in its iron grip, and he has painful memories of the lean years when his friends and relatives in the Bend were battling starvation. The day that the white people came and seized whatever they could find is indelibly etched in his memory. He recalls, "They took everything. They took cows, they took hogs, [even] corn out of the cribs." Pettway also has vivid memories of the changes that occurred in Gee's Bend after federal officials with the Farm Security Administration came into the area. Later, when World War II started, Pettway joined the army, and in a short time he found himself on a ship bound for Europe.

As the ship he was on got closer and closer to the war in Europe, a thoughtful Monroe Pettway realized that he had more than one goal in mind when he decided to join the military. Of course, he was intent on defending his country, but he was also determined to stay alive and save enough money from his serviceman's wages to pay off the mortgage on his land. By the end of the war, Monroe Pettway had achieved all of his goals: he had helped to defend his country, and he had returned uninjured to his beloved Gee's Bend with enough money to pay off his mortgage. As soon as he got home, he went straight to the bank to pay off the debt on his land in full. He gleefully recalls that white bank officials were "surprised." Thus, the night of the inaugural meeting of the WCCPL, Monroe Pettway was an independent Gee's Bend landowner, a veteran of the war to make the world safe for democracy, and a proud black Wilcox County resident with a burning desire to vote.

The WCCPL continued to meet through 1961, and by late 1962 they began formulating a strategy to dramatize the painful fact of total black disfranchisement in their county. At that point, Bernard Lafayette, a young Student Nonviolent Coordinating Committee (SNCC) staffer, made a trip to Wilcox County from nearby Selma where he was based. He met with members of the WCCPL, and after some deliberation, they all agreed that a delegation from the organization would go to the courthouse in Camden and attempt to register to vote. They decided to schedule their confrontation in early April of 1963. After they made their decision, the next few weeks passed quickly as WCCPL members continued their normal routines. Finally, the eve of the day they had chosen to challenge their disfranchisement arrived, and members gathered one last time that night.

That meeting was characterized by an atmosphere of grim determination. Everyone knew that voting was the first step they had to take on the long road to equal rights in their county, but they also knew what a dangerous first step it was. Reverend Brown explains, "Really, that's what it came down to when we organized in that room that day, we had said we were willing to die if we knew our death would mean that people would get registered to vote. That's how serious it was."[10] As those present discussed their hopes and fears about the attempt to register the next day, the discussion naturally turned to the question of who should go. A consensus rapidly emerged among the men in attendance. Brown explains, "We didn't want them [women] to go the first time, cause if we were going to get killed, or beat[en] up real bad, we would rather the women be home [be]cause they had children." The women present were comfortable with this decision and did not question it: they understood the gravity of the undertaking, and they also understood that they needed to be there to care for their families regardless of the outcome.

As the meeting continued that night, the young SNCC staffer Bernard Lafayette sat quietly listening to the discussion. He was quite comfortable in the easy familiarity of these husbands and wives whose families had shared the land in Gee's Bend for generations. Lafayette concentrated intently on the discussion about the makeup of the delegation that was to go to the courthouse the next day. While it was clear that the women in the room were willing to abide by the decision that they stay at home the next day, it was also clear to the young activist that it was inevitable that these strong black women would be equal participants in the African American struggle for civil rights in Wilcox County.[11] Reverend Brown confirms Lafayette's impression when he insists, "After we got started, they [the women] were just as bold as we were."[12]

As the meeting continued that night, Lafayette was particularly struck by the religious overtones. Ironically, it was held on a Wednesday evening: weeknight prayer services in black Christian churches across the South were traditionally held on Wednesday evening. Lafayette concludes, "It was like a comin' of Jesus meeting."[13] Those in attendance sang hymns in the call and response pattern that was so characteristic of black church music. Yet, even though they found solace in all the prayers and hymns, those gathered together that night could not escape the prospect of death that seemed to have invaded their meeting: many clearly expected that county authorities would shoot and kill members of their delegation when they arrived at the courthouse the next day. In fact, in hushed tones they discussed a story that was part of the county's collective consciousness. According to that story, "the last time a [black] person went to register to vote, it was an older minister, retired. He was in his eighties, and he said it was something he [had] wanted to do all his life. . . . He had nothing else to live for. . . . And he needed to at least attempt to register to vote." All of those in the room had heard this story many times before. They were also well acquainted with the tragic ending. When the elderly minister went to the courthouse to register, "he was shot and killed."[14] Lafayette looked around at the circle of somber faces surrounding him. The subdued glow of the table lamps in the room softened their grim expressions somewhat, but the intense commitment in all those pairs of eyes cut through the dim light that night, and twenty-two-year-old Bernard Lafayette was both awed and inspired.

The next day dawned crystal clear. As the golden ball of the sun peeped over the horizon in the east, the droplets of dew on the tender young spring foliage and on the grass began to sparkle like millions of diamonds. The families of Gee's Bend were already awake and preparing for the new day. But their minds were not on the fields they had to work, or the animals they had to tend, or the fences they had to mend. Their normal routine was the furthest thing from their minds because this was destined to be a day like none other.

This was the day that twelve men who had been their friends and neighbors for many years were going to the courthouse to try to register to vote.

At the appointed hour, after the sun was fully up, all the men gathered at the house of Monroe Pettway. In a short time the SNCC staffer, Bernard Lafayette, arrived. The group silently climbed into their pickup trucks for the forty-five-mile trip to Camden. The men in this voter registration caravan were all dressed in their Sunday best: new or nearly new denim overalls that were stiff and deep blue because of their newness, and crisply starched long sleeved shirts. The caravan of pickup trucks driving single file through the community of Alberta and then south toward Camden was an unusual sight on the nearly deserted back roads of Wilcox County. Sunlight glinted off the metal trucks, nearly hiding the dents, scratches, and dirt that clung to their sides from years of work on the farm. Except for the sound of the tires making contact with the dirt road, and the growl of their engines, the caravan was silent. The men in the trucks were motionless; their backs were ramrod straight, and their stern countenances almost seemed as if they could have been carved from granite. The gentle breeze coming in through the open truck windows carried just the faintest perfume of the wildflowers dotting the roadside. Nobody noticed. Instead, as their caravan rolled closer and closer to the courthouse, each man was acutely aware that the gun rack mounted behind his head was conspicuously empty: the young SNCC staffer had persuaded them to leave the guns they routinely carried at home.

When the caravan finally arrived at the courthouse, the men silently and deliberately climbed out of their trucks and walked single file toward the white columns that marked the entrance to the structure. White county employees furtively peeked out of windows at the awesome sight of this line of black men from Gee's Bend grimly marching into the courthouse. There were reporters milling around outside, along with FBI agents and representatives from the Justice Department. If the men noticed all this activity, they gave no sign of it. Instead, they marched straight into the building without looking left or right. When they approached the door marked Voter Registration, they noticed to their dismay that a Closed sign had been posted on the office door. Undaunted, one of the men boldly walked up to the closed door and rapped on it sharply with his gnarled knuckles. Seconds dragged by as mounting tension settled itself on this group of Gee's Bend farmers in their stiff overalls. Finally, the door opened just a crack, and an authoritative voice punctuated by a thick south Alabama accent informed the men that nobody would be available to take their applications until after lunch. Before the group could react, the door slammed shut. The men looked at each other searchingly, and almost as if on cue, they walked over to the benches lining the hallway, and they all took seats, determined to wait. The minutes stretched into an hour, then an hour and a half. They all sat stiffly on their benches, their rich brown faces impassive. From time to time, white county employees peeked out of nearby offices at the strange sight of twelve grimly determined black farmers sitting in the hallway of the Wilcox County Courthouse, waiting to register to vote. Finally, the door to the voter registration office opened again. All the men instinctively stood up just as one of the registrars stepped into the hall to inform them that they could come into the office one at a time to fill out an application. Without hesitation, the man closest to the door took a deep breath, squared his shoulders, and strode bravely through the open door, determined to face whatever demons might be on the other side. The others tensely sat down again. As the afternoon wore on, every member of the Gee's Bend delegation was summoned into the registrar's office one by one to fill out an application.[15]

After the last man had taken his turn, the group walked out of the courthouse and back to their pickup trucks. Bernard Lafayette paused for just a minute to watch the group of Gee's Bend farmers cross the courthouse lawn in front of him. Even though these men were all much older than he, Lafayette beamed like a proud father. Despite his tender age, the young SNCC activist was a seasoned civil rights veteran who fully understood the danger these men were facing. He explains, "It was a good feeling to see those mature black men, rural. They had the courage to stand up and be men, and to face that situation without weapons . . . and they were demanding their rights."[16] As the caravan of trucks turned around and headed toward home, their occupants seemed to release a collective sigh of relief. Then, once they picked up speed, leaving Camden, and heading back into the familiarity of rural Wilcox County, the faces of the Gee's Bend farmers split into broad grins as they realized the importance of what they had just done: They had demanded the right to vote, and they had lived to tell about it. Later that evening, the men were treated like conquering heroes at a community gathering that had been organized to commemorate the occasion. The enthusiastic cheers and sincere congratulations of their neighbors echoed in their ears. But, even as they basked in the admiration, each of these men had no doubt that their attempt to register to vote that day was only the opening salvo in a long and bitter struggle that was just beginning. As Bernard Lafayette sat quietly enjoying the celebratory mood and replaying the day's momentous events in his mind, he also understood that the struggle these men had just begun would be long, difficult, and dangerous.

The path that had brought young Bernard Lafayette to Wilcox County had been long and roundabout. The young activist had been a seminary student in

Nashville, Tennessee, in 1960 when the sit-ins started. He quickly became involved in the fledgling SNCC and the very next year, 1961, participated in the Freedom Rides. By this time, Bernard Lafayette was sure that for the foreseeable future, his place was in the southern freedom struggle. Just as Lafayette made his decision to work full-time in the movement, a number of students from the Nashville movement decided to take time off from school to go south and work to register and educate prospective black voters. Ironically, they made their decision just as the country's young idealistic president, John F. Kennedy, created the Peace Corps. It was against this background of American idealism and voluntarism that the Nashville students began their voter registration work. Not all of the students who volunteered for this hazardous work were Southerners, but all were acutely aware of the danger that awaited them. For Bernard Lafayette, the young ministerial student who was convinced of the righteousness of the cause, the call was irresistible.[17]

As soon as he volunteered, Lafayette was immediately dispatched to Detroit and Chicago to raise money for students who had been jailed in Louisiana when they tried to organize local African Americans to register to vote. The incarcerated students, Dion Diamond, Chuck McDew, and Bob Zellner, were charged with conspiring to overthrow the government of the State of Louisiana. By the time Lafayette finished raising the money for their bail and returned to Atlanta, all of the field assignments had been made. The eager young activist was terribly disappointed. Jim Forman, SNCC's newly appointed executive secretary, clearly saw the disappointment in Bernard Lafayette's face, and heard it in his voice as he talked to the young ministerial student. Forman could also see the determination in his young colleague's face, so he told Lafayette that even though the field assignments had already been made, there were options: Lafayette could join SNCC's Arkansas project and work with its director Bill Hanson, work with Charles Sherrod in Southwest Georgia, or work with Bob Moses in Mississippi. As Forman discussed these possibilities, he watched his young colleague's face very carefully. Lafayette's face continued to reveal his disappointment. Clearly, the young movement veteran had his heart set on directing his own project. Forman paused for just a moment, and then finally he offered his young colleague one last option. He informed Lafayette that there was only one place left where he could go and direct his own project: Selma, Alabama. The young activist immediately perked up, and his face split into a broad grin. "But," Forman cautioned, "we've crossed that off." He went on to explain that SNCC had sent workers into Selma previously, "but it was too hard."[18]

Forman was not surprised when he realized that Lafayette had stopped listening to him. Instead, the young movement veteran was looking off beyond

SNCC's executive secretary, and he appeared to be consumed by a sense of anticipation. Forman knew that look; he had seen it on the face of other eager young activists, and he was certain that it meant that Bernard Lafayette had already made up his mind: he had decided to take on Selma, Alabama. Soon after his meeting with Forman, Lafayette began doing research on Selma. Even though he quickly realized that SNCC's executive secretary had not overestimated the danger, he was not deterred. Thus, in the fall of 1962, Bernard Lafayette, Selma's new project director, drove down to Montgomery, Alabama, to meet with activists there before continuing south to Selma. Upon arriving in Montgomery, one of the first people he met was Rufus Lewis, a local black funeral director who had been canvassing for voter registration in Montgomery and surrounding counties. Lewis shared some of his experiences with the young activist, and he warned that some areas were just too dangerous to organize.

Undaunted, Bernard Lafayette left Montgomery and drove on down to Selma. Once he arrived, he immediately set about the task of forming a local committee, and they soon resuscitated the almost moribund Dallas County Voters League. One of the black Dallas County residents who worked closely with the eager young SNCC staffer was James Gildersleeve, a teacher at Selma's black Lutheran Academy. When Lafayette made it clear that he was interested in organizing black voter registration campaigns in surrounding counties, Gildersleeve, a seasoned activist, warned him about neighboring Wilcox. Lafayette recalls that at the time, "Wilcox County had such a tough reputation."[19] One of the reasons for the county's reputation was its sheriff, Lummie Jenkins. Lafayette recalls that before he ventured into Wilcox he heard a story about Sheriff Jenkins that was particularly troubling. According to the account Lafayette heard, Jenkins went to interrogate a black woman in a wheelchair because he was unable to locate her son who was wanted for questioning, and he was convinced that she knew his whereabouts. When the woman was unresponsive to Jenkins's repeated queries, the sheriff allowed his frustration to get the better of him, and he slapped her repeatedly. Actually, so the story went, the woman was unable to answer Jenkins because she had had a stroke, and she was unable to speak. A short time later, the woman had a heart attack and died.

When he heard this story, the young activist recoiled in horror at the image of a helpless, disabled black woman in a wheelchair being victimized by her county's chief law enforcement officer. Although the story remains an unsubstantiated legend, it clearly indicates the popular perception of Lummie Jenkins in the minds of African Americans in the Alabama Black Belt. At the time, Lafayette concluded, "Jim Clark [the notorious sheriff in Dallas

County] was like a Sunday school kid compared to Lummie Jenkins."[20] In fact, Jenkins himself cultivated the image of a tough lawman who was clearly in control. For example, when he served as the umpire for local baseball games, he routinely strapped on his Colt .45 before taking his place behind home plate. Local white residents laughingly insisted that nobody would dare argue with the umpire. Local black residents did not laugh at all.[21] As Bernard Lafayette thought about all the difficulties facing anyone trying to register black voters in Wilcox County, he was acutely aware of the central importance of the office of sheriff in rural southern counties like Wilcox. In this setting the sheriff was the one county official with whom black residents routinely had contact. He had the right to come into their neighborhoods at any time, and his word could mean the difference between freedom and incarceration, or even life and death.

Yet, despite Jenkins's reputation, and all the other dangers waiting for him in Wilcox County, Bernard Lafayette would not be deterred. As he prepared to enter the county for the first time, the young activist recalled the advice that Montgomery activist Rufus Lewis had offered just a few weeks ago. Lewis had advised him to go into tough areas like Wilcox as quietly as possible under cover of darkness. Accordingly, one evening in early 1963, Selma activist James Gildersleeve accompanied Lafayette into Wilcox County. As the two men prepared to leave that night, young Bernard Lafayette had a lot on his mind. He thought about the progress of the organization in Selma that he had been working with for some weeks now, and he wondered about what awaited him in Wilcox. At the same time, he also realized that many of the local black people he had met since coming into Alabama routinely carried guns. By this time in his activist career, Bernard Lafayette had faced danger many times in the field, but he still remained completely committed to the principle of nonviolence. Consequently, in preparation for that first visit to Wilcox County, he thought he had better explain his commitment to James Gildersleeve. Lafayette clearly recalls the discussion. "We got ready to leave, and I said, 'Listen now, we can't carry guns. . . . I don' t want to get in that kind of situation.'" Gildersleeve's response? "You don't have to do anything, you know, I'm just kind of going with you, and kind of riding shotgun." Gildersleeve, a native of Dallas County, patiently explained to the young outsider, "You know, [we need to] have a little something, protection or something, just to scare them off in case they come at [us]."

Lafayette looked thoughtfully at his older companion. Since spending time in the Deep South, he was beginning to understand and even sympathize with the tradition of carrying firearms that was such an important part of rural southern culture, both black and white. Despite his understanding, however,

Lafayette still refused to compromise his principles. He looked Gildersleeve in the eye and insisted in a soft voice that they could not carry any weapons. "Absolutely not," he told Gildersleeve, "I just can't take a chance like that." James Gildersleeve broke eye contact with the young activist and shrugged his shoulders. Moments later, the two men climbed into Lafayette's 1948 Chevrolet for the ride into Wilcox County. Neither man said another word about guns until years later when a considerably older Bernard Lafayette saw James Gildersleeve for the first time in over three decades. The occasion was the commemoration of the Selma-to-Montgomery march on March 5, 2000. The two men embraced as each expressed his delight at meeting again after all this time. They chatted pleasantly for a while, and then Lafayette posed a question to Gildersleeve that had nagged him ever since the night they made that lonely first trip into Wilcox County. "Hey Gildersleeve," Lafayette said, "I have a question I need to ask you." With a twinkle in his eye, Lafayette continued, "Tell me the truth, now, [the night we went to Wilcox County] do you remember whether you carried a gun? You told me you weren't going to carry a gun." Gildersleeve paused for a minute, and as he looked deep into Lafayette's eyes, the years seemed to melt away. He sighed and briefly looked up at the ceiling as he tried to summon the memory of that night so many years ago. When he again looked at Lafayette, James Gildersleeve was smiling broadly. He chuckled as he answered, "I believe I did."[22]

But that night in 1963 when he drove into Wilcox County for the first time, Bernard Lafayette was blissfully unaware that James Gildersleeve was literally riding shotgun. Lafayette was unsure of what he would find when he arrived, and his anxieties seemed to be magnified by the inky blackness of the dark Wilcox night. Finally, the long ride was over, and Bernard Lafayette had his first glimpse of a handful of members of the WCCPL. After he was introduced to members of the group, including Lonnie Brown and Monroe Pettway, the young SNCC activist listened intently to the participants express their hopes and fears. What he heard fired his optimism. It was obvious to Lafayette that these God-fearing courageous people were totally convinced of the righteousness of their cause, and they were prepared to give their lives if necessary.

There was something else about these people that also resonated with the young activist: they seemed to have an obvious independent streak and an unstudied orneriness. Many of those present that night were Gee's Bend residents, and Bernard Lafayette perceived the same independent streak in these people that many had recognized over the years. Furthermore, it seemed to the young activist that many of those who were present that evening seemed to be free of many of the attitudes and mannerisms that he associated with the black middle class. Lafayette considered this a definite advantage because by this time, he and many of his SNCC colleagues had become frustrated with some members of the black middle class. All too often, some in SNCC reasoned, the black middle class was resistant to change because they had a stake in the system as it existed. Of course, members of this class were subjected to racism like all African Americans. However, some members of the black middle class had managed to carve out a relatively comfortable existence for themselves and their families within the confines of their segregated society. Change, any kind of change, might threaten that position. Against this backdrop of increasing class-consciousness, many in SNCC began to believe that the future of the freedom struggle lay in the hands of the "common" people. Many SNCC field workers became so intent on identifying with "the people" that they started dressing in the same kind of denim overalls that many rural black people wore. The accompanying change in the demeanor of these young activists would soon provoke some curious reactions from many rural African Americans, including some in Wilcox County. It was in the midst of this increasing class-consciousness in his organization that Bernard Lafayette had his first meeting with members of the WCCPL before their fateful first trip to the courthouse.

The course of the freedom struggle in Wilcox County emphatically underscored class differences among members of the local black community as they struggled to organize themselves effectively. A particularly illustrative case in point is offered by the example of the Pettway family. Fiercely independent, the sons of Roman Pettway, including fiery farmer Monroe Pettway, became intimately involved in the freedom struggle, and they paid dearly. This thrifty branch of the Pettway clan had been independent landowners since the Depression. Yet, despite their economic independence, they were still not considered part of the middle class. They always had plenty to eat, but like so many of their poor neighbors, they still had to struggle to make ends meet. Both Tydie D. and Paulette Pettway, granddaughters of Roman Pettway, recall how hard everyone in the family had to work to maintain their independence. Tydie D. Pettway explains, "They [her family] were somewhat achievers. So, we had to work hard, and people saw us different[ly]. We was kind of set apart from day one." All of the children were expected to share the hard work with the adults. Tydie D. insists that neither she nor her brothers and sisters were allowed to leave the fields until "the last corn was pulled, and all the potatoes was [sic] dug, all the cotton was picked, and the millet was stripped, and the syrup was made."[23]

Paulette, Tydie D.'s first cousin, remembers that she and her brothers and sisters, Monroe Pettway's children, also worked hard. She insists, "When I was old enough, I started to babysit my younger siblings while they [her parents] worked in the cotton field." Paulette's babysitting chores did not last long: by the time she was nine years old, her father decided that she was old enough to go out in the fields and pick cotton. But, as little Paulette struggled to fill her sack with the snowy cotton bolls, it was clear that her heart was not in it. She confesses, "I always would dream of becoming a nurse and leaving." Paulette's ambition distressed her father. She recalls, "He [her father] didn't want to hear about that." Instead, "He wanted you to really take interest and be proud of it [the land]." Paulette Pettway concludes, "He has a thing about the land. He wants to hold on to it." Paulette also recalls that sometimes after the field work was done, she would go outside and try to play. It seemed that she was never outside more than a few minutes before her mother would call her in that distinctive tone of voice that clearly meant that playtime was over. "Paulette," her mother would say, carefully emphasizing each syllable. Paulette knew that she had better get in the house right away to start on the endless round of household chores that never seemed to be finished. Like Paulette, Tydie D. remembers that she and her sisters also worked in the house after their field work was done. It was more than a little ironic that when she and her siblings were working in the fields, they were all expected to do equal amounts of labor. She explains, "And it didn't matter if you was [sic] a girl . . . because the girls would work just like the boys. It wasn't no boys jobs and no girls jobs." Yet, when it came to housework, both Paulette and Tydie D. agree, "We had to make those boys' beds up every morning . . . we had to wash their clothes and iron them. We did all the cooking and all the dishwashing and the mopping." Tydie D. concludes, "My brothers didn't do any of that."[24]

Both Pettway cousins also agree that along with their rigorous work routine, they were subjected to extremely strict discipline. Paulette insists that she lived with the constant threat of a whipping if she did not pick enough cotton each day she worked in the fields. Tydie D. adds, "They [her parents] were strict. I'm not talking about word strict, I'm talking about stick strict." Both Paulette's parents and Tydie D.'s parents used to cut switches from one of the many peach trees growing on their property, and they regularly used them on all their children to ensure absolute obedience. Tydie D. still has vivid memories of the many mornings she went to school with stinging welts on her arms from the whippings she received from one of those peach tree switches. Clearly, this hardworking, God-fearing, ambitious branch of the Pettway clan thought that the use of corporal punishment to ensure absolute obedience from their children was right and proper. While Americans have become sensitive to issues of family violence in recent years, prior to this time, "[d]iscussions of corporal punishment of children or domestic violence played little part in American life in the early twentieth century."[25]

In fact, through much of the last century the use of corporal punishment was an accepted and expected part of the rural black southern culture in which the Pettways lived. In his recent biography of Reverend Fred Shuttlesworth, who was a native Alabaman and a leader in the Southern Christian Leadership Conference (SCLC), Andrew Manis explains that "the South has had a reputation for violence, typically expressed in greater support for the military, corporal punishment of children, gun ownership, and recreational fighting. Although these tendencies have been most pronounced in white southerners, blacks have shared their region's comparatively violent ethos."[26] Manis asserts that in addition to being part of their region's culture, the violence evident in so many rural black families is a characteristic of their economic class as well. As he put it, "regardless of race, families of lower economic status experience more frustrations and have fewer resources for coping with them. As a result, such families resort to violence more often than those in higher status groups."[27] Both Paulette and Tydie D. Pettway agree with this part of Manis's assessment. Paulette explains that she is sure that one of the reasons why her parents whipped her is because they were so overworked and stressed that "they sort of took it out on us. That's how they handled it."[28] Clearly, rural black lives were punctuated by hardship and deprivation, and in such an atmosphere the Pettway children developed a toughness, and a realistic understanding of the harsh conditions that would confront them when they grew to adulthood. At the same time, however, these children were comfortable with their identities as part of a gregarious, ambitious, and rambunctious family that was secure in its sense of place, imbued with a sense of mission, and motivated by a profound love of their land.

Many of the first members of the WCCPL were from this tough, no nonsense background, and as they listened intently to young Bernard Lafayette from SNCC at that initial meeting, they all filtered his message through the prism of their own experience. They admired his courage and his deep commitment to the black freedom struggle. They were also comforted by his quiet demeanor and his devotion to his Christian beliefs, because religion was a critical part of their own belief system. But, the young man's commitment to nonviolence left many shaking their heads in bewilderment. Most were completely comfortable around firearms. Moreover, they recognized the extreme danger that was bound to accompany their organizing efforts. Consequently, many had reservations about Lafayette's deep commitment to the principles of nonviolence. Despite their reservations, however, they were very glad to have this young man from Nashville to help them.

During the early spring of 1963 Lafayette became well acquainted with the members of the WCCPL as he helped them organize for their assault on black disfranchisement in their county. After their initial attempt in April, miraculously, most of the men who had gone to the courthouse that day were eventually notified that they had passed the test, and they were now registered voters. That only whetted their appetite for more. In the meantime, Bernard Lafayette was continuing his organizing efforts in Selma. By this time, the young activist's presence was beginning to make Dallas County authorities very nervous. Unlike his quiet efforts in Wilcox County, Bernard Lafayette's organizing efforts in Selma were very public. One of the most important reasons for this difference was Selma's location: It was the largest town in the Alabama black belt, and it was centrally located in the region. Consequently, it was a logical place to locate the headquarters for SNCC's voter registration project in the region. Still another reason why organizing efforts in Selma were so much more public than those in Wilcox County was because Lafayette and other SNCC personnel were aware that there was a black business community in Selma, and also a practicing black attorney there. Organizers were convinced that this provided a measure of protection that allowed them to carry on their efforts more openly. By contrast, Wilcox County "was more rural . . . so they [white supremacists] had a lot more kind of things that they could do and get away with."[29]

Despite his optimistic view of conditions in Selma, Bernard Lafayette quickly realized that his very public efforts in this Black Belt town were putting him in grave danger. In fact, after he had been in Selma only three months, the local newspaper, the *Selma Times-Journal*, published a story profiling his voter registration efforts, and also revealing his address. If he had any doubts about his status before, they completely vanished after the article's publication: Bernard Lafayette realized that he was a marked man.[30] Not surprisingly, then, barely two months after Lafayette led that historic male delegation to the Wilcox County Courthouse, his worst fears were realized. It happened the night of June 12, 1963. The young activist had just arrived home after a mass meeting when he was accosted by a very large white man wearing a white T-shirt with the sleeves rolled up. In his deep south Alabama drawl, the man asked Lafayette to help him push his stalled car. Eager to help, the young ministerial student turned to walk over to the man's car. Practically before he had taken a step in the car's direction, the heavyset stranger began to beat Lafayette in the head with the butt of a gun. The pain that the young activist felt was almost unbearable as his assailant continued beating him over the head unmercifully. It seemed to the wounded activist that the beating continued for an eternity. Finally, a neighbor came out on his porch brandishing a shotgun, and the assailant ran away.[31]

Word of the attack spread rapidly through Selma's black community. Initially, people were horrified and angry, but their anger soon turned to fascination and admiration when they realized that despite his wounds, Bernard Lafayette refused to quit. As soon as he was able, the young civil rights worker resumed his hectic schedule. Selma's black community responded enthusiastically to the young outsider's determination: attendance at mass meetings was up sharply after the attack. Lafayette was pleased. By the fall of 1963, the young ministerial student was convinced that the voter registration beachhead he had helped establish in Selma was permanent. Consequently, at that point Lafayette made the decision to return to Nashville to resume his studies at Fisk University that had been interrupted by his decision to go to Selma.[32] Bernard Lafayette would never again work in Wilcox County, but others would soon follow.

These early beginnings of Wilcox County's organized voter registration campaign in the spring of 1963 were unfolding against the backdrop of one of the most important campaigns of the civil rights movement: Birmingham. Just previous to this in the fall of 1962, Martin Luther King's Southern Christian Leadership Conference had suffered a crushing defeat in Albany, Georgia. In Albany the local sheriff, Laurie Pritchett, had made careful preparations before King's forces came to town: he secured extra jail space to hold all the activists who might be arrested, and he warned his officers not to brutalize the demonstrators. Because of the sheriff's actions, demonstrations dragged on for an interminable length of time, the press soon lost interest and left town, and the campaign ground to a halt. Finally, when it became clear that local officials were not going to yield, SCLC members realized that they had no recourse, and so they left town. Albany, Georgia, remained a segregated town.

On the heels of that crushing defeat, SCLC leaders realized that they had better be very careful in selecting their next target because they could not afford to make the same mistake twice. At this point, Birmingham activist Reverend Fred Shuttlesworth urged King and other SCLC leaders to join the fight in Birmingham. After some discussion, they agreed. By early 1963 as his organization prepared to take on Birmingham's power structure, Martin Luther King Jr. commented, "If we can crack Birmingham, I'm convinced we can crack the South."[33] Thus, in April of that year, just as members of the WCCPL were planning their first trip to the courthouse to register, demonstrations were heating up in Birmingham just a few miles to the north. Before long, the eyes of the nation and the world would be focused on this southern industrial city as Eugene "Bull" Connor, the city's infamous commissioner of public safety, directed his officers to unleash German Shepherd attack dogs on helpless demonstrators, many of whom were children. Pictures of these vicious attacks and of the Birmingham Fire Department turning their high-pressure water hoses on these civil rights activists appeared on the front pages of newspapers all over the world. In Washington, D.C., the news of the Birmingham campaign began to generate support for a new and comprehensive federal civil rights law.

That fall, after the historic march on Washington, the state of Alabama was the site of still another widely publicized event that was related to the civil rights movement: the bombing of the Sixteenth Street Baptist Church in Birmingham. The Sixteenth Street Church had been the site of many of the mass meetings that were held during the Birmingham campaign that previous spring. Furthermore, it was located right next to Kelley Ingram Park; the site of the most vicious attacks on civil rights demonstrators by the city's fire and police departments. The nation was transfixed in horror as it watched the film footage of the bodies of four little black girls covered by white sheets being removed from the smoking ruins of the church after that Sunday morning bombing on September 15, 1963. A short time later when Martin Luther King Jr. preached the eulogy for the young victims, he would characterize them as "martyred heroines of a holy crusade for freedom and human dignity."[34] Coincidentally, the same day that the Sixteenth Street Baptist Church was bombed, SNCC staffers Julian Bond and Worth Long were headed down to Selma. They had flown to Birmingham that morning from SNCC headquarters in Atlanta and rented a car to drive to Selma. But, once they picked up their rental car in Birmingham, they were irresistibly drawn to the site of the terrible bombing. They had heard the news just before leaving Atlanta, and they still could not quite believe it had happened.

By this time, both Long and Bond had experienced countless demonstrations, endless strategy sessions, and the wrath of white supremacists who were furious at these young people for challenging their system. However, nothing in their experience prepared either of the young activists for the sight that confronted them when they pulled up in front of the mangled ruins of the Sixteenth Street Baptist Church that afternoon. When they got out of their car and approached the church, they were greeted by stony-faced Alabama National Guardsmen ringing the building. Just inside the circle of guardsmen, Long could see the rubble of bricks and shards of stained glass littering the ground. As he replayed in his mind the film clip that he had seen earlier of the bodies of the four young girls being taken from the wreckage, Long was hit by an overpowering wave of disgust that soon turned to anger as one of the National Guardsmen shouted at him to move along. Later that afternoon, a profoundly disturbed Worth Long continued on to Selma with Julian

Bond. The very next day Long, energized by his anger over events in Birmingham, organized a demonstration, and soon found himself arrested and incarcerated. Ironically, he and some of the other demonstrators wound up serving their sentences at a work camp in neighboring Wilcox County, christened by the locals "Camp Camden."[35]

Upon his release, Long continued his efforts to organize African American residents in Dallas County. In fact, he had come down for the specific purpose of directing SNCC's Alabama Voter Education Project, and one of the things he was most anxious to do was "to look to see where to branch out" from Selma.[36] As the new director considered the possibilities, he was both unnerved and intrigued by Wilcox County's tough reputation. Long recalls that almost as soon as he arrived, "We decided we were going to look at Wilcox, but they [white authorities] were so well-organized in their system of resistance there that we [already] had our hands full in Selma." Long also recalls that the county's tough reputation was common knowledge among local people, and they always made sure to inform the young civil rights workers coming into the area. One of the stories that Long particularly remembers hearing about Wilcox County involved two brave black residents who publicly complained about the restrictive racial atmosphere. According to the account Long heard, they "had to leave for the North at night [just] because they spoke up about conditions."[37]

Despite the county's reputation, or perhaps because of it, Worth Long, the brash, young SNCC staffer, could not resist at least exploring possibilities for organizing in Wilcox County. Consequently, in the late fall of 1963, he climbed into the little rear-engine Chevrolet Corvair that had been issued to him from the SNCC Sojourner Motor Fleet and slowly drove through the county. He recalls that he was immediately hit with the powerful impression of just how closely the reality of conditions in the county matched the expectations he had. Even though it was fall, the Alabama heat was still stifling as Long drove down the county's dusty roads. Everywhere he looked, the young SNCC activist saw acres and acres of neatly planted fields tended by black farm laborers. Sometimes, if the breeze was just right, snatches of the songs sung by the workers in the fields would drift through the open windows of his little Corvair as he drove along. However, not all of the county's land was under cultivation, the young activist noticed. On the contrary, some of the areas he passed had vast expanses of land fenced off, and large herds of cattle grazed contentedly in these fields. In other areas, he passed acre after acre of timber. Yet, regardless of what the land was being used for, Worth Long realized with a sinking feeling that Wilcox County, Alabama, was overwhelmingly rural, and that meant that it would be incredibly difficult to organize. Despite his growing belief that there were almost insurmountable obstacles to creating an effective movement in the county, however, there was still one possible avenue to organization: Gee's Bend. As Long puts it, "But, Gee's Bend was the place to look. It was the ideal spot."[38]

Long had first become aware of the unique character of Gee's Bend and its residents when he began to encounter some of them in Selma. Because of the geographic proximity of the Bend to Dallas County, many Gee's Bend residents routinely shopped and conducted other business in Selma. Long was fascinated by the area's unusual history, and by the independent spirit he sensed coming from many of those he met. Given Worth Long's personal history, it is completely understandable that he would be drawn to the residents of Gee's Bend. The young SNCC staffer was born in Durham, North Carolina, and he grew up in neighboring Chatham County. Long's father was a presiding elder in the African Methodist Episcopal Church, and he was also a race man who espoused black self-determination and the importance of black land ownership. Indeed, Long has vivid memories of how much his father admired the self-sufficiency of Booker T. Washington's Tuskegee Institute. At the same time, the elder Long was a staunch Pan-Africanist, and he never missed an opportunity to preach the importance of black self-sufficiency and Pan-African unity to his young son. Thus, by the time that Worth Long joined SNCC, he had developed his own unique philosophy of activism that was defined by the teachings of Pan-Africanism and black self-determination that were such an important part of his upbringing.

The young SNCC activist eagerly talked to the Gee's Bend residents he encountered in Selma, and a short time later, he decided to visit Boykin High School, the black public school in the Bend. He especially liked to hear the students sing, and he fondly recalls that they talked very fast, and he had to develop an ear for the rhythm and cadence of their speech that seemed almost musical in its quaintness. Obviously, Worth Long was not the first outsider to comment on the unique cultural characteristics of Gee's Bend residents. What Long and so many others before him noticed was what scholars have labeled the retention of Africanisms: the survival of a greater concentration of African cultural characteristics. This process occurred in areas where there was a highly concentrated and relatively stable slave population, few white inhabitants, and relative geographic isolation.[39] Clearly, Gee's Bend fit this profile. Worth Long was thrilled to find this group of independent black residents who he thought would be interested in his organizing efforts. However, the young activist's optimism began to wane considerably when he took a closer look at the conditions confronting him.

Indeed, although the students had given him a warm welcome at Boykin High, Long quickly realized that the teachers were far less enthusiastic about his visits. Paulette and Tydie D. Pettway corroborate Long's impression. Both have painful memories of the treatment they received at the hands of teachers who resented their family's involvement in the movement. Paulette explains, "Some of the teachers really resented us and . . . [we were] really verbally abused." Teachers were particularly angry at her father because of his leadership role. As Paulette puts it, "One of the teachers said, my father thinks he knows everything."[40] Taking their cues from the teachers, many of their fellow students also expressed resentment at children from this branch of the Pettway clan. Paulette and Tydie D. agree that they could never talk to their parents about this treatment, because within the confines of the absolute obedience to authority required by their parents, they simply were not allowed to complain. The cousins understood that many of their teachers were not free to act because their fate was dependent on the continued goodwill of the same county authorities who were bound and determined to maintain segregation. Tydie D. concludes, "It wasn't the people [like the teachers] who were out in front. . . . But then, they didn't want to lose their jobs . . . so it had to be like lay people who'd get out there and really step out front, uneducated people, really, and the educated people had to hang back."[41] Worth Long agrees that differing perspectives based on class made it difficult to organize in Wilcox County. As he puts it, "there's a class contradiction" among black people in Wilcox County. He further explains that when he went into the county "there [were] certain people who [were] not going to do liberation involvement. . . . they're not going to do it because they [had] an investment in the system."[42] Clearly, the views of SNCC's fiery young project director were out of step with the views of some African American residents of Wilcox County.

Yet, even as Long was becoming discouraged after his first tentative efforts in the county in late 1963, there were other civil rights workers who continued to be interested in exploring organizing options in Wilcox County. From late 1963 on into 1964, both SCLC and SNCC continued to send personnel into the Black Belt in an effort to expand the central Alabama Voting Rights campaign, which was designed to enfranchise the vast African American population in the region. Consequently, over the next two years, a changing cast of characters representing these two civil rights groups were in and out of Wilcox County to help organize civil rights activities. Many of those who ventured into Wilcox County during these years came in response to direct requests from local Wilcox activists. Reverend Lonnie Brown remembers that he and the other members of the WCCPL contacted both SNCC and SCLC for help on more than one occasion. One of those who were sent to Wilcox County by SCLC during these years was Reverend Daniel Harrell.

Once Harrell came to Wilcox, Brown remembers, he played a critical role in helping the WCCPL to organize communities all over the county. Under Harrell's tutelage, these communities began holding citizenship classes, and this paved the way for the massive voter registration campaign that would erupt in 1965. The citizenship classes that Harrell organized were based on an SCLC model. For some time previous to this, the organization had sponsored a citizenship school program. The first of these citizenship schools was located at Dorchester Center in southern Georgia.[43] SCLC staffer Andrew Young clearly explains the citizenship school concept:

> The basic idea at Dorchester was to establish voter registration using a few key people in 188 counties that had black majorities across the Deep South but almost no black registered voters. Our hope was that the first people registered would in turn begin registration campaigns in their own counties. Our South-wide focus was on the Mississippi Delta, *the black belt of Alabama*, scattered areas of Georgia and Florida, the eastern shores of North Carolina and South Carolina, and the Tidewater area of Virginia (emphasis added).[44]

Armed with this SCLC Citizenship School concept, Reverend Daniel Harrell helped Wilcox residents in various areas of their county set up classes where prospective black voters could come to discuss politics, practice filling out registration forms, or even tackle issues of basic literacy. Harrell had come to the Alabama Black Belt from southern Louisiana. While organizing for SCLC there in the spring and summer of 1963, he had worked as an assistant to Major Johns, SCLC's project director in Shreveport. Johns and Harrell organized sit-ins in Shreveport, and thirty people were jailed. But their movement soon fizzled out because it seemed that the local black residents did not have the collective commitment necessary to effect change. Johns reported in despair, "Unless additional people come into this city . . . not too much will be accomplished."[45] Johns went on to insist that what local black residents really wanted was for Dr. King to "come in and direct a freedom movement."[46] After such unspectacular results, SCLC abandoned Shreveport, and Johns and Harrell moved farther south to Lake Charles. But, while the black apathy in Shreveport had been disappointing, the organized black opposition that greeted them in Lake Charles was extremely discouraging. There, a local black organization, the Calcasieu Parish Coordinating Committee, barred SCLC activists from their churches, and they eventually asked the men to leave the area altogether. Harrell was stunned, and he was also disillusioned. His feelings clearly came through in the field reports he sent back to SCLC headquarters. When SCLC staffer Andrew Young, a member of the group's inner circle, read Harrell's reports, he was troubled. He immediately sent a reply to Harrell advising him to "bear with our brethren of the clergy, [and] remember they have been brainwashed for 300 years."[47] Johns and Harrell continued to work in Calcasieu Parish, but their efforts were rewarded with only a modest increase in the number of registered black voters in the parish.

Such experiences prepared Daniel Harrell well for the complexities of organizing in Wilcox County. When he first entered the Alabama Black Belt, Harrell spent a short time working with the movement in Selma, but he would soon come to concentrate almost all of his time and energy on the fledgling movement in Wilcox County. His arrival could not have come at a better time as far as African American activists in Wilcox County were concerned. Buoyed by the successful attempt made by the black caravan that had been led by Bernard Lafayette in the spring of 1963, the WCCPL was anxious to unite with activists in other areas outside of Alberta and Gee's Bend. WCCPL members who met Harrell when he first came to the county were favorably impressed. He was a tall, brown-skinned man with broad shoulders, a commanding voice, an unshakable commitment, and seemingly limitless energy. Initially, Harrell and his wife stayed with Reverend Lonnie Brown and his family. Brown clearly recalls how dedicated his houseguest was to the civil rights revolution. During these hectic months Harrell seemed to be everywhere at once in the county, organizing precincts and teaching citizenship classes. Finally, Harrell and his wife moved out of Brown's house and built a house in Coy. It was clear that Daniel Harrell had come to Wilcox County to stay.

In the meantime, as organizing efforts expanded throughout the county in the early sixties, white residents became very concerned even though they took some solace in the combative attitude of their political leaders. In fact, one of the most potent symbols of Alabama's white resistance was the state's popular governor, George Corley Wallace. Wallace's fierce resistance to federal attempts to protect black rights elevated him to the status of a folk hero among segregation supporters in Alabama and throughout the South. The determined promise that was part of his inaugural address, "segregation now, segregation tomorrow, and segregation forever," resonated with many white residents all over the state, including Wilcox County. It was against this backdrop of official state resistance that some white Wilcox residents were emboldened to act. Reverend Lonnie Brown clearly remembers the retaliation that was directed at him because of his voter registration work. Because Brown was an insurance agent, he frequently went on plantations where his clients worked in order to conduct business. What many white plantation owners correctly guessed was that Brown was discussing more than insurance with their sharecroppers; he was encouraging them to register to vote.

White landowners were furious, and determined to stop him. Brown recalls that a group of them got together and signed a petition denying him access to their land and the black people who worked it. After all the white landowners had signed the petition, one of the group approached Brown to tell him he was no longer welcome on their plantations. Brown explains,

> He told me that as long as I was connected with this activity, but he didn't say what activity, they wouldn't want me on their land, and that I was turning their people against them. He said Negroes liked things the way they were. . . . I replied that I wasn't trying to turn anyone against them, that I was only trying to get Negroes registered to vote.[48]

Brown soon received official notice by registered mail. He laughingly recalls that the letter did not have enough postage on it, and he had to pay the postage due before the post office would release it.[49] Lonnie Brown immediately tore open the official-looking envelope, and even before he had walked out of the post office, he had finished reading the brief notice: "This is notice to you, your agents, representatives, and employees: Under Title 14, Section 426, Code of Alabama of 1940, to stay off any premises and lands, owned or controlled by us, and not to trespass at any time."[50] Brown quickly forwarded the letter to the U.S. Justice Department. The response was immediate. The Justice Department dispatched John Doar to the scene, and when he questioned those who had signed the petition they became quite defensive, and they offered reasons like, "He [Brown] left the gate open and the cows got out." One white woman who had signed the petition even claimed that she was afraid of Reverend Lonnie Brown. When Doar pressed her, she could not explain why she was afraid, but she declared unequivocally that she was afraid.[51] Satisfied that the landowners' charges were only convenient inventions, and that their real intent was to keep Lonnie Brown from encouraging their tenants to register to vote, the Justice Department filed suit on his behalf. Brown remembers that the federal government handled the whole thing: they did not even call on him to testify.[52] After numerous hearings and appeals, the suit was finally settled in Reverend Brown's favor in November of 1965, three months after the passage of the historic Voting Rights Act.[53]

In the meantime, Wilcox County's white supremacists were not content to limit their resistance to such official activities, and Reverend Brown vividly remembers the evening that the harassment turned violent. That evening in 1963 started off uneventfully just like so many others. Reverend Brown and his wife went to a voter registration meeting, leaving their two teenaged children at home as they had so many times before. Only, this evening was different. After participating in the discussion and prayer at the meeting, the Browns climbed into their car for the return trip home. Almost as soon as Reverend Brown turned into his driveway, he was greeted by the unusual sight of his children running out of the house and up to the car before he had brought it to a complete stop. The only light on the driveway came from a porch light just a few yards away, but even in that feeble light, Brown and his wife could clearly see the frightened looks on their children's faces. The teenagers were both talking at once, their voices rising hysterically as they tried to tell their parents about the shots that had been fired into their house. As Reverend Brown stood quietly listening to his children, the horror of the near miss they had just suffered began to sink in, and he was almost overwhelmed by a sense of relief that was mixed with anger at the perpetrators. At the same time, he experienced an almost suffocating fear for his family's welfare, and he knew he had to act. After spending a few precious minutes calming his family down and making sure the house was secure, Lonnie Brown climbed back into his car and drove off, determined to seek protection for his family, but also equally determined to continue his voter registration activities.

Because Reverend Brown had been born and raised in Wilcox County, he knew better than to seek help from local law enforcement officials. Instead, he drove to Selma that night to ask the advice of Selma activist James Gildersleeve. Brown rushed into Gildersleeve's living room, his concern for his family etched in his face as his words tumbled out, recounting the details of the shooting at his house. Without hesitation, Gildersleeve advised his friend to call Robert Kennedy's Justice Department. Brown complied. The staff person who answered the phone that evening told Brown to go home and someone would contact him. Shortly after Reverend Brown returned to his anxious family, there was a knock at the door. Brown answered it, and standing there on his porch was Wilcox County's sheriff, Lummie Jenkins, accompanied by a white man dressed in a business suit who Brown did not recognize. Brown later discovered that Jenkins's companion was actually an FBI agent from the closest field office. After the men exchanged a few words, Jenkins walked around the outside of Brown's house, examining the holes left by the pellets that had struck the house. Finally, Jenkins concluded his examination, cleared his throat, and turned around to face Brown. "Lonnie," he addressed Reverend Brown with that familiarity that white county residents claimed as their birthright when addressing their black neighbors, "maybe your children were fooling around with their BB guns, and maybe they were just afraid to tell you." Jenkins grinned at Brown as he concluded, "You know how kids are."[54] A visibly angry Reverend Brown struggled to control the tone of his voice as he informed the sheriff that his children could not possibly have shot up his house because they did not even own BB guns. That night in his living room, Brown vowed to redouble his efforts in the struggle for equal rights because he knew that the only way his family would ever be truly safe was if they were truly free.

Such incidents of white resistance did not stop the quiet black organizing that continued in the county. In response, white residents became more and more alarmed. They were especially sensitive to the appearance of white outsiders in their county: white Wilcox residents automatically assumed that all unknown outsiders were civil rights workers who had come to stir up their "Negroes." White Wilcox resident Viola Goode Liddell explains the actions her friends and neighbors took when they spotted "suspicious visitors from outside, riding the roads, and roaming the back country by day and night." She observed, "Trespass signs went up on some property, gates were locked, tenants were warned, and some were put in the road. A few of these strangers were arrested on various charges, but on and on they came."[55] In the spring of 1964 a group of Presbyterian ministers learned firsthand the deadly consequences of that white fear of outsiders. The stage was set when the Presbyterian Church decided to send three representatives to check on the condition of its Wilcox County missions. The delegation included two white ministers; one was the moderator for the Presbytery, while the other was a clerk, and Reverend James Reese, the black minister who had tried to register to vote in Wilcox County back in 1958. As the only African American member of the group, Reese was acutely aware of segregation's rules. Consequently, as they got closer to Wilcox County, even though Reverend Reese and the two white ministers thought of themselves as colleagues and equals, Reese insisted on driving the car, with the two white ministers riding in the back. As their car approached the Camden city limits, a tense silence descended on its occupants. It was May 12, a beautiful spring evening, when the three men finally reached their destination. The white ministers immediately checked into the local segregated hotel, while Reese stayed with James Hobbs, the principal of Camden Academy.

Later that evening the three ministers met with a group on Camden Academy's campus. It was a pleasant and encouraging meeting, and the visitors expressed their appreciation for the work of the school's faculty and administrators. After the meeting broke up, the two white ministers returned to their hotel, and Reverend Reese gratefully settled himself into the soft, comfortable bed in the Hobbs's spare bedroom. Almost before Reese's head hit the pillow, his mind began to drift into the twilight zone between wakefulness and deep sleep. Just briefly, an awareness of just how tired he was flitted across the exhausted minister's mind, and in that last instant before he lost consciousness,

Reese decided, "It must have been all that driving." But just as his conscious mind surrendered, it seemed that there was a nagging noise that would not quite let him slip all the way into the deep sleep he craved. At first, Reese's conscious mind refused to be dragged away from its retreat into deep sleep, but the annoying noise persisted. Gradually as the fog of sleep enveloping his brain began to dissipate, Reese became aware of frantic knocking. Just as his brain reached full awareness, Reese heard loud footsteps and shouting. He quickly jumped out of the comfortable bed, all traces of his tiredness swept away on the rising tide of adrenaline that began pumping into the minister's system. It was clear that something was very wrong, and James Reese ran out of the guest room just in time to see his host open the front door, and his two white traveling companions rush into the living room. They were both out of breath, and they were both clearly terrified. Reese stepped into the room and attempted to calm his colleagues as one of them began to relate the evening's events in a very shaky voice. He explained that well after the two had gone to bed they were awakened by loud pounding on their door, and an angry voice that demanded, "Get up and get out of here. You're civil rights agitators, and we don't want you in this hotel."[56]

The frightened ministers quickly ran to the closet and yanked their clothes off the hangers. In their haste, it seemed that the ministers' hands were all thumbs as they fumbled with buttons and zippers amid their mounting fear. But, before they could finish dressing, the impatient intruder rushed into the hotel room and began beating the two men with the butt of a shotgun. Clutching their clothes, they hurried from the room as fast as they could and ran the short distance to safety at Principal Hobbs's house on the Camden Academy campus. As Reese stood there listening to his colleagues, the full horror of the situation began to dawn on him. He shook his head in disbelief as he struggled to comprehend the reality confronting him right there in the Hobbs living room. The shaken ministers were bruised and bloody, and one had a broken arm. Reese immediately advised, "We can't stay here."[57] As news of the attack spread among a select few of Camden's black citizens, lights began to come on in previously darkened households. One of those was the Threadgill household, and Sheryl Threadgill vividly remembers being awakened that night by the sound of voices in her living room. By the time she became fully aware of what was going on, her father, Reverend Thomas Threadgill, was meeting with other men of the community, trying to decide what the safest way would be to spirit the men out of town.[58] Everyone recognized that time was of the essence. Consequently, shortly after the two white ministers first ran from their assailant, Reverend Reese recalls that he was given a set of keys to a car that just seemed to have materialized in front of the Hobbs house. Everyone agreed that it was not safe for the ministers to retrieve their own car from its parking spot in front of the hotel.[59]

Sympathetic bystanders helped the two white ministers into the getaway car's backseat, and covered them with blankets. Reverend Thomas Threadgill and Principal James Hobbs directed Reese to drive to Selma, and not to stop for any reason until he crossed the county line into Dallas County. Reese did not have to be told twice. A small, cold knot of fear formed in the minister's stomach as he climbed behind the wheel. After quickly glancing in his rearview mirror to make sure that his passengers were properly concealed, Reese started the engine, and cautiously headed the car toward Selma and safety. He recalls the apprehension that settled over him like a cloak that night as he drove. In fact, Reese was so fearful that he drove without headlights until he was sure they were not being followed. A short time after their escape, a good Samaritan in Camden volunteered to retrieve the ministers' car from in front of the hotel. The man carefully looked around before climbing into the driver's seat. When he turned the key in the ignition, the car refused to start. The man got out and raised the hood. It did not take him long to diagnose the problem: the wires had been pulled off the distributor cap. After reconnecting the wires, he drove the car out of Camden. A cold shiver of fear traveled down his spine as he realized that had the ministers tried to escape in their car that night, they would have been sitting ducks.

Through the summer of 1964, after the attack on the ministers, the anger and suspicion of Wilcox County's white residents seemed to blossom into full-blown paranoia. An important part of the motivation for such a drastic white reaction was an ongoing federal inquiry into the county's voter registration procedures. In fact, as early as 1958 the U.S. Civil Rights Commission had attempted to examine Wilcox County's voter registration records after they received complaints from black residents who had not been allowed to register to vote. County officials moved quickly to convene a grand jury, and then to place the records in the custody of that grand jury, which refused to give the Civil Rights Commission access to those records. Over the next few years, the records were passed from one grand jury to another, and as late as 1961, attorneys from the Civil Rights Commission were still trying to gain access to them.[60] In the meantime, white Wilcox residents received still another political shock: their representation in the state legislature was reduced as a result of the state legislature's new redistricting plan. The *Wilcox Progressive Era* reported the bad news: "Wilcox County will lose one representative and divide its senator with Monroe County."[61] In the wake of these developments, many white residents became convinced that the political influence they had always enjoyed in state and national politics was waning. They had already lost enough influence, many reasoned; they simply would not allow their black neighbors to vote because this would only further erode what was left of white political power in their county.

Then, when they looked next door to neighboring Mississippi later that summer of 1964, white Wilcox residents saw developments that truly confirmed their worst nightmare: that summer of 1964, Freedom Summer, marked the occasion of the biggest and most public black voter registration effort yet. By bringing hundreds of outsiders into the state to dramatize the fact of black disfranchisement, the civil rights groups that participated in Freedom Summer succeeded in shining a spotlight on black powerlessness that made many white Alabamans distinctly uncomfortable. It was against this background of hardened white resolve and heightened federal attention that the WCCPL continued its quiet organizing efforts through the summer and into the fall of 1964. Throughout this time, a few brave black souls made periodic visits to the courthouse to attempt to register. But, by the end of that year, developments outside the county would finally provide the catalyst for a series of dramatic confrontations over the issue of black voting right there in downtown Camden, in front of their own county courthouse.

The fate of Wilcox County's developing registration drive was directly affected by decisions made in Atlanta at the headquarters of SCLC. In the aftermath of Freedom Summer, some in SCLC began to advocate a major voting rights drive in the Alabama Black Belt. They reasoned that while the publicity generated by the Mississippi voting rights campaign was still fresh in peoples' minds, they should continue to dramatize the persistence of black political powerlessness. These activists were convinced that the Alabama Black Belt would provide just the right backdrop for their efforts. It had all the right ingredients: recalcitrant racism, black poverty, and a spark of black resistance. By late 1964, the organization dispatched C. T. Vivian, SCLC's director of affiliates and a member of Dr. King's inner circle, to Selma to evaluate the situation.[62] The group had decided that their effort would be centered in Selma for the same reasons that SNCC had chosen the town as the headquarters for its Alabama Project some months before: It was the largest town in the region, it had black attorneys who were willing to work with the movement, and it already had a thriving local movement. Yet, even though this SCLC initiative was headquartered in Selma, it was not limited to Selma and Dallas County. On the contrary, as things began to heat up, activists spent a great deal of their time venturing out into the surrounding counties to support the growing voter registration campaigns in those areas.

By January and February of 1965, the growing momentum of the voter registration campaign in Selma resulted in a series of dramatic confrontations between Dallas County sheriff Jim Clark and civil rights activists on the steps of the Dallas County Courthouse. These very public confrontations generated widespread publicity. Furthermore, by early February of 1965 Dr. Martin Luther King Jr. began to make regular visits to the region to attend rallies. It was in this atmosphere that Wilcox County's voter registration efforts reached a crescendo. Mass meetings were held in a number of churches, most notably Antioch Baptist Church near the Camden business district and Pleasant Grove Baptist Church in Gee's Bend, and demonstrators began a series of marches to the courthouse, demanding the right to vote. Paulette Pettway vividly remembers the night that Andrew Young spoke at a mass meeting at Pleasant Grove Church. She also remembers that her father regularly took her to mass meetings. She was expected to sit quietly and listen.[63] But it was very difficult for most in attendance simply to sit still and listen. The inspirational words of the speakers and the sheer power of the civil rights songs never failed to generate shouts of affirmation and approval from the audience. In mid-February in the midst of their enthusiasm, local activists got the thrill of their lives when Dr. Martin Luther King Jr. visited Camden and spoke at a voting rights rally. He addressed his audience from high atop a raised platform that had been built just for the occasion on the Camden Academy campus. The scene was almost surreal. Those who were familiar with Camden Academy's history could almost imagine the Presbyterian missionaries standing beside King on the platform and nodding their approval. Many standing in the crowd that day had goose bumps as they listened to Dr. King's musical and eloquent speech encouraging them to continue the struggle. It was hard for them to believe that this famous man was actually standing in front of them and speaking to them. A little later, Dr. King joined the marchers as they walked to the courthouse.[64]

Waiting for the marchers and their famous leader that day was none other than Wilcox County's sheriff Lummie Jenkins. Jenkins stopped the group just as they reached the courthouse door. The eloquent preacher politely addressed the sheriff. He asked Jenkins if he would vouch for any of the African American Wilcox residents who had come with him to register to vote. King asked that question because at that time, state law required that anyone wishing to register had to have a registered voter to vouch for them. King's request seemed to catch the sheriff by surprise. Jenkins shifted his weight as he thought about how to answer the minister's question. Finally, the sheriff cleared his throat and said, "They don't allow me to . . . it's not my work. The voucher can't be in politics." Jenkins went on to advise King, "Get anybody who's willing and is not in politics."[65] King politely thanked Jenkins for his advice.

Barely two weeks later, on March 2, local black residents staged another voter registration demonstration. About fifty people participated in that march led by John Lewis, chairman of SNCC. Before the marchers got very far, Sheriff Lummie Jenkins and Camden mayor F. R. Albritton blocked the demonstrators' path. "Go on home," both the mayor and the sheriff ordered. As the demonstrators and the authorities stood glaring at each other, some of the marchers began to kneel, right where they were in front of the offices of the *Wilcox Progressive Era*. Jenkins and Albritton watched helplessly as the other demonstrators followed suit and fell to their knees. Then, everyone began to sing the movement anthem, "We Shall Overcome." Finally, the demonstrators all stood up again, but their path to the courthouse was still blocked by the mayor and the sheriff. After a short pause, Lewis turned the group around and they retraced their steps. There would be another day, Lewis soothed, as he and the marchers walked back toward Antioch Baptist Church.[66] Coincidentally, this march in Camden was held on the same day that funeral services for Jimmie Lee Jackson were conducted. Jackson had been killed just days before when he was shot in the stomach by an Alabama State Trooper during a night march in neighboring Perry County.

The very next day after the aborted march, Wilcox County protesters were marching again. They came in two waves on that Friday. The first group marched in the morning, but a group of armed police on the outskirts of Camden blocked their way before they could get very far. They dispersed. Later, after lunch, the group of demonstrators reorganized, and about 150 began marching toward the courthouse again. Camden Mayor Albritton and eight helmeted and armed policemen stopped this later group of marchers, but this time they refused to disperse. Instead, they knelt down and prayed by the side of the road. It was a chilly March afternoon, and there was a brisk north wind blowing. Many in the group pulled up their collars and huddled down in their coats as the wind blew over them. But the cold wind could not cool the heat of their commitment. After praying for a while, the group began singing freedom songs. "Ain't gonna let nobody turn me round; turn me round; turn me round. Ain't gonna let nobody turn me round. Gonna keep on a' walkin'; keep on a' talkin'; marchin' up to freedom land." Verse after verse they sang. Finally, after an hour and a half of kneeling and singing in the cold, the group began to disperse. Yet, even though Albritton and his policemen had succeeded in stopping the demonstrators, they were profoundly disturbed by the commitment that these activists had shown. Furthermore, they were even more alarmed by the apparent lack of fear coming from some of the group. The press reported, "When they left in the late afternoon, many of the teenagers in the Negro group waved and shouted, 'Goodby, goodby,' to the officers. The police did not answer."[67]

The demonstrations in Camden were accompanied by similar demonstrations in other parts of the Alabama Black Belt. Such widespread unrest prompted both of the state's senators, John Sparkman and Lister Hill, along with Armistead Selden, one of Alabama's representatives in the U.S. House of Representatives, to ask President Lyndon Johnson to discourage voting rights demonstrations in their state. They insisted that "voting registration in Alabama is being conducted under the law but is being impeded in areas where demonstrations and 'outside agitators are being employed.'"[68] After defending their state's registration practices, the Alabama lawmakers went on to implore the president to let the state handle its own affairs without federal intervention. They argued, "voter registration can be effectively accomplished under prevailing state and federal laws without further federal legislation."[69] Within two days of their talk with the president, the Alabama legislators' arguments rang hollow when pictures of the bloody confrontation on the Edmund Pettus Bridge in Selma that came to be known as Bloody Sunday were beamed around the country and around the world. In the aftermath of that very public confrontation, calls for a federal voting rights bill increased.

Activists working for voter registration were encouraged as the nation focused its attention on the Selma-to-Montgomery march that unfolded in the days after the initial clash at the foot of the bridge on Bloody Sunday. Indeed, some black Wilcox County residents were so moved by events in Dallas County that they actually participated in the march to Montgomery. Yet, while some marched to the state capital to dramatize the fact of their disfranchisement, demonstrations in Wilcox County continued without a break. In one of those demonstrations Monroe Pettway remembers that the route of the march passed right by Sheriff Lummie Jenkins's house. The sheriff was not at home that day, but his wife was. As the marchers drew even with the Jenkins home, the sheriff's wife ran out onto the porch, screaming at the demonstrators at the top of her lungs. The anger in her voice gave her words a strident quality as she yelled at the demonstrators, "Y'all better go on home, Mr. Lummie's gonna kick y'all's ass." Pettway clearly recalls the look of frustration on Mrs. Jenkins's face when the demonstrators ignored her warning, and actually laughed in her face as they kept marching straight to the courthouse.[70]

When the group reached the town square, Jenkins and several armed deputies stepped up to block their way. Pettway was at the head of the column of marchers. The short, wiry farmer drew himself up to his full height and strode right up to the sheriff. Jenkins glared at Pettway, and everyone on both sides held their breath as they waited to see who would make the next move. They did not have to wait long, because after a few seconds, Pettway started speaking in a dead calm, but authoritative voice. "I've been to Germany, fought for this country during World War II." The little farmer's steady gaze remained on the sheriff's angry face as he continued, "I saw dead men from our side laying on the banks of the Rhine River. I promised God I wouldn't smoke or drink or gamble while I was over there, and he brought me back in one piece." Monroe Pettway paused before he concluded his speech, his eyes seemed to grow dark with anger, the cadence of his words slowed perceptibly, and the tone of his voice seemed to drop an octave. He looked deep into the sheriff's eyes as he declared, "DAMMIT; I'VE EARNED THE RIGHT TO VOTE."[71] Those standing behind Pettway silently cheered him on, all the while keeping their faces impassive.

Through the rest of the spring and summer of 1965, scores of black Wilcox residents attended the citizenship classes begun by SCLC's Daniel Harrell, and eager activists continued their regular demonstrations at the courthouse. Among the most enthusiastic participants in those voter registration demonstrations were some of the county's black children. In fact, some of these students became so heavily involved that they began to boycott classes. A very large proportion of the students involved were enrolled at Camden Academy, and one of those students, Pat Kemmons Pettway, remembers how excited she and her classmates were about getting the chance to participate in the marches. Outside civil rights workers coming into the county noticed the eagerness of these young people right away, and at the same time, these young Alabamans were mesmerized by the bold activists. Pettway recalls, "They were like a revolutionary army." She continues, "And they were willing to die for a cause. We hadn't seen that . . . you just don't know. To come here and to say the things they said. They didn't have to say, 'I'm willing to die for this cause.' Their presence said that."[72] The encouragement of such committed activists galvanized the students. It put an extra spring in their step as they marched, and an extra lilt in their voices as they sang freedom songs. The inspiration provided by the energetic outsiders helped many of these young freedom fighters to reach deep inside themselves and discover a courage that many did not even know they had.

Reverend Charlie Pettway remembers a dramatic demonstration of that courage by one of his classmates. The march that day started just like all the others had. Students assembled at Antioch Baptist Church, and then the column of marchers moved off in the direction of the courthouse, singing freedom songs and clapping. But, on this day, the students did not get very far before they were confronted by a line of Alabama State Troopers who were blocking their path. Despite this show of force, there was a determination that emanated from the group that angered the already edgy lawmen. One of the troopers, who was determined to halt the march's progress, stepped right up to a young girl who was in the front of the group. The defiance he saw in her face angered him, and in one swift motion he raised his double-barreled shotgun with both barrels cocked, and aimed it right between her eyes. Another Alabama trooper stationed right behind the trooper with the gun could barely control the snarling German Shepherd that was straining at the end of the leash he held in his right hand. The freedom song that the marchers had been singing died on everyone's lips as they watched the confrontation unfold between their classmate and the troopers.

After the briefest pause, the young girl spoke to the trooper in an even voice without so much as a trace of nervousness. She said, "You'll just have to pull the trigger." It was as if the quiet determination in the girl's voice reached out and pushed the trooper. He blinked his eyes a few times in rapid succession, and then he quietly stepped aside. The other troopers just stood there watching in befuddled silence.[73] All this student enthusiasm was sustained at fever pitch despite an increasing aura of confusion swirling around the developing demonstrations. Gerald Olivari, a SNCC field worker assigned to Wilcox County, was convinced that much of the confusion was rooted in a split that he perceived between SNCC and SCLC workers. He explained, "The first time I noticed a definite split between SCLC and SNCC was a registration day in March. We took 117 people to the old jail house (where they were registering people) and Danny Harrell [SCLC staff] had called a march (which we didn't know about), to the courthouse itself and presented grievances—about 200 people participated." Olivari concluded in frustration, "The people were confused because of the split."[74] As the school boycott continued that spring of 1965 Olivari charged that interest in it began to wane because "there weren't concrete ideas behind it."[75]

Edith Ervin Brooks was a Wilcox County student during the boycott, and she agreed with Olivari's assessment. In 1965, she attended the Presbyterian school at Annemanie where her mother was a teacher and her father served as the principal, the basketball coach, and also as a teacher. Brooks vividly remembers the day that Ralph Eggleston, a Camden Academy student who became a boycott leader, came to her school to convince the students there to join the demonstrations. They were all sitting in class when Eggleston, a tall, well-built, confident young man who Brooks thought was arrogant, swept into her classroom and ordered the students to join the boycott. Brooks was horrified when her classmates immediately got up and followed the charismatic student outside. Her horror quickly turned to anger when Brooks walked outside and saw her classmates just milling around. In the center of the throng stood Ralph Eggleston. Edith Brooks found the scene very disconcerting be-cause in her estimation, "He acted as if he was God." She knew that she had to confront him, so she marched right up to him in the middle of all those stu-dents, and she declared in a firm and steady voice, "We're better off being here for now because leaving here is not going to do us any good at this particular time." She concluded, "Yeah, we'll march at the appropriate time, but you don't have anything planned for today."[76] Because he did not have any con-crete plans for his student recruits that day, Eggleston did not even try to ar-gue with Brooks. Instead, he got back in his car and drove away.

Despite such confusion, Camden Academy students continued to boycott classes and participate in the marches throughout the spring. The students were shocked and disappointed when they learned that the principal of their school, James Hobbs, was careful to keep the county's white school superin-tendent, William Jones, informed about their activities. At this point, even though the students were not attending classes, they routinely met at the school every morning before going on to the courthouse to demonstrate. One of those mornings, an incensed superintendent Jones decided to visit the school to put a stop to this student defiance once and for all. When Jones drove onto the campus that morning he was greeted by the sight of black stu-dents milling around in front of the classroom building. He quickly parked and got out of his car. The students noticed the white stranger on their cam-pus immediately, and a number of them realized he was the superintendent of their county's school system. An ominous tension settled over the campus as Jones stormed past the group of students on his way to the office. Many of the students brazenly stared at Superintendent Jones as he walked by. This obvious lack of deference enraged Jones, and by the time he reached the principal's office, his rage was threatening to overwhelm him. He immedi-ately screamed at Hobbs, demanding to know why the principal could not keep his students under control. Hobbs swallowed and blinked his eyes in rapid succession as he tried to compose himself. When the superintendent's tirade subsided, Hobbs timidly informed Jones that the ringleader was Cam-den Academy's student body president, Ralph Eggleston, the same student activist who had crossed swords with Edith Ervin Brooks when he had at-tempted to recruit protesters at Annemanie. The principal went on to reas-sure the superintendent that Eggleston was not a local boy; he was from California, and he had fallen under the spell of some of those outside civil rights workers. This seemed to calm Jones somewhat.

Superintendent Jones then demanded to see the troublesome student. Hobbs sent for him, and when the unsuspecting student body president ar-rived at the principal's office, the superintendent immediately began chas-

The Camden Academy's faculty, c. 1916. The school's principal, William Green Wilson, is second from left in the front row.

Camden Academy's baseball team, c. 1925. The principal's house is in the background.

Camden Academy's band, c. 1925.

Antioch Baptist Church, in Camden, Alabama, the scene of many mass meetings.

Farmer in Gee's Bend. Courtesy of the Birmingham Public Library.

Far right, Sheryl Threadgill. Middle, Larry Threadgill. Sheryl was one of the first black students to attempt to integrate Wilcox County High School. Larry was one of the leaders of the student boycott.

Brenda Bussey Carson, one of the leaders of the school desegregation struggle.

Wilcox Central High School. Photo by Charles Thompson.

1978 parade celebrating the election of the first black candidates to office. Left, Bobby Jo Johnson, wagon driver Levon Pettway. Right, Prince Arnold. Photo by Ralph Ervin.

Activist Presbyterian minister Thomas Threadgill at the National Guard Armory celebrating the election of the first African Americans to office in Wilcox County in 1978. Photo by Ralph Ervin.

Circuit judge Edgar Russell swearing in the first African American elected to the Wilcox County Commission in 1980. Left, Bobby Jo Johnson. Right, Percy Luke Hale. Photo by Ralph Ervin.

Group picture of Wilcox County's early black elected officials. The picture was taken in 1982. Front row, left to right: probate judge Reg Albritton; first black county coroner, Roman Pettway, county commissioner Eddie Beverly; first black circuit clerk, Willie Powell; Prince Arnold, sheriff. Back row, left to right: Bobby Jo Johnson, first African American elected county commissioner; county commissioner Charles Hayes; Percy Luke Hale, also elected to the county commission. Photo by Ralph Ervin.

Two of the founding members of the Wilcox County Civic and Progressive League, Rev. Lonnie Brown (left) and Mr. Monroe Pettway. Photo by Charles Thompson.

Artur Davis, freshman congressman from the seventh district in Alabama, which includes Wilcox County. Photo by Charles Thompson.

tising him. Eggleston squared his shoulders and gazed directly into the superintendent's eyes with a look of pure defiance as he proudly informed Jones that he had been encouraging his fellow students to boycott classes, and he intended to continue. Eggleston's defiant stance finally dissolved the last of what was left of the superintendent's self-control. Before anyone could react, the white superintendent drew back his hand and slapped Ralph hard across the face. The resounding sound of the slap seemed to echo off the walls of the principal's small office. Word spread rapidly to the group of students gathered outside. The tension that had settled over the students when the superintendent first arrived on campus immediately turned to outrage. When teachers inside the school heard the news, many promptly walked out to join the students. Soon the group vented its rage on Jones's car, turning it over. In the meantime, Jones and Hobbs remained in the principal's office, afraid to come out and face the angry crowd. Eventually, Hobbs called the police, and Sheriff Lummie Jenkins was only too happy to come on campus with a show of force to disperse the crowd.

Lawrence Parrish recalls that after this incident, Jones decided that he would try and "persuade" the teachers to help him reestablish his control. He promised the teachers that they would be allowed to keep their jobs if they did not participate in the demonstrations. Of course, teachers were left to conclude that if they did participate, they would be fired. Despite the superintendent's warnings, Parrish continued to participate in the marches. His activities did not go unnoticed, and soon after the Eggleston incident, Superintendent Jones summoned Lawrence Parrish to his office. He quickly expressed his disapproval of Parrish's activities, and he added, "You know your job is with the board of education; your first loyalty is to the board."[77] Undaunted, Parrish told Jones that there were some things that were more important than his job. The frustrated superintendent did not even bother to argue with Parrish, he simply ordered the defiant educator to leave his office. Once Parrish stepped outside, he breathed a sigh of relief. His relief was short-lived, however, because just a short time later, both Parrish and his wife, who was a teacher, were fired. Mrs. Parrish's dismissal added a strange twist to this tragic tale. Principal Hobbs dismissed Mrs. Parrish because he alleged that she brought a gun to school and tried to shoot him. Not surprisingly, this was considered grounds for dismissal. When the distraught Mrs. Parrish came home and told her husband what had happened, he was incredulous because he knew his wife was afraid of guns. In fact, some time before this when he had bought a gun for protection and brought it home to show her, his wife was so upset that she ran outside, jumped in the car, and drove all the way to Selma to tell her mother-in-law. Parrish quietly disposed of the gun.[78]

Despite the consequences, there were other black school employees who also participated in civil rights activities. One of those was Priscilla Charley Washington. Washington was a native of Wilcox County. Her family owned a small farm in Coy, and during her early years she attended Coy Elementary School. When she was a student there, J. E. Hobbs, who would later become the principal of Camden Academy, was the principal. Later, after Washington had grown up and left the county for a time, she returned to take a job as the registrar at Camden Academy. She soon met Johnnie Young, another single young black woman who worked at Camden Academy, and the two became fast friends. By 1965 after the boycott began, Albert Gordon, a Camden Academy teacher who was active in the WCCPL asked the two young women if they would be interested in participating in demonstrations. They readily agreed. A short time later, Reverend Thomas Threadgill, Camden Academy's chaplain, introduced the new converts to some SCLC workers. Unfortunately for the two young women, Principal Hobbs got wind of it, and the very next morning he summoned them into his office. The young registrar was shocked and disappointed when Hobbs told the two women that he did not want them to participate in the demonstrations. Priscilla had respected Hobbs since she was a child; but here he was saying things that were profoundly disappointing. She recalls, "He told us not to participate. . . . [He said] let them do whatever they want to do in Selma and other places, but he did not want them [civil rights workers] to come on the campus . . . cause he said he didn't want no mess." Priscilla looked at Hobbs sadly, and with tears in her eyes she said softly, "It's already a mess."[79]

Clearly, by 1965, Camden Academy had become the center of student participation in the voting rights demonstrations. Outside civil rights workers noticed and appreciated the energy and commitment of the Camden students. SNCC and SCLC staff spent a good deal of time and energy nurturing this student discontent, and they encouraged their young Camden Academy charges to go out and recruit student demonstrators from some of the other schools in the county. One of those recruiting trips set the stage for a showdown that painfully exposed a generational conflict that some of the county's young African Americans felt very keenly. The day of this particular recruiting trip in the spring of 1965, Pat Kemmons Pettway remembers that she was joined by two other students, Ebbie Williams and James Ephraim Jr. Coincidentally, both Pat and James Jr. had parents who were principals. Pat's mother was principal of Canton Bend Elementary School, and James Jr.'s father was the principal of Coy. The three student recruiters excitedly settled themselves in the car that afternoon for the drive to Pine Apple, where they had decided to go recruit. It was a warm spring day, and they rolled the windows down. The breeze felt good on their faces, and the girls did not even worry about the wind blowing their hair out of place. On the contrary, they did not have time to worry about such details because they were completely focused on the task ahead of them. On this important day, they had stepped outside their teenage lives and into the tradition of resistance that connected them to their ancestors. They knew they were doing a big thing today.

When they arrived at the school in Pine Apple, the principal was particularly surprised to see the children of two of his fellow principals, and displeased that they had chosen to recruit at his school. The nervous principal quickly called the white school superintendent to inform him that Mrs. Kemmons's daughter and Mr. Ephraim's son were at his school stirring up trouble. As the superintendent listened to the news, his face turned red, and then even more red. He promptly called Principal James Ephraim Sr. at Coy. He did not call Mrs. Kemmons only because her school did not have a phone. Consequently, he vented all his anger on Ephraim. The superintendent demanded to know why the principal could not control his son, and in none too subtle language, he warned the elder Ephraim of serious consequences. Later that afternoon when the three student recruiters returned to Camden, an agitated James Ephraim Sr. confronted them. As he looked at their eager young faces, his gaze softened, but he remained steadfastly determined to warn them about the consequences of their activities.

Principal James Ephraim Sr. could not forget how hard his family had struggled to provide him with educational opportunity. He would forever carry with him the vivid memory of his mother out in the fields in the early morning struggling along behind the mule-drawn plow all by herself while he and his siblings went off to school. As he grew to maturity, Ephraim was bound and determined to live up to his mother's expectations. He graduated from Tuskegee, and later when he joined the service, he faithfully saved his salary, and he was eventually able to buy part of the land on which he and his family had sharecropped. After completing his education, he returned to Wilcox County, began a career in teaching, and eventually became a principal. But as Ephraim Sr. looked at his son and the other two students standing in front of him that day, he realized that they had no idea how hard life had been for him, and how far he had come from his humble beginnings. He also feared that they did not fully appreciate the dire consequences that could result from their voter registration activities. He had lived with the deadly reality of white supremacy all his life, and he knew the lengths to which local white residents would go to preserve the county's racial status quo. As he puts it, "These are diehard [white] people here."[80]

When he opened his mouth to talk to his son and the other two students with him, all of these issues were swirling around in the elder Ephraim's head. He spoke to the young people in a soft voice, trying to explain his feelings. He warned them that their actions could "cause black people to lose everything they had." The younger Ephraim replied in an equally soft voice, "If you don't have the right to vote, you don't have anything."[81] Father and son stood motionless for just a moment longer, looking deep into each other's eyes, probing the depths of each other's understanding, and then the moment ended. As student participation in the demonstrations continued unchecked through the spring and summer months of 1965, black families all over Wilcox County were forced to confront the same issues that James Ephraim Sr. and James Ephraim Jr. confronted that day.

As the voting rights struggle gathered momentum, one black family after another was forced to contemplate the impact that movement participation was likely to have on their economic well-being. Camden Academy student Larry Threadgill remembers how some of his friends reacted. He explains that the eager and idealistic youngsters from sharecropping families were in a particularly vulnerable position. They were painfully aware that their involvement in the marches would undoubtedly put their family's economic well-being at risk because they could be evicted from the land at any time. Everyone knew that local plantation owners and law officers carefully scanned the crowds of marchers day after day hoping to identify participants who they could intimidate. Despite their vulnerability, however, Larry recalls that these young people were determined to march anyway, and many of them began to disguise their identity. They regularly came to marches wearing sunglasses, bandanas tied over the lower parts of their faces, and big, floppy straw hats. The disguised demonstrators clapped, sang, marched, and prayed along with everyone else. Larry and the other marchers noticed and sympathized with their disguised comrades, and local authorities noticed the disguised youngsters too, but they were frustrated and powerless to do anything about them. Camden Academy student Alicia Parrish Foster remembers one girl in particular who wanted to march so badly, but she was worried that this would ensure her family's eviction from the land where they were sharecroppers. This short, brown-skinned attractive student's name was Helen Hicks, and when she finally decided to risk the consequences, she showed up for a demonstration one day wearing a hat, sunglasses, and a scarf. Alicia vividly remembers that Helen was so excited that she just kept exclaiming, "I'm gonna march; I'm gonna march."[82]

In the midst of all the problematic issues just barely beneath the surface of the struggle, the students continued to boycott schools and demonstrate for voting rights through the spring and early summer of 1965. Most did not think about all the complicated undercurrents swirling around them. Instead, they demonstrated their youthful exuberance as they continued to march with a spring in their steps and sing with enthusiasm in their voices. Their spirit led some white observers to believe that they were too immature to understand fully the significance of their actions. White Wilcox resident Viola Liddell expressed the opinion of many of her white neighbors when she insisted that the young demonstrators "were said to have been enticed into playing hooky by 'outside agitators.' Many of them probably did not know why they were demonstrating, but they had a lot of fun after they were stopped before reaching the courthouse; they sang, they clapped hands, and made faces and stuck out their tongues at passing whites."[83] Liddell, like so many of her friends and neighbors, did not understand just how profoundly committed these young people were to bringing change to their county. Because there had been a number of highly publicized murders of civil rights activists by the time of these demonstrations, these young people fully realized what they were risking, but they also knew what was at stake. As one commented, "To be an organized black group of people trying to get the right to vote; trying to get the right to do anything . . . out of the status quo was saying *you were willing to die*."[84]

The efforts of local activists and civil rights organizers in the Black Belt finally paid off when President Lyndon Baines Johnson signed the historic Voting Rights Act of 1965 into law on August 6, 1965. African Americans all over the country rejoiced, but particularly in the Black Belt many were convinced that this would be the start of a new day. Immediately after the passage of the act, African Americans began to register in unprecedented numbers. In Wilcox County the registration of large numbers of black voters could very well result in revolutionary change because the county's population was 78 percent African American at that time. White residents openly expressed their fears for the future, and they could not help but reflect on that other time in their history when black voters had held the balance of power in their county: Reconstruction. At that time their ancestors had vowed *never again*. Yet, here they were almost one hundred years later, about to be visited by the ghosts of Reconstruction. They had just suffered the recent redistricting in their state that had resulted in a shift of political influence away from their agrarian Black Belt to the industrial districts and urban areas. Now the prospect of a further and overwhelming reduction in their status with the enfranchisement of the huge black majority in their midst was more than most white Wilcox residents could stand. Many vowed to do whatever they had to in order to prevent implementation of the new voting rights law.

In that unsettled atmosphere, white residents resisted in a variety of ways, and for some time, their resistance was very effective. One of those methods of resistance employed by white Wilcox residents was accomplished by manipulating the registration apparatus. Because the county's registrars remained all white in the days immediately following the passage of the voting rights act, the registration process was still totally under white control. Large numbers of the county's black residents complained to the federal government about the obstacles to registration they still faced. In fact, within days of the passage of the new law, the *Mobile Register* reported that "civil rights workers said they have drafted a 32-point complaint against the Wilcox County Board of Registrars, alleging non-compliance with the 1965 Voting Rights Act."[85] The federal government responded by agreeing to send federal registrars to the county. White Wilcox County officials were furious, and they responded immediately. According to the *Mobile Register*, "The chairmen of the Wilcox and Perry County boards of registrars said that they could see no reason for the assigning of federal voting examiners to their counties."[86]

However, Attorney General Nicholas Katzenbach and the Justice Department were convinced that there were plenty of reasons to send federal registrars into Wilcox and surrounding counties. He argued that although reports "indicate extensive and encouraging voluntary compliance with the new Voting Rights Act . . . such responsible compliance is neither uniform or complete." The attorney general went on to insist that the five counties most recently designated for federal supervision, Jefferson Davis and Jones, Mississippi; Ouachita Parish, Louisiana; and Perry and Wilcox, Alabama, "have continued to discriminate and have given no substantial indication that they will comply with it [the Voting Rights Act]." The attorney general concluded, "Consequently, I believe it is my responsibility under the new act to designate them as counties to which examiners should be sent." Katzenbach tried to reassure white residents that federal intervention would last only as long as necessary. As he put it, "When local officials demonstrate their willingness to deal fairly with Negro as well as white applicants, the examiners will be withdrawn promptly."[87]

Such assurances of prompt withdrawal were small comfort to white Wilcox residents. Most felt like their county was under siege. First the civil rights workers had come to stir up trouble, and now they were confronted by federal examiners telling them how to handle their Negroes. It was like the dark days of Reconstruction were happening all over again. The question uppermost in the minds of many was, How would it all end this time? After the end of Reconstruction, their ancestors had managed to regain control.

But, this was a new day and time, and many feared that the outcome would be different. The possibility of any real substantive change in their county's race relations was just too horrible to contemplate, and as a feeling of utter desperation settled over white Wilcox residents, their congressman, Jack Edwards, pleaded their case to the U.S. Attorney General. Speaking on the floor of the House of Representatives, Edwards "asked the Attorney General to use a sense of fairness, common sense, and reason in application of the voting rights law in Wilcox County." Edwards went on to complain bitterly about aggressive federal action that was bound to ensure the registration of large numbers of black Wilcox voters, many of whom were illiterate. He argued that "over-application of a stringent law . . . on the part of Federal officials . . . will work against the goals of the civil rights laws of 1964 and 1965." In Edwards's estimation, the actions of federal registrars were "vindictive." The congressman concluded by asking "that the Attorney General consider his actions in Wilcox County from the standpoint of how racial harmony is really achieved. I ask him what price he is prepared to pay, for the mass voting registration of illiterate [black] persons by Federal order."[88]

Undoubtedly, many white Wilcox residents noticed and appreciated their congressman's attempt to plead their case. However, in the aftermath of the passage of the Voting Rights Act, few of the county's white citizens expected the federal government to sympathize with their position. Consequently, white Wilcox residents resisted the effective implementation of the new act by doing everything they could to "persuade" their African American neighbors that becoming a registered voter was not in their best interests. Predictably, among the most vulnerable of Wilcox County's black residents were the thousands of sharecroppers who were landless, impoverished, and powerless. The landowners who employed these people threatened to fire them if they registered to vote, and it is important to note that when sharecroppers lost their jobs, they also lost their homes because most of them lived in houses owned by their employers. As more and more of these poor sharecroppers suffered eviction because of their determination to register to vote, members of the WCCPL felt obligated to help them. SNCC staffer Gerald Olivari observed, "They [WCCPL] wanted to buy land in Coy and build homes for the people thrown off the land, and also to encourage people out of work because of the movement by paying them to clear the land and build the homes."[89]

In the months after the passage of the Voting Rights Act the eviction of black tenants and sharecroppers continued unabated. Civil rights workers expressed concern that soon turned to alarm. In one report, a civil rights activist bluntly observed, "The economic intimidation has also increased as a direct result of people registering to vote. Therefore, in Lowndes, Wilcox, Bullock, and Greene counties those who have registered have been used as examples."[90] The report went on to explain, "The landowners on the larger plantations will come around to those who have registered to vote and, in front of the rest of the tenants, say 'We just can't use you anymore.' The others who are completely dependent on the land quickly get the message."[91] Despite such widespread use of economic intimidation, black Wilcox residents, including scores of landless farm laborers, refused to be dissuaded. Many paid dearly for their determination, and as black evictions reached epidemic proportions in the late fall of 1965, SCLC workers began collecting affidavits from black victims. The affidavits told heartrending tales of defiance and deprivation. For example, Mrs. Lizzie Miller had lived on the Henderson Plantation in Miller's Ferry for eighteen years when the demonstrations started. All of her children, with the exception of her oldest son, graduated from Miller's Ferry High School. She explained that her oldest son "left and went to Detroit, Mich. After he participated in demonstrations they no longer wanted him on the place."[92] A short time after Mrs. Miller's son was forced to leave, the mistress of the plantation asked Miller not to vote. She explained, "After I became a registered voter, one day Mrs. Sarah Henderson, Mr. Bain Henderson['s] Mother said to me, 'when time come to vote, you hide out and don't vote.'" Later, as the Christmas holidays approached, Lizzie Miller was looking forward to a visit from her eldest son, but she was told in no uncertain terms that her son "couldn't come on the place." She explained that "if he did I would have to move, so I am on my way because I will stay no place where my children can't stay."[93] Mrs. Mary Charley, a widow and a mother of thirteen children, had lived on Fred Sheffield's plantation for twenty-eight years when the demonstrations started. But, she reported, "I participated in demonstrations back in March 1965, we marched on a Monday and the following Friday I had to move."[94]

Still another black Wilcox resident, Leathia Foster, who lived on Don Henderson's plantation, complained about retaliation that affected him. He reported, "After I became a registered voter I was fired and I knew this is the only reason because he [Henderson] has a nurse maid who is not yet registered and he did not fire her." Foster went on to explain, "Everyone else I know who is registered and he [Henderson] found out about it[,] he made them move." Foster's circumstances became desperate after he was fired. He was a widower with seven children and an elderly mother to support. He lamented, "I do need some financial aid immediately." But when he tried to get federal assistance he discovered that the government would not help him or any of his neighbors as long as they continued to demonstrate for their freedom. He explained, "I have tried to get wellfare [sic] aid but was told at the time, they were not issuing checks as long as the civil rights marches were taken [sic] place."[95]

Thus, in the months immediately following the passage of the Voting Rights Act, regardless of the consequences, scores of Wilcox County's rural black residents proudly registered to vote. The statistics are very revealing. In July of 1965, just previous to the passage of the Voting Rights Act, some 3,135 white residents were registered to vote in Wilcox County; this number represented more than 100 percent of the 2,624 white residents of voting age living in the county. At the same time, only 280 of the 6,086 eligible black citizens in the county were registered to vote. That number represented only 4.6 percent of the black voting age population in the county at that time.[96] After the Voting Rights Act was signed into law, however, some 3,900 black county residents soon registered to vote. Even though this represented a dramatic improvement, this still left 42.7 percent of eligible black Wilcox residents unregistered.[97] Yet most remained hopeful, and they were at least cautiously optimistic about the impact their votes would have on the way their county was governed.

While black Wilcox residents knew that even with the new law on their side, change would not come easily, and most were still unprepared for the ferocity and tenacity of the white resistance that was in store for them. It seemed that nobody was safe: In addition to targeting landless powerless sharecroppers and tenant farmers, the county's white supporters of the racial status quo also attacked members of the black middle class, and, of course, the most vulnerable members of this economic class were those who taught in the public school system that was still under the control of the all-white school board. Lawrence Parrish and his wife were two of the first teachers to lose their jobs, but they were not the only ones. In fact, Parrish reports that before the demonstrations ended, sixteen teachers were fired by the board.[98] Eventually, after they filed suit, the court ordered the school to reinstate all sixteen teachers, and although the board complied it showed that it was still determined to punish these civil rights sympathizers. Board strategy was to assign these teachers to schools that were as far as possible from their homes, and in the cases where both spouses were teachers, husbands and wives were assigned to schools at opposite ends of the county. If the family did not own two cars, it was very difficult for both spouses to get to work on time. In that atmosphere Lawrence Parrish was convinced that the school board would make life difficult for him, and so he took a job selling real estate for a while. Parrish's daughter Alicia vividly remembers how the school board's treatment of her parents made her feel. She explains, "I was very upset, particularly, I think about my mother because she wasn't involved."[99]

Alicia Parrish Foster also recalls that while all of this was happening, she saw her father exhibit behavior that seemed to be totally out of character. She explains that her father was always a quiet, soft-spoken, and unassuming man. But one day as demonstrations were going on around them, and the school board was threatening him, Lawrence Parrish's frustrations finally bubbled over, and he violated his county's racial etiquette in a very public way. The stage was set when Alicia and her father were sitting in their family car parked on Broad Street in Camden's business district. Alicia sat in the back seat, and her father sat in the driver's seat. Mrs. Parrish had gone into one of the stores on Broad Street to make a purchase, and both her husband and her daughter had decided to stay in the car and wait for her after she assured them both that she would not be long. Father and daughter sat quietly, thinking about nothing in particular, but suddenly they both jumped at the sound of a white man tapping on the driver's window of their car. Before Parrish could finish turning around to confront the white man, he heard the disrespectful tone in the man's voice as he demanded, "Boy, let this lady in this space. Move that car on up so this lady can get in."

Parrish looked over his left shoulder to see a white woman motorist who was attempting to park her car behind his, but it was clear that she did not have enough space. Without even thinking about it, Parrish's resolve hardened, and he turned back around in his seat, and stared impassively out the windshield, refusing to respond to the white man's request. The white man was furious. The flames of his anger were fanned by the noisy voter registration demonstrations going on at the courthouse just a short distance away, and he was determined to assert his white authority. In an even louder voice he demanded, "Boy, did you hear me? Get that car on up there."[100] As the white man's voice became increasingly shrill, young Alicia unconsciously began to dig her nails into the armrest next to her. Just when it seemed that the tension had reached the breaking point, Lawrence Parrish, the quiet, unassuming educator, stunned his daughter, and the white man confronting him. He turned to face the white man, boldly locked gazes with him, and with his eyes blazing while he carefully enunciated each syllable, Parrish said, "Who in the hell do you think you're talking to?" Alicia's mouth flew open in amazement: she had never even heard her father curse before. In the meantime, the unidentified white man simply turned and walked away. Just a few minutes later, Mrs. Parrish came out of the store, climbed into the passenger seat, and Mr. Parrish turned the car around and drove home as though nothing had happened. As Alicia sat in the back seat lost in thought, her amazement began to turn to fear as she thought about the possibility that the white man might come and find them to exact his revenge for the racial slight he had suffered. She explains, "I didn't think it was over."[101] But the Parrish family never suffered any repercussions from the confrontation. Clearly, in the face of increasing black activism, the county's time-honored racial deference patterns could not withstand the strain.

Black Wilcox residents were not the only ones who had to contend with the angry reactions of the county's white residents. Predictably, white fury was also directed at some of the outside civil rights workers who had come into Wilcox County to help local black residents. For example, John Golden, an SCLC field worker, reported a frightening incident that occurred the night of October 30, 1965:

> At 10:00 P.M. October 30, on the outskirts of Camden, Alabama, I was chased by a pickup truck which was joined by another about one mile out of town. Having been followed by an unidentified car three weeks earlier, which had followed me through town twice and waited for me on the edge of town for nearly a half hour, I was certain that the two pickup trucks meant to shoot at me (I should say their occupants).[102]

To his dismay, Golden looked in his rearview mirror after he had driven several miles at breakneck speed, only to realize that the lead truck had flashing red lights just above its bumper. His pursuers were the police. Yet, the fact of their status provided the young civil rights worker little comfort: he knew that in this jurisdiction police officers were much more interested in preserving white supremacy than in upholding the law. As the adrenaline pumped through his body, John Golden clutched the steering wheel and consciously tried to steady his breathing. He carefully steered the car off the road, and both pickup trucks stopped behind him. According to Golden's account, he tried to explain his initial decision to flee, but the angry lawman who approached his car "said he wished someone had shot me." The lawman went on to add that he "would as soon kill me [Golden] as look at me." The angry lawman sneered at the young civil rights worker and challenged him to "report this to the mayor or [Attorney General] Katzenbach." Then, according to Golden, the lawman warned that "the FBI being on my side wouldn't help me when I was dead."[103] Finally, the deputy grabbed Golden, handcuffed him, and took him to jail. After spending the night in jail, the young civil rights worker was released only to discover that his car, which had been impounded by the police, had been vandalized.

The forces of white supremacy were not content with just harassing and intimidating a wide variety of individuals who were active in their county's voting rights struggle. On the contrary, by late 1965 they decided that the time had come to strike at one of the main institutions in their community that was supporting civil rights activities. Their target was the Presbyterian school up on the hill, Camden Academy. For some time, many of Wilcox County's white residents had grumbled about the school's open support of outside civil rights workers and their activities. Things came to a head early in the summer of 1965 when Wilcox County's sheriff, the county's school superintendent, and the mayor of Camden all went on campus and confronted Reverend Thomas Threadgill, the school's resident pastor. County officials had been aware for some time that Threadgill had taken a leading role in helping to organize the movement. Furthermore, the fiery minister also participated in demonstrations and arranged to house civil rights workers on the campus.

The three local officials confronting the activist pastor that summer day in 1965 thought that it was time they exerted their authority over the Presbyterian school and its uppity minister: they demanded that Threadgill file a trespassing complaint against the outside civil rights workers who had been living in the dorms and using the school's chapel. They threatened that the school would be subject to dire consequences unless Threadgill cooperated. Reverend Thomas Threadgill was furious: he glared at the three white intruders, flatly refused their request, and sent them packing. The white officials were incensed. After this confrontation, white anger at the uppity black Presbyterian school on the hill and its resident pastor continued to grow throughout the long hot summer as the demonstrations at the courthouse continued. Finally, by August, just before school was scheduled to start, the Wilcox County School Board was convinced that the time had come to act: they instituted legal proceedings to condemn Camden Academy. They succeeded. By December of 1965, the school board agreed to pay the Presbyterian Church $40,000 for the campus, which included forty acres of land, all of the school buildings, and the parsonage where Reverend Threadgill and his family lived.

Anyone who wondered about the county's true motive for seizing the Presbyterian school on the hill soon learned the truth: almost before the ink was dry on the deed, county officials gleefully took action against the militant Thomas Threadgill. On December 23, 1965, Wilcox County's school superintendent sent a letter to Threadgill informing him that he and his family would have to vacate their house on the Camden Academy campus by January 1, 1966. Only the Threadgill family and the outside civil rights workers who had been staying in the school's dormitories were evicted. Everyone else was allowed to stay, at least for the time being. Ironically, when the eviction notice arrived at the parsonage, Thomas Threadgill was not even home. He had become ill some time before this, and he was hospitalized at the Veteran's Administration Hospital in Tuskegee.[104] As soon as the letter arrived at his house, however, the sick minister received a frantic phone call from his wife. He immediately checked himself out of the hospital and returned to his family.[105] It was just two days before Christmas, and nobody could believe this was happening. The Threadgill children were devastated and frightened. They had always felt so safe in their house on the Camden Academy campus. But in an instant, that short, terse letter from the county school superintendent had shattered their sense of security. Their house was all decorated for the holidays, but the children scarcely seemed to notice as they worried about what would become of them. Threadgill's young son, Larry, clearly remembers the fear that gripped him after his family received the eviction notice. He explains, "That was more scary than marching [in demonstrations], because I remember thinking, we're going to be homeless, and I don't want to be homeless."[106]

As soon as their father walked through the front door, both Sheryl, who was thirteen years old, and her brother Larry, who was only eleven, recall that they were instantly flooded by a sense of relief. Their daddy had always taken care of everything, and they never doubted for a minute that he would make things better this time too. Yet, even though Larry was relieved, his young mind still struggled to make sense of his family's eviction, and he was left to wonder, "What did we do to deserve this?"[107] As his family pondered their circumstances, Thomas Threadgill immediately set about making arrangements to move his family out of their home. Initially, the Threadgills moved into a house in Miller's Ferry. They stayed there for almost a year, and during much of that time, the parsonage from which they had been evicted remained vacant. The Threadgill children continued to attend Camden Academy even after they had been evicted, and every time they passed the empty parsonage on campus, it bore silent witness to the county's determination to silence their outspoken father. Later, one of Camden's African American citizens, Nathaniel Hill, offered the Threadgills a half acre lot in Camden. Reverend Threadgill gratefully accepted, and over the next several months, the determined minister built a comfortable new house for his family.[108] Young Larry remembers how amazed he was when he realized his father, an ordained Presbyterian minister and civil rights activist, actually knew how to build a house. As far as twelve-year-old Larry Threadgill was concerned, his father was Superman. As he put it, "This man [his father] can do everything. He can build a house, he can preach . . . he can tell jokes, he can drive anything—a tractor, a truck, a car . . . any kind of stick shift."[109]

The determination with which Thomas Threadgill attacked the problem of providing a home for his family was the same determination that characterized everything he did, including his civil rights activism. He was clearly outspoken and unafraid. Not surprisingly, county officials carefully scrutinized the fiery pastor's activities. They knew that he was an ordained minister, and they could not understand how he could act the way he acted and say the things he said. It was hard for local white residents to believe that the militant pastor had been born among them. But, in fact, Thomas Threadgill had been born in Wilcox County in 1926. He was one of five children born on the family farm in Annemanie. Even though the Threadgill family owned their own land, they still had to work hard to make ends meet. Yet, older brother Willie recalls a secure childhood: They always had enough to eat, and their parents made sure that all the children attended school regularly. The enterprising Threadgill children made their own toys. They were particularly fond of using an old board to slide down a hill covered with pine needles, and they also enjoyed regular dips in the local swimming holes.[110]

As the Threadgill children grew, they spent a lot of time in their safe close-knit community. But, when they did venture out, they were sometimes stung by the ugly racism that confronted them. Thomas's older brother Willie clearly recalls that if they were walking on the side of the road when the white school bus passed by, the bus driver would often veer off the road in their direction as if he meant to hit them. As the bus got closer, the white children would lean out the windows to call them names and throw rocks. Willie Threadgill still recalls how much this bothered him initially. He would run home and rush breathlessly into his house with the laughter and taunts of the white schoolchildren still ringing in his ears. His parents' calm demeanor would always still his anxieties. The elder Threadgill remembers that his younger brother Thomas was also calmed by his parents' reassurances, but he also remembers that there was a restlessness in young Thomas, a refusal to accept the racial injustice that was all around him.[111]

While the family tried as much as possible to shield their children from the ugly racial realities of their county, their father, Obediah, would make sure that they understood their county's racial past. He would sometimes share the stories of slavery in Wilcox County that had been passed down to him by his grandparents. The Threadgill children would sit in rapt attention as their father described heartrending scenes of separation and loss. There was one scene the elder Threadgill described that was particularly poignant. That scene involved his grandmother, who had been born in slavery and was only a young mother when her master decided to sell her twin daughters. The girls were loaded into a wagon, and as their hysterical mother clung desperately to the sides, it began to pull away. The driver touched his whip to the horses, and they picked up the pace, but the slave mother ran alongside for a few strides, refusing to let go. Finally, the pace proved to be too much for her. Her heaving chest felt like it was on fire, her aching fingers could not hold on anymore, and she collapsed in a heap right in the middle of the dirt road as a high-pitched cry of grief and frustration escaped her tired lungs. The Threadgill children could almost feel the frustration of their great-grandmother as their father finished his account. But in the same breath, the elder Threadgill, who was a very gentle man, would reassure his children that God was a forgiving God, and they must learn to forgive the sins of the past too. As young Thomas sat there with his brothers and sisters absorbing these images of the past, he would often frown in concentration. The images of his ancestors in slavery filled his young mind, and he tried to forgive the sins of the past. But, even as a child, young Thomas Threadgill was motivated by a keen sense of fairness that quickly turned to moral outrage if it was violated. And, in young Thomas's mind, the forced separation of his great-grandmother from her children was the ultimate violation. Years later, a mature Reverend Thomas Threadgill fondly admitted that his father was "more forgiving in things like that than I am." The minister went on to explain, "It makes my blood boil, and while I know that there are things that we need to forget, there are things that I hope you ask me never to forget." He continued, his voice rising slightly, "Don't ever ask me to forget how they sold my great-grandmother and her sisters. . . . There is no justification anywhere to treat a human being like that."[112]

After finishing Arlington Literary and Industrial Institute, one of the Presbyterian high schools in the county, young Thomas Threadgill enrolled in Morehouse College in Atlanta. All-male Morehouse was one of the most prestigious black colleges in the country, and it counted among its alumni some of the most notable black men in America, including Dr. Martin Luther King Jr. After completing his undergraduate work, Threadgill went on to complete a masters of theology degree at Pittsburgh Theological Seminary. During World War II he served in the U.S. Army and saw combat in the Pacific theater.[113] Through all of his experiences, Thomas Threadgill never lost his passionate sense of fairness, and his commitment to justice: even his status as an ordained Presbyterian minister failed to alter his beliefs. In fact, Threadgill's understanding and interpretation of the Bible placed him squarely in the more militant camp of civil rights activists. As many around him were espousing the principles of nonviolence and advising demonstrators to turn the other cheek and love their enemies, the fiery Thomas Threadgill had other ideas. He explained, "There is nothing in the New Testament anywhere to suggest that a Christian is called upon to lie down and let other people trample over him. It was done, but nowhere in the New Testament does it recommend that, and I just can't subscribe to it." As he reflected on past racial injustices in his county, he added ominously, "I can't forget."[114] Local white residents were not sure what to think of such a militant preacher. At the same time, black residents who were fearful of white retaliation were sometimes vaguely uneasy in the presence of Thread-gill's uncompromising commitment to the crusade for social justice. Yet, even though he held such uncompromising beliefs, Reverend Thomas Threadgill was still widely known as a gentle and compassionate man. His children recall that people in the community often came seeking his help and advice in times of trouble. He never turned anyone away, and this some-times meant that he was not home very much: when he was not doing move-ment work, he was conducting weddings, preaching eulogies, visiting the sick, or helping neighbors and church members in the community with a whole host of problems.[115]

Through the fall of 1965 after the passage of the Voting Rights Act, Thread-gill advised black county residents to be vigilant. He was sure that the passage of the new law did not mean the end of their struggle. On the contrary, he and many others in the movement understood that they would have to continue their voter registration and education efforts if they were ever going to change the balance of power in their county. By December of 1965 in the wake of the school board's seizure of Camden Academy, any remaining doubts that black residents may have had about the determination of their white neighbors to re-sist change were put to rest. They realized that white residents were willing to use any means necessary to maintain their political hegemony in Wilcox County. The battle lines were drawn: black and white residents were now on a collision course that would have immediate and tragic consequences.

Things came to a head right after the Christmas holidays. The stage was set on January 23, 1966, scarcely three weeks into the new year. The place was Antioch Baptist Church, the staging area for so many of the voter regis-tration marches that had taken place during the chaotic spring and summer of the previous year. But, on this chilly January day, there was barely a hint of the anticipation that had marked those earlier gatherings of voter regis-tration demonstrators. Indeed, many of those now gathered at the church had been a part of those earlier mass meetings, clapping, singing, and prepar-ing to march on the courthouse. But on this gloomy January day, the people gathered at Antioch Baptist Church had come to attend a funeral. The gloominess of the day seemed to be magnified by the dark, conservative clothes worn by the mourners and by the somber expressions on their faces. The stark white paint of the little frame church provided a dramatic contrast to the dark mourners beginning to arrive. As little knots of mourners began to gather in front of the church, they spoke in hushed tones, but with just a hint of excitement in their voices. They were excited because they had come not only to attend the funeral of one of their neighbors, but also to have a voter education meeting after the service.

Within a few minutes some people began to enter the church while others were still driving up outside. One of those who pulled up in his car just then was David Colston. Colston, a local black resident who was a veteran of World War II and who had also participated in the recent marches and mass meetings, was driving a green, two-door 1963 Chevrolet Impala. He paused in front of the church with his car's smooth eight-cylinder engine idling quietly as he looked around for a parking space. While Colston was sitting in his car, some of the mourners who were still milling around on the sidewalk in front of the church looked up just in time to see a car driven by a white man come out of nowhere and plow into the back of Colston's Impala. As far as the onlookers could tell, the white motorist had hit Colston's car deliberately. The witnesses' amazement soon turned to horror when they saw what happened next. Before anyone could react, the white motorist, forty-six-year-old James T. Reaves, exited his car, calmly walked up to the green Impala, pulled out a .32 caliber pistol, and shot David Colston at close range in the head.[116] The sharp report of the gunshot seemed to freeze the action in front of the church for just a split second. The only movement was the collapse of David Colston's mortally wounded body, and the calm retreat of his assailant. As the onlookers gathered in front of the church recovered from their initial shock, the scene erupted in pandemonium. There were screams of outrage, cries for help, and calls for revenge. Reverend Thomas Threadgill was among those gathered at the church that day, and he expressed his feelings in no uncertain terms. Threadgill insisted in a grim tone, "This is very definitely a civil rights killing." He continued, "It's not against David Colston, but against the Negroes of Wilcox County."[117]

Black Wilcox residents were horrified, angry, and disillusioned in the wake of David Colston's murder. They had picketed and protested peacefully, and after the passage of the Voting Rights Act they had risked everything to register to vote. But still, their white neighbors refused to do the right thing and obey the law. Many were wondering what they should do now, and even what they could do now. Shortly after this when Dr. Martin Luther King Jr. stayed overnight at the Threadgill home, Reverend Thomas Threadgill could not restrain himself from expressing the pent-up anger and disillusionment that so many of his neighbors felt. Threadgill's son Larry vividly remembers the conversation he overheard between the two ministers that night. Larry explains that the men stayed up and talked into the wee hours of the morning. Often, their voices were so low pitched that the little boy had to strain to make out the words. But, at one point, young Larry heard unmistakable anger and agitation in his father's voice, and he could imagine the fierce light in his father's eyes as the elder Threadgill declared, "You know, Dr. King, we ought to just pick up guns, and just fight back." Larry could not believe his ears: he had never heard his father talk like this before. There was a long pause, and finally King replied in a soft, reassuring voice, "Reverend Threadgill, they're the ones with all the weapons. If we try to fight fire with fire, we'll be destroyed." King concluded, "We've got to do this nonviolently." Reverend Threadgill looked sadly at his famous houseguest and said, "I'm kind of mad right now, but I know you're right."[118] Despite King's reassurances, anger, fear, and disillusionment were the constant companions of black residents of Wilcox County in early 1966, and despite all the progress their movement had made, many were becoming increasingly doubtful that racial equality would ever be a fact of life in Wilcox County, Alabama.

CHAPTER SIX

∿

Ain't Gonna Study War No More: The Struggle to Desegregate Wilcox County's Schools

The winter of 1966 was particularly bleak for black citizens in Wilcox County. Just that previous fall, they had been so hopeful because President Johnson had signed the Voting Rights Act and the Justice Department had sent federal election supervisors to their county. At the time it had all seemed so miraculous. But now, as they desperately struggled to come to terms with the news of their neighbor's violent death, these recent political developments did not seem so miraculous after all. Instead, it was clearer than ever to black Wilcox residents that regardless of any federal intervention, the same white supremacists were still running their county. This painful reality became even more obvious to black residents when they learned that the sheriff refused to arrest James Reaves, the white farmer who many had seen shoot David Colston. Reaves had turned himself in right after the murder, but Sheriff Lummie Jenkins had sent him home. Reaves was never charged. News of the injustice traveled throughout the county very quickly and left black residents shaking their heads in disgust and complaining about business as usual.

One who was particularly shaken by Colston's murder was his son, David Jr. A shy boy who was an only child and the apple of his father's eye, young David could only wonder how he and his grieving mother could possibly go on with their lives. He remembers sadly that his father had been a man of few words, but there were those special times when David Colston Sr. would talk about his navy experiences during World War II. His young son would sit spellbound, trying to visualize the exotic Pacific locations his father described. But, more often, father and son just enjoyed each other's company with few words passing between them while they fished, played catch, or visited friends together. The elder Colston always advised his son to be honest and work hard, and he often took his little boy to church with him.

David Colston Jr. vividly recalls that his father warned him about white people. He explains, "We were taught to not ever take them lightly because they were capable of doing anything . . . for nothing. I mean you could just be gunned down for nothing."[1] Despite the warning, David Colston Jr. never imagined that his father would become a victim of his county's racial violence, and in the days and weeks after his father's murder, the little boy had trouble understanding how it could have happened. He recalls, "It was a shock. It was a hurtin' thing."[2] Young Colston's mother became very protective of him, and some of his friends offered him their support and sympathy. Colston explains that all this attention "spoiled me rotten. . . . I think they were too protective of me sometimes."[3] Yet, in spite of the best efforts of all of those around him, the pain of his father's death was never far from young David's consciousness. He was particularly frustrated by the refusal of county authorities to punish his father's murderer, and with each passing day, the injustice continued to gnaw at him until finally young David Colston decided that he had to act. As he puts it, "I remember . . . I said well . . . it's about time I got some justice myself." At the time, Colston had just graduated from high school. He explains, "So I went riding one evening with some friends." That evening was a typical Wilcox evening, warm and humid. David Colston Jr. was sweating, but it was not because of the heat and humidity. On the contrary, it was the anticipation of the act he was contemplating that made him sweat: he intended to go to Coy and confront the man who killed his father, once and for all. An involuntary shiver ran down Colston's spine as he reflected on the anger and frustration that had been gnawing at him for almost a decade. But, before the carload of teenagers reached Coy, cooler heads prevailed, and they decided to turn around. Yet, even though he never made it to Coy that night, David Colston Jr. still aches for justice for his father. He explains sadly, "Thirty years, sixty years, or even two hundred years is not too long for justice to be served."[4]

However, back in Wilcox County in 1966 young David and his mother were not the only ones trying to cope with the pain of David Colston Sr.'s murder. Their friends and neighbors were also struggling with their pain and outrage. At the same time, black residents were also being forced to confront the pain of the deep conflicts within their own community that had been slumbering inside segregation's restrictive walls for generations. In the midst of the upheavals of recent civil rights demonstrations, these conflicts had erupted with a ferocity that residents found most unsettling. One of these conflicts was rooted in class divisions. While it is clear that the majority of the county's black residents lived at or near the poverty line, everyone was aware that there were exceptions. In many instances, the black residents who were in salaried positions that were not dependent on agriculture were able to escape the poverty that ensnared so many of their neighbors. Of course, the overwhelming majority of salaried positions open to black Wilcox residents were in the field of education. Thus, as the movement in Wilcox County unfolded, many of the county's black teachers and principals found themselves caught between the security of their jobs and the advancement of their people, and the reaction of some only served to underscore black class divisions. On one hand, some were quite reluctant to support the movement, fearing retaliation from the county's white school officials. They were acutely aware that there were almost no other employment opportunities for college-educated African Americans in Wilcox County, and they knew that only the income from their teaching positions saved them from the desperate poverty that ensnared so many of their black neighbors. On the other hand, others were openly supportive regardless of the consequences. Interestingly enough, there were some instances when husbands and wives who both taught in the school system disagreed about movement participation, and this often led to tense times in the household.

For example, Alicia Parrish Foster, a Camden Academy student during these years, clearly recalls the disagreement of her parents, who were both educators. Her father, an outspoken supporter of the movement, was the principal of Camden Academy's Junior High School, while her mother, a teacher at the school, expressed reservations about movement participation. Foster explains, "There was . . . sort of a conflict in our household because my father was involved . . . but my mother wasn't. She was reluctant because of her job, and because she had some very good friends who were white."[5] Regardless of his wife's reluctance, Lawrence Parrish was determined to encourage his students to participate in the struggle. Parrish was a native of Wilcox County, and he had attended Camden Academy in the years leading up to World War II. After fighting in a segregated military during the war, Parrish returned to Alabama, finished his college training, and was hired as the principal at Canton Bend in 1948. By the time of the voting rights demonstrations, Parrish had moved on to become principal of Camden Academy's Junior High School. Lawrence Parrish soon found that his willingness to encourage the students to demonstrate put him at odds with his fellow administrator James Hobbs, who was principal of Camden Academy's Senior High School. Relations between the two men quickly became strained because Hobbs was an outspoken opponent of student participation in the voting rights marches. Parrish remembers one particular occasion when students boycotted classes. Hobbs tried, but was unable to prevent the boycott, and he was so upset by this challenge to his authority that he broke down and cried.

Indeed, many black Wilcox County students have fond memories of supportive teachers during the voting rights struggles. For example, Camden Academy student Pat Kemmons Pettway vividly remembers how supportive one of her teachers was. The teacher's name was Rudolph Cooper, and he taught shop class at Camden Academy. He was a short but powerfully built man who had a commanding voice with just a hint of a West Indian accent. Pettway recalls that on one occasion, Principal Hobbs ordered Cooper to corral as many students in the auditorium as he could in order to prevent them from going out to join the demonstrations. The shop teacher pretended to follow the principal's instructions. He made a great show of locking the auditorium's front door, but in a stage whisper that was loud enough for the students to hear he advised them, "Go to the side door; go to the side door." Cooper made sure that the side door was unlocked.[6]

Despite the support of sympathetic educators like Parrish and Cooper, however, there were a number of others who were not just reluctant; they were actually hostile to the movement, and Reverend Thomas Threadgill, the outspoken Presbyterian activist, criticized them in no uncertain terms. He insisted, "The black teachers and the black principal are doing pretty good with eight or nine thousand dollars a year, and they don't want to integrate. Now they're just like the white man—they don't bother about anything."[7] In such an atmosphere, black Wilcox residents became more sensitive than ever before about the economic and social rift within their community. Of course, they had recognized the presence of this division all along, but the existence of a segregated system that oppressed all black people, irrespective of class, had served to minimize the importance of such class distinctions within the black community. However, as people began to choose sides during the movement, those distinctions took on added significance. Black Camden native Alicia Parrish Foster vividly recalls that she was blissfully unaware of the economic inequities separating black residents in her county until the civil rights movement brought them into sharp focus. Both of her parents worked very hard to shield their young daughter from the harsh realities of life that were all around her. Alicia recalls an idyllic childhood. She lived with her family in faculty housing on the Camden Academy campus, and the school and church activities there were the center of young Alicia's world. In fact, when she was growing up in the years before the civil rights era, Alicia Parrish Foster had almost no impression of white people at all. She explains that she did understand "the separate part [but] that is the only impression that I had because I was very sheltered and very protected.

And my parents went the extra mile to keep me from any harm at all from the hands of the white people, whether real or imagined."[8] Likewise, young Alicia did not have the slightest idea that the majority of African Americans in her county continued to be mired down in an abject poverty that had afflicted their families for generations. During the movement, when the truth about life in Wilcox County finally dawned on her, Alicia Parrish Foster was amazed at the state of her own ignorance. She exclaims, "I lived in such a cocoon that I don't think I was aware, really."[9] With her dawning awareness came anger: Alicia was not angry at her parents for keeping this knowledge from her. Instead, she was angry about the very existence of such abject poverty and misery in her county.

Another conflict that was highlighted in the bright glare of the spotlight cast by the civil rights movement in Wilcox County was the racial divide that had shaped the lives of the county's residents for generations. Of course, everyone understood that white supremacy was the law of their land, and life had settled into a predictable rhythm over the years as Wilcox citizens accommodated their lives to their county's racial realities. Despite the apparent calm on the surface, however, black anger and resentment had never been far from the surface. Yet, in order to survive, black residents had always carefully kept their feelings in check, but when the civil rights movement came to their county, it was almost as if a dam burst. The black anger and resentment that had been swirling around beneath the surface for generations erupted, and scores of black citizens were emboldened to confront segregation head on in a way they had never done before. The county's white citizens looked on in disbelief as their previously peaceful "Negroes" defied white authority. Many of the county's white residents simply could not believe that their "Negroes" were doing this on their own. It must be those outside agitators causing this, they reasoned. In that white miscalculation were the seeds of the county's continued racial conflict: by refusing to acknowledge the existence of legitimate black discontent in their county, white citizens made it clear that they had no intention of treating their black neighbors any differently than they ever had.

Another conflict spotlighted by the movement was actually part of the movement itself. That conflict was rooted in the fundamental differences between the Student Nonviolent Coordinating Committee (SNCC) and the Southern Christian Leadership Conference (SCLC). By the spring of 1965 during the Selma campaign, SNCC members emphasized those differences in a very dramatic way when they invited Malcolm X to Selma during the voting rights campaign to address a mass meeting. Clearly, increasing numbers of SNCC members had begun to identify more closely with the uncompromising

militancy in Malcolm's tone than with the continued commitment to nonviolence that characterized SCLC's message. At the same time, as many in SNCC
became more class conscious, they became more critical of what they perceived
as SCLC's middle-class emphasis. One SNCC staffer who was assigned to
Wilcox County, Gerald Olivari, insisted that SCLC's middle-class emphasis
only served to circumscribe the organization's effectiveness because it meant
that they "didn't involve the mass of the people in the movement, i.e., instead
of just holding mass meetings, they should have gotten out, especially in the rural [areas], and talked to people and shared their problems."[10] Olivari's charges
clearly reflect the organizing philosophy held by many in SNCC by this time:
they wanted to be sure that they were reaching the most impoverished and dispossessed members of society, the ones who were least likely to come to mass
meetings. Olivari's frustration finally overwhelmed him, and he decided that he
had had enough. He knew he could not be content working only with the students and other black middle-class residents who had been drawn to the mass
meetings, so he announced, "I am definitely frustrated with the situation, and I
am quitting."[11] This serious organizational conflict was played out against the
background of Wilcox County's civil rights struggles.

In the meantime, some of the eager young fieldworkers in SNCC began
influencing Wilcox County's black youngsters in ways that some of their elders found quite disturbing. The most common complaint from black
Wilcox residents was that civil rights workers were teaching the county's
youth to be disrespectful. In fact, SNCC staffers were encouraging the
county's young people to challenge authority. These young activists were
convinced that black people had to break through the deferential behavior
patterns that had defined their lives in Wilcox County for generations before they could successfully challenge segregation. Regardless of their motives, many black Wilcox residents simply did not like the result of such
teaching. Principal James Ephraim Sr. was particularly alarmed by the impact of all of this on the attitudes of his students. He understood the appeal
of the outside civil rights workers to the county's black young people. It
seemed that these civil rights workers exuded a charisma that was practically irresistible. Yes, he had to admit that many of the things they said
made sense, but there was still something about these outsiders that made
him uneasy. In Ephraim's estimation, they were brash, aggressive, and disrespectful. He explains, "They weren't concerned about your feelings, they
wanted to make you angry."[12] Ephraim and his wife, a teacher, had discussed
the disrespect displayed by these outsiders many times, and he remembered
his wife's criticism of their behavior. She complained that these outside activists were systematically teaching disrespect to their young people. As she

put it, "They would teach the children don't [say] miss [to] anybody. Don't even say Mississippi."[13] James Ephraim Sr. simply could not understand how this could possibly help their cause.

Edith Ervin Brooks, a black Wilcox native, was also particularly troubled by this part of the SNCC philosophy. As far as she could tell, it had a devastating impact on the county's black young people. Brooks explains that before the movement, "boys, in particular, wore blue jeans . . . [but] not a single boy ever came to school with wrinkled or dirty blue jeans on. Those jeans were starched with a crease right down the middle. I mean, they took pride in that." But after the voting rights campaign drew so many outsiders into the area, things changed. Brooks observes, "All of a sudden, because these white folks from the North were wearing dirty jeans, rumpled clothes, [and] straggly hair, black kids began to wear dirty jeans." Brooks observes sadly, "That's the one thing that stands out for me. Values." In short, she concludes, "This is when the students then began to become rebellious and disregard authority."[14]

Edith Ervin Brooks has particularly painful memories of the movement's impact on her school and her community. Prior to the movement, she recalls, her parents had very cordial relations with Annemanie students and their parents. Indeed, many in the community really looked up to the Ervins because of the sacrifices they had made for their school over the years. Annemanie, like so many of the other black schools in the county, was chronically underfunded. Even though Edith's mother taught English at the school, she also functioned as the school's dietician, and on many occasions, Edith remembers, her mother would buy chicken and fish with her own money to supplement the meager provisions allotted to the school by the county. Furthermore, Edith's father, the school's principal, sold candy and showed movies in the school auditorium in order to raise money to construct a playground and a cement basketball court. When the first skirmishes in Wilcox County's voting rights struggle occurred, Brooks remembers that her father was very enthusiastic. In fact, he was prepared to "tutor parents in the community to help everybody to get ready." She continues, "[But] when the outside civil rights workers came, it became a different story. It was like them against us. It became so ugly, and it was disheartening."[15] Clearly, when SNCC workers encouraged students to stop deferring to authority in their county, many did not distinguish between the authority of the county's white racists and that of the black middle class. Thus, with this disruption of traditional deference patterns within the black community, the issue of economic class began to occupy increasing importance in the midst of Wilcox County's civil rights struggles.

Caught in the middle of all of these conflicts were the county's young people. They were getting a variety of mixed signals as their struggle unfolded. Civil rights workers were encouraging them to abandon the deference patterns that had been instilled in them from an early age, while many of their elders were encouraging them to remain true to their upbringing; some of their elders were encouraging them to work in the movement while others were not. It was all so confusing. Regardless of what anyone thought, however, these young people had come of age in a country that was optimistic about its ability to effect change. In the early 1960s, the idealism of the Kennedy administration's New Frontier heightened American expectations. Later, during the Johnson administration's Great Society, American optimism was sustained, at least for a while. These forces shaped youngsters in Wilcox County and throughout the country in some profound ways. "For these young people, the traditional constraints on blacks had lost their legality and their legitimacy. . . . They grew up with the sense that they were as good as whites and therefore were entitled to equality. . . . They refused to abide by the white South's stalling tactics designed to delay implementation of the *Brown* decision into a far distant future."[16]

In Wilcox County, some black youngsters who were in the midst of the voting rights struggle simultaneously began to articulate their dissatisfaction with their segregated school system. By this time the *Brown* decision had been in effect for over a decade, but nothing had changed in Wilcox County, so increasing numbers of students, teachers, and parents began to articulate increasingly forceful demands for change. In fact, members of the Wilcox County Teachers Association, a group of African American teachers, were so frustrated that they finally contacted the National Education Association (NEA) to request that they launch an investigation into the conditions in Wilcox County. The NEA complied.[17] The testimony of both students and teachers painted a dismal picture of conditions in the county's black schools. One witness explained,

> One reason for the low quality science classes is a simple lack of supplies and equipment. Row upon row of bottles, chemicals, flasks, crucibles and Bunsen burners greet a visitor to the science rooms at the white high schools. At the Negro schools, one sees a closet of five desk drawers that contain a dozen or so jars of chemicals (Boykin and Lower Peach Tree) and storage rooms with less than half the shelf space for chemicals as at the white schools (Camden Academy and Wilcox Training School).[18]

Inequities in science classes were just one part of the problem. In fact, NEA investigators uncovered inequities in every category they investigated from teacher–pupil ratio to availability of textbooks, and from transportation to toilets. As investigators concluded their study they were appalled to discover that conditions in black schools not only affected the quality of education received by the students, but they also affected the students' physical health. For example, severely overcrowded school buses posed a serious health hazard. There were often as many as eighty-seven black school children loaded on a bus designed to accommodate forty-five, and in 1965, teachers reported that thirty students had inhaled fumes on a bus that made them so sick that they required medical treatment.[19] NEA investigators also reported that the majority of the black schools in the county did not have indoor toilets. Instead, they had only outhouses, "most of them in miserably unsanitary condition." Furthermore, "in some schools, it was reported, there are no facilities even for washing hands."[20] When the NEA special committee confronted the former state superintendent of public instruction about the unsanitary conditions in the county's black schools, he glibly explained that, "Since so few of the [black] homes in the county have indoor toilet facilities . . . there would be resentment on the part of parents if the schools provide what the homes could not provide."[21]

The county's black students were tired of excuses, and many echoed the sentiments contained in the NEA report. Larry Nettles, a Camden Academy student at the time, recalls that "through the whole time there was a constant [refrain] that their school [Wilcox County High School, WCHS] was better. They had more educational tools; not so much that the teachers were better, but the . . . library was better, the facilities [were] better."[22] Brenda Bussey Carson, another Camden Academy student, recalls that she and some of her classmates noticed that white students had many amenities that were unavailable to black students. For example, Brenda and her friends were exposed to the weather anytime they walked from their classroom building to their cafeteria, but they knew that the white students had covered walkways that sheltered them when they walked between buildings. Furthermore, the Camden Academy students discovered that the lunch menu in their school was different from that in the white school. Carson explains that she and her classmates were served food like pork and beans and biscuits while the white students could choose from a menu that included more appealing dishes like spaghetti and strawberry shortcake.[23] Yet, while fellow student James Ephraim Jr. agrees with the assessment offered by his Camden Academy classmates, his explanation of their situation clearly exposes the ambivalence that so many of these black young people felt about the prospect of school integration. As Ephraim puts it, "My sense personally, I've never been about integration, because in all honesty, I always felt that we had good teachers. That was not the issue. The issue for me was facilities and equipment and things. It was never a thing of being around white folk."[24] While Ephraim was concerned about the inequality of facilities in general, he emphatically declares that there was one deficiency that he found particularly galling. He explains, "All I wanted was a gym." At that time, Camden Academy did not have a gym.[25]

During the spring and summer of 1965 a group of black Wilcox students applied for admission to the county's all-white schools. Even though eleven years had passed since the United States Supreme Court had ruled in the *Brown* case that segregated schools were unconstitutional, Wilcox County school officials quickly denied the black students' request. Ironically, that same summer a group of white students from neighboring Dallas County applied for admission to Wilcox schools after one of their schools had been closed. Wilcox officials quietly admitted them.[26] Paulette Pettway vividly recalls that during this time she and her father were among those who tested the school board's compliance to the *Brown* decision in the spring of 1965. This particular group targeted Camden High, the county's other white high school. When the black parents in the group attempted to enter the school to register their youngsters, they were met by a solid wall of mounted policemen and a small group of white bystanders. Out in front of the group was Lummie Jenkins, the Wilcox County sheriff, and behind him the edgy horses of his deputies pawed the ground and tossed their heads. Sheriff Jenkins looked directly at Monroe Pettway, and in the most authoritative voice that he could muster he ordered Pettway to tell his people to go back before somebody got hurt. The two men stood there glaring at each other as the horses' bits jingled and the policemen nervously fingered their billy clubs. Finally, after what seemed like an eternity, the wiry farmer ordered the rest of the demonstrators to turn back. The group complied, but they decided to return the next day.

The next morning, the same group of black students and their parents assembled at Antioch Baptist Church and marched to the school. The crowd confronting them was even bigger than the one that had been on hand the day before. Paulette recalls that this is the day when the situation turned ugly. Because news of the school demonstrations had spread, there were a few reporters in the crowd in front of the school on the second day when they returned. Paulette was a scared seventh grader, and when she saw the size of the crowd awaiting them, her fear threatened to overwhelm her. Everywhere she looked, it seemed that there were white people with hateful expressions on their faces screaming racial epithets at her. It felt like her legs had turned to rubber, and she felt herself slowing down as she walked toward the school with her father and the others. Then, time suddenly seemed to stop altogether as young Paulette watched a white man with a hatchet step out of the crowd. He held the hatchet high up above his head, and the sun glinted menacingly off its polished metal surface. In one smooth, swift motion, the man swung the hatchet directly at the head of a nearby news reporter. Paulette describes what happened next: "Blood just shot out. . . . It scared me so bad, I was just shaking, and they turned us around and told us to go back."[27] Some of the adults in the crowd were advising quietly, "Don't react," as they tried to keep everyone calm on their walk back to Antioch. By this time, Paulette remembers, she was practically trembling with fright. It seemed that it was taking forever to get back to the safety of the church, and just then, her uncle, Roman Pettway Jr., came up behind her and put his hand on her shoulder to reassure her, but it had the opposite effect. She explains, "I didn't know that was him, and he touched me, and it scared me so bad."[28] A short time later, Paulette's parents made the decision to send her to Mobile to attend school. In fact, they sent all of their children out of the county after this experience because it was clear that Wilcox County officials had no intention of addressing the deficiencies in their segregated school system any time soon.

By the late fall of that year, the defiance of the county's school officials came to the attention of the federal government, and in November of 1965, the Justice Department filed suit seeking the desegregation of Wilcox County Schools.[29] This set the stage for an ugly confrontation. No one would emerge unscathed from the protracted struggle that would soon follow. The Wilcox County Board of Education made the first move in January of 1966 when the superintendent threatened that the board might "have to" dismiss as many as twenty-four black teachers. Barely two months later, board members sent out a letter to all of the black parents in the county. The tone of the letter is quite revealing: it clearly demonstrated their expectation that black residents would continue to defer to white authority. Board members insisted that in "an effort to prevent the destruction of the school system of Wilcox County as we know it and realizing *what is best*, we are asking that you promote and encourage your children in the schools in which they are now attending" [emphasis added].[30]

As the letter continued, board members unequivocally articulated their position on the school integration that had been mandated by the federal government: "In our honest opinion, integration or desegregation is not good for education; it is against sound educational principles and works to the disadvantage and to the detriment of both races."[31] The stance of Wilcox school board officials on the question of school integration was completely in line with the sentiments expressed by white officials in other parts of the state. In fact, in May of 1966, members of Alabama's congressional delegation openly preached defiance when they "urged Alabama school officials to continue to resist the new federal school desegregation guidelines and requested districts that had already submitted compliance agreements to withdraw them."[32] Despite all the vocal white resistance, in August of 1966, a federal appeals court ordered Wilcox County to begin desegregating its public schools immediately.

The order handed down by the three-judge panel on August 30, 1966, left absolutely no room for compromise:

> IT IS FURTHER ORDERED, ADJUDGED AND DECREED that said persons [Wilcox County School Board] be and they hereby are required to adopt and put into effect for the 1966 fall term of school in Wilcox County, Alabama, a free-choice plan for the first, second, third, seventh, eighth and ninth grades in which all students in the affected grades will be afforded a reasonable time up to and including September 12, 1966, in which to exercise a free and unrestrained choice of schools they wish to attend.[33]

This order, which was issued just days before the fall term started, caused quite a stir all over the county. White residents realized that they could no longer keep black children out of their schools, while black residents realized that their moment of truth had finally arrived. The word spread rapidly through the black community that parents and children who were interested in helping to integrate their county's schools should meet at Antioch Baptist Church. One of those excited about the meeting was Sheryl Threadgill, the daughter of activist Presbyterian minister Thomas Threadgill. Sheryl remembers that when her parents discussed the prospect of their daughter becoming one of the first black children to attend WCHS, they did not expect that she would encounter any real trouble. However, just to be on the safe side, they decided that they would not allow their younger son Larry to go to the white school because they were afraid that his temperament might get him into trouble. But they were confident that Sheryl's calm demeanor would minimize the impact of any harassment she might encounter. Because Sheryl had grown up influenced by her father's commitment, she was excited about being one of the first black students to enroll in Wilcox County High School.

On a warm September evening, Sheryl Threadgill accompanied her father to Antioch Baptist Church to meet with other black students and their parents. As the anxious ninth grader walked into the church's familiar sanctuary, the scene of countless mass meetings during the recent voting rights campaign, her excitement froze, and she was hit by the first pang of uncertainty. There were only eight black students and their parents sitting nervously on the wooden pews. Where was everybody, she wondered. They had fought so long and hard to get to this point that Sheryl had expected the church to be full to overflowing. As the disappointed ninth grader took a seat next to her father, she was only half listening to the quiet discussion going on around her while she wondered what her experience at Wilcox County High would be like with so few black children to accompany her. Despite her misgivings, within days of the Antioch meeting, Sheryl and twenty other black students were officially admitted to Wilcox County's formerly all-white public schools.[34]

Sheryl vividly remembers her first day at WCHS. Her father went with her to school that morning, and he walked her to the school's auditorium where she officially registered for classes. She was very nervous, but not really apprehensive. Initially, it seemed that the people she met were cordial, and while Sheryl noticed that a lot of the white students stared at her, she had expected this. Things did not seem so bad after all, and gradually the butterflies in her stomach began to subside. Finally, the elder Threadgill bid his daughter goodbye after giving her money for lunch. As he left the building, Reverend Threadgill stole one last glance at his brave daughter, and then he was gone.[35] Sheryl Threadgill had never felt so alone in her whole life. She had always been surrounded by the love and support of her immediate family, and the care and concern of the teachers and students at Camden Academy. But on her first day at WCHS, Sheryl Threadgill felt like a foreigner. The sights, the sounds, and the feel of her new school were so alien to her that she might as well have been attending high school on the moon. As her father disappeared through the front door, Sheryl realized to her dismay that the butterflies in her stomach were quickly taking flight again. The nervous ninth grader paused for a moment, took a few deep breaths, and by sheer force of will focused all her attention on walking to her first class. The morning passed uneventfully, and when lunchtime came, Sheryl started out in the direction of the cafeteria. But, before she had gotten very far, she saw one of the other black students walking toward her. His name was Erskine Scott, and his class had been scheduled to eat lunch the period before Sheryl's. As the two students approached each other, Sheryl could scarcely believe her eyes: Erskine Scott's head and shoulders were dripping with chocolate milk. In a shaky voice, Scott explained that several male students had taken his lunch tray and thrown it on him.[36]

As she looked at the disheveled boy standing in front of her, Sheryl decided that she had better avoid the cafeteria, at least for now. She quickly retraced her steps, and on that first day of school, Sheryl Threadgill did not eat lunch at all. From then on she brought her lunch to school, but she still refused to go to the cafeteria. Instead, she stood in front of the principal's office where she felt relatively safe and ate her lunch. Sheryl ate her lunch in front of the principal's office every day for the whole school year: she never even saw the inside of the cafeteria. Yet, while her lunchtime strategy saved her from harassment in the cafeteria, Sheryl soon found that there were dangers lurking in other parts of the building that she could not avoid. Indeed, as the semester wore on, physical assaults became a routine part of Sheryl Threadgill's day: she does not remember a single day that whole year that she was not subjected to some form of physical attack.

As a student at Camden Academy, Sheryl Threadgill had always trusted and admired her teachers. But, as a student at WCHS, Sheryl quickly learned that many of her teachers supported and protected the white students who were harassing and attacking her and the other black children. In fact, some teachers actually turned their backs while black students were attacked in their classrooms. Sheryl has particularly vivid memories of the pain she felt in her back when one of her assailants caught her off guard one day and used all his strength to ram the desk behind her into the back of her chair.[37] The teacher sitting in the front of the classroom refused to intervene. Sheryl also recalls that white students often put chalk dust in her hair. It seemed that as the semester wore on, the level of harassment and intimidation escalated. The worst incident that Sheryl remembers occurred in her science class. One day after the teacher had passed back a test that the students had taken, she briefly left the room. While the teacher was absent, one of the white boys who regularly tormented Sheryl turned around and said in a hateful and menacing voice dripping with his southern Alabama accent, "Nigger, if you make more than me on this test, I'm gonna kill you." Something in the tone of his voice let Sheryl know that he meant it. As the reality of the threat sank in, the next few seconds seemed to pass in slow motion. She sat transfixed in horror, and her tormentor walked to Sheryl's desk, reached down, and turned her test paper over. At this point, Sheryl was only dimly aware of all the details of her surroundings: the other students, the teacher's empty desk, the beakers, and the Bunsen burners all faded to the indistinct edges of her consciousness. With the hulking bully standing over her, the frightened ninth grader, who had kept her eyes glued to her desk up to this point, risked a quick glance at her tormentor's face. What she saw made her blood run cold: it was clear by the look on the boy's face that Sheryl had made a better grade.[38] She flinched involuntarily as the bully's gaze shifted from the 88 percent marked in red on the top of her paper to her face. In that menacing look Sheryl saw the boy's unmistakable determination to make good on his threat.

Sheryl Threadgill was more frightened at that moment than she had ever been in her life.

After her science class ended and she was walking to her next class, Sheryl tried very hard to put the threat out of her mind. *If I can just get through the rest of the day, maybe everything will be alright,* she tried to reassure herself. But, before she had gotten very far, she noticed the bully running toward her. The adrenaline started pumping through her veins, and her whole body stiffened as Sheryl anticipated the attack that was sure to come. That was Sheryl Threadgill's last deliberate act: her assailant hit her so hard that he knocked her unconscious. After the attack, school officials called Reverend Threadgill and he rushed to the school. Sheryl's assailant was never punished, and to this day, she does not know what he used to hit her. Fortunately, young Sheryl suffered no permanent injury from the attack, and she soon resumed her studies at WCHS.[39] Her worried father observed, "She came home every day with a swollen lip or a bleeding nose. She was fifteen at the time. Boys hit her across the head with crutches. They tore her books and clothes and put chewing gum on her seat." Reverend Threadgill clearly recognized that his uncompromising activism made a bad situation even worse for his young daughter. He insisted bluntly, "Of course they knew she was my daughter. And I wasn't exactly the kind of nigger they wanted around. So they decided to take it out on her."[40]

Every morning as the black students prepared to step through the front door of WCHS, they felt almost as if they were stepping onto a battlefield. The only thing they were certain of as they walked through the school's front door was that they would not get through the day without being attacked. The only question was when and how. The NEA investigators observed, "All of the Negro high school students have stated that the butts of closed knives have been used as weapons against them. They have been hit in the nose and in the back by white male students using knife butts. Cigarette lighters have also been used against the Negro students as weapons with which to hit them."[41] It seemed to the black students that they were not safe anywhere in school, but clearly, some areas were more dangerous than others. One place where students were particularly vulnerable was in the restroom. NEA investigators wryly observed that because of their vulnerability "they [the black students] attempt to use the rest room during times when it is fairly empty which, during the day, poses a considerable problem."[42]

As the beatings continued, all the male black students left and went back to black schools. Before long only Sheryl Threadgill and Donna Gordon, an eighth grader, remained of the older children, but all the elementary students stayed because they were not brutalized as badly as the high school students.

In the midst of this tense atmosphere Threadgill recalls that there was one bright spot: Bonnie Mitchell, a white teacher who treated her fairly. Mitchell made it clear that she would not allow any of her students to be harassed, and Sheryl insists that this special teacher helped her to discover the joys of reading. Yet, despite Mitchell's support, facing the hostile atmosphere in school became increasingly difficult. It got to the point where Threadgill admits, "I didn't want to go to school," but somehow, she managed to continue going to school day after day that whole academic year, 1966–1967. She explains, "I guess it was because of what we had gone through to get there, and I would say to myself, if I could just make this year out."[43]

During their whole ordeal, the brave black students who attempted to integrate Wilcox County's public schools were never given any protection or help by any federal, state, or local police agency. Yet, in some of the more publicized school integration cases preceding this, such as the attempts to integrate Little Rock's Central High School, the University of Mississippi, and the New Orleans Public Schools, the federal government actually dispatched law enforcement officers to protect black students. Indeed, during the Little Rock crisis in 1957, President Eisenhower actually sent a battalion of the 101st Airborne division of the United States Army: the "Screaming Eagles" of the 101st were recognized as one of the most elite fighting forces in the world. However, the bruised and bloodied black students in rural Wilcox County, Alabama, received no such consideration. Instead, they were left all alone to cope with an exceedingly dangerous situation. Local law enforcement made absolutely no attempt to help the black students. For example, in one instance, a Camden policeman actually witnessed a white student administering a beating to one of the black students enrolled at Wilcox County High. The officer refused to intervene.[44]

When black students were not being brutalized or harassed, they were often subjected to what NEA investigators termed "in-school segregation." Such treatment only served to reinforce black students' feelings of isolation. Investigators described one particularly egregious example of this internal segregation that occurred during the homecoming festivities. They explained,

> The Special Committee was told of a homecoming day parade that was held during 1966–67. In order to maintain racial segregation among the spectators, the teachers in the high school locked the classroom door on the two Negro high school girls. They were required to remain there while the festivities were in progress—that is, until the father of one of them learned about it and came to the school, obtained the classroom door key, and took them home.[45]

Such treatment was not limited to the high school students. Third grader Dolores Ray described the pain that in-school segregation caused her:

> My mother sent me to the white school. People were talking about mixing up, and she thought I should try it for a while. But it didn't mix up well. I was in the third grade and sat in the back of the room. The teacher wasn't nice to me. I had to let my books stay in school, 'cause I was colored. So I did my assignments in the daytime. I got D's and F's.[46]

Such treatment deeply wounded the black third grader. She concluded sadly, "They acted like I wasn't there–like I was invisible."[47]

Finally, mercifully, the school year ended. When she woke up the first morning of her summer vacation, Sheryl Threadgill felt like a great weight had been lifted off her shoulders. She could go back to being just a normal teenager. However, Sheryl did not have long to savor the wonderful feeling of normalcy. It seemed that the precious weeks of summer just flew by, and before she knew it, the beginning of a new school year was looming. As she reflected on the unremitting harassment and brutality that she had suffered inside the walls of Wilcox County High School last year, Sheryl Threadgill knew that she could not go back. But, how could she tell her father, she fretted. She was, after all, Reverend Thomas Threadgill's daughter, and everyone expected a lot from her. As the last few days of summer flew by, Sheryl worried about how to approach her father. Then, just before school was scheduled to start, she finally found the right opportunity.

It was a leisurely afternoon, and her family had all gone to visit Sheryl's grandmother in Snow Hill. The Threadgill family was relaxed and happy, enjoying each other's company far from the concerns of the movement, but Sheryl could not relax. Instead, as the quiet conversation and gentle laughter swirled all around her, she could not get the image of WCHS out of her mind. During a lull in the conversation, a worried Sheryl pulled her father aside. The elder Threadgill could tell that his daughter had something on her mind, and he waited patiently for her to explain. Sheryl cleared her throat and looked sadly at her father as she began expressing her feelings about going back to Wilcox County High. As the anger, anxiety, and frustration that she had repressed all summer came to the surface, her words of explanation tumbled out with increasing rapidity. At the end of her soliloquy, the fiery pastor smiled knowingly at his young daughter and reassured her that she did not have to go back, and in the same breath he was sure to let her know how proud he was of her. Sheryl exhaled a huge sigh of relief. A short time after that conversation, Sheryl Threadgill stepped comfortably back into her old life at Camden Academy; the apprehension and anxiety from the previous school year quickly melted away.

As the fall term in 1967 approached, none of the black high school students who had attended the white high school the previous year returned. Instead, two new recruits, a young boy from Camden and a young girl from Coy, prepared to continue the struggle. The male student, Larry Nettles, had participated in some of the earlier voting rights marches. He remembers how exciting those demonstrations were, and he remembers the sense of camaraderie he felt as he marched with the other demonstrators and sang freedom songs. He explains, "There was singing, freedom songs . . . that was exciting . . . because some of the songs were very emotional and catchy . . . you found yourself walking around the house humming them."[48] And so it was with those freedom songs ringing in his ears and the excitement of the movement fresh in his mind that young Larry Nettles attended the first few strategy sessions as members of the black community planned their next assault on their county's segregated school system. Nettles observes, "I can remember a lot of excitement about it during the planning and preliminaries . . . there were quite a few parents that supported it, and [had] no problem with their kids going."[49] One of the major topics of discussion at those sessions was the question of defensive strategies. Students were advised to "stay in groups, [and] avoid being caught alone in certain parts of the building."[50]

Young Larry knew that his mother, Mattie Nettles, was very supportive of his desire to attend WCHS, and he was convinced that he also had the support of many in the black community. Those attending the strategy sessions had already decided that on the first day of school all the black students would meet at Antioch Baptist Church, and then they would go to school together. So on that first day Larry Nettles walked to the church. It was a warm, sunny day, and young Nettles, a husky, powerfully built youngster, had on a new shirt, new jeans, and new shoes. As he approached the church, butterflies began to fly around in his stomach, competing with the freedom song that kept going around in his head. "Ain't gonna let nobody turn me round, turn me round, turn me round"; the words echoed reassuringly in Larry's consciousness. When he arrived at the church, Nettles reached out, grasped the knob, pulled open the door to the sanctuary, and an audible gasp escaped his lips. He stopped short and just stood there staring uncomprehendingly at the empty sanctuary. He was thunderstruck: The civil rights song in his head stopped abruptly, and the butterflies flew away. They were replaced by a feeling of sheer, naked panic. On rubbery legs Larry Nettles entered the sanctuary, and he soon found that the room was not completely empty. Seated up near the front was a young girl from Coy. Larry did not know her, but she looked as scared and forlorn as Larry felt. The two made eye contact and exchanged a brief look of sympathy and understanding. Larry Nettles was sorely tempted to turn around and run out of the church all the way back to Camden Academy. But he knew in his heart that his strong-willed mother would never allow him to quit.

The two black students felt almost as if they were in a fog as they arrived at Wilcox County High School on that first day of class. Despite their fear, however, the atmosphere that greeted them was actually quite calm. Nettles explains, "At that time, I was very scared, not knowing what to expect." He continues, "It was frightening, but the principal was cordial."[51] The first day passed uneventfully; a number of the white students stared curiously at them, but nobody said anything. The two black students quickly registered for classes, and then they were separated because they were assigned to different homerooms. Nettles recalls that his homeroom teacher immediately put him at ease because she was "very nice." At the end of the first day, young Larry Nettles was pleased that he had actually gone through with it, but he was assailed with doubts about the wisdom of continuing his solitary stand. He remembers this moment in his life as a turning point. As he puts it, "At that time, my strong support for the movement in Camden was totally shattered . . . we [he and the young woman from Coy] both felt that we were hung out to dry. ABANDONED."[52] When Nettles went home and told his mother that there was only one other black student with him, his mother fixed him with the stern stare he knew so well and advised him, "You can't let that stop you." She did not say another word on the subject, and Larry knew that was the end of it.

As the days and weeks wore on, Larry Nettles settled into a familiar routine. He knew what to expect every day: stares, snickering, and taunts; but mostly Nettles was ignored. He was treated as a nonperson, and he quickly learned to disregard all of this as he concentrated on his studies. Indeed, Larry Nettles's response was typical of the responses exhibited by other black students who were similarly situated. For example, Melba Patillo Beals, one of nine black students who integrated Little Rock's Central High School in 1957, recalled that once she became accustomed to the hostile atmosphere, her school experiences seemed routine. It is not that black students were comfortable in such situations, but rather that the uncomfortable atmosphere they faced in white schools was one of the few certainties in their uncertain existence. Consequently, it came to define a new reality for them, and most adjusted accordingly. Larry Nettles vividly remembers that in most of his classes students and teachers alike ignored him. He explains, "There was never any . . . in class participation unless you forced yourself into the

conversation . . . you were never picked by the teacher." Despite such treatment there were times when Nettles made his presence known, but he insists, "[I] felt very self conscious and unless I felt I was absolutely right in what
I was going to say, [then] I wouldn't say anything."[53]

Larry Nettles clearly recalls one day in class when he knew he could not
keep silent. The stage was set when his civics teacher decided to mention
some facts about Alabama history. Larry describes the exchange: "We were
talking state history, and she [the teacher] was saying the nigras, the nigras,
the nigras." As the teacher talked on, Larry could not resist the impulse to
raise his hand. The teacher quickly recognized the one black student in her
class, and she smiled and said, "Yes, Larry." The civics teacher was clearly surprised when Nettles responded, "Isn't that pronounced Nigger?" Larry's face
remained carefully neutral as the question rolled off his tongue. The embarrassed teacher's surprised face flushed a deep shade of crimson, and she stam-
mered as she tried to think of a response. Finally, the awkward moment
passed, and the flustered teacher finished her lecture on Alabama state history. Nettles recalls that she never said anything to him about her use of the
word nigra that day. In fact, he insists, "I never heard her use that word
again." Furthermore, Nettles insists, "I think at the end of the year, she was
one of the ones that always greeted me every morning." However, while Nettles savored small victories like this, he still understood that he could never
let down his guard completely because the harassment continued unabated,
and the potential for real danger was never very far beneath the surface. Nettles was reminded of this fact from time to time, like the day when he saw
the black student from Coy walking toward him in the hall with fresh eggs
dripping from her hair and clothes.[54]

The most graphic reminder of the depth of white intransigence, however,
was the attempt to burn down the Nettles house. The evening of the fire
started quietly like so many others. Larry had gone to bed after finishing his
homework. He was tired from all the work and from all the tension at
WCHS. It seemed that his head had just hit the pillow when he was dragged
out of a deep sleep by the sounds of his mother's shrill screams. She was
screaming for her children to come help her extinguish the flames that were
casting eerie shadows outside her bedroom window. The flames were greedily licking at the roof of the Nettles's ramshackle frame house. Fortunately,
because the family had just washed clothes, there were big tubs filled with
wash water sitting on the side of the house. Mattie Nettles and her children
quickly extinguished the flames with the soapy water, and nobody was hurt.
They had no doubt that the fire had been deliberately set: they found an
empty gas can on their front porch. Before that night ended, Sheriff Lummie

Jenkins came by the Nettles house and confiscated the gas can, assuring the family that he would have the can fingerprinted and he would get to the bottom of this. The Nettles family never heard another word from Sheriff Jenkins. The next day when Nettles went to school, nobody said a word about the fire—even though he was sure that everyone knew about it. Despite this attempt to burn him out, Larry Nettles continued to attend Wilcox County High day after day.

Nettles quickly devised strategies to ensure his survival and success in that atmosphere. He always made sure that he avoided situations where he might get hurt. For example, he never participated in any extracurricular activities, particularly sports. Larry was a husky boy, and he had enjoyed playing football at Camden Academy. Yet he knew better than to try out for the football team at WCHS. If he had played football at his new school, he explains, "You could get mangled, and it would be perfectly legal."[55] Nettles was also reluctant to try out for the WCHS Band. At Camden Academy Larry had played trombone in the band, but he was afraid that participation in the band at his new school might expose him to unanticipated danger. Even though he realized that forfeiting these extracurricular activities was the safest course of action, it was still hard for his seventeen-year-old mind to accept. He says simply, "It hurt."[56]

As he continued his struggle to remain at Wilcox County High that year, Larry Nettles did not have much contact with students at Camden Academy. He admits that he had trouble coping with his feelings of abandonment, and so he deliberately kept his classmates at arm's length. Consequently, throughout much of his ordeal, Larry battled a profound sense of isolation: He was isolated in his new school, and he was virtually isolated from many members of his own community. Yet, through this whole experience, Larry could always count on the support of his mother. Larry's mother, Mattie Nettles, had seen her share of hardship over the years. A large woman with rich, medium brown skin, she was born in Wilcox County in 1915 on Christmas Eve to a poor family of sharecroppers. Because the family had trouble making ends meet, Mattie's mother worked as a domestic in white people's houses when she was not out in the fields. Young Mattie watched her mother's struggle with growing frustration: it seemed that no matter how hard she worked, she could never get ahead. Mattie was particularly troubled by her mother's attitude. She explains that her mother never seemed to think about doing anything for herself. Instead, "she just did what the white man told her to do."[57] Witnessing her mother's submission only fueled young Mattie's determination to resist.

She got married during the depths of the Great Depression in 1934 when she was only nineteen years old, and the hard times continued. Mattie Nettles and her husband had ten children before they finally separated. Yet, through all of this, her will to resist continued. Thus, when the civil rights movement came to town, Mattie Nettles was drawn to the struggle. Larry clearly remembers that his mother attended some of the mass meetings during the voting rights campaign, and there were times when Reverend Threadgill would come by their house to discuss voter registration. At the same time, however, Mattie Nettles continued to keep a tight rein on all her children, including Larry. She made sure they all understood that hard work was a necessary part of life. Indeed, Larry clearly recalls that she never allowed him to just hang out with his buddies. On the contrary, when he was not in school, Larry's mother expected that all his time would be occupied by farmwork or schoolwork. Thus, Mattie Nettles's high expectations for her children, coupled with her commitment to resistance, ensured that she would be strongly supportive of Larry's efforts as he attended the white high school day after day.

Shortly after her son enrolled in WCHS, Mattie Nettles's uncompromising attitude combined with her high expectations for her son to set her on a collision course with school authorities. The stage was set when Larry left school one day after being harassed by some of his white male classmates. After that incident, Mattie Nettles received a letter from the school informing her that her son had left school without permission and warning her that if he did it again, he would be suspended. After reading that letter, Nettles was livid. She immediately went to the school board and walked straight to the superintendent's office without looking left or right. As the angry Mattie Nettles stormed into the office, a startled secretary looked up and inquired in a timid voice, "May I help you?" In a loud, commanding voice Mattie Nettles demanded to see the superintendent. The secretary quickly announced with just the barest hint of a tremor in her voice, "He's not in." Mattie Nettles drew herself up to her full height and announced, "I'm not leaving until I see him." She had just taken a step in the direction of a row of chairs against the wall when a door to an inner office opened and Wilcox County's school superintendent appeared and reassured her that she would not have to wait. He ushered her into his private office, and before he could close the door, Larry's mother declared, "I understand that they've been trying to run Larry away from up here." The superintendent quickly replied, "Oh no, that won't happen." Before the superintendent could continue, Nettles said, "Yeah, they ran a bunch of [black] children off from up here." She concluded in a resolute voice, "Larry's not going, *we're* not going to run." The superintendent continued to try to reassure the angry black woman in his office. He spoke soothingly, "Larry's a sweet boy."[58]

Mattie Nettles went on to assert that she had told her son to come home whenever he felt threatened. The superintendent tried to explain that Larry had left school without permission. Nettles cut him off. She declared emphatically, her voice rising, "I told him to do so if they tried to [gang up on] him." She further insisted, "I told him I'd be sitting on my top step with my gun across my lap, and for him to come home." Even though Nettles's combative attitude clearly unnerved Wilcox County's school superintendent, he continued to try to calm his black visitor. She refused to be calmed. Instead, she went on to warn the flustered administrator that any white student who tried to attack her son would be in for a rough time because, "I told him [Larry] don't try to fight a gang of 'em, but get you a brick or a piece of iron, and back [them] up in a corner, and knock [the] hell out of 'em as fast as they come to him."[59] Nettles stood there with her eyes blazing, and when the superintendent looked deep into those eyes, his sense of unease increased because he knew that she meant every word. Trying very hard not to reveal his uneasiness, the superintendent replied in a steady voice, "Oh no, oh no."[60]

Not content with just meeting with the county's school superintendent, Mattie Nettles decided to write a letter to the principal of WCHS, C. C. McKelvey. In no uncertain terms Larry's mother declared, "What he [Larry] is looking for is an education not a mob. . . . As I told the Supt. on yesterday, *unless they start at him,* he is not going to give anybody any trouble. But you know him being one [he] cannot protect himself against a 'mob' . . . threatening his life." Mattie Nettles went on to express her opinion of the white students harassing her son: "If boys that size and age don't know right from wrong, they are in a bad condition." Finally, she concluded her letter with a postscript advising, "Maybe it would be good to read this to all concern[ed]. Children usually show their rearing in public."[61]

Larry Nettles returned to school without incident, and even though the snickering and name-calling continued, Nettles encountered no real trouble. In fact, by the end of the first year some of Larry's white classmates actually began to speak to him when they passed him in the hall. Of course, they would never speak if their white friends were around, but Nettles would smile secretly to himself as he savored this small victory. Despite this hint of a thaw in the attitudes of the white students that spring, however, Larry Nettles received a graphic reminder of the continued existence of white intransigence the day after Dr. King was assassinated. Because King had visited their county and expressed support for their struggle, many black residents took his death particularly hard. When Nettles arrived at school that morning, he saw little knots of students gathered in the hall around their lockers talking about the assassination. All the conversations stopped when Larry entered the hallway, and a tension settled over the scene. But one boy separated himself from one of the little groups of students, turned toward Larry and taunted, "Oh Larry, they got your nigger last night, didn't they?" Then he threw back his head and laughed a too-loud exaggerated laugh, "HA, HA, HA, HA." His performance was greeted by a scattering of nervous giggles from the students in the hall. Larry Nettles did not respond. Instead, he squared his shoulders, looked straight ahead, and continued his walk down the hall.[62]

Finally, the school year came to a close. Larry Nettles had managed to make it through the whole year with passing grades, and as he looked back on that year he thought, "Wow, I've done it."[63] Over the summer, Larry never doubted that he would go back in the fall to do his senior year at WCHS. Indeed, by this time, Larry had had time to reflect on the importance of his struggle to integrate the white school. He concluded that "as the fear of being abandoned completely [engulfed me] I was away from bettering my people, it strictly became [about] me at that point."[64] Thus, in the fall of 1968, a grimly determined Larry Nettles returned to Wilcox County High. He and the young girl from Coy were still the only two black students at the school, but this time they were not surprised. However, Larry was surprised at how easily he slipped back into his school routine. As his senior year began, Larry followed the strategy that had ensured his success the year before: He tried to blend in with the others as much as possible by doing "what the other kids did; I wasn't there to be different." Larry diligently followed his strategy, and it seemed that the weeks and months raced by. In no time, the spring semester was about to end, and Larry Nettles prepared to become the first black student ever to graduate from WCHS. On the eve of his graduation Nettles briefly worried about his safety. But he quickly banished such dark thoughts from his mind when he realized that even though the graduation exercises would not be held until 6:00 the next evening, it would still be broad daylight.

That next evening Larry Nettles made history when he marched into the auditorium with his white classmates, and became the first and ultimately the only black student ever to graduate from WCHS when it was still all white. Nettles clearly remembers walking up on the stage to receive his diploma. He looked out at the sea of white faces in the audience, but in the midst of that big white sea there was one small group of black faces smiling broadly. Larry recognized a few community supporters like the Threadgills and the Gordons, an assortment of relatives, and sitting right there in front of the group was his mother, Mattie Nettles. She still had that fierce light of determination in her eyes, but her gaze softened and her eyes misted just a bit as she watched her son receive his diploma. As Nettles reached out to accept his diploma, he recalls, "I felt proud that I had accomplished my goal."[65] After his graduation, Larry had to decide what college he would attend. For some time, Nettles had been debating between Tuskegee and Alabama State.

However, just as he was about to make his decision, his employer for the summer presented Larry with an opportunity to attend a church-affiliated school in the North. He jumped at the chance. Because he was still feeling abandoned by members of his own community, Nettles was anxious to leave his hurt, pain, and disillusionment behind: he graduated on Thursday, left the state on Sunday, and never looked back. Larry Nettles has never lived in Alabama again.[66]

In the meantime, just as they showed no interest in integrating the student bodies, the school board made absolutely no attempt to integrate any of the teachers in the system. NEA investigators reported that they could find no "evidence of any intention on the part of Wilcox County School officials to plan for faculty desegregation."[67] NEA officials further observed that the county's superintendent would not even communicate with the black teachers. Investigators reported, "Following the teacher dismissals in August 1965, the [black] Wilcox County Teachers Association repeatedly requested a meeting with the superintendent to discuss the dismissals and . . . other concerns. . . . Not until May 1966 did the superintendent agree to meet with the Association." Yet, even though the superintendent finally met with the county's black teachers, nothing was resolved. Instead, the superintendent abruptly "left this meeting in apparent anger."[68] A short time later, a number of white teachers would begin to teach in some of the county's black schools. However, this faculty integration occurred despite the school board's efforts, not because of them, and none of these white teachers was local.

The first white teachers assigned to Wilcox County's black schools were young, idealistic, white Volunteers in Service to America (VISTA) volunteers who had been assigned to the county. VISTA was a federal program sometimes known as the domestic Peace Corps, and it was designed to give assistance to poor communities at home while the Peace Corps served people in other countries around the world. VISTA personnel were assigned to serve impoverished Americans all over the country, and African Americans in Wilcox County were very grateful for the services of the VISTA teachers who came to help them. James Beardsley, a white LeHigh College student who joined VISTA and then was assigned to Wilcox County, was one of those first white teachers. He recalls, "The schools were segregated. We later found out that we were here to satisfy the superintendent integrating faculties because most of the VISTA workers were white, and he could say that he had whites on the faculties of the black schools." Beardsley adds pointedly, "That's why they put up with us."[69] Thus, as the decade of the 1960s came to a close, it seemed that black and white residents in Wilcox County were at an impasse on the issue of school integration.

Because of the recalcitrant attitude of Wilcox school officials, the U.S. Justice Department continued to monitor the state of the county's schools throughout this period. In fact, the very next academic year after Larry Nettles graduated, the Justice Department filed a report with the district court complaining about the lack of progress toward integration in the system. The report charged, "all of the white students continue to attend the schools traditionally maintained for white students, and more than ninety-seven percent of the Negro students attend schools traditionally maintained for Negro students."[70] In the same report, the Justice Department asked that the district court order the "complete disestablishment of the school system based on race in the Wilcox County School District." Essentially, the Justice Department wanted the county to establish a unitary school system in which the student body in each school in the system would mirror the racial ratio of the county's student population as a whole.[71] County officials were furious and totally uncooperative. McLean Pitts, the attorney for the Wilcox County School Board, fired off a scathing denunciation of the Justice Department's recommendations. In it he warned that "the [white] people of Wilcox County will not take anymore at the present time and they have considered the matter individually and they are ready to have complete segregation in Wilcox County *without public schools* if it becomes necessary [emphasis added]."[72] As the controversy continued, the Department of Health, Education, and Welfare (HEW) filed a plan with the district court in March 1970, recommending that the county should be divided into attendance zones. The black and white students in the schools in each zone were to be combined to achieve racial integration. The county's school board officials did not like this plan either.[73] The stalemate continued.

In the meantime, by the spring of 1971, the *Wilcox Progressive Era* proudly announced that "Wilcox Academy will graduate first seniors in exercises Wednesday."[74] The article went on to outline the schedule for the graduation exercises and the accompanying activities. What the article did not discuss was the school's racial composition: this brand new private school that was established with the donations of local white contributors was unashamedly all-white. Clearly, the school's founders recognized that at some point the integration of their public school system was inevitable, and so the only way they could continue to keep their children in an all-white school environment was to establish a private school that would not be subject to federal mandates.

The new academy grew out of the Wilcox Education Foundation, which was established in 1970 in response to the threat of school integration. Many of the county's leading white citizens, including the Hendersons of Miller's

Ferry, were staunch supporters of the foundation. However, at least a few of the county's white residents had reservations about pulling their children out of their county's public school system. Dale Henderson, who had two children enrolled at Wilcox County High School, recalled, "A lot of people were very much against it."[75] Many were particularly concerned about the added expense they would have to bear if they sent their children to private school. Bruce Lowe, a white resident who had just moved to Wilcox County, expressed the concern that was on the minds of some of his white neighbors: "Our children go to public school. Now I make five dollars and thirty cents an hour and I'm not able to pay twelve hundred dollars a year to send them [sic] children to a private school when we've got a public school here." Despite the concern articulated by many white residents about the cost of private school tuition, Lowe realized that many of these people were still unalterably opposed to integration. He explained, "when we came here, they tried to put niggers in the white school, and all hell broke loose." Regardless of the opposition of his neighbors, however, Lowe concluded, "but it's going to happen. They've got to come into the twentieth century and integrate. They can't afford not to."[76]

In response to this reluctance, proponents of segregation started a campaign to convince white parents to pull their children out of the county's public schools. One white Wilcox parent reported,

> Along about March 20 of '71, I had a phone call early one morning [from someone] that would not identify herself. . . . She said that for us to keep our children at home and keep them out of school, that all the white children were going to be pulled out of that school. We kept our children out the rest of the year.[77]

Many were convinced that the school board was behind the campaign to vacate the public schools. Yet, regardless of who was responsible, many white students whose parents did elect to send them to Wilcox Academy found that conditions were less than desirable in their new school. One observed, "We did without a lot of things." He continued, "We had to make do with desks that were the old-timey desks that were hooked on rails. You didn't have a lunchroom. You paid for everything you got. You didn't have [free] books."[78] The continuing debate over the private school issue highlighted the existence of an economic divide that had separated white residents for generations. Over the years, the feeling of white unity resulting from the profound impact of segregation had always worked to soften the edges of this economic schism. But, with segregation being shaken to its very foundations, the economic differences separating white residents took on added significance. The schism exposed a raw nerve that generated a great deal of emotional feeling. Wilcox Academy student George Fendley insisted, "There were hard feelings." Fendley went on to lament, "Two of my best friends stayed at the public schools. We grew apart based upon that, because their parents didn't believe that a private school should be started."[79] There was a practical reason why some white parents balked at sending their children to private school: they could not afford the tuition. Many of these parents continued to hope against hope that integration would not come to their county, at least not before their children managed to graduate.

It was against this tumultuous background of white recalcitrance that a number of Camden Academy students decided to take a stand. One of the main leaders of this group, Brenda Bussey Carson, recalls that students began complaining to each other that spring about the obvious differences between facilities in the white schools and those in the black schools. This vocal group, which numbered about a dozen, soon became known as "the Bad Bunch." Because most of these young people were veterans of their county's voting rights struggles, they were completely comfortable with the concept of protest, and so they decided that the time was right to protest their county's unequal educational facilities. Initially, Brenda wrote a letter to their superintendent, Guy Kelly, outlining the group's grievances, and they scheduled a meeting with the local PTA. Even before the meeting, news of the students' demands leaked out into the community. Thus, that evening as black adults filed into the Camden Academy auditorium for the PTA meeting, a somber mood seemed to envelop the crowd. Many in the audience were veterans of their county's bruising voting rights struggles of the mid 1960s, and they were tired. They were also disillusioned, because even though they were now able to vote, it seemed that the power relationship in their heavily black county had not changed: White people still had power; black people did not. Consequently, it was with a great deal of uneasiness that many in the audience waited to hear what their young people had to say.

The auditorium was packed, and as she climbed the steps to the stage that evening, Brenda Bussey was just a little nervous. But as soon as she began to read a copy of the letter the students had already sent to the superintendent, a soothing calm settled over the Camden Academy junior. She seemed to gather strength from each word, and her voice was steady and clear. After Brenda finished, the students asked that their principal, J. E. Hobbs, and members of the PTA approach Superintendent Kelly to convey their demands in person. For just a moment, the audience was motionless and silent. Then, many began to squirm restlessly in their seats as they contemplated the awful consequences if they complained. Although some of the adults sympathized with the students' position, it seemed that the majority of the audience was unalterably opposed to the students' suggestion that the adults should complain to the superintendent. Led by Principal Hobbs, PTA officials flatly refused to approach the superintendent and the school board with the students' complaints. The students were stunned momentarily by the vehemence of the refusal, but they quickly recovered. Undaunted, they announced quietly, "We will go." They paused briefly to look searchingly at their worried elders, and then they quietly filed out of the meeting, determined to follow through on their threat. Carson vividly recalls the adult reaction, "that made everybody pretty much hot with us."[80] Once they were outside, the students breathed a huge sigh of relief. They had really done it; they had stood up in public and taken a stand. Yet, the sense of pride they felt was mixed with a profound sense of disappointment. They knew that their grievances were legitimate, and they had expected the adults to stand with them. When most did not, the students were disappointed and disillusioned. The young people were particularly troubled by the reaction of their principal because before that meeting, they had been certain that they could count on Hobbs's support. Carson explains that Hobbs was considered the "principal of principals." She continues, "You know, we respected him. If Mr. Hobbs walked down the hall, I mean, you could hear a pin fall. I guess we expected him to want to do it."

Despite their disillusionment, or maybe because of it, the "Bad Bunch" became more determined than ever to carry their demands to the superintendent and the school board. Carson observes, "When he [Hobbs] refused to do it, that just made us more determined that we were going to see it through."[81] After that emotional meeting, Reverend Thomas Threadgill became involved. He had been sitting in the audience that night, and he had been appalled at the PTA's refusal to support the students.[82] Threadgill quickly arranged for the students to meet with some individual members of the school board, and with Reg Albritton, Wilcox County's probate judge. Carson remembers that when she presented the letter of grievances to Albritton, he looked at her sternly and said, "If you wrote this letter, you have no business in this system anyway. You should be in college somewhere."[83] Carson also recalls that when the students met with the individual board members, some of them actually admitted that Camden Academy students deserved better facilities, but "nobody wanted to make the first move to do anything about it."[84] As adults, both black and white, continued to stall, the school year came to a close, and the seniors graduated.

If the adults thought that student enthusiasm would cool over the summer, however, they were sadly mistaken. Instead, the student activists continued to meet during the summer months. Those members of the group who left the area to accept summer jobs were careful to stay in touch with the others as they debated the question of how to continue their fight. The stand taken by Camden Academy students that spring was set against the background of a growing Black Power movement. All over the country, the demands for Black Power were increasing in intensity. Many African Americans were wearing Afros—the bigger, the better—demonstrating their pride in their blackness. In Wilcox County, many black youngsters were also wearing Afros. They were influenced by the rhetoric of Black Power, and they were also influenced by the explosion of black movies coming out of Hollywood: *Superfly*, *Shaft*, *Sweet Sweetback's Baadasssss Song*, and many others. These films simultaneously celebrated and exploited black culture, but in the end, the good guys always won, and in these movies, the good guys were always black. Black Wilcox youngsters danced to music by black artists like Marvin Gaye, who sang about the most pressing issues in black communities all over the country. In the popular song "What's Going On," released in 1971, Gaye's silky voice crooned,

> *Mother, mother, there's too many of you crying*
> *Brother, brother, brother, there's far too many of you dying*
> *You know we've got to find a way*
> *To bring some lovin' here today, yeah*
> *Father, father, we don't need to escalate*
> *War is not the answer, for only love can conquer hate*
> *You know we've got to find a way*
> *To bring some understanding here today, oh*
> *Picket lines, and picket signs*
> *Don't punish me with brutality*
> *Talk to me, so you can see, oh-oh*
> *What's going on; what's going on.*

Wilcox County's black young people were convinced that they knew what was going on during the summer of 1971. It was clear that they had to be the agents of change in their county because it seemed that the adults, both black and white, were at an impasse. Consequently, during their weeks of summer vacation, a conviction was born in their young, idealistic hearts and minds: when the fall term started, they would not go back to school. Instead, they would boycott classes to dramatize the inequities in their public school system.[85]

Coincidentally, just as the students decided on this course of action, the U.S. District Court issued a new integration order that Wilcox County officials were directed to implement "forthwith." According to the terms of that order, "A transfer shall be granted to any student attending a school in which his race is in the majority to a school in which his race is in the minority."

The order went on to direct that "transportation [for students] be provided by the School Board if desired by the student or his parent or guardian."[86] Thus, the court gave the Wilcox County School Board the responsibility for facilitating the integration of their county's schools. Finally, the order went on to direct the school board to begin integrating its faculty "at the earliest possible date, but in no event, no later than the beginning of the second semester of the 1971–72 school term."[87]

Despite the court's unequivocal directions, it soon became clear that county officials would continue to drag their feet. School superintendent Guy Kelly made his position clear when he indicated that "these things cannot be done overnight and . . . it will take some time to affect all the changes ordered by the court."[88] Kelly went on to threaten, "104 Negro teachers must lose their jobs in order for the local Board of Education to comply with the court's order that teaching staffs be equalized according to race."[89] This part of Kelly's interpretation of the court order was undoubtedly intended to dampen black student enthusiasm for school integration. It failed. Indeed, Superintendent Kelly would soon learn that despite his dire predictions of black teacher layoffs, the county's black young people were poised to act. However, just as the students were bound and determined to fight for the court ordered integration of the schools, Superintendent Kelly was determined to block it. Guy Kelly was a staunch segregationist. He had been hired in 1965 to replace the aging W. G. Jones, who had served as Wilcox County superintendent for forty-two years. There were some in Wilcox County who suspected that the school board had hired Kelly at that time because they needed just the right man to spearhead the fight against school integration.[90] Albert Gordon, a black teacher and the vice president of the WCCPL, stated bluntly, "I hate to say it, but he was a redneck out of this world. That's why they [the school board] hired him."[91] Kelly did not disappoint his new employers. As the fight for school integration began to intensify, the new superintendent proved that he could be "blustering and combative." On some occasions when he was forced to deal with one of the endless court rulings designed to enforce desegregation, he would "storm through the outer office and into his own. He frequently called in the Assistant Superintendent at such times. They would close the door and . . . discuss what was to be done. He gave the impression that he was determined to beat them."[92] As the new school term started, the confrontation between the students and the superintendent was about to turn nasty.

On September 7, 1971, just as the new school year began, a group of Camden Academy students, led by the "Bad Bunch," boycotted classes and marched to WCHS, where the superintendent himself blocked the entrance.

At this point, the students were tired of all the excuses and delaying tactics. Their impatience and their determination clearly showed on their faces, and Guy Kelly could almost feel the anger and resentment coming from the group. But the superintendent was equally determined. His face was red, and his eyes blazed as he addressed the assembled students in his most stern voice. Kelly ordered them to return to Camden Academy, and he threatened them with expulsion if they did not comply immediately. Guy Kelly became enraged when the students refused to disperse. Instead, they milled around for a few more moments, and boldly voiced their opinions of the school board's actions. Through the red haze of his anger Kelly noticed that one of the male students seemed to be more vocal than the others. The superintendent quickly grabbed this student by his shirt and turned him over to a nearby police officer. That student, Larry Threadgill, was later released to his father, Reverend Thomas Threadgill. A short time later, all the student boycotters were expelled by their principal, James E. Hobbs.[93]

After this initial demonstration, student demonstrators knew that they had reached a point of no return: they were determined to fight until change occurred. At the same time, Superintendent Kelly remained adamant in his opposition. Somewhat disingenuously he argued that he could not make any progress in his attempts to implement the court's order if he had "to sit on the school house steps every morning" to keep the black students out.[94] Much to his dismay, Kelly would soon learn that this was just the beginning of a whole year of boycotts and demonstrations. What the superintendent failed to recognize was that this new generation of students with their Afros and bell bottoms were fired by a determination that would not allow them to be dissuaded from their goal, regardless of what black or white adults in their community said or did. From that time on through the fall semester the expelled students met day after day to plot strategy and continue their demonstrations. Their principal, J. E. Hobbs, refused to confront them directly. Of course, he did not support them either. On the other hand, there were some black adults, most notably Reverend Threadgill, and educators Albert Gordon and Lawrence Parrish, who openly demonstrated their support. As the boycott continued, there were other black adults who openly expressed their support to the students as well.

The demonstrations continued into the fall, and both Brenda Bussey and Larry Threadgill continued to play leadership roles. However, these two young activists approached that fateful fall from two very different backgrounds. Larry Threadgill was born into a middle-class family with two college-educated parents. Although Larry's childhood had been punctuated by some uncertainty and occasional insecurity because of his father's civil

rights activities, he and his siblings never felt the sting of economic deprivation. Moreover, as the son of one of the most respected activists in the
county, Larry Threadgill grew up with the notion that every African American was obligated to work for the liberation and the betterment of black people. As a youngster he attended mass meetings with his father, and he remembers how famous civil rights activists would often visit their home. Larry
and his older sister Sheryl would sit on the floor of their living room for hours
listening to their father plot strategy with the likes of Andrew Young, Hosea
Williams, and even Martin Luther King Jr. Larry admired his father a great
deal, and he closely watched everything the elder Threadgill did. Like so
many young boys, Larry tried to imitate his father. He laughingly recalls how
he would organize his little friends in the same way that he had observed his
father organizing the adults in their community.[95] Furthermore, as Larry prepared to join his comrades in their challenge to the segregated school system
in their county, the memory of his sister coming home from WCHS day after day with a bloody nose, torn clothes, and tears in her eyes was never far
from his mind. Thus, in September of 1971, Larry Threadgill was supremely
confident that he was ready to confront the forces of segregation in Wilcox
County.

On the other hand, Larry Threadgill's female counterpart, Brenda Bussey
Carson, was from a very different background. She was born and raised in
Camden, and she had nine brothers and sisters. Brenda was next to the
youngest: her youngest sibling, a brother, was born only eighteen months after her. When she reflects on her childhood, Carson concludes, "Growing up
was very hard."[96] The family never had much money. Her father worked at the
local mill, and her mother was a housewife, but she also picked cotton, worked
in white people's kitchens, and "did whatever she had to." Although they
farmed and grew most of their own food, Carson remembers some evenings
when she and her brothers and sisters had only grits or eggs for supper. She
also remembers some days when her mother was gone all day, and the children
were left with only baked sweet potatoes for lunch. From an early age, she and
her siblings tried to do whatever they could to supplement the family's meager income. They often picked berries and plums and sold them to local white
residents for fifty cents a gallon. Later, when Brenda turned thirteen, she got
a job washing and ironing for a young white couple who lived nearby. The
wife was only sixteen years old, and Carson remembers how strange she felt
when she realized that her employer was only three years her senior.

Even though her parents had not gone very far in school—her father went
to the second grade, and her mother finished the seventh—they advised
their children to get all the education they could. Brenda was only too happy

to oblige. She loved school, and she has many fond memories of Camden Academy, the only school she ever attended until she attempted to integrate WCHS in the fall of 1971. Carson insists that Camden Academy's teachers were strict and their expectations were high, but she blossomed while she was in their care. She remembers that many teachers helped their students to form a positive self-image. For example, Carson remembers how they all smiled when their principal, J. E. Hobbs, addressed them in chapel. He smiled broadly as he looked out over his audience of students, and he never tired of telling them, "Black people make such a beautiful bouquet."[97] Carson also remembers that her home economics teacher, Mrs. Parrish, frequently told the girls in her class, "All girls are beautiful." Yet, despite all the positive reinforcement that students received, Carson still insists that there were times when students who were economically disadvantaged were treated differently. She explains, "We were poor. You had a lot of teachers who encouraged us, regardless of what our status was, but you also had some teachers who looked over you if you weren't in a certain [economic] group." However, Carson recalls that even though she was from a poor background, she was a straight-A student, and this fact ensured that she received a great deal of attention from her teachers despite her economic status.[98]

When Brenda reached the seventh grade, the voting rights demonstrations started. She remembers how the whole school was buzzing with excitement. Even though she was quite young at the time, she clearly recalls that some students and some of her teachers participated. In particular, she recalls the day when her teacher, a young woman named Johnnie Young, went off to march in the demonstrations and left her class in the care of a soft-spoken SNCC worker. Brenda and her classmates were fascinated by the young man from SNCC. He was so different from all the other adults she had known: His accent was different from any she had ever heard, and he talked about issues that most adults would never think of discussing with children. Yet, long before the voting rights struggle came to her county, young Brenda Bussey had been acutely aware of local racial realities. She has particularly sharp memories of the time when she and her brother were walking along the railroad tracks near their home. It was a lazy summer afternoon, and she and her little brother were just killing time. They looked down the tracks and noticed a big lump of something in the distance. Their childish curiosity quickly got the better of them. They could not resist investigating the unusual sight, and so they ran down the tracks as fast as they could, their childish laughter streaming out behind them. But as they neared the mysterious lump, their steps slowed, and their laughter died in their throats. To their horror, the mysterious mound was actually a young black man who had been beaten until he was bloody. He lay on the tracks groaning, his limbs twitching. Brenda and her brother, who had been momentarily paralyzed by shock, knelt down to help the young man off the tracks. They took him to their house, and Brenda's family was able to get word to the young man's family in Coy. They quickly came to get him. Even though nobody ever said it explicitly, they all understood that "the white folks" were responsible for this outrage. Carson also remembers when the father of one of her classmates, Clifford Martin, was beaten and killed while he was in jail. Again, everybody understood that "the white folks" were behind it.[99]

During her early years in school, some of Brenda's teachers discussed the county's racial realities with their students. She particularly recalls some of the lessons she learned from Mr. Thomas, her social studies teacher. She explains, "He would talk about our right to be where we were, and we deserved any opportunities [we got] because our foreparents had paid for them, and he would cry sometimes when we'd read stories about what had happened . . . he just made it exciting." Thomas also tried very hard to educate his students about their place in their county and in the rest of the world. Carson laughingly recalls that when Thomas informed her and the other students that African Americans were only a minority of their state's population, they were incredulous. Many of them had never been out of Wilcox County, and so they figured that the population in the rest of the state was heavily black like the population in their county. When Thomas told them that this was not the case, Carson recalls, "We just couldn't believe it."[100] Thus, in 1971 against the background of heightened expectations coming out of Wilcox County's voting rights struggle, Brenda Bussey's Camden Academy experiences combined with the lessons from her childhood to propel her into the midst of the struggle for school desegregation.

Through the fall of 1971, the students continued their attempts to demonstrate at WCHS. Larry Threadgill remembers that by the second day of the demonstrations when the students marched to the white school, they were met by a line of white policemen nervously fingering their billy clubs. The column of students halted right in front of the officers just as one of them growled, "We don't care what you do, you're not coming in this school." The students refused to move. Then, without warning, the line of police began advancing, using billy clubs to push students back. Threadgill remembers glancing up at the school and being surprised to see fear on the faces of the white students who were looking out the windows just before a large white policeman shoved him so hard that he almost lost his balance. Threadgill quickly recovered, and walked forward until his face was only inches from the red face of the angry policeman who had just pushed him. Pure defiance seemed to radiate from the black teenager's body as the officer thrust his billy club forward and pushed Threadgill again.

Undaunted, the youngster again began walking toward the policeman without missing a beat. But before Threadgill had taken more than one step toward the officer, an authoritative voice said quietly, "Don't push him anymore." The voice startled Larry. He quickly turned his head, and he was amazed to see his father, Reverend Thomas Threadgill, standing only inches away. In the meantime, the policeman had taken a step backward. For just a split second the cop and the preacher stared at each other, and finally, the officer lowered his billy club. Then, without taking his eyes from the officer's face, Reverend Threadgill calmly advised the students to come with him. He promised them that they could come back to WCHS the next day. Without a word, the students turned and followed the elder Threadgill back down the street to the community center. After they had all gathered around him, Threadgill offered the youngsters words of encouragement and support, but he also advised them to be careful. He warned, "Don't get in a shoving match with these cops because they're looking for a reason to kill you anyway." He continued, "The white folks are crazy, they're scared, they're mad."[101]

Day after day the student boycott continued, and increasing numbers of supporters began to join the demonstrations in front of WCHS and the board of education office. New supporters included parents and students from other schools. Brenda Bussey Carson vividly recalls that they were joined by students from all over the county: Pine Hill, Alberta, Boykin, and Pine Apple. She insists, however, that the Pine Hill students were the strongest supporters of the Camden Academy students. Of course, not all of the students participated in the boycott. Some parents refused to allow their children to participate for a variety of reasons including fear for their children's safety and concern about the detrimental effect that an extended absence from class would have on their children's academic progress. Carson vividly remembers that one of her close friends, Louise Moody, did not participate in the boycott because her mother would not allow it. Yet, even though Louise continued to attend school every day at Camden Academy while Brenda protested, the two girls remained close. They frequently talked to each other about the complex paths their lives had taken because of the school desegregation struggle. Sometimes Louise felt guilty because she wanted to be with her classmates and friends, protesting the continued segregation in her county. On the other hand, there were times when Brenda longed for the uncomplicated life she led before she was thrust into daily demonstrations. But then the girls would sigh, promise to stay in touch with each other, and go their separate ways: Louise Moody went back to school, and Brenda Bussey went back to protest.[102]

By mid-September, with no end to the demonstrations in sight, Wilcox County's new sheriff, Reg Albritton, who had unseated long-time sheriff Lummie Jenkins in the 1970 election, decided to confront the students directly. Accordingly, on a warm September morning, the new sheriff accompanied Superintendent Kelly to WCHS. Kelly and Albritton stood side by side awaiting the arrival of the demonstrators, and wondering about the inevitable confrontation that was sure to follow. They did not have long to wait. Initially, Albritton tried to reason with the students by discussing the exact wording of the desegregation order:

> He explained in considerable detail that Mr. Kelly was within his rights to turn the group away because of the wording of the court order. Albritton read a portion of the order to the black students and pointed out that Kelly is relying on a sentence which states that the ordered integration must take place "in the school year."[103]

The sheriff's voice droned on in his deep Alabama drawl, but his words were greeted by looks of skepticism and mistrust. The student demonstrators stood there, arms crossed, seething with anger as the sheriff explained that the precise wording of the court order meant that "Kelly could wait until the last day of the year before fully complying with the order."[104] The sheriff's attempt to justify the superintendent's refusal to admit them to WCHS elicited only angry groans from the assembled students. On a slightly more conciliatory note, Superintendent Kelly insisted that "he and the Board of Education are taking all deliberate steps to fully comply with the order of the court." The students stared at him with stony faces. Kelly tried to conclude on a positive note. He insisted that "some pupil transfers are expected to begin shortly once the problems of transportation and logistics are worked out."[105]

Despite Kelly's feeble attempt to reassure the students, the school board was actually doing all it could to delay and prevent school integration. In fact, just the year before, Superintendent Guy Kelly had publicly admitted that he and other members of the board had "deliberately harassed and stalled [federal officials]" who were attempting to supervise the desegregation of the Wilcox County school system.[106] All through the 1970–1971 school year, federal officials and Wilcox school board members had been sparring over the issue of school integration. At one point, a frustrated HEW official exclaimed, "Hell we have integrated the entire South, and Kelly and Wilcox County are fighting just as hard today as they were in the beginning."[107] Predictably, Kelly's foot-dragging was greeted with hearty approval by the *Wilcox Progressive Era*, which editorialized, "This remark should stand as the highest possible tribute to Mr. Kelly and the

Board."[108] Given Kelly's uncooperative attitude, his words of reassurance to the students rang hollow.

In the meantime, members of the WCCPL decided to support the student demonstrations by calling for an economic boycott. A negotiating committee of fifteen WCCPL members issued a list of thirty-one demands, and sought an audience with local white officials. White officials refused. In the wake of this refusal, the committee called for a boycott of downtown stores. The boycott, which dragged on for several months, was only partially successful. In the meantime, however, the group was able to publicize its list of demands, which included a wide variety of recommendations such as the hiring of black policemen, black salespeople in department stores, black cashiers in food and liquor stores, black bank tellers, and a black clerk in the post office. The list also included the demand for a black majority on the welfare board and a black case worker. The negotiating committee also asked for improvements at Camden Academy, including an enlarged cafeteria, a replacement for the classroom building, which had been condemned for six years, a paved driveway, the rehiring of a bus driver and cook who had recently been fired, and the reinstatement of the students who had been expelled because of their protest activities. The committee further recommended that J. E. Hobbs, Camden Academy's principal who had been particularly hostile to demonstrators, should be replaced. Other education-related demands included the hiring of black assistant principals in every school that had a white principal and the hiring of white assistant principals in every school that had a black principal. The committee's demands also included improvements in the black community, such as paved roads in all black subdivisions, equal service from the telephone company, and vigorous enforcement of the city's sanitation code. Finally, because the committee was also concerned about safeguarding their newly won right to vote, they demanded black workers at every polling place and black registrars at the courthouse annex.[109] These ambitious demands fell on deaf ears and the standoff continued.

As the demonstrations dragged on, some of the student activists tried to reason with police officers. Policemen could scarcely believe their ears. How could these black children be so disrespectful, they fumed. Larry Threadgill remembers that demonstrators often reminded law enforcement officials that because their parents were taxpayers they had a right to attend any school they chose. Apparently, the police officers remained unconvinced. Brenda Carson vividly recalls the day that she decided to speak out during a demonstration. As usual, the students came face-to-face with a solid wall of police officers blocking their path. However, on this particular day as Brenda stood there looking into the stony face of the officer directly in front of her, she felt compelled to try and reason with him. She started slowly, "On Sunday morning every church in Camden is full. And then Monday through Saturday you treat black people as if they were nothing." Brenda's voice rose just a bit and her eyes glowed with intensity when she looked into the faces of the other policemen closest to her. She continued, "And if we serve the same God, how can that be? And if God is as good as you say He is, how can you justify acting that way?" the teenager's impassioned speech was greeted only by impassive stares from the police officers.[110]

Initially, frustrated school officials tried to cajole, and then to threaten the students into submission. Nothing worked. Everyone realized that the longer the demonstrations dragged on, the more potential there was for violence. Finally, in the middle of October, violence struck when angry residents vandalized school property. On the night of October 12, 1971, vandals slashed the tires on "virtually every Negro school bus in Wilcox County." Sheriff Albritton characterized the vandalism as "an organized effort to disable the buses." He also announced that concrete was poured in all the locks and around the doors of the Negro school in the Coy community. Albritton went on to lament that the damage to the school and the buses was very costly, and he quickly jumped to the conclusion that the black demonstrators must be the perpetrators. It is important to note that the sheriff did not present any evidence to substantiate this charge. At the same time, the conclusion is inescapable that disabling black school buses would virtually halt integration because it would mean that most black students would be unable to get to school. Clearly, this conclusion should have convinced the sheriff to look outside the black community for the perpetrators. However, he did not.[111]

These Tuesday night acts of vandalism had followed a hectic day of demonstrations that left Camden city officials pointing fingers at each other and complaining about the attitude of the Alabama State Troopers who had been dispatched to the scene. The first march earlier that day had started at 7:30 in the morning when a group of demonstrators left Antioch Baptist Church for the short march to downtown Camden. Before the group had gotten very far, Camden police chief Clinton Luker and a group of his officers confronted the demonstrators and ordered them to disperse. By this time, many of the students in the crowd had been demonstrating for almost five weeks, and they were in no mood to obey Luker's demand that they disperse because they did not have a parade permit. After the group stubbornly refused to retreat, Luker gave the command to fire tear gas canisters into the crowd.[112]

The gas quickly spread over the group of students like a foul smelling blanket. Larry Threadgill remembers that people were stumbling around disoriented. They were gagging and vomiting, and the delicate membranes in their eyes and noses felt like they were on fire. From behind the protective anonymity of their gas masks the police watched smugly as the protestors staggered uncertainly back in the direction of Antioch Baptist Church. When the youngsters entered the safety of Antioch's sanctuary, they slumped over on the pews, greedily gulped the untainted air, and dried the tears that were streaming from their irritated eyes. But in many cases their tears were not just the result of the gas. Instead, many were shedding tears of frustration and rage; and as their tears dried, and their breathing steadied, they began to get ready for the next confrontation. In a short time, the protestors lined up again and marched resolutely out of the church in the direction of downtown Camden. The police, who had positioned themselves very close to Antioch, were in various stages of relaxation when the demonstrators started streaming out of the church. The officers quickly snapped to attention and resumed their positions blocking the path of the marchers. Behind their gas masks the officers' faces registered surprise that the demonstrators were confronting them again so soon. The officers' faces also registered annoyance: they were tired of these brash young people sporting their Afros and singing their freedom songs. Once again, their chief gave the order to fire the tear gas. The officers planted their feet, took aim, and fired. Disoriented protestors blindly stumbled back to the safety of Antioch once again.

Officers breathed a sigh of relief. However, their relief was short-lived, because the demonstrators quickly regrouped and began advancing on the line of police officers once again. After the third encounter the police realized, much to their dismay, that they were out of tear gas. They quickly began "making a frantic effort to locate more tear gas." They were successful. Police braced themselves for the next confrontation, and their reaction this time proved to be particularly aggressive. The *Wilcox Progressive Era* reported,

> The needed tear gas was obtained shortly before noon Tuesday and was in the hands of officers by the time the blacks prepared for their fourth attempt at marching. That effort was made at precisely noon. In that instance the blacks were met with the largest barrage of gas they had seen during the day. Many of them were observed stumbling and falling down a bank beside the road way.[113]

Despite this police reaction, the protestors regrouped and confronted the officers one last time that afternoon. Again, they were turned back by a barrage of tear gas.

Against the background of that chaotic scene, local officers were infuriated by the presence of Alabama State Troopers who absolutely refused to lift a finger to help them subdue the demonstrators. Instead, the troopers sat about a block away from the action under a shade tree observing the long succession of confrontations. Both Sheriff Albritton and Chief Luker were puzzled about the reason for the troopers' presence in their jurisdiction: neither of them had requested state help. They both agreed bitterly that "the troopers will not become involved in anything until it may be too late."[114] Sheriff Albritton was so incensed that he confronted the troopers and had "some harsh words with Trooper officials over the Trooper's refusing to take an active part in maintaining order."[115] Albritton and other county officials were further angered by the attitude of Colonel Walter Allen, the state director of public safety. Allen had accompanied the contingent of Alabama State Troopers who had been dispatched to Camden, and it was he who informed city officials that the troopers would not provide the tear gas requested by the local police. Then, Allen proceeded to add insult to injury when he implied that local officials precipitated the disorder confronting them because of their refusal to allow the demonstrators to complete their march. Beleaguered local officials felt like they were under siege. On the one hand, black demonstrators were defying their authority, while on the other, the state director of public safety was second-guessing their judgment. A short time later Colonel Allen decided to confer with Irby Ratcliffe, Camden city councilman and mayor pro tem. The two met for a time with Camden mayor D. F. Dees, Sheriff Albritton, and Chief Luker. But, after Allen criticized their handling of the protestors, Dees, Albritton, and Luker all stormed out of the meeting. In their absence, Allen and Ratcliffe decided to countermand the orders of city officials by granting permission to the demonstrators to hold their march the next morning. Local law enforcement officials were furious when they got word of the change in policy. The next day,

> As late as two hours before the march was scheduled to begin local Police and Sheriff's officers were still protesting the decision and objecting to the fact that no officially constituted *local* body had authorized the march. They have also noted that they have not been instructed by the Council as to the official position of the town in these matters [emphasis added].[116]

A short time later the Camden Town Council met to clarify procedures for obtaining parade permits. At that time, they decided that they would only allow three black marches a week.[117]

In the meantime, black demonstrators were only dimly aware of all the administrative infighting and bureaucratic posturing behind the scenes as they continued their protests that fall. As the impasse continued, the effect of the school boycott deepened. Because the amount of state education funds allotted to county school boards was based on school attendance figures, the funds available to Wilcox County's schools had been severely curtailed. Predictably, officials were becoming desperate. In that atmosphere, Superintendent Guy Kelly decided it was time for some members of the black community to be punished. Clearly, the most vulnerable African Americans were the county's black teachers. Accordingly, Kelly recommended that "any school which has lost 60% or more of its enrollment because of [the] black walkout be cut by whatever number of teachers is necessary to bring the pupil–teacher ratio in line with state standards of 1 teacher for every 28 pupils."[118] Kelly made that pronouncement knowing full well that the numbers of students missing class were staggering. For example, the Pine Hill Consolidated School had an enrollment of 1,100, but at the height of the boycott only 40 were attending class. At the same time, out of an enrollment of 389, only 22 students were regularly attending class at Boykin. Coy Public School had an enrollment of 102 students, but only 3 students reported for class during the latter part of October.

Curiously enough, even though the leadership and much of the impetus for the boycott came from Camden Academy, a much smaller percentage of their students boycotted classes than students at other schools.[119] The explanation for this seemingly contradictory behavior is undoubtedly rooted in the difference in economic class between students at Camden Academy and students at the county's other black schools. While it is true that Camden Academy's student body included students from economically disadvantaged backgrounds, it still had more middle-class students than other black schools in the county. At the same time, emphasis on education was clearly a core value of the black middle class. Consequently, many middle-class parents, whether they sympathized with the aims of the boycott or not, simply refused to jeopardize their children's education by allowing them to miss classes.

Despite the reluctance of some black middle-class parents to allow their children to boycott classes, however, a huge number of black students all over the county were missing classes, and that prompted Superintendent Kelly to threaten that as many as one hundred black teachers would lose their jobs. By this time, the superintendent was clearly fed up with black student defiance, and he was ready to act immediately. He assured white residents that if the school board accepted his recommendation, "it [would] be only a few days before the teachers [would] be dismissed from their duties."[120] Kelly's action pitted the interests of black students against the interests of their teachers, with the principals caught in the middle. In this chaotic atmosphere, many of the black principals were desperate to convince students to return to class. Because they correctly sensed that their careers were in jeopardy, some principals pressured their faculty to try to convince their students to end the boycott. Reverend Thomas Threadgill observed, "The principals were encouraged to support freedom of choice by the superintendent. Then the principals pushed it down the teachers' throats." Threadgill insisted that this was just another delaying tactic because according to the terms of the freedom of choice plan, students would be reassigned to other schools only if they *requested* a transfer to a school where students of their race were in the minority. Most black residents agreed that the voluntary nature of the freedom of choice plan doomed it to failure. Reverend Threadgill was horrified when his wife came home one afternoon and announced that her principal, J. E. Hobbs, had insisted that his teachers must support freedom of choice. According to Threadgill, "When my wife came home and told me she'd signed supporting freedom of choice, I told her if she didn't take her name off the support, I'd send her to Vietnam the next morning."[121]

Students were painfully aware of the dilemma facing their principals, but many still continued to hope that these community leaders they had always respected would do the right thing. Sometimes Wilcox County's idealistic young people were disappointed. For example, boycott leader Brenda Bussey Carson has particularly painful memories of an incident that illustrated the lengths to which some of the county's black principals were willing to go to keep their jobs. The stage was set when Wilcox County school officials were summoned to federal court in Mobile to report on the progress of school integration in their county. A number of students, including Brenda, were also called to court to testify. That morning, a nervous Brenda Bussey dressed very carefully as she prepared for her court appearance. When she arrived at the courthouse in Mobile, Bussey paused for a moment to compose herself before taking her first step into the long hallway that would lead her to the courtroom. Brenda was only dimly aware of the polished marble of the floor and the pictures hanging on the walls in the corridor leading to the courtroom. She was too busy concentrating on the points she wanted to make in her testimony to worry about such details. She wanted to be sure not to forget anything.

Because she was totally lost in thought, Brenda did not see the group of black principals until she was practically right in front of them. She recoiled in anger and disgust when she saw Wilcox County superintendent Guy Kelly in the midst of a gathering of black principals. He was relaxed and smiling, dressed in a cowboy hat and cowboy boots. Brenda Bussey Carson explains, "That morning when we got down to federal court, Guy Kelly was superintendent at the time, and every black principal in this county was standing there with him [dressed in] cowboy boots and hats [too]." She concludes sadly, "They were there together."[122] This show of solidarity between the black principals whom the students had always respected, and the superintendent whom most had come to view as their enemy, was almost more than Brenda could bear. In that awful moment Brenda Bussey felt like she had been abandoned. When these principals whom she had always admired let her down, Bussey was robbed of some of her childhood innocence and idealism. In particular, she insists that she and her Camden Academy classmates were terribly disappointed by their own principal, J. E. Hobbs. After Hobbs refused to support the students at their initial meeting with the PTA the previous spring, most had still hoped that he would change his mind. However, when it became clear that he would not support their cause, Carson explains, "Everybody pretty much lost respect for him at that point."[123] But James Hobbs was a man caught in the middle. On one hand, the students refused to listen to his pleas to return to school. On the other hand, the Wilcox County Board of Education demanded that he control his students. The untenable nature of his position took its toll on Hobbs, and before that eventful school year ended, he had a nervous breakdown.

While many of Hobbs's students could not forgive his treachery, their anger at him was tinged with sadness when they realized what a pathetic figure he had become. Years later when Brenda Bussey Carson returned to Camden, she decided to take a night class, and that class met at the school where Hobbs was working at the time. Carson had not seen Hobbs since that tumultuous year of the boycott, and she hoped desperately that she would not run into him. Even though those painful events had happened a long time ago, the feeling of betrayal caused by her former principal's treachery was still fresh in her mind. She was careful to sit in the back of the room where she thought her presence might be less conspicuous. Yet, despite her best efforts, Hobbs spotted her in class one evening. He walked right up to her and said cordially, "Nice to have you home." Carson was so surprised at his affable and calm demeanor that all she could do was smile and nod her head. As Hobbs walked away, Carson exhaled noisily: she had not even realized that she had been holding her breath through the entire encounter. After all, the last time she had seen him, Hobbs had been caught in the throes of his nervous breakdown, and he was known to carry a gun. In fact, that night in the classroom Carson had wondered just briefly, "Is he still carrying a gun?"[124]

However, back in the fall of 1971, the demonstrations continued, but now officials decided that it was time to play hardball: they began arresting the protestors. Because there were so many demonstrators, law enforcement officials had to find a large enough facility to house them all. The county and municipal jails did not have nearly enough space, and so officials made arrangements to transport prisoners to Camp Camden, a state penal institution that was located nearby.[125] Larry Threadgill has vivid memories of being incarcerated at Camp Camden. He recalls that the demonstrators were all herded onto big yellow school buses that were lined up on Camden's main street right in the center of town. As the cops roughly pushed Threadgill and his fellow protestors on board those buses, he could not help but smile as he thought about the irony of the situation. Here he was, a high school student, being loaded on a school bus with other students: But they were not being taken to school; they were being taken to jail. The students looked out the windows as their county's familiar scenery flashed by, and many of them wondered what jail would be like. They did not have to wonder long. After the buses arrived at the prison, the student demonstrators were separated by gender, and the males were housed together in one large cell while the females were confined to another. Even though the accommodations were not very comfortable, many of the youngsters still managed to pass the time pleasantly. They talked, sang freedom songs, and many of the young men tossed a balled-up sock back and forth, pretending that they were playing football. At most meals they were served either peanut butter or cheese sandwiches. Finally, after a few days the demonstrators were released, and the marches continued until the Christmas holidays.

When school resumed after the holidays, black students continued to boycott classes. School officials were desperate to resolve their school integration crisis because the student boycott was continuing to cost them precious state education funds. Finally, county school officials extended an olive branch to the black community: they sent word that students would be allowed back in school without any penalty. In fact, they even declared that seniors who had participated in the boycott would be allowed to graduate on time. There were only two exceptions: Larry Threadgill and Brenda Bussey. Thus, in January of 1972, black student boycotters returned to school. The school board made promises about better conditions, and everyone breathed a sigh of relief. Everyone, that is, but Brenda Bussey and Larry Threadgill. The board was careful to send stern letters to these two students informing them that they would not be allowed to come back to school. Brenda Bussey Carson recalls that she was told that she would be barred from returning to school because she had called the superintendent a liar. According to Carson, what she really said was, "The superintendent has lied to the students." However, this was too fine a distinction for the school board to make, and Carson was kept out of school. Finally, the board relented in March and Brenda was allowed back in school. She was so glad to be back; she had missed her friends, her routine, and even her class work. Carson had always been a good student, and she had high hopes for her future once again. Even though she was a senior, Brenda did not expect to graduate that spring because she had been out of school almost all of her senior year. So, she was truly amazed when the school board informed her that she would be allowed to graduate with all the other seniors. The young student leader had mixed feelings about the school board's decision: she knew that her diploma represented her scholastic achievement, but she also knew that it represented the board's decision to rid their school system of the students whom they viewed as troublemakers. She recalls sadly, "We didn't expect to graduate [but] they gave us a diploma to get rid of us."[126]

Even though the board decided to let Brenda Bussey return to school and graduate with her class, they refused to extend the same consideration to the other boycott leader, Larry Threadgill. Threadgill remembers how he felt when he realized that he was the only one of the student protestors who was punished with permanent expulsion. He declares, "I was mad." But, in addition to his anger, Threadgill felt a profound sense of betrayal. He desperately wanted his fellow demonstrators to support him by refusing to return to school as long as he was not allowed back. However, many parents were quite anxious for their children to resume their studies, so that even if the other students had wanted to support Threadgill, most of their parents would not have allowed them to remain out of school any longer. After the others returned to school, Larry Threadgill sometimes went to Camden Academy to talk to his classmates through the fence: he was not even allowed to come on the school grounds. The isolation was very difficult for seventeen-year-old Larry. In his spare time the restless young man watched a lot of television, and he read a lot, too: *The Invisible Man*, *The Autobiography of Malcolm X*, *Native Son*, and *I Know Why the Caged Bird Sings* were only a few of the books he read that spring. A short time later, the preparation of Threadgill's classmates for their senior prom and their graduation exercises only served to underscore his sense of isolation and disillusionment.

At this point, Threadgill's parents wisely decided that their son needed to get away, so they sent him to Chicago to stay with one of his uncles. Although he would later return to Camden and become involved in local politics for a time, Larry Threadgill would never be a permanent resident of Wilcox County again.[127] It seemed that there were powerful feelings of disillusionment and disappointment lurking everywhere in the county waiting to remind him of his part in the 1971–1972 school desegregation struggle every time he came home. Ironically, the year after Larry left, large numbers of black students were finally welcomed into WCHS and all of Wilcox County's formerly all-white schools. But the victory was bittersweet: at the same time that black students entered, the white students fled. *The Wilcox Progressive Era* told the dramatic story of the white exodus:

Public education as Wilcox County had known it for more than 100 years died Tuesday. The schools, which produced the doctors, lawyers, farmers, ministers, storekeepers, mothers, and fathers who made Wilcox County great in the eyes of all Alabama, have taken their place in history. They truly exist no more and we doubt they will again. . . . The last white students at Wilcox County High School walked out the door that afternoon. A few came back Tuesday morning, but only to gather their personal belongings. . . . The destruction of the schools is already proving to be a hollow victory.[128]

The white students enrolled in the private all-white academies that had just been established in various parts of the county. Thus, in the fall of 1972, it seemed that the desegregation the black students had struggled so hard for just the previous spring remained just beyond their reach.

CHAPTER SEVEN

~

After the Movement

In the aftermath of the dramatic school desegregation struggles of the 1971–1972 school year, Larry Threadgill, the only student who was permanently expelled because of his leadership in the struggle, sadly contemplated his future. Despite his sense of disappointment and betrayal, young Larry had to go on with his life. Accordingly, his father, Thomas Threadgill, attempted to get a copy of his son's school records so that the younger Threadgill could continue his education elsewhere. Father and son were both shocked when they learned that Larry's records had fallen victim to the school board's vindictiveness: his records had been completely obliterated. It was as if he had never attended school in Wilcox County. Larry never found out who was responsible for the destruction.

Undaunted, Reverend Threadgill enlisted the aid of sympathetic teachers who had taught his son. One of them managed to obtain an official Wilcox County transcript form, and they were able to reconstruct the young activist's school records. Armed with his reconstructed transcript, Larry applied for admission to Mary Holmes College in West Point, Mississippi. He was accepted, but he hated it, and he only stayed one year. A short time later, he decided that the place for him was Morehouse College in Atlanta. The young activist was drawn to the all-male college because it had been a hotbed of student activism during the glory days of the Student Nonviolent Coordinating Committee (SNCC). Furthermore, it was his father's alma mater, and the alma mater of the recently assassinated Dr. Martin Luther King Jr.[1] Young Larry gladly left Wilcox County that fall to enroll in Morehouse College.

In the meantime, as Larry Threadgill was trying to regain his equilibrium in Atlanta, the educational system in his county had lapsed into an uneasy peace as it tried to adjust to a new reality. Many expected that the swift and sure exodus of white students from the county's public schools that had begun in the spring of 1972 would soon be complete. As the fall term approached the *Wilcox Progressive Era* confidently predicted,

> Several hundred white students walked out of the public schools last year, and most are expected to remain out. The largest number of those students are enrolled in private schools throughout the area, and others are expected to do so between now and the first of September.[2]

It soon became clear, however, that things were not nearly this definite. For some time, a number of white students continued to attend their county's public schools. For example, when Wilcox County High School (WCHS) opened that fall some 99 white students enrolled for classes along with 115 African Americans. Furthermore, the school's previously all-white faculty was now all black with the exception of the principal and the home economics teacher.[3] In the meantime, as the county's remaining white school officials alternately fretted and fumed about enforced desegregation, they allowed conditions in the system's traditionally black schools to go from bad to worse. In this regard most black schools in the county were particularly hard-hit by classrooms that were even more overcrowded than they had been prior to the integration upheaval of the 1971–1972 school year. The pupil–teacher ratio at Camden Academy was one of the highest: it was more than eighty to one. While other black schools in the system had lower pupil–teacher ratios than Camden Academy, they still suffered from serious overcrowding. For example, Pine Hill Consolidated's ratio was sixty to one. At the same time, however, the white schools in the system had much lower pupil–teacher ratios.[4]

All the while, the county's combative white superintendent, Guy Kelly, was alternately furious and despondent as he saw control of the public school system in his county slipping out of his grip. In fact, just the previous spring, right after the black students ended their boycott and returned to school, Kelly had decided that the situation was spinning out of control. At that point, motivated by feelings of impotence, Kelly decided that there was only one person who had the power to put things back the way they were. That person was Richard M. Nixon, the president of the United States. Although most white Wilcox County residents had been staunch Democrats for generations, by this time many had begun to look with increasing favor on the Republican Party. Part of the reason for the switch was the conviction held by many white Southerners that the Democratic Party under Kennedy and Johnson had moved much too far to the left in their support for civil rights initiatives.

At the same time, Richard Nixon, the Republican nominee who was elected to the presidency in 1968, began to make promises that endeared him to the white South. For example, in a 1968 campaign promise, Nixon insisted that if he were elected, he would "reverse the flow of power and resources from the states and communities to Washington and start power and resources flowing back . . . to the people."[5] Kelly and other white residents were overjoyed to hear such a promise because most of them were furious with what they thought of as federal meddling in their affairs. After he was elected, Nixon made good on his promise. Indeed, in his zeal to "start power and resources flowing back . . . to the people," the new president promptly cut the funding for many War on Poverty programs that had been started by his predecessor. Nixon also dismantled the Office of Economic Opportunity in 1971. Furthermore, it quickly became apparent that Nixon had virtually no interest in "extending the gains of the civil rights movement."[6]

Not surprisingly, then, Wilcox County's desperate superintendent of education thought he recognized a kindred spirit in Richard M. Nixon, and he wrote a series of letters to the president during the spring and summer of 1972. In his first letter, Kelly made sure to let the president know the identity of the culprits who were responsible for his county's predicament. He explained, "In March . . . the Fifth Circuit Court issued the order which sealed the doom of the Wilcox County School System. This order was issued as a result of continuous attacks on the school system by the Justice Department, HEW, and a little group of civil rights activists living here in this county."[7] Kelly pleaded with the president to intervene. He insisted, "We have a judicial system which is clearly violating the law and you are our only hope."[8] In his second letter to the president, Kelly blamed the victims of unequal education for the destruction of the whole system. He charged, "Public education is being systematically destroyed in the name of negroes [sic]."[9]

There is no indication that the busy president ever answered the frustrated superintendent. By the time that Kelly's last letter reached him, Richard Nixon was in the midst of campaigning for his second term, and the Watergate scandal that would eventually bring down his presidency was looming on the horizon. In the meantime, however, back in Wilcox County, Superintendent Guy Kelly finally decided that he simply could not face a future of integrated schools and federal intervention. Consequently, just as the fall 1972 term was getting underway, Kelly decided that he had had enough. He

abruptly resigned. For some time after his resignation, Kelly offered no public explanation. Finally, some time later, he expressed anger and bitterness in
a letter he wrote to the *Wilcox Progressive Era*. As far as Kelly was concerned
the blame for his county's bleak educational outlook rested squarely with the
federal government. He charged,

> When . . . [President] Johnson and the federal government ordered officials to
> allow and protect Martin Luther King and his motley gang to march down
> Highway 80 from Selma to Montgomery [in 1965], they opened a Pandora's
> box that let loose on this land a reign of violence and rebellion unparalleled in
> the history of this country.[10]

After Kelly's resignation, his assistant, Morris Ward, was appointed as his replacement. There were some who heralded Ward's appointment as an important step forward. For example, Albert Gordon, one of the black teachers
Kelly had fired, and a vice president of the Wilcox County Civic and Progressive League (WCCPL), recalled that Ward was much less abrasive than
his predecessor. Gordon insisted, "He [Ward] would listen to you. He would
sit down and listen to you and talk to you any time about the situation."[11]
Yet, despite the new superintendent's more affable personality, there were
some who had serious concerns about his educational vision. Volunteers in
Service to America (VISTA) teacher James Beardsley recalls that when the
new superintendent hired him to teach full-time at Boykin, he did not discuss serious issues like curriculum or even discipline at Boykin Elementary
School. Instead, Ward told the young teacher, "I want you to go over there
and see if you can get the bathrooms clean."[12]

One of the reasons why Superintendent Ward was so concerned about
clean bathrooms was because the issue of bathroom sanitation in black
schools had been addressed specifically in an appeals court order dated May
15, 1973.[13] The condition of the bathrooms in black schools was part of a
larger judicial concern regarding the air of neglect that seemed to envelop all
the black schools in the system. It was that concern that prompted the court
to issue an order on June 28, 1973, directing the Wilcox County Board of Education to "provide janitorial service, maintenance and upkeep for each
school."[14] Furthermore, this court found that when the county began to desegregate its schools, the school board began charging black students a fee to
cover the cost of janitorial services in their schools. The court decreed that
this was improper, and it unequivocally instructed, "the School Board to provide janitorial service," and it further prohibited the board from "collecting
fees from the students for this purpose."[15] In fact, the issue of sanitation in

the county's black schools had long been a bone of contention. Just the previous decade when the National Education Association (NEA) investigated conditions in black Wilcox schools, they reported,

> Lower Peach Tree students reported that the classrooms are cold when they arrive in the morning and that they have to build their own fires and sweep their own floors. They said that the school does have a janitor, but that he is paid only $38 a month for janitorial services and also drives the school bus, making two trips each morning and evening. The time he has to spend on janitorial tasks is extremely limited, and what he does not do, the students and teachers must do or it does not get done at all.[16]

The association was quick to point out that Lower Peach Tree was not exceptional. On the contrary, "the [Wilcox County] Board of Education provides little, if any, more in the way of janitorial services in other Negro schools than it does in Lower Peach Tree."[17]

Yet, while sanitation was clearly a concern, over the next few years Superintendent Morris Ward would have a lot more to worry about than the condition of school bathrooms, because through the early part of the decade of the 1970s the U.S. District Court for the Southern District of Alabama and the United States Court of Appeals for the Fifth Circuit sparred over the question of the most effective way to implement the desegregation of Wilcox County's schools. District Court judge W. Brevard Hand insisted that although the Wilcox County School Board had not zealously implemented the desegregation directives mandated by his court, still, "there was total acquiescence by counsel and the School Board, and insofar as this Court has been informed or advised or has received testimony on point, the School Board has attempted to fully comply with these orders within the limits of their capabilities and understanding."[18] In contrast, the U.S. Court of Appeals insisted that, "the record here indicates that the Wilcox County School Board has yet to objectively demonstrate its will to operate this system in a manner calculated to remedy past discriminatory practices and achieve unitary status." The appeals court went on to charge that Wilcox County's attempt to implement school desegregation was so feeble that it placed the county squarely in "the shadow of contempt."[19]

One of the most important issues on which the two courts disagreed was the method that should be used to achieve desegregation. District court judge Hand was convinced that the only way for the Wilcox system to achieve any desegregation at all would be for the court to give white students special consideration because of their small numbers. Hand explained, "The court finds that the minority involved in this respect is not the black community but the white community and as part of the resolution of the problem . . . an effort was made to preserve in part the integration of the races by devising some means by which the whites attending the schools of Wilcox County would remain in the system."[20] However, in their ruling on Hand's remedy, the U.S. Appeals Court candidly discussed the way Hand's desegregation method was designed to work: "the district court, in the face of a preponderant black student majority and a white student exodus, sought to preserve some semblance of racial integration by permitting the relative handful of white students to elect to concentrate themselves in a formerly all-white facility—the Wilcox County High School."[21] Appeals court judges were highly critical of Hand's remedy. They insisted, "In Wilcox County, the minority to minority transfer provision imposes a condition that is racially biased in every respect except literal appellation."[22] The judges continued, "the district court erred . . . in adopting a minority to minority transfer provision." The judges concluded by ruling, "these portions of the order appealed from are reversed."[23]

In the midst of all this wrangling by the courts, the Wilcox County Public School System continued to deteriorate as the exodus of the few remaining white students proceeded unchecked. At this point, one of the major issues facing the embattled system was the problem of accreditation: not one of the county's schools was accredited. As early as October of 1972, the court of appeals had issued a consent order directing the Wilcox County School Board to "achieve accreditation in every district school where financially possible."[24] Appeals court judges realized that a large part of the reason why accreditation problems along with a whole host of other issues continued to plague the Wilcox system was because of the county's impoverished condition. The court asserted that, "Economically the county is among the nation's poorest, and some of the impediments to achieving a unitary school system are directly attributable to fiscal disabilities under a system of financing in which declining enrollment and lack of local effort reduce state funding."[25] The court had already issued an order "enjoin[ing] all parties to seek outside financial assistance and to assist the [Wilcox County] Board with other financially related efforts." In frustration the appeals court explained that despite its previous order, "the [Wilcox County] Board has taken the position that its direct financial involvement is limited by Alabama law to allocation of funds based upon average daily attendance and that it has no authority to make 'a special case' of Wilcox County."[26]

Indeed, the Alabama state formula for public school funding at that time was based on the daily attendance statistics for students in each district. Thus, when large numbers of black students had boycotted classes, first during the voting rights campaign, then later during the school desegregation struggle, the state withheld a significant portion of funding from the already impoverished system. A short time later when large numbers of white students began to desert the system, Wilcox County's public schools lost even more precious state funding. Furthermore, it is important to note that the Wilcox County Public School system had been badly underfunded for many years prior to the black student boycotts and the white student defections during the civil rights movement. Consequently, when the state withheld funds in the late 1960s and early 1970s, the already inadequate Wilcox County school system came close to the brink of collapse. In the meantime, even though both the district court and the Fifth Circuit Court of Appeals had directed the Wilcox County School Board to reinstate the black teachers who had been dismissed during the demonstrations and give them back pay, the board had continued to drag its feet. It was not until 1976 that the cases of the last two black teachers who had been unlawfully dismissed were finally settled.[27] By this time, the Wilcox County Public Schools were virtually all black, but the superintendent and members of the school board remained all white.

Caught in the middle of all the legal maneuvers of the 1970s were Wilcox County's black students. At the very beginning of the decade they had publicly and forcefully demanded equal treatment. At the beginning of their struggle, they had no doubt that their county's school system unfairly favored the white students, and in the aftermath of the *Brown* decision, they simply refused to accept this. Armed with their youthful idealism, the county's black students looked forward to the future with a great deal of hope. However, as the decade wore on, and the equality they had been seeking continued to elude them, student optimism gave way to a sense of unease and despair, and then ultimately to a sense of resignation. Hannah Bell Ramsey, a black Wilcox native, clearly recalls those years of transition in the Wilcox County Public School system. She was born and raised in Camden, the youngest girl in a family of ten children. When she was a youngster, she remembers how frightened she was during the most chaotic days of the civil rights movement in her county. At one point her mother was arrested during a voting rights march, and she spent two days in jail. By this time Ramsey's father was dead, so she and her brothers and sisters were left alone the whole time their mother was incarcerated. Hannah remembers feeling particularly vulnerable during those two days.[28]

Later, when Ramsey was older, she clearly remembers the student boycott that would finally force public school officials to face the issue of school integration. It seemed to young Hannah that the boycott would drag on forever, and she almost lost hope that anything would ever change. Finally, it was over, and an eager Hannah Ramsey was able to return to school. During her first days back her expectations were high, but very quickly, she says, "I saw a little bit of change, [but] not really much."[29] Later, she was one of the black students who were assigned to attend the formerly all-white Wilcox County High School. By the time she enrolled in classes there, only a small number of white students remained, and she was convinced that the only reason they were there was because their parents could not afford the tuition at one of the county's private academies. Ramsey has vivid memories of the first day she entered the formerly all-white school. She observes, "it felt kind of funny." As she settled into a routine at her new school, Ramsey recalls that she could never quite shake that initial sense of unease she had felt the very first day. She explains, "I felt out of place even though I went to school there."[30] Clearly, even though Ramsey and her black classmates were now a majority of Wilcox County High's students, ghosts from the school's segregated origins and traditions seemed to roam the hallways and haunt the classrooms spreading a sense of unease. S. C. Collier, a black teacher during the tumultuous days of the school integration crisis, recalls that many of his students talked to him about their feelings of isolation and vulnerability in the midst of the struggle. Collier was convinced that the current generation of students was so badly scarred by the impact of the school integration struggle that the system would fail to make any real progress until these students had finished school. As he put it, "I said that after the movement was over it would take thirteen years in order to . . . see an advance . . . [because by then] we would have a new crop of students."[31]

At the same time, many of those black teachers who lost their jobs at the height of the crisis were irreparably harmed. In a county as impoverished as Wilcox there were few job opportunities besides teaching for educated African Americans. Consequently, the loss of their teaching jobs often wreaked financial havoc on the families of these unemployed educators. Black fellow teachers sympathized and tried to help as much as they could. Clark Thomas, a black Wilcox principal, recalls that the Wilcox County Teachers Association provided some support for their unemployed colleagues; but usually the best they could do, given their financial limitations, was to provide $200 a month, but only for two or three months.[32] Against this background of economic uncertainty and job insecurity the county's white school superintendent blatantly tried to sow the seeds of dissension by pitting black principals against their teachers. A graphic illustration of Superintendent Kelly's tactics is contained in the case of Reverend Frank Smith. Smith was a teacher at Lower Peach Tree during the school desegregation conflict. Because of his energetic support of the movement, Smith soon became recognized as a leader of the struggle in his area. Predictably, word came down from the board of education that Reverend Smith would be dismissed from his teaching position. Of course, the official reason for Smith's dismissal was that fewer teachers were needed because of the low attendance resulting from the student boycott. Everybody was sure, however, that the real reason for the popular teacher's dismissal was his unequivocal support of the movement. The unfair treatment stung Reverend Smith, and he was particularly disappointed by the role he thought his principal had played in the whole affair.

In fact, Principal Ferdinand S. Ervin of Lower Peach Tree had been approached by Superintendent Kelly about Smith's movement activities. The superintendent demanded that the principal fire the troublesome teacher. Ervin refused. Instead, he looked the superintendent in the eye and said in a soft, but stern voice, "If you want to fire him, you fire him." The principal added resolutely, "I'm not going to do it. He does a good job."[33] At the time, Reverend Smith was totally unaware of this exchange between his principal and the superintendent. Instead, he assumed that Principal Ervin had helped to engineer his dismissal. Smith did not find out the truth until years later when he was elected to the Wilcox County Board of Education. In his capacity as a board member, Smith had access to all the documents detailing the board's past activities. One day, he ran across some old documents from the civil rights era. His eyes widened and the blood drained from his face as he read about the dismissal of black teachers who were staunch supporters of civil rights activities. As he read down the list of names, his name jumped out at him, and he realized that the superintendent and the school board had been solely responsible for the dismissals. His principal had not had anything to do with it. At that moment, Smith realized that he had been nursing a grudge for over a decade against a man who was blameless. A short time later, he went to see his former principal, and with tears in his eyes, he grasped Ferdinand Ervin's hand and offered his sincere apology.[34]

Smith was not the only one who, rightly or wrongly, felt that they had been betrayed by other black educators in their county. Moreover, the picture became even more complicated because of the board's attempt to blame teacher dismissals on student boycotters. Because state policy tied teacher employment to student attendance statistics, the board reasoned, they were only following state policy by reducing the number of teachers in light of the student boycott. It was clear to everyone, however, that the only teachers who were being dismissed were those who had expressed support for the movement. This link between student activism and teacher job security only served to inject even more insecurity into an already insecure system. It was against this background of suspicion and dissension that Wilcox County's black educators and students faced an uncertain future. They were painfully aware that they were inheriting a fractured system of public schools that was flat broke and unaccredited. They were also aware that because there were few white students left in the system, it was highly unlikely that white Wilcox residents who still controlled the county's finances would be inclined to try to improve the system. Thus, after the school integration struggles of the 1970s, Wilcox County's public education system was virtually all black— that included students, teachers, and administrators—but the leadership of the bankrupt system, the school board and the superintendent, remained all white.

The struggle of Wilcox County's black residents to integrate the county's public schools was part of their larger struggle to integrate their county's po- litical structure. By the early 1970s just as the leadership of the school system remained all white, the county's political structure also remained firmly un- der white control. Ever since the passage of the Voting Rights Act in 1965, African Americans in Wilcox County had registered and voted in every county election. Yet, despite their superior numbers, black voters had been unable to elect a single black candidate to any county or municipal office. Even in the face of a federal commitment to protect the voting rights of newly enfranchised black Southerners, white Wilcox residents unequivocally and constantly demonstrated their refusal to yield any political power in their county. Consequently, through the late 1960s and well into the 1970s black residents encountered a solid wall of white resistance. One of the most widespread tactics used by determined white residents was the tried and true method of intimidation. Black residents reported a continuous stream of white attempts to intimidate black voters. For example, Reverend Thomas Threadgill reported,

> When some [black] people had gone to register, they'd been evicted from their homes. They were afraid of being fired. You couldn't just slip in and vote. Peo- ple stand in line. And if you're a landowner and you have ten families living on your place, you come to town on voting day, drive by the courthouse and see your cook standing in line—waiting to vote. So you go back that night and tell her, "Mary, I don't need you anymore."[35]

Because of their fear of economic reprisals, many black residents agonized over the question of whether or not they should register to vote. Black resi- dents often discussed their plight with Reverend Threadgill, and he was deeply moved by their plaintive pleas. He explained, "I'd have people come to me and say, 'Reverend, my landlord told me that if I go up tomorrow and vote, I've got to go.'" After commiserating with them, Threadgill advised, "I'd tell them to make up their own minds. But if they decided to go and vote, and if they were evicted, I'd do whatever I could to find them a place to stay."[36] Threadgill's son Larry has vivid memories of seeing some of those sharecropping families who had been evicted. Many came to Camden in mule-drawn wagons piled high with their possessions. They did not know where to go or what to do, and the expressions of despair on the faces of the parents and their frightened children haunted Larry.[37] The threat of eviction was not the only form of intimidation employed by determined white Wilcox residents. One of the more common forms of intimidation was the none-too-subtle reminder of racial deference patterns. Reverend Charlie Pettway, a black Wilcox resident who was a poll watcher in 1970 and 1971 recalls that white residents routinely gathered around the polls on election day and glared menacingly at black residents who were forced to walk past them as they made their way to the voting booth. One of Pettway's jobs as a poll watcher was to assist illiterate voters by reading the names on the ballot to them. The county's white election officials were furious at Pettway for assisting illiterate voters, many of whom were black and elderly. They warned him over and over again in a strident tone, "You cannot tell them who to vote for." Pettway patiently replied, "I know that."[38] Pettway recalls that the tense and menacing atmosphere at the polls was extremely upsetting to many black residents who were attempting to exercise their right to vote for the very first time.

White Wilcox residents were unapologetic for their opposition to black voting. For example, white Wilcox resident Pat Nettles clearly expressed his opposition in no uncertain terms. As he put it, "The nigger ain't got no business voting." Nettles continued,

What's the nigger across the road going to do with the vote? He doesn't know there's such a thing as a Probate Judge. If it's up to him to vote, he'll vote for the one who gives him a nickel, or a dime, or a quarter. . . . You take an old nigger who can't read or write. Now who's he going to vote for in Wilcox County?[39]

As it became clear that African American voting had become a fact of life in Wilcox County, some of the more blatant expressions of white disapproval began to subside, and some of the white candidates for county offices actually began to court the black vote. All too often, however, their appeals were characterized by insulting and demeaning behavior that clearly indicated their continued belief in black inferiority. Charles McCarthy, a white candidate for probate judge, accused long-time sheriff Lummie Jenkins of this kind of behavior. According to McCarthy,

> Lummie told the whites he was their candidate. But Lummie Jenkins went to the Boykin Prom, over there dancing with niggers. Lummie Jenkins spoke at Boykin class night. He brought three jugs of whiskey, and they all got so drunk they lost the third one. He brought three hundred pounds of fish.

McCarthy went on to describe the fish fry sponsored by Jenkins for local black residents. He concluded disgustedly, "some political rally."[40] Recognizing the frequency of such appeals and the temptation they posed because of the impoverished condition of the county's black residents, one local African American clergyman exhorted his parishioners, "This man comes down here and he comes to me and he comes to you and he says he'll give us a little money for his vote. His pocket's full. But we've got this franchise. We had a hard time getting it, but you all have it." He concluded, "now the Lawd give you one little job—to vote. And you don't let this little ole white man tell you how to do it."[41]

In an atmosphere where white residents were willing to do anything to blunt the impact of black voting strength in their county, charges and countercharges of fraud were leveled in one election after another. In fact, accusations of fraud surfaced immediately after the very first election since Reconstruction in which black candidates ran. In that election, which was held on May 3, 1966, just months after the passage of the Voting Rights Act, the first slate of black candidates ran for county offices. Walter J. Calhoun ran for sheriff, pledging to "put honor and dependability back into law enforcement." Donnie Irby and James Perryman ran for road commissioner, James Robinson ran for tax assessor, and Lonnie Brown ran for state senator in District 19.[42] Reverend Brown vividly recalls that they were all very hopeful in the initial stages of the campaign. He observes, "Sometimes when you go into these things, you go in kind of naive." Many felt empowered just to have the opportunity to run for political office. Brown explains, "[There were] two things we had in mind; if we could get those positions, and [even] if we didn't get them, we ran for them to let younger people understand that you can do it. It's there for you."[43] Throughout the campaign, an optimistic Reverend Brown continued to believe that when the election results came in, Wilcox County would have its first black elected officials since Reconstruction.

Finally, the big day came. African American voters all over the county excitedly went to the polls, determined to make the promises of the civil rights movement a reality. However, the excitement of Wilcox County's new black voters was tempered by a nagging sense of unease that accompanied them to the polling places. They knew how angry their white neighbors were, and they could not help but wonder if that white anger would result in white retaliation at some point. Despite their fears, however, most proudly marked their ballots and then waited, secure in the knowledge that they far outnumbered the county's white voters. By that evening the anxiety had become almost unbearable as the candidates waited to hear the vote tallies. Brown recalls, "It seems to me that up until about ten o'clock the night of the election I was leading, but that changed. What we really think happened [is that] it changed in the counting." Brown goes on to lament that the votes were counted in a room inside the courthouse, and nobody black was present to witness it. Brown concludes, "We felt that it [the election] was stolen."[44] Not a single black candidate was elected. Such an overwhelming defeat in their heavily black county left local black political activists reeling. Most were disappointed, some were angry, but all remained determined. Brown explains, "We were discouraged some, but you got to remember, we had been discouraged all of our lives about something. So, it wasn't enough to kill our spirits . . . it just intensified [our desire]."[45]

Through the late 1960s and well into the 1970s, success continued to elude every black Wilcox candidate who ran for political office. Just like Reverend Brown, most African Americans were convinced that their county's white election officials were continuing to manipulate the vote count in one election after another. One of those unsuccessful black candidates, James Thomas, recalls just how blatant the manipulation was during his 1978 bid for a seat in the Alabama House of Representatives. On election day Thomas was hopeful, and as the ballots were counted, his confidence soared. By late that night, all the boxes, except one from Arlington, had been counted, and Thomas held a convincing lead. It was two o'clock in the morning, and James Thomas could not hide his small smile of satisfaction as he contemplated his victory. He explains, "I was certain that I had won . . . because . . . there had never been over sixty or sixty-five people voting in that box [the one that had yet to be counted]." With the lead he had, he knew that those sixty-five votes should not have made any difference, but to James Thomas's surprise those counting the votes claimed that the Arlington box contained over one hundred votes, and that was enough to change the outcome. His opponent, white incumbent William Edwards, won by ten votes.[46]

Thomas had no doubt that the vote count was fraudulent, and when he went to the courthouse the next morning, his suspicions were confirmed.

That morning as he approached the antebellum structure that was still a symbol of white control in his county, Thomas spotted a group of white men standing near the entrance. They were laughing and talking with easy familiarity. As Thomas got closer to the group of men, one of them casually turned toward him and said, "Yeah, there's James Thomas." Looking directly at Thomas the white man continued, "I want you to know I voted twenty damn times, and I'll vote twenty more damn times if necessary."[47] Thomas, a tall, lean man, drew himself up to his full height and continued to make his way into the courthouse. The statement hung in the air like an unanswered challenge, but James Thomas did have an answer to that challenge even if he did not say it out loud. As he puts it, "I said to myself that day, it will never happen again," and by that afternoon he had already begun looking forward to the next election in 1982 when he could run again for the same seat. He confirms, "I started running that day."[48] Through all the early defeats they suffered, African American candidates in Wilcox County learned an important lesson. As Reverend Brown puts it, "We knew how they [white people] were thinking. People don't give up power." He repeated emphatically, "They don't give it up. We had sense enough to know that you have to . . . I hate to use that word, you have to force them and take power."[49]

Clearly, the battle lines were drawn. Despite the existence of an overwhelming black majority in their county, African American residents realized that they would have to go to extraordinary lengths to change the balance of power because their white neighbors continued to exercise virtually complete control over Wilcox County's election apparatus. Thus, as they plotted strategy, most black Wilcox residents quickly became convinced that the key to their success lay in seizing control of the electoral process. It is against that backdrop that insecure white Wilcox residents regularly urged their black neighbors to ignore the race of the candidates for political office. At every opportunity, white residents insisted that experience was of paramount importance. Because black candidates obviously had no political experience, the conclusion was inescapable, according to prevailing white wisdom, that African Americans were unfit to hold any political office in Wilcox County. One political ad that blatantly articulated this message appeared in the May 2, 1974, edition of the *Wilcox Progressive Era*. In big, bold type the ad declared, "DON'T ENTRUST YOUR COUNTY TO INEXPERIENCED MEN. A FIRST GRADE BOY SHOULDN'T BE PRINCIPAL OF A SCHOOL AND INEXPERIENCED MEN CAN'T RUN COUNTY BUSINESS."[50]

In a long editorial in the same edition, the paper's editor consistently advised county residents against voting for black candidates in one race after another. For example, in the race for probate judge, the *Wilcox Progressive Era* endorsed incumbent Roland Cooper, calling him "an experienced business-man and administrator" who will "fairly represent all the county's residents." In the very next sentence the paper's editor quickly dismissed Cooper's black opponent by claiming "his opponent, Reverend Albert Suggs, has no qualifi-cations whatsoever. He seems to be an honest, religious man and . . . aside from the fact that he is black . . . that is about all. Voters of both races should not waste their vote by casting it for Suggs because of racism or personality."[51] Furthermore, despite the precarious position of the county's school system due to the mass exodus of white students, the *Wilcox Progressive Era*'s editor doggedly endorsed only white candidates for positions on the school board. He argued, "many people have said that blacks should have these jobs since most of the students in the public schools are black." The editor conceded, "there may be merit to that argument in the minds of many[,] but we don't think so." Using a farfetched comparison he warned, "those who say 'black for black's sake' ought to stop and think whether they would want a black hospital orderly doing brain surgery simply because he is black. The same is true of school administration . . . color has nothing to do with it."[52]

Even as their white neighbors argued against the election of black candi-dates in those early years after the passage of the Voting Rights Act, Wilcox County's black political activists refused to be dissuaded. However, as they continued to organize and plot strategy in an effort to elect black candidates to office, they were faced with the question of their party affiliation. At that time, many of their state's most rabid racists continued to be affiliated with the Democratic Party. At the same time, however, the National Democratic Party led by President Lyndon Johnson was widely perceived to be a friend of the civil rights movement. The existence of such dramatic differences be-tween local Democrats and the national party establishment set the stage for the formation of a rival Democratic organization in Alabama that would provide black Wilcox residents with a clear choice. That organization, the National Democratic Party of Alabama (NDPA), was eagerly embraced by black county residents. Predictably, white Wilcox residents were extremely critical of the NDPA. In fact, after the general election in the fall of 1974 when NDPA candidates were once again defeated by white incumbents, the *Wilcox Progressive Era* insisted that the election results indicated that "a number of black voters rejected the NDPA and what it has come to stand for. This gives rise to the notion that most of the responsible black leaders around Wilcox County are not affiliated with the NDPA and that more and more black voters are turning their backs on the NDPA in favor of proven leadership."[53]

Regardless of the *Progressive Era*'s wishful thinking, a majority of the county's black voters continued their affiliation with the NDPA, and later, after this organization became part of the Alabama Democratic Conference, they remained loyal to this Democratic alternative. The all-black Alabama Democratic Conference had been established well before the passage of the Voting Rights Act. The impetus for the establishment of this group was rooted in the extraordinarily close presidential election of 1960. Louis Martin, a black newspaper publisher and Kennedy supporter, called a meeting of black leaders from all over the South in the summer of 1960 in an effort to cultivate southern black support for the Kennedy–Johnson ticket in the upcoming election. Conferees met in Atlanta, and representing the state of Alabama were Orzell Billingsley, Peter Hall, and Arthur Shores from Birmingham; C. G. Gomillion of Tuskegee; and Rufus Lewis of Montgomery.[54] As they thought about the most effective way to influence the black vote in their state, the Alabama delegation came up with the idea of establishing a statewide organization of black voters' leagues and improvement associations. They named their new organization the Alabama Democratic Conference (ADC).[55] This black alternative to the white Democratic Party would later play an important role in the election of black Democratic candidates all over the state—including Wilcox County. According to J. L. Chestnut, a black civil rights attorney in Selma, "after the Voting Rights Act was passed and thousands of blacks got registered, ADC gave the black vote in Alabama an organized impact, and it became the most powerful statewide black political organization in the country."[56]

Despite the ADC's effectiveness, however, as the 1970s drew to a close, the African American enfranchised majority in Wilcox County had yet to elect a black candidate to any office in the county. Although many were frustrated, and most were disillusioned, there still remained a core of black political activists who continued to work to make the dream of black elected officials in their county a reality. One of those activists was a wounded Vietnam veteran named Bobby Jo Johnson. Johnson was a native of Wilcox County who came up the hard way. His mother was a struggling single parent who made the difficult decision to send him to live with his grandmother when he was just a youngster. Johnson's grandparents farmed, and even though they owned their own land, there never seemed to be enough money. As he was growing up, Bobby Jo Johnson, like most other black boys in Wilcox County, experienced firsthand his county's code of racial conduct that demanded absolute submission from black residents. At the same time, however, he was also aware of the ever present undercurrent of black resistance.

Things came to a head in his young life when he was about sixteen years old. The stage was set when a tragic house fire in his community killed an elderly woman. Wilcox authorities quickly decided that young Johnson was a suspect. One of Sheriff Lummie Jenkins's deputies picked up the unsuspecting teenager, took him down to the jail in Camden, put him in a small windowless room, and tried to extract a confession from him. As a young black boy growing up in Wilcox County, Bobby Jo Johnson had heard the lurid details of the brutal treatment black suspects routinely received at the hands of white law enforcement officials. But here it was happening to him, and he could not believe it. Johnson realized the danger he was in, and it frightened him even though he knew he was innocent. Without warning, the deputy slapped the teenager viciously across the mouth. Before Johnson could react, the deputy slapped him again and again. All the while the deputy demanded that his prisoner confess. With every slap, Johnson's fear began to recede, and in its place a terrible anger grew. The angry teenager was careful to keep his facial expression neutral, but he was seething inside. When the slaps did not work, the deputy began punching Bobby Jo, but still the teenager refused to utter a word. Finally, the frustrated deputy realized that his prisoner was not about to admit anything, and he released young Johnson. Relieved to be out of his tormentor's clutches, the bruised and battered teenager began walking home, careful to stay close to the side of the road. Unable to shake an unsettling feeling of vulnerability, Johnson was careful to step off the side of the road and into the bushes every time a car approached. Before long, he looked at a passing vehicle from his vantage point in the bushes and realized that it was Sheriff Jenkins and his deputy. Johnson was sure they were looking for him, and he was sure there was only one reason they would want him: to lynch him. He was innocent, but they did not seem to care. The injustice of his predicament struck the teenage Bobby Jo Johnson like a lead weight, and it proved to be a defining moment in his life.[57]

In the meantime, after Jenkins and his deputy drove past their quarry in the bushes, they continued on in the direction of Bobby Jo's grandmother's house. They arrived at the house without ever having spotted the young fugitive, and they brazenly went up to the old woman's front door to demand that she produce her grandson. She quietly opened her door, stepped outside, and allowed the door to bang shut behind her. She stood motionless for just a moment, but as the white lawmen repeated their demand, they noticed that the old woman was holding a shotgun by her side. Without hesitation she responded, "I don't think you're going to talk to him no [sic] more . . . the only thing you'[re] going to talk to is my shotgun, and I want you out of my yard."

The irritated lawmen quickly realized that the old woman meant every word, so they turned and left.[58] As Bobby Jo matured, he never forgot his near-fatal encounter with Wilcox law enforcement authorities, and a righteous indignation began to simmer in him. That indignation continued to simmer in Bobby Jo Johnson when he joined the United States Army and shipped out to southeast Asia to fight in the Vietnam War. After a short time in combat, he was seriously wounded, and he was sent to Japan to recuperate. Because of the severity of his injuries, Bobby Jo Johnson received an honorable discharge from the service as soon as he was well, and he returned to Wilcox County to try to resume his life. However, the Bobby Jo Johnson who returned to the Alabama Black Belt was not the same man who had left. The most obvious difference was in his appearance: his combat wounds resulted in the loss of one leg and four fingers. There were also other changes in Bobby Jo Johnson that were not quite as obvious. The most important difference was that the simmering righteous indignation that had accompanied Johnson to Vietnam had begun to boil over by the time he returned.[59]

It was 1968 when Johnson arrived home in Wilcox County, and by that time he had decided that he was ready to settle down. Consequently, on July 5, 1968, he married his high school sweetheart, Astoria Mason, and the two settled into married life in the months that followed. It was not long before the new Mrs. Johnson detected that righteous indignation that burned so brightly in her husband. She recalls that he regularly commented on the unjust treatment suffered by black Wilcox residents at the hands of their white neighbors. It seemed to Johnson that even though the laws had changed because of the civil rights movement, white residents were having trouble adjusting to the new racial reality. He was furious at white Wilcox residents who still expected their black neighbors to continue to observe the same racial deference patterns. Astoria Johnson remembers a particularly illustrative incident. One day her husband went to an auto parts store, and after he had selected the items he intended to purchase, he walked up to the cashier. As he was reaching for his wallet, the cashier looked up casually and remarked, "Okay, boy, I'll be with you in a minute." The cashier was totally unprepared for the fury her comment unleashed. Johnson's face seemed to turn to stone, and the words he spoke seemed to come from a place way below his throat, deep in the wellspring of his anger. "Boys don't go to goddamn Vietnam," he spat at the flustered clerk as he stalked out of the store.[60]

Over the next few years of their marriage, his wife watched her angry husband go from one confrontation to another. His outrage was never far beneath the surface, and he made no secret of his feelings. Because of his outspoken manner, many of his friends began to urge Johnson to run for political office. Johnson scoffed at the idea initially, and whenever anyone tried to convince him he should run, he always replied, "Hell, I'm running for the county damn line." Everybody chuckled at Johnson's remark, but they still continued to ask him to run for office. The wounded Vietnam veteran continued to resist the entreaties of his supporters until he finally reached a turning point: He realized that nothing would change in Wilcox County until black residents could elect their own candidates to office, and he felt he had to help make that happen. Astoria Johnson vividly recalls that when that realization hit him with full force, her husband made a remarkable change. He began putting all of his considerable energy into political organizing. It was clear to all those who knew him well that after his conversion, Bobby Jo Johnson would not rest until Wilcox County had black elected officials. His wife explains, "When it changed with him, he ate it. I mean he lived it day and night."[61] In fact, it was Bobby Jo Johnson who helped engineer the first successful black challenge to the white Wilcox political order.[62]

The stage was set when Prince Arnold, a young teacher and a graduate of Alabama State University, decided to run for the office of Wilcox County sheriff. Arnold had only recently returned to Wilcox County in 1977. Upon his return, he was terribly disappointed when he realized that his home county still did not have a single black elected official, and he demanded to know, "Where are the black folks?" The young teacher vowed to change things, and he started going to political meetings. After attending a number of meetings and talking to a variety of black Wilcox residents, Arnold decided to run for sheriff. He explains,

> I had looked at the history. I had looked at counties that had made the change. Like Greene County had a black sheriff. By getting that sheriff, that man set the tone for the whole thing. . . . It had a domino effect. It got the fear out of the people, because the sheriff, believe it or not, in these small rural counties, he or she sets the tone.[63]

By this time, most other Black Belt counties had black sheriffs, including Lowndes County, Wilcox County's notorious neighbor to the north.[64] After making the decision to run, the eager young teacher attended a political meeting at a local black church and announced his intentions. He was stunned by the reaction of his friends and neighbors. He recalls, "Half [of] the people walked out of the church,"[65] but there was one man in the crowd that night who listened intently to Arnold's announcement: Bobby Jo Johnson. The wounded Vietnam veteran's eyes lit up when he realized that the young teacher was quite serious about running for sheriff. Like Arnold, Johnson firmly believed that the position of sheriff in rural Wilcox County was the most powerful elective office in the county. Johnson reasoned that the sheriff was the one elected official with whom black residents were most likely to have direct contact. He had the power of freedom and incarceration, or even life and death over the county's African Americans. As Johnson sat there in the church savoring the prospect of having a black sheriff in Wilcox County, he could not help but remember that day in the distant past when Sheriff Jenkins and his deputy had come looking for him after they had questioned him and beaten him. Johnson shook his head slightly to banish that frightening image back to the distant past where it belonged. Then, when he refocused his eyes and his mind on the scene in front of him, he saw his friends and neighbors turning their backs on the earnest young teacher in front of him.

Bobby Jo Johnson positioned his crutches in front of him and leaned on them to stand. He looked directly at the young teacher, but he began addressing those who remained in the church. He declared, "If the boy is a big enough fool to run for sheriff, I'll help him."[66] Over the next few months Prince Arnold taught school during the day and campaigned at night. He reached out to residents of the county, and they knew he understood their plight because he was one of them. Prince Arnold had grown up in a poor family in Wilcox County. He and his nineteen brothers and sisters had worked hard in the fields to help their parents make a profit from their rented land. He explains, "It was hard, but all the people around me did the same thing. We all were poor, and we worked in the fields. We all plowed mules, and we all did the same thing."[67] Yet, even though his neighbors lived in the same poverty that he did, Arnold was still keenly aware of the deprivation he suffered, and he understood that poverty seemed to be one of the most important defining characteristics of black life in his county. As he puts it, "I knew we were poor. You know, we had food to eat, we had clothes on our back, [but] I knew that we didn't have many of the things that other folks had. *When I say other people, it was white people at the time,* [be]cause all the black folks were basically like me."[68]

After announcing his intention to support Arnold's candidacy at that meeting in the church, Bobby Jo Johnson actively campaigned for him. Black Wilcox native and political activist Ralph Ervin vividly recalls that Johnson's campaign style made white residents a bit uncomfortable. During the course of the campaign, Ervin recalls, a group of black students in Pine Hill were passing out campaign literature in front of their school. The mayor of Camden heard about the students' activity and took it upon himself to go to Pine Hill to stop them. He cursed at them, and ordered them off the sidewalk. Word spread quickly about the mayor's bold action, and when Ervin heard, he immediately jumped in his car and raced to the scene. He arrived just in time to see Bobby Jo Johnson getting out of his van in front of the school. What happened next would leave many white Wilcox residents red-faced and angry.

The reaction of black residents, on the other hand, ranged from fearful consternation to supportive enthusiasm. Johnson asked one of the students to go into the school and get him a chair. The student quickly complied. Johnson directed him to place the chair in the middle of the sidewalk, and the disabled veteran carefully lowered himself into the chair, placing his crutches right next to him on the sidewalk. In the meantime, the mayor, who was still on the scene, positioned himself directly in front of Johnson's chair, leaned over, and said with an air of authority, "Bobby Jo, you gonna have to get off this sidewalk." Johnson replied evenly, "Let me tell you something, mayor. You're over here showing your white ass to try to make sure your candidate gets elected, well I'm over here to show my black ass to make sure mine gets elected." The students looked on in stunned silence, and Johnson addressed them without dropping his gaze from the mayor's startled red face. He said, "Pass me my gun." When an obliging student retrieved Johnson's .357 magnum from his van, the disabled veteran carefully placed it across his lap. For just a brief moment the mayor stood motionless, looking deep into the eyes of his seated adversary. What he saw there finally made him take a step back. In Bobby Jo Johnson's gaze was the frustration of the Black Power generation and the memory of the brutal war that had taken his leg and four of his fingers. The mayor turned on his heel and left the scene, and the students continued their election activities.[69]

Finally, election day came, and to the amazement of many, Prince Arnold won the race for sheriff of Wilcox County, thus becoming the first black elected official in Wilcox County since Reconstruction. He was sworn in on January 16, 1979. Arnold observes that he was only twenty-six years old at the time, and that made him the youngest sheriff in the history of the state. He also recalls laughingly that he had never shot a pistol in his life before this. He had fired a rifle and a shotgun, but never a pistol.[70] This was just one of many adjustments facing Wilcox County's new black sheriff. The main adjustment, as far as Arnold is concerned, however, was rooted in the attitude of some county residents toward law enforcement. The sheriff explains, "What they [the deputies] were doing . . . they weren't educated. They couldn't do nothin' [sic] but hit you upside the head. . . . I know now [be]cause I kept one or two of them. . . . That's kind of what they [the white people] wanted: big with a big stick. We had to change all of that, and we did."[71] The election of a black sheriff proved to be the beginning of the end of complete white political control in Wilcox County. Over the next few years, African Americans would be elected to a variety of county offices.

Very early in their terms many of the new black office holders found that their battle to get elected was only the first phase of their struggle. Wilcox native Ralph Ervin ran for tax assessor in 1985—a full seven years after Prince Arnold's historic victory in the 1978 election. By that time, according to Ervin, running for office was not nearly as difficult as it had been for the earlier black candidates. Ervin explains, "A lot of the anguish was gone." However, it still presented unique challenges. For example, as Ervin campaigned around the county, he quickly began to realize how difficult his job would be if he were elected tax assessor in such an impoverished county. He explains, "I went into homes of people where you could literally feed the chickens through the cracks." While the living conditions of these black county residents bothered Ervin, he found that the attitude displayed by some of these people was even more troubling. He explains, "[Some of] these people who live in poverty have . . . totally given up on life itself. [They do not believe] that their condition will change, or that of their children."[72]

All of this was a revelation to the idealistic young candidate for tax assessor, because even though he was a Wilcox native, Ralph Ervin had been unaware of how widespread the desperate poverty was that affected so many black county residents. His parents had shielded him from the unpleasant truth by providing him with a comfortable upbringing on the Annemanie campus where his father served as principal and his mother taught. After graduating from high school, Ervin attended Alabama A&M University in Huntsville, majoring in urban planning. Ralph Ervin was a very ambitious young man, and after graduating from college he had every intention of moving to a major city where he could put his urban planning degree to work. He only planned to return to Wilcox County to visit his family from time to time. Yet, a chance remark by one of his professors changed all that. Ervin heard that remark when he was sitting in a history class one day. During the class, the professor began talking about the political situation in Wilcox County. Ralph sat up a little straighter and began to listen more intently and he heard the professor say, "Those dumb niggers down in Wilcox County got [an] 80 percent advantage, and they can't elect anybody to public office." Those harsh words were like a cold slap in the face that served to trigger a fierce determination in the young Wilcox native right then and there to go home and help change things.[73] Consequently, when he graduated from college in 1975, Ralph Ervin went straight back to Wilcox County, got a job with the regional planning commission, and started attending political meetings. Finally, in 1985, a full ten years after he had returned home, he was convinced that the time had arrived when he should run for office.

After his successful election campaign, Ervin became the first black tax assessor ever to serve Wilcox County. He quickly realized that his new job would not be easy: in addition to black poverty, he would also have to deal with white resentment. Right from the start many white residents made it clear that they were unwilling to respect the authority of their new black tax assessor. Whenever they could, most white residents tried to ignore him altogether. Ervin received the first hint of the difficulties awaiting him when all but one of the white employees in the tax assessor's office quit as soon as he was elected. Then, after Ervin was sworn in, white landowners refused to speak to him. Instead, when they came to the tax assessor's office, they would talk only to the one remaining white clerk on Ervin's staff. Ervin explains, "They would stand in the hallway and ask her to come out. She would come out and I would hear them cursing." As the conversation continued, the clerk tried to calm the agitated white landowners, but she steadfastly insisted that they would have to talk to Mr. Ervin. This only fueled their anger and most exclaimed, "Don't be calling that nigger mister."[74] When they finally relented and came in to talk to him, Ervin recalls, many of the large white landowners tried to tell him how he should appraise their land. He refused to give in to their demands, however, and eventually most were able to work with their new tax assessor. Throughout those difficult early days, Wilcox County's new black tax assessor had to keep reassuring himself. He recalls, "I [would] say to myself that I had a degree of intelligence about the job. I had done my research even though I was new, and I was basically brought up to treat people the way that I wanted to be treated."[75] Undoubtedly, Ervin's calm demeanor and soft-spoken manner helped to soothe resentful white landowners.

Having a black tax assessor and a black sheriff was bad enough, but as far as many white residents were concerned, the change in the composition of the county commission was even more disturbing. The beginning of that change had come some time before Ralph Ervin had successfully campaigned for the office of tax assessor. In 1980 two black candidates won seats on the four-member commission. The two new black county commissioners were twenty-three-year-old Percy Luke Hale and thirty-four-year-old Bobby Jo Johnson, the disabled Vietnam War veteran. The men were sworn in on January 19, 1981. The *Wilcox Progressive Era* glibly noted that the date of the swearing-in ceremony was significant for two reasons: "Wilcox Countians made note Monday of two historic events: one, the anniversary of the birth of Robert E. Lee; the other, the swearing-in of the county's first negro [sic] commissioners."[76] The paper pessimistically predicted that this historic change in membership would result in a commission at war with itself.

Wilcox County's governmental body will now be composed of two negroes [sic] and two caucasians [sic] with Judge Reg Albritton serving as chairman. Albritton has expressed the wish that voting not become divided . . . racially. Expectations are, however, that numerous occasions will arise where the Commission does vote two-to-two with the burden of breaking the tie falling to Albritton.[77]

As the two new commissioners prepared to take their seats, white residents were more than a little uneasy about the impact these black men could have on the commission. Of course, their uneasiness was magnified by the reality that one of their new commissioners, Bobby Jo Johnson, had a reputation for having a chip on his shoulder when it came to issues of race. Predictably, almost from the beginning of his term, Johnson was outspoken and uncompromising during commission meetings. In the emotional atmosphere that always seemed to surround these meetings, Johnson's blunt comments were often laced with a steady stream of curse words. At last, Bobby Jo Johnson had found a forum where he could express his feelings of frustration and rage over the many racial injustices in his county. Regardless of white opinions, he proved to be enormously popular with his black constituents and consequently, he was reelected to serve on the county commission through the 1980s and beyond. During these years Bobby Jo Johnson continued his outspoken attacks on racial injustice, and because of his bold and uncompromising attitude, Commissioner Johnson became a lightning rod for white anger and resentment.

In late 1988 things came to a head when Johnson was accused of making a series of obscene phone calls to a white woman in Pine Hill. While Johnson's supporters cried foul, white Wilcox residents gleefully anticipated their chance to rid county government of the troublesome commissioner. Astoria Johnson, Bobby Jo's wife, steadfastly maintains that his political enemies manufactured the charges just so they could get Johnson off the county commission. Astoria Johnson insists that it all started when a local white man complained about having a county dumpster near his property. Even though it had been placed on the corner of a county road, the man insisted that it was too close to his land. Despite the man's complaints, county officials refused to move the dumpster. The man then decided to take matters into his own hands: he hooked the dumpster to his pickup truck and dragged it to a nearby creek. When Commissioner Johnson heard about the man's defiant action, he was furious, and he would not rest until the county forced the man to pay restitution for the dumpster. Astoria Johnson charges that the sexual harassment allegations surfaced just a short time after the dumpster incident.

Furthermore, according to Astoria Johnson, the woman who made the accusations was the wife of the man who had tangled with Commissioner Johnson over the dumpster.[78] Astoria Johnson vividly recalls that day in early 1989 when her husband first heard about the woman's allegations. She could hear his crutches thumping on the floor as he stomped around in the next room, railing against the woman's husband, who he was sure was behind the charges. Then, for a brief moment there was an ominous silence as Johnson stopped pacing. The next thing Astoria Johnson heard was the sound of her husband dialing the telephone. She did not have to be told who he was calling: the woman's husband. Almost before the connection was complete, Commissioner Johnson yelled a string of obscenities into the phone and after he had finished cursing the man, Johnson could not resist saying in parting, "Why don't you record this?"[79]

Astoria Johnson vividly recalls how difficult things became for their children when the allegations were made public. At the time the Johnsons had three children, two of whom were in high school. One day their youngest son was at school talking to one of the girls in his class. Just then, another boy passed by and teased, "Hey, what [are] you gonna do, harass her like your daddy?" The girl who was talking to the younger Johnson was in midsentence when the other boy interrupted her, and before she could tell the other boy to apologize, Johnson whirled around and punched him in the mouth. Blood spurted from the surprised student's lip, and when he gingerly explored his upper gum with the tip of his tongue, he realized that there was a broad space where two teeth had been just a split second before. Johnson looked the injured student in the eye and declared in a low but even voice, "My daddy is innocent, and don't you forget it."[80] Commissioner Johnson's son was not the only one of his children who felt compelled to defend him. It turns out that his daughter also found herself in a situation where she felt that she needed to defend her father's innocence. One day when Johnson's daughter was on the school bus, another girl made a disparaging comment about her father. Without hesitation, Bobby Jo Johnson's daughter quickly slipped her belt from around her waist and beat the other student with it until she apologized. Seeing her children get in fights at school saddened her, but Astoria Johnson understood and sympathized with her children's anger and frustration. Sometimes, it almost seemed too much to bear, but Astoria Johnson concludes, "For him to stay strong, I had to be strong for him . . . you know how it is. I said, we expect things like this, you know, and we should be able to deal with it."[81]

Commissioner Johnson went on trial in the summer of 1989. According to the *Wilcox Progressive Era*, "Johnson was the only witness called by the defense. No one took the stand in his behalf to try and sustain his claim that he was out of town when some of the calls were made."[82] For the prosecution, Kathy Huckabee, the alleged victim, "testified that Johnson had made a series of sexually offensive calls to her residence beginning in early December of 1978 and ending on March 24 of 1988 when a telephone call-trapping device locked in on a call Johnson placed from his own residence some miles away."[83] Huckabee's damaging testimony proved to be a turning point, and despite the encouragement of his family, friends, and many political supporters, Bobby Jo Johnson was convicted on August 23, 1989. In reporting on the verdict the *Wilcox Progressive Era* reasoned that the outcome of the trial was not surprising because "over the years Johnson has been sharply criticized for the use of what some perceive to be 'foul language' during meetings of the county commission and other public gatherings."[84] Many of the county's white residents openly speculated that the conviction might lead to Johnson's dismissal from the county commission. However, Donnie McLeod, the assistant district attorney handling the case, asserted that Johnson's conviction of this Class C misdemeanor was probably not serious enough to provide the necessary grounds to remove him from office. Despite the DA's warning, he still offered some hope to Johnson's enemies when he declared that "the DA's office is researching Alabama's moral turpitude laws to see if any of those provisions might result in Johnson being removed from public office."[85] In a separate proceeding Judge Harold Crow sentenced Commissioner Johnson to ten days in jail and one year's probation. William Pompey, Johnson's lawyer, "denounced the conviction and sentencing as further evidence of 'racism' in Wilcox County."[86]

Within a matter of days, even before the dust had settled from the guilty verdict, the Johnson family received another major shock: on Friday afternoon, September 8, their home was heavily damaged by two explosions. Ironically, the explosions occurred on the same day as Commissioner Johnson's sentencing hearing. Astoria Johnson has very vivid memories of that afternoon. After she had been at work for a while that day, she received a phone call. When she picked up the receiver and identified herself, a mysterious voice on the other end of the line told her that her house had been bombed. Before she could recover from her shock enough to question the caller, Johnson heard a loud click, and the line went dead. At that moment on the other side of town, her husband was in his van driving up to what was left of their house. He and the children had all gone to a high school football game that afternoon, and as they pulled up their driveway, they could scarcely believe what they were seeing. Commissioner Johnson stopped his van and exclaimed, "What the hell?" Astoria Johnson estimates that the hole in their house was so big, "You could drive a Volkswagen through it." Commissioner Johnson immediately called the sheriff's office on his CB radio and within a matter of minutes, Sheriff Prince Arnold responded. The nearest fire department was at Pine Hill, however, and they did not respond nearly as quickly. Instead, according to Astoria Johnson, Pine Hill authorities, who were all white, offered the Johnsons only excuses: First they said their fire truck did not have any water; then they said they were unable to locate a driver. As the agitated commissioner heard one excuse after another, his fury mounted. By the time reluctant Pine Hill firefighters arrived on the scene, Bobby Jo Johnson was in a rage. He ordered them to turn their truck around and get off his property.

Predictably, almost before the dust settled from the explosions, the charges and countercharges began to surface. William Pompey, Johnson's lawyer, was convinced that the Ku Klux Klan was responsible for the explosions and for Bobby Jo Johnson's recent conviction, because "it takes a lot of power and money to get something like that done."[87] At the same time, authorities began questioning Johnson about his experience with explosives while he was in the army. Johnson was furious at their insinuation that he had something to do with the bombing, and he vehemently denied that he ever had any training in the use of explosives. In the meantime, because of the circumstances of the blast, federal agents of the Bureau of Alcohol, Tobacco, and Firearms (ATF) launched an investigation from the nearest field office in Birmingham. ATF agents promised a thorough investigation, and they insisted that "if evidence of a criminal nature is uncovered, the government will devote every possible effort to apprehend[ing] and convicting whoever is responsible."[88] Despite such assurances, nobody was ever prosecuted for the bombing.[89] Astoria Johnson is convinced that the bomber was not trying to injure or kill any member of her family. Instead, she insists, they were probably trying to frighten her husband into silence. If that was the bomber's intent, he failed miserably, because in the days after the explosions, Commissioner Johnson became more outspoken than ever. As his wife puts it, "He got even worse. He sure enough got worse."[90] The Monday following the bombing Commissioner Johnson insisted on offering the invocation to open the regularly scheduled county commission meeting. He thanked God for sparing him and his family from the explosion, and then he proceeded to conduct business as usual.[91] By this time, Bobby Jo Johnson had been elected chairman of the Wilcox County Commission.

Racial tension, white resentment, and the troubles of its chairman were not the only troubles plaguing the Wilcox County Commission. In fact, one of the most serious issues faced by commissioners was the broad gap that existed between the expectations of newly enfranchised black constituents and the ability of black commissioners to effect change. After the 1982 election when control of the commission finally passed to the county's African Americans, black citizens expected immediate changes. It was difficult for eager black residents to understand that their commissioners' power was severely limited by their county's dismal economic realities. Selma civil rights attorney J. L. Chestnut worked with the Wilcox County Commission during these turbulent years, and he vividly recalls the frustration of black commissioners and their constituents in Wilcox County:

> On any given night, we'd have about twenty-five people, mostly black, in attendance . . . sessions always opened with a prayer. These meetings sometimes lasted four or five hours because everyone wanted their say. Black people who'd been reluctant to pressure a white county commission were hardly reluctant to make all kinds of demands on a black one. We tried to cut the personal speeches and complaints at least in half by requiring advance permission to get on the agenda. But, it didn't work. Black people saw this as their government and they would say what they wanted when they wanted. So it often was midnight before we were able to complete our business.[92]

Against this background of raised black expectations and long black memories of brutal racism and segregation, it seemed that race insinuated itself into almost every issue confronting the new majority black commission. Chestnut explains,

> At its first meeting, the newly elected Wilcox County Commission fired five white county employees, and there was some public sentiment for firing all of them. Some of the new commissioners felt that the employment disparity between the races should be corrected immediately; others thought it should happen by attrition. It was a damn thorny issue.[93]

Chestnut goes on to explain, "there was no question that something had to give because of the built-in unfairness."[94] The commission tried to compromise. They fired five white county employees, and retained a number of others. At the same time, they placed newly hired black employees as assistants to experienced white directors in a number of departments so that those black assistants could gain the experience they needed to take over their departments in the future. Chestnut recalls that this compromise angered many Wilcox residents, both black and white, but he goes on to conclude, "I don't think there's any way that situation could have been handled without someone being hurt. No way could a black commission come into power after decades of struggle and then tell black folk they'd have to wait on jobs until all the white people retired. There were some black people who thought we didn't go far enough."[95]

As Wilcox County's new black county commissioners struggled to translate their victory at the polls into meaningful gains for their constituents, new black members of the county's board of education waged a similar struggle. Their victory at the polls had been a long time coming because even after virtually all of the white students deserted the public schools, white administrators in the system and white members of the board of education had stubbornly continued to hold onto their positions. This absolute white control over the education of their children proved to be an emotional bone of contention for many black Wilcox parents. Not surprisingly, one of the most outspoken critics of Wilcox County's all-white public school administration was Bobby Jo Johnson. Johnson strongly urged black candidates to run for the school board. One of those who Johnson contacted was Reverend Lonnie Brown. After his unsuccessful run for the state senate in 1966, however, Brown had no desire to run for public office again. Brown remembers that Johnson called him at the office one day to gauge his interest in running for the school board. A surprised Reverend Brown quickly informed Johnson that he was far too busy even to consider running for the school board. Typically, Bobby Jo Johnson refused to take no for an answer. Every argument against his candidacy that Brown offered, Commissioner Johnson quickly countered. Brown concludes, "He [Johnson] was very aggressive."[96]

Thus, Reverend Lonnie Brown soon found himself running for office again. This time, however, he won. Along with Reverend Brown, four other black candidates were elected to the Wilcox County School Board in 1982. The other victorious candidates were James Ephraim, a school principal; K. P. Thomas, a teacher; Reverend Benjamin Thompson, a Presbyterian minister; and Reverend Frank Smith, a minister and a teacher. That historic election signaled a shift to black control of the Wilcox County School Board. Brown remembers that during the campaign leading up to this historic election he and the other black candidates were convinced that "color has nothing to do with brain power."[97] While he was campaigning, Reverend Brown traveled all over the county. He spoke anywhere and everywhere: churches, private homes, and businesses. His slogan was "better education for all people," and his audiences were wildly enthusiastic. It was obvious to Brown that his listeners were hungry for black control of their children's education.

After the black school board candidates triumphed at the polls in 1982, everyone, both victorious black candidates and their constituents, had high hopes that positive change for the educational system was right on the horizon. The new school board members felt a keen sense of urgency because they were all painfully aware that their county's school system was in disarray. They understood that some of the system's problems were rooted in the massive disruption that had occurred during the school desegregation crisis of the 1971–1972 school year. At the same time, however, they also suspected that another cause of the system's problems could be found in the ineffective leadership of the white officials who had continued to administer the system after 1972 when the student body became virtually all black. Some black critics charged that white officials had shown little interest in implementing programs that would improve the system, and this had only compounded the problems.

There were other black critics who went one step further and charged that vindictive white school officials had deliberately sabotaged the county's public school system. One of those critics, James Thomas, state representative and principal of Wilcox Central High School, charges, "They [white school officials] tried every way possible to derail it. . . . When the courts ordered the school system integrated, the [white] superintendent said, 'okay, I'll show you how to integrate,' and he took a hat and put all the teachers' names in. Then he pulled names out and randomly assigned teachers to various schools in the county with no regard to subject area."[98] This reckless shuffling of teachers created further disruption and ensured that schools would not function at maximum efficiency. The resulting chaos would eventually come back to haunt the new black school board members who were left to untangle this personnel mess. Whatever the reason for the system's problems, Wilcox County's new black school board members recognized that they were facing an uphill battle. They had inherited a system that was unaccredited, underfunded, and unorganized. New black school board member Lonnie Brown concludes, "We knew we had to get down to hard work."[99]

One of the first major decisions facing the new black school board members was the selection of a new school superintendent. Board members had no doubt that the appointment of the right superintendent was an important first step in their effort to overhaul their county's public schools. Brown recalls that he and his fellow board members felt like they were trapped between a rock and a hard place. They knew that everyone, both black and white residents, would scrutinize their decision very carefully, and at the same time, no matter who they chose, they were likely to be criticized. As soon as the board of education advertised the position, a steady stream of candidates submitted their applications. For the first time in Wilcox County's history, some of those applicants were African American. Most of the applicants were local people, and this placed new black board members in the unenviable position of having to pass judgment on the qualifications of some of their friends and neighbors. They decided that the best way to handle the situation was to follow established procedures as carefully as they could, but they still received a lot of criticism. One of those critics was the principal of Wilcox Central, James Thomas. After Thomas submitted his application, he watched the board's deliberations very carefully. He charges that the board decided against his candidacy because, "The powers that be just didn't want me. They wanted somebody from the outside." He concludes bitterly, "They had rigged the whole system."[100]

Reverend Brown is quick to admit that he and his fellow board members considered hiring a candidate who was already working in the Wilcox County system, but they decided against it. He explains, "We had some people [in the system] who could do a good job, but we figured if we get some of those [inside candidates] they would have ties to family . . . so, we wanted somebody [from] outside."[101] The candidate board members decided to hire was Odell Tumblin, a black woman from outside the county. Brown characterizes her as being a "dynamic, hardworking woman." Brown goes on to insist that her status as an outside candidate was only part of the reason why they chose Tumblin. He explains, "We persuaded her to take that job. After we looked at the candidates, she had more of what we wanted."[102] There were others, however, who had a far less flattering view of Odell Tumblin. For example, Wilcox Central Principal James Thomas insists, "She was so controversial." He goes on to charge that "she got here and she got to feeling that she was invincible and tried to control the apparatus of the black community."[103] Regardless of anyone's view of her, Odell Tumblin made history when she became the first female and the first African American school superintendent in the history of Wilcox County. From the beginning it seemed that the new superintendent was destined to become the eye of the storm that swirled around Wilcox County's crippled system of education. One of the most critical issues confronting the county's new school superintendent was the problem of funding. For years, Wilcox County's students, both black and white, had suffered because their system had been inadequately funded. By the decade of the 1980s when the election of the first black school board members ushered in an era of black control, the system's long-standing problems with funding had escalated into a full-blown crisis. It seemed that the system was being hit from all sides. For example, in 1982 the Pine Belt Telephone Company of Arlington won a judgment against the Wilcox County Board of Education. The company had filed suit against the board, alleging that a seven mill school tax had been collected illegally every year since 1965. The mix-up occurred because "the taxes were put on a referendum vote in 1955 and were to have been collected for ten years. In 1965 the tax was supposed to have come off but did not, for reasons that have not as yet been made public."[104] Even though the statute of limitations would prohibit taxpayers from seeking a refund for all the taxes collected since 1965, the plaintiffs could still expect to recover taxes paid for the last three years. "Even so, a three year refund to all taxpayers would exceed $1 million and would virtually bankrupt the already financially-strapped county."[105]

In the short term, while the legal wrangling over tax refunds continued, the tax collector stopped collecting the seven mill school tax, and that resulted in an "immediate loss of about $240,000 to the local public school system."[106] The very next year when voters were asked to pass an eighteen mill tax increase, they refused. Had the measure passed, ten mills of the increase would have gone to the schools. The *Wilcox Progressive Era* reported that in the aftermath of that election, "school officials and parents genuinely concerned about the schools have expressed their disappointment that the measure failed." The paper consoled, "officials say the schools are not in any danger of closing," but it went on to warn, "without the hoped-for funds it will be virtually impossible to . . . institute many of the plans for upgrading the system."[107]

It was against this background of economic deprivation that the new superintendent, Odell Tumblin, began her work. Tumblin, a brown-skinned, solidly built woman with an intense and determined glint in her eye, quickly realized just how difficult her new job would be. She faced an economic crisis of monumental proportions and at the same time, she also faced a variety of personalities, and an undercurrent of disunity in Wilcox County's African American community. Reverend Brown is convinced that Tumblin's problems were compounded by her gender: he and other board members were well aware that many of their black friends and neighbors vigorously opposed the appointment of a woman to the superintendent's position.[108] Yet, regardless of the undercurrent of uneasiness swirling around her, Odell Tumblin systematically set about implementing the plan she had to improve the Wilcox County School system. She attacked the system's problems with a zeal that some found a little disconcerting, and she soon found that she was making a number of enemies. In Principal James Thomas's estimation, her technique left a great deal to be desired. At the same time, he does concede that "her motive was good." However, he continues, she fancied herself the "savior" of their school system, and he concludes that her "arrogance" sealed her fate. According to Thomas, Tumblin was just the first in a long line of superintendents appointed by the Wilcox County School Board who would follow the same pattern. He bluntly insists:

> I fault a lot of it on the board, in making the proper decision in terms of who they brought in. I guess they were so eager to bring what they thought were the best folks, and sometimes the better people are the ones who are right there with you. And they went out and got, in my mind, a lot of rejects from other places and brought them in, and they . . . were going to be the savior.[109]

As Superintendent Tumblin continued to focus on her plans for the future, she and James Thomas eventually crossed swords. Thomas explains that initially he was able to work well with the new superintendent. However, he alleges that after she directed him to examine old records for the purpose of uncovering corruption and he refused, their relationship became strained. Right after this, he charged, "She went after me with a vengeance; I mean, with a vengeance."[110] In the midst of all of this, Superintendent Tumblin continued to work to implement her plan for improvement of the system. The focal point of this plan was the creation of a centralized high school. Tumblin reasoned that Wilcox County really needed this facility because the education of high school students had suffered a real blow during the school desegregation crisis. When she presented her proposal for a new high school to the school board, she argued that a brand new state-of-the-art centralized high school would greatly improve the quality and efficiency of secondary education in the county. Even James Thomas, one of Tumblin's most vocal critics, grudgingly admits that her idea to build a central high school was a good one. He continues wistfully, "If anything, her dream was too extensive for the resources. A lot of things were left undone, simply because the money wasn't there."[111] The school board eventually approved Tumblin's plan, and construction began on the new Wilcox Central High School.

In the meantime, the board's new black members were learning just how difficult it was to please their constituents. Reverend Brown recalls that before they were even sworn in, many of their constituents had a low opinion of the new black school board members' capabilities. As Brown puts it,

> Wherever there are black people in the Black Belt in office, I feel that white folk, and some black folks think that . . . just because they're black people, they're not going to do anything. They can't do it, or they won't do it.[112]

Brown concludes, "We were determined to prove them [wrong]."[113] As they set about trying to prove themselves, one of the most important tasks facing the board was the need to reorganize their teaching force. Back in 1972 when the white superintendent responded to court-ordered desegregation by randomly shuffling teachers around, it resulted in many teachers being forced to teach subjects that were outside their area of expertise. The new board decided that if the system were ever to function effectively, the teaching force would have to be reorganized to ensure that all Wilcox County teachers were teaching in the fields in which they were certified. Confident that they were doing the best thing, the board began reassigning teachers. New board members were totally unprepared for the reaction. Some teachers became angry: they felt like they were being singled out for some sort of punishment. Brown explains, "People made it a personal thing rather than look at the whole picture. They could not see . . . that we were not after them, we were trying to do what was better for the young kids who were coming on."[114]

Still smarting from the reaction they received when they attempted to reorganize system personnel, Reverend Brown and his colleagues moved cautiously as they sought to address some of the system's other problems. Yet, no matter what they did, it seemed that the community was always ready to criticize, but rarely ready to compliment their new school board's initiatives. Brown is convinced that a large part of the reason for the steady stream of criticism was rooted in the community's perception of its relationship to this new school board. Brown explains, "Many people with influence in the county thought that they ought to dictate to the board. And sometimes, I felt that some of those black folks were influenced by [the] white folks."[115]

All of the school board's regularly scheduled meetings were open to the public. Reverend Brown recalls that because of the developing friction between school board officials and their constituents, many people from the community attended the meetings every week, and the meetings soon became quite contentious. As the school board members attempted to conduct business, they were frequently interrupted by their friends and neighbors in the audience. Many of these black people, still dressed in the overalls and dusty shoes that they had worn out in the fields earlier that day never thought that they would live to see a time when they would be able to express their opinion in a school board meeting. Most offered their opinions with enthusiasm, completely unselfconscious about the broken language and split verbs that characterized their speech. Reverend Brown observes, "Sometimes they [the meetings] were packed . . . you couldn't hardly do anything. But then sometimes they would get kind of rowdy."[116]

The reaction of their constituents notwithstanding, school board members continued to propose solutions to the system's many problems, but of all the problems they faced, the problem of funding proved to be the most difficult. Board members enthusiastically supported the adoption of new local taxes to help solve the system's funding problems and to pay for the construction of the new high school. However, board members soon realized that this was a very unpopular position. In fact, relations between members of the school board and their constituents in the county became quite strained. Reverend Brown explains sadly, "It hurts for people that's been your friends and all, and that you go to church with sometimes to hate you and call you names. . . . You don't want people to be angry at you, but when you get into that kind of a situation, you still have to make the tough decisions of what is right, according to what you think is right."[117] Brown goes on to conclude, "I expected to get some [negative] feedback from white folks cause we could understand that . . . but the thing that puzzled me was how could you get this kind of thing from black folks?"[118]

Despite the controversy surrounding some of the school board's initiatives, they were eventually able to corral enough support to ensure the completion of the county's centralized high school. However, just as construction on the new school was completed, the board of education and Superintendent Tumblin became embroiled in a nasty controversy. For some time, Tumblin and the board had been at odds over some of the board's decisions. Things finally came to a head when Superintendent Tumblin withdrew her support of James Thomas's application for the principal's position at the new high school. Originally, the superintendent had endorsed the board's decision to appoint Thomas. However, she abruptly withdrew her support, explaining that she did not think he would be able to perform the functions of a state legislator and a high school principal at the same time. Thomas and the board were furious, and board members took the extraordinary step of offering a one-year contract to Thomas over Tumblin's strenuous objections. He promptly accepted. When Tumblin objected, the board suspended her. In the tense atmosphere that followed, charges and countercharges swirled around the controversial superintendent. The *Wilcox Progressive Era* reported,

> Tumblin began to run afoul of the system soon after coming to Camden when it was learned by this newspaper that she did not possess the "earned doctorate" which the BOE had asked for when it first sought applicants for the post. When Tumblin came here she was introduced from the very beginning as "Doctor Tumblin" when she only held a masters degree.[119]

The paper went on to reveal that "Dr. Tumblin also had problems with certification on the state level. When she came here she did not have the required 'AA' certificate."[120] The question of credentials was not the only source of controversy. In fact, Tumblin also found herself in a difficult situation because she had managed to offend a variety of county residents during her time as superintendent. For example, the *Wilcox Progressive Era* reported, "Dr. Tumblin drew sharp criticism statewide after a confrontation with state health department officials at which time she disputed a finding of warm-blooded animal feces in school drinking water."[121] Superintendent Tumblin made sure that reporters were present when she drank out of one of the polluted water fountains at Snow Hill. She pronounced the water safe because it tasted fine to her.[122] Her lack of diplomacy and questionable credentials notwithstanding, many county residents were most uncomfortable with Odell Tumblin's insistence on interweaving religious activities into school programs. Tumblin, who was deeply religious, "said publicly on several occasions that God sent her here to serve the local system."[123] A short time after she crossed swords with the board over Principal James Thomas's appointment, Odell Tumblin was fired.

Since Tumblin's departure, the Wilcox County Board of Education has appointed a succession of superintendents, none of whom has occupied the position very long. Through all of this the Wilcox County School System, which was unaccredited when the first black members were elected to the school board, has remained unaccredited. At the same time, the system has continued to suffer from a chronic shortage of funds even though school officials have worked diligently throughout this period to find new sources of funding. As recently as June of 1989 just as new Wilcox Central High School was about to open, members of the board of education sought help from the county commission. Board members tried to persuade county commissioners that one-half cent of a countywide two cents sales tax should be given to the schools. William Pompey, one board of education member, told commissioners that the schools were in desperate need of the money because they were "$1.5 million in the hole."[124] Although everyone agreed that the schools were in debt, there was some disagreement over the size of that debt. For example, Ira Bradford, the county administrator, insisted that state auditors would not know exactly what the shortfall was until the next month. Bradford speculated that the shortfall was probably closer to $500,000.[125]

Through the decade of the 1990s, the Wilcox County School Board and the Wilcox County Commission remained at odds over the question of taxation to benefit the school system. After one particularly nasty encounter between the two governing bodies, the board of education sued the county commission. It all started when the county commission certified a final vote tally that spelled defeat for an ad valorem tax that would have benefited the schools. The county commission claimed that the tax referendum had been defeated by a vote of 2,691 to 2,561.[126] The board of education cried foul and immediately filed suit alleging that "the results certified by the Commission is [sic] predicated on bribery, intimidation and other malconduct calculated to prevent a fair, free and full exercise of the elective franchise."[127]

The board of education's charge of election fraud in the last decade of the twentieth century was nothing new. Of course, there had been numerous charges leveled by black citizens in the years immediately after the passage of the Voting Rights Act as one black candidate after another went down to defeat. At that time black county residents were convinced that white Wilcox officials desperate to hold on to power were responsible for the fraud. However, even after the complexion of county officials changed with the election of large numbers of black candidates, charges of vote fraud and other irregularities continued. For example, in 1979, just one year after the election of the county's first black sheriff, the United States Circuit Court ordered the Wilcox County Board of Registrars to purge their voting rolls of all "dead persons, non-residents who have registered elsewhere, and individuals convicted of disqualifying crimes."[128] The order was issued in response to a suit filed by Hollis Curl, the *Wilcox Progressive Era's* publisher. However, local black voters concerned about the fairness of such a purge appealed the ruling. In response district court judge Brevard Hand issued a consent order directing that purged voters be restored to the county's voting rolls. Hand's order did not mean the reinstatement of all purged voters, just "those voters, mostly black, who were registered here in the 1960s as part of the civil rights effort of that period."[129] In the midst of this electoral uncertainty, the *Wilcox Progressive Era* dropped a bombshell in the fall of 1980 when it reported that the U.S. Bureau of the Census calculated that the county's total population numbered only 13,695 people, but the county claimed to have 14,310 registered voters. The paper went on to report that "knowledgeable observers here and in Washington are betting on the Bureau of the Census as having the final, and most accurate word."[130]

By that next spring county officials were still wrestling with the discrepancy between federal census figures and local voting statistics. In an effort to resolve the controversy, the state adopted a voter reidentification ordinance that required all of the county's voters to reidentify themselves or be stricken from the voting rolls. Many of the county's white residents thought the new ordinance was a good idea. However, black residents were not so sure. The new law drew "strong opposition from black politicians prior to its passage in both houses. Black leaders opposed to the re-identification law have charged that it will violate their civil rights by diminishing their base of voter strength."[131] The *Wilcox Progressive Era* reported that a court challenge to the new law was likely, but the paper confidently predicted that it would withstand any legal challenge because "those close to the drafting of the new law say . . . that it was carefully researched and complies with all applicable federal voter rights requirements."[132] Despite the paper's confident prediction, by the fall of 1981 the U.S. Justice Department moved to halt compliance with the new law because federal officials were afraid that it "would impose a much greater burden on blacks than on whites and would make it much more difficult for registered blacks to preserve their voting status."[133] Justice Department officials expressed particular concern about the impact of the new law in Wilcox County because "their [black voters] lower socio-economic status in Wilcox County made it difficult for them to comply with the requirements of the re-identification law."[134]

Well into the 1980s allegations of voter fraud and irregularities continued to plague Wilcox County's elections. For example, after the Democratic primary in the fall of 1982, more allegations of election fraud surfaced. First, the district attorney's office impounded five ballot boxes after local officials uncovered counting errors and "possible criminal law violations in the illegal numbering of ballots."[135] After the same election, the DA's office announced that it was about to present a number of cases of voter fraud to the Wilcox County Grand Jury. District Attorney Roy Johnson "did not say exactly how many cases of possible fraud his assistants have uncovered but he did indicate that they were widespread and involved mainly black voters whose absentee applications may have been falsified."[136] Coincidentally, that election was the first time that the county's black sheriff, Prince Arnold, faced reelection since his historic victory in 1978. Most expected that Arnold would win reelection easily. He did. Despite his victory, local white observers refused to give Arnold any credit for his ability to attract the support of white voters. Instead, they insisted that the white support he did attract was for the wrong reasons. As the *Wilcox Progressive Era* explained, "the main surprise in Sheriff Arnold's victory is the apparent fact that he received upwards of 500 white votes. Most of those are thought by local analysts to have come from the 18 to 25 year old marijuana users who view Arnold as less strict than Robert Rogers [his white opponent]."[137]

In that same election, Larry Threadgill, one of the main leaders of the student boycott during the school desegregation struggle, lost his bid for the office of probate judge. When Threadgill attempted to contest the vote count, the local Democratic Executive Committee refused to hear his complaint, ruling that he filed his petition one day too late. However, state party officials overruled local Democrats, and Threadgill, represented by civil rights attorney J. L. Chestnut, was allowed to present his case. Despite Threadgill's best efforts, however, local Democrats decided to accept the vote count that resulted in victory for his opponent, white incumbent Reg Albritton.[138] After Threadgill's loss in the primary, his father, Reverend Thomas Threadgill, decided to become a write-in candidate for the office of probate judge in the general election later that fall. Reverend Threadgill explained that he decided to run for the office in order to "work to change the image of Wilcox County." He conceded that the county's image had become tarnished, but he insisted that "all of us are to blame—black and white—for how other people see us." He reasoned that the most obvious problems plaguing Wilcox County, inadequate education and a failing economy, were only symptoms of a larger underlying problem: lack of effective leadership. Threadgill went on to charge that without effective leadership the county's prospects for progress were slowly being strangled without anyone around to resuscitate them. He declared that the county desperately needed leaders who would work together for the good of everyone, and he pledged "to provide the kind of leadership that will make it easier for local officials to work [together] harmoniously."[139]

In his typical energetic fashion, the ever zealous and ever idealistic Thomas Threadgill campaigned vigorously after his late entry into the race for probate judge. He trusted his friends and neighbors to do the right thing. Yet, despite his highly visible role in the county's civil rights struggles, his reputation as an honest man, and his popularity among county residents because of his kindness and generosity, Reverend Thomas Threadgill was defeated by white incumbent Reg Albritton. The loss was extremely hard for Threadgill to accept because during the civil rights struggles he had risked his life, his health, and even his own career ambitions to lead and support the movement. Yet, when he counted on the same people who had looked to him for leadership during the movement, they had deserted him. Threadgill's son Larry remembers that the loss devastated his father.[140]

Despite his profound sense of disappointment after the election, however, Reverend Thomas Threadgill went right back to looking out for his friends and neighbors like he always had. He never seemed to be too busy to help a promising student secure a college scholarship, or to talk to bank officials to convince them to give an extension on a loan, or to help raise money for a family who needed food or funds to pay their electric bill. At the same time, however, in those years after the 1982 election Thomas Threadgill sadly watched his county become more deeply embroiled in disunity and mired down in charges of election irregularities. He never ran for office again, and if anyone asked him what it would take to change things in Wilcox County, Reverend Thomas Threadgill would reply quietly, "Only God." Just six years later Reverend Thomas Threadgill died of sarcoidosis, a disease that attacks the internal organs. He was only sixty-two years old.[141]

When Reverend Threadgill died in 1988, the board of education and the county commission were still at odds, the schools were still unaccredited, the county's tax revenues were still inadequate, and many black Wilcox residents who had had such high hopes right after they had elected their first black candidate were becoming increasingly disillusioned. Of course, the faces in the courthouse were almost all black now. Just that superficial change seemed like a miracle, but replacing white faces with black ones was only a small part of the fundamental change that black Wilcox residents expected. Most had expected a county government that would finally hear their concerns and respond to their needs. Yet, many are convinced that this is not what they got.

In fact, some disillusioned black residents complain that black officeholders have not done things any differently than the white officials they replaced. For example, Jessie Pettway, a resident of Gee's Bend whose family was an integral part of the movement, insists, "After putting people in office then you expect them to do some of the things that would help the black folks. But, to my understanding, most of the black people we put in office, *they turn white*."[142] Former Wilcox resident Hannah Bell Ramsey adds, "Racism is still there," and even though there are a lot of black elected officials in the county, they have very little real power.[143]

Even black officeholders themselves expected that their presence would make more of a difference than it has. State representative James Thomas explains that many of them had totally unrealistic expectations about what they could accomplish. These high expectations were born of the enthusiasm and idealism that these political novices brought with them to office. As Thomas puts it, "The whole perception was that we was [sic] going to be able to do miracles overnight, and I was even a little bit naive. I thought that I could just transcend everything that had taken place." Thomas soon learned a hard lesson, however. He explains, "It was only after having gotten there, and beginning to learn the system and work in the system, you find that it is much different from what you thought." He concludes pessimistically, "The system is still in place even today. The power structure, the powers that be still control it, and it's very difficult [to make any substantive changes]."[144]

Some observers insist that the problem with black officials in the county is rooted in the character of the people who were elected to office. Many of the early black officeholders in Wilcox County were from middle-class backgrounds, and SNCC staffer Worth Long, who spent time organizing in Wilcox County before the passage of the Voting Rights Act, declared prophetically that the black middle class in the county might protest segregation, but they were still wedded to the social order that segregation produced. As he put it, "There are certain people who are not going to do liberation involvement. They're not going to do it because they have an investment in the system, and you're trying to challenge a system that they have spent their whole lives trying to be a part of."[145] In short, because of their middle-class perceptions, some of the county's early black office holders defined the problems and solutions in ways that were almost foreign to their poor constituents.

By the 1980s with legal segregation no longer an issue, the reality of race was no longer enough to unify black Wilcox residents. In this brave new world, early black officeholders who had successfully unseated white incumbents became incumbents themselves. To the dismay of some observers, in some instances well-educated black incumbents were defeated by poorly ed-ucated black challengers from underprivileged backgrounds. For example, Jack Bonham, a black educator who taught for years in Gee's Bend, remem-bers how distressed he was when he learned that the people of the Bend had voted against their incumbent black representative on the school board. They elected one of their own to replace him. The new school board mem-ber, Eddie Mingo, was a member of one of the oldest families living in Gee's Bend, but he had not even finished elementary school.

As Wilcox County's African American residents fought over the elective offices and appointed positions that were finally open to them for the first time, one critical factor that helped shape that struggle is abundantly clear: this group of jobs, both elective offices and appointed positions, represented practically the only hope to secure a good job and a decent living for African Americans in Wilcox County. Reverend Lonnie Brown, one of the first African Americans elected to the school board, declares that the Wilcox County Board of Education employed more people than any other employer in the county.[146] Thus, as black residents scrambled to secure elective offices and other county positions, a lot more than public service was at stake. This climate of aggressive competition for county positions was further compli-cated by the example that had been set by previous white officeholders. In fact, a culture of nepotism and favoritism had characterized public service in Wilcox County for generations before the passage of the Voting Rights Act. In many instances, white officeholders had routinely rewarded their friends, family members, and supporters by putting them on the county payroll. Black residents obviously had no experience with government service prior to this time, and as they tentatively explored these new opportunities, they operated in the shadow of this well-established, long-standing tradition. In such an at-mosphere the contests between black candidates often got downright nasty. Predictably, sharp competition for various county positions only served to exacerbate the hurt feelings, suspicion, and feelings of betrayal that had been plaguing black county residents for years, ever since the first black residents had begun to take advantage of new opportunities opened up by the civil rights movement.

Reverend Threadgill's earlier warning about the lack of effective leader-ship resonated with many as they sadly watched these developments in Wilcox County near the end of the twentieth century. By that time, increas-ing numbers of black county residents had become convinced that only ef-fective black leadership could put their county back on the right track. How-ever, it is important to note that regardless of their motives and their vision, any African American seeking to assume a leadership role in Wilcox County would find himself caught between practical realities and historical truths. Indeed, black leaders in America have always found themselves in a similar situation, where their ability to lead has been circumscribed by a severely limited range of options because they are part of the powerless minority they are attempting to lead. As British scholar John White explains,

> Like their supporters, black leaders have had to contend with a caste system based on racial discrimination and proscription. For long periods, they were also effectively denied the franchise, entry into the major political parties or access to the centres of power. By definition, black leaders occupied tenuous and vulnerable positions in their own and surrounding white community.[147]

In addition to the aforementioned limitations, *Southern* black leaders have been further burdened by the long shadow of slavery and its direct descendant, de jure segregation. As John White put it, "southern black leadership was forced to operate within the 'separate but [un]equal' confines of a system predicated on and pledged to the maintenance of white supremacy."[148]

Because of these severe limitations that have circumscribed the scope of their accomplishments, it has seemed to many African Americans that their leaders are not doing enough. Furthermore, at times it has even seemed that black leaders were exhibiting contradictory characteristics, and this has led to charges that they are "selling out." However, historian John Cell, who compared southern segregation to South African apartheid, explained how adopting these seemingly contradictory modes of behavior allowed black leaders to navigate the fine line between black expectations and white power. He explains,

> Most individuals, as well as most institutions, movements, and strategies . . . fell between the poles of collaboration and resistance, combining elements of both in complex, shifting ways. Through collaboration . . . positions of power might be consolidated. On the other hand, by helping through trial and error to define the boundaries of practical opposition, as well as by providing the justification for strengthening the state coercive machinery, resistance itself might be functional, feeding back into the system and legitimizing it.[149]

Clearly, the tenuous position of black leaders who are attempting to help other African Americans find their way through this oppressive system defined by economic deprivation and racial discrimination is fraught with contradictions. Thus, black leaders everywhere, including those in Wilcox County, have attracted a steady stream of criticism over the years. Famous novelist James Baldwin expressed a cynical view of black leadership that many African Americans have accepted at one time or another. According to Baldwin, "the problem of Negro leadership . . . has always been extremely delicate, dangerous, and complex. The term itself becomes remarkably difficult to define, the moment one realizes that the real role of the Negro leader, in the eyes of the American Republic, was not to make the Negro a first-class citizen but to keep him content as a second class one."[150]

The black leadership picture in Wilcox County has strongly mirrored national trends. During the early years of the civil rights movement, many black Wilcox residents were naturally drawn to the courageous and charismatic activists in their community who helped organize their struggle. This attraction to charismatic leadership is remarkably consistent with the definition of black leadership offered by historian Manning Marable. Marable explains,

> The leaders who have come from a series of black political and social movements in the twentieth century represent very different personalities, organizational affiliations, and political ideologies. There is however, one powerful model or tradition of leadership that has evolved within black political culture. To some extent, this tradition has been characterized by a charismatic or dominating political style.[151]

Marable goes on to insist that such a charismatic/autocratic style of leadership grew directly out of the black church because "the political culture of black America since slavery was heavily influenced by the Bible, particularly the Old Testament saga of Moses and Joshua as 'deliverers' of an oppressed, enslaved people who found themselves in a foreign land."[152] It is against this historical background that certain black ministers assumed leadership positions in the civil rights struggles of the 1960s.

One of the best examples of this kind of black leadership in Wilcox County is offered by the case of Reverend Thomas Threadgill. Threadgill clearly exhibited all the characteristics of charismatic leadership, and in the eyes of the black people in his county Threadgill had a high standing among them because of his position as an ordained minister. Black residents were also drawn to him because he had a riveting oratorical style and an uncompromising commitment to the civil rights struggle. In fact, his commitment was legendary, and he readily made his feelings known whenever the he had the opportunity. On more than one occasion the fiery minister insisted, "If we have to eat bread and water, we're not going to bow down to them [white people]."[153] Threadgill was a tireless organizer who seemed to be everywhere at once during the movement, encouraging people when they became weary, cracking jokes to cheer them up, and all the time ministering to their needs: preaching eulogies, conducting weddings, and raising money for needy families. Sheryl, Threadgill's daughter, remembers that during the civil rights years "he wasn't in the house that much." She was only a little girl, and she missed having her father around, but it was only after she was practically grown that Sheryl and her brothers were finally able to spend any significant amount of time with their father.

Because of Threadgill's charismatic style and his high visibility in the community, African Americans in Wilcox County were drawn to him. Most scholars agree that the black southern masses are primed to respond to this kind of charisma, and some observers even argue that such a response frequently results in the formation of a cult of personality. This kind of relationship between leader and followers can have a positive impact because it can help to unify the masses. In the case of Wilcox County, the sheer force of the attraction to charismatic leadership like that displayed by Reverend Threadgill helped to unite black Wilcox residents in the midst of the stresses and strains of the crusade for civil rights in their county. Conversely, however, too much reliance on the strength of a leader's personality can help retard the growth of the long-term strategies and programs necessary to change people's lives. Historian Manning Marable uses the example of Harold Washington, the first black mayor of Chicago, to illustrate this point.

> The lesson of Harold Washington is that black leadership in the civil rights and Black Power periods depended too heavily upon personalities. The charisma of a Harold Washington was no substitute for an effective political organization, which could have kept together the various class and ethnic forces that had challenged the Democratic machine during the 1980s.[154]

In those early days of the civil rights struggle in Wilcox County, other black residents who, like Threadgill, were perceived as leaders were most often from Wilcox County's tiny black middle class. They were either ministers, like Lonnie Brown, or they were educators, like teacher Albert Gordon or principal Lawrence Parrish. Some scholars argue that black leaders often came from this class because the white power structure was more comfortable negotiating with the educated black people from this class. What this suggests, obviously, is that white approval has had a profound impact on the perception of the legitimacy of black leadership. British scholar John White explains, "whatever their ideological (or psychological) complexion then, black American leaders have historically depended on white as well as on Negro recognition of their claims to speak for their race."[155] White goes on to conclude that "one of the anomalies of Afro-American history is that blacks, as an ethnic group, have had only limited opportunities to select their own leaders."[156]

Although most of the county's civil rights leaders came from the middle class, there were exceptions to this general rule of black leadership. A case in point is offered by the example of some members of the Pettway clan of Gee's Bend. A number of members of this family were perceived as leaders, particularly the fiery farmer Monroe Pettway. Although Pettway enjoyed an independent economic status as a landowner, he clearly lacked the professional standing and the educational attainment possessed by some of the others who were perceived as movement leaders. At the same time, however, Pettway had gained the respect of many in his community because of his outspoken commitment to justice and his willingness to help those in need, and this served to elevate him to a leadership role during his county's civil rights struggles.

Irrespective of the class background of Wilcox County's civil rights leaders, they were all confronted by the challenge of learning to work with the outside civil rights workers who came into their county. It was not always easy, and it is important to note that the leadership styles of SNCC and SCLC were very different. SNCC's approach tended to be more "egalitarian and participatory" while SCLC's style was more "charismatic and patriarchal."[157] Perhaps because they were already primed to respond to charismatic leadership, or maybe because of SCLC's superior resources, those who were active in Wilcox County's civil rights movement more often involved themselves with SCLC's field staff. In fact, one SCLC worker, Daniel Harrell, became so involved with the community that he became a permanent resident of Wilcox County. He lived there for over a decade after the movement until his untimely death.

In the meantime, because the changes promised by the movement were extremely slow in coming despite the best efforts of the county's black leaders, some of the county's black youth began to take matters into their own hands. These young people had cut their teeth on their county's voting rights demonstrations, and they had soaked up the ideas of some of the outside activists who came to their county. By the late sixties, however, they were becoming impatient. Two of these young people in particular, Brenda Bussey Carson and Larry Threadgill, clearly emerged as the leaders in the difficult school desegregation struggle that began in the early seventies. Initially, these new leaders were united by their youthful idealism, but when their idealism suffered a huge blow because many of the adults in the community refused to support their school protests, they were also united by their feelings of betrayal. These two young leaders provide a fascinating study in contrast: They were from two different economic classes, and obviously, they were different genders. Regardless of their differences, however, both of these young people were strongly influenced by the times in which they lived. They had come of age in an America that was very different from that of their elders. They only dimly remembered the 1950s, but they were old enough to be aware of current events in the early 1960s when the federal government began to demonstrate its sympathy for civil rights. By the time they reached high school in the early 1970s, the Black Power movement was at its height, and that spirit of pride and assertiveness resonated with these young people. Against this background of youthful black assertiveness, Brenda and Larry's classmates appreciated the willingness of these young leaders to speak out in their behalf.

That spirit of assertiveness that had been spawned by the Black Power atmosphere of this era continued to linger long after the school desegregation struggle, and by the time black candidates began to win election to Wilcox County offices, a new breed of black leader had begun to emerge. That new breed was also influenced by Black Power assertiveness, but one of the critical characteristics that separated them from pre–civil rights movement leaders was the legal reality in which they operated: they were the first group of black leaders who were able to function outside the confines of legal segregation. That meant that unlike their predecessors whose options had been limited by de jure segregation, the new black leadership had a wider range of options as they searched for ways to help their constituents. Conversely, the group cohesiveness that had flourished in the presence of segregation had begun to break down in its absence. Obviously, hatred of de jure segregation had been a powerful rallying tool that had united African Americans across economic and educational lines. Without it, the new generation of black leaders was left wondering if they would ever be able to enjoy the kind of group unity that had existed before the civil rights movement.

The ascendancy of Bobby Jo Johnson is symbolic of this new age of African American leadership in Wilcox County. Clearly, Johnson was not from a middle-class background, but by the 1980s his assertive and confrontational style proved to be extremely popular with black constituents who were frustrated with the slow pace of change. When they sat in the audience at Wilcox County Commission meetings and listened to the fiery Vietnam veteran speak, many of the county's African Americans silently cheered as he articulated their hopes and fears at the same time that he "put the white people in their place." Predictably, most of Wilcox County's white residents feared and loathed a leader like Bobby Jo Johnson. His blunt outspoken demeanor, especially regarding issues of race, made his white neighbors extremely uncomfortable.

Finally, as the 1980s drew to a close, it was clear that an era in Wilcox County politics was also drawing to a close. By that time, Reverend Thomas Threadgill, the most visible symbol of the earlier civil rights leadership, was dead, and Bobby Jo Johnson, symbol of the new assertive, confrontational style, was chairman of the Wilcox County Commission. This black leadership shift in the 1980s occurred against a background characterized more by continuity than change. Black residents still faced the same desperate poverty that they had faced for generations. That had not changed. It seemed to most that even though their elected officials were now almost all black, their lives were not any better, and their prospects for the future were not any brighter. African Americans in Wilcox County had fought long and hard during their civil rights struggle, and they had fervently believed in the movement's promise of a better life. Yet, when they realized that the movement's promise was not coming true, they became angry, bitter, and disillusioned. Predictably, many focused their anger on the most accessible and convenient targets: the county's black elected officials. At the same time, white residents, who had predicted disaster if African Americans were allowed to vote and hold office, were quick to blame all the county's problems on the new black elected officials. Of course, they refused to admit that when they had been in charge of the county's political apparatus, the lives of the county's black majority had not been any better then either.

Thus, as the last years of the twentieth century approached, Wilcox County's black elected officials and community leaders were left scratching their heads in consternation. The political winds blowing over their county were tainted by anger, suspicion, and disillusionment. Ordinary citizens, both black and white, apparently had little faith in the ability of their leaders to make any substantive change. Consequently, even in the twenty-first century, the people of Wilcox County remain trapped in twentieth-century problems that were spawned by the county's twisted racial history reaching all the way back into the nineteenth century. After all they have been through, most still see no way out.

CHAPTER EIGHT

∽

The More Things Change,
the More They Stay the Same

As Wilcox residents face the new millennium, they are confronted by thorny economic, social, political, and educational problems. Their search for solutions continues to be complicated by the sharply divided racial past that has characterized life in Wilcox County for generations. These days, the civil rights campaigns of a generation ago that were supposed to address racial issues are only a distant memory to many residents. At the same time, the county's young people, who had not even been born when all the marching, singing, and protesting occurred, know absolutely nothing about this chapter of their county's history. However, back in the 1960s most black residents were hopeful that their movement would finally bring fundamental change to their county, but to this day many are disappointed that the change did not go far enough.

Of course there are some obvious changes. For example, today, anyone entering Wilcox County's old red brick courthouse cannot help but notice the abundance of black faces peering from behind computer monitors, answering phones, filing motions, and just generally conducting business. Just off the courthouse square sits the public safety building with police cruisers parked in front. There is a steady flow of law enforcement officers in crisp brown uniforms armed with their service revolvers going in and out of the building. Some get in official cars and hurriedly drive off to answer calls; others go into the station to file incident reports as their shift ends; but regardless of their rank or their assignment, nearly all of these officers have black faces. In light of the difficult relationship between black residents and county law enforcement officials, the sight of so many black faces in the ranks of the county's law enforcement officers seems almost miraculous.

Black Wilcox native Paul Washington recalls his reaction the first time he ever saw black police officers in Wilcox County. Years earlier in 1949, Washington had graduated from Camden Academy, and he laughingly recalls, "I caught the first thing smoking" to get out of Wilcox County. Even though he moved all the way to Detroit, Michigan, where he made a new life for himself, Paul Washington stayed in touch with events in Wilcox County over the years, and he came home regularly to visit family members who stayed behind. He made one of those routine visits just after the remarkable change in county personnel had occurred. When Washington arrived at the courthouse square that day, sleepy little Camden seemed to be exactly the same as he remembered it. However, when he looked more closely, he let out an audible gasp as he examined the faces of the law enforcement officers climbing into official police cruisers in front of the police station: they were almost all black.

An equally dramatic surprise was in store for Washington when he entered his county's antebellum courthouse. As he walked through those massive white columns into the building that had always symbolized white supremacy, Paul Washington felt that familiar tension begin to tie his stomach in knots. However, once he actually entered the building, he could scarcely believe his eyes, and the tension in his stomach melted away. Instead, he felt goose bumps on his arms, and his jaw dropped as he stared in disbelief. His mind was having trouble processing the miraculous scene in front of him. Finally, Washington shook off the paralysis that had seemed to affect every part of his body, and he walked up to a young black clerk in one of the offices. Washington paused, cleared his throat, and said, "Please excuse me for staring at you, but I just can't believe this is Camden." When the puzzled young woman asked Washington what he meant, Washington replied, "You would never know, but anyway, congratulations."[1] Wilcox native Clifford Crowder is also amazed by the change in personnel in his county. Like Washington, Crowder left the county right after he finished high school, and he has never lived there since. Crowder now makes his home in Washington, D.C., but he returns to Wilcox County to visit friends and relatives. He explains, "Sometimes you get a feeling of disbelief. You can't believe what's going on there now."[2]

Another signpost pointing to the changed racial reality in post–civil rights movement Wilcox County involves a member of one of the county's most prominent families. The stage was set when Bain Henderson, a descendant of the Hendersons of Miller's Ferry and a staunch segregationist, shot and killed a young white poacher who was illegally hunting deer on his land. Because the murder happened in Wilcox County, the trial was held in the old county courthouse right in the middle of Camden. Henderson retained Wyman Gilmore, a white criminal defense attorney from nearby Clarke County. Gilmore, an astute and experienced lawyer, recognized that because the trial would be held in a majority black county, the jury would likely be majority black, and it would be in his client's best interest to have a black lawyer on his defense team. After convincing his reluctant client, Gilmore approached his old friend and colleague, black Selma civil rights attorney J. L. Chestnut. Chestnut was incredulous. He declared, "You must be kidding."[3] Gilmore tried to convince his old friend to join the Henderson defense team. He argued, "He's [Henderson's] not such a bad fella, J. L. You really need to get to know him." Chestnut retorted, "I already know him. . . . It would be a plus for the county if he was convicted." Chestnut concluded, "I hope they put his white ass in the penitentiary."[4]

After thinking about Gilmore's proposal for a while, however, Chestnut decided to accept after all. There were a number of reasons why Chestnut decided to represent Bain Henderson, a staunch segregationist. One of those reasons was an exceedingly practical one. Chestnut explained simply, "I knew representing Bain Henderson would boost our [his and his law partners'] credibility." Chestnut continued, "Many white people were surprised, and most black people were proud. In some kind of way, it signaled that we had arrived."[5] Ironically, even though many Wilcox County citizens regarded this as a real breakthrough, Bain Henderson, whose freedom hung in the balance, was distinctly uncomfortable with the situation. Chestnut observed, "At first, Bain was self-conscious around me because he wasn't used to dealing with blacks as equals." After a while, however, "He loosened up a little when he saw how Wyman and I carried on with each other."[6] Yet, even though he "loosened up" some, Bain Henderson was never completely comfortable being represented by a black lawyer. But, in the end, those feelings seemed to matter very little because a Wilcox County panel of seven black and five white jurors found Bain Henderson not guilty.[7] Overnight, white prospective clients began to come to J. L. Chestnut's law firm. Many observers were convinced that this was an important signal that the racial atmosphere in Wilcox County was finally changing.

Besides these obvious changes that many viewed as positive, there were other changes in the post–civil rights years that left some black residents worried and upset. For example, residents of Gee's Bend had always cherished the nurturing atmosphere of their exclusively black peninsula. However, in the unsettled years immediately following the movement, increasing numbers of

white people began invading this all-black domain. The details of their struggle to buy and retain the land are seared into the community's collective consciousness, and consequently, this unexpected invasion has made some long-
time residents very uneasy. Gee's Bend resident Paulette Pettway, activist
Monroe Pettway's daughter, explains, "Years ago, there were no white people
here, and now lots of white people want to get in here and get the land. I really don't want that to happen, and if there was a way I could stop it, I would."
Paulette concludes sadly, "But [black] people now, a lot of them, have moved
away and they have no interest, so they're selling their land."[8]

Despite these visible changes in the racial atmosphere in Wilcox County
in the years since the movement, many black residents still refuse to be persuaded that any fundamental change has occurred. Black activist and educator Lawrence Parrish laments, "I expected it to change and stay changed . . .
[but] it hasn't changed as much as I expected it to change." Furthermore, he
concludes sadly, "I was expecting more courtesy than we're getting from our
own people who . . . benefited from the change."[9] Longtime black resident
and retired teacher Lucy Ephraim expresses an even more pessimistic view.
As she puts it, "They're really just as segregated today as they were back
then."[10] Black Wilcox native and retired teacher Gwendolyn Bonham agrees
and adds, "The mind-set of the white man in Wilcox County is one of never
relinquishing what he thinks he has."[11] David Colston Jr., the son of the
black shooting victim who was killed in front of Antioch Baptist Church in
1966, also sees white attitudes in Wilcox County as a problem. He explains,
"Far as attitude . . . I don't think it has changed any."[12] Black Wilcox native
Clifford Crowder, looking back at his birthplace from his vantage point as
a resident of Washington, D.C., agrees that white attitudes are a problem.
He insists, "The racism is still there. It's going to be there forever."[13] Black
Wilcox native and Olympic track star Mabel Walker Thornton adds,
"They've [white people] had years to change. They haven't changed."[14]
Tydie D. Pettway, Gee's Bend resident and member of the activist branch of
the Pettway clan, sums it all up. She declares, "I think white people will al-
ways be white people."[15]

It seems then, that even though the laws have changed and segregation is
no longer legal, white supremacy in Wilcox County has not been entirely
eradicated. In such an atmosphere, even though white residents continue to
make up only a small minority of the county's population, their attitudes still
continue to matter a great deal. The reason for this continued white influence is squarely rooted in the county's continuing economic problems. David
Colston Jr. succinctly sums up the situation: "We just don't control
enough."[16] Black Wilcox native and Philadelphia resident Matthew Wilmer

offers an even more detailed assessment. As he puts it, "The jobs are not there."[17] In short, the overwhelming majority of the county's black population remains mired down in the same desperate poverty that has trapped their ancestors since slavery ended. Selma civil rights attorney J. L. Chestnut points out that the unequal economic relationship is glaringly obvious: "The courthouse squares in these rural counties [like Wilcox] symbolize the division. There sits the courthouse in the center, now with black people in charge. Ringing it are the banks and businesses, all owned by white people." Chestnut goes on to conclude that the consequences of this economic reality have been quite serious. He explains, "The two [the black political apparatus and the white business community] were at a standoff and progress was at a standstill."[18]

It is important to note, however, that there were at least some white people who demonstrated their willingness to do what they had to in order to advance their own economic position in the new order. Attorney Chestnut recalls, "Even though white business people thought a black government was bad for the county and didn't want to help it succeed, they came in to bid on the contract for gasoline for the county's road equipment or printing or office equipment."[19] Matthew Wilmer observed the same white willingness to at least pay lip service to the new racial order in an effort to protect their economic position. He explains, "That's one thing they [white residents] know well is what the bottom line is. If the bottom line is that money, then whatever they got to do in order to get that money, then they [are] gonna do it . . . down there now they're saying yes ma'am and no ma'am [to black customers] when you go in these stores."[20] Despite the cooperative attitude displayed by some white residents, however, there were others who just could not seem to resist using their economic position to punish black people for the changes ushered in by the civil rights movement. For example, black Wilcox native Priscilla Charley Washington clearly recalls that in the aftermath of the movement some white store owners stopped extending credit to black customers. This proved to be disastrous for many black residents who were barely getting by even in the best of times. These people were dependent on credit to help them make ends meet, and Washington explains that this prompted some of them to charge that the movement actually made things worse. She explains, "People said, 'you all came down here and started this, you know . . . you all didn't do nothing but make it hard for us.'"[21]

Thus, the conclusion is inescapable that in the new post–civil rights movement atmosphere while black people appeared to have political control, white economic hegemony remained a fact of life in Wilcox County, Alabama. Artur Davis, the new congressman from the seventh district in Alabama, which includes Wilcox County, succinctly sums up the new reality. As he puts it, "Seg-regation nationally has been eroded by economics. When you haven't had eco-nomic change, you're going to have socially segregated and politically segre-gated patterns continue because blacks have gained political power in Wilcox County. But political power uncombined or unmatched with economic power is still not going to be very transformative."[22] In short, life has remained bleak for the vast majority of black residents of the Black Belt in general and Wilcox County in particular. Recent statistics reveal that the Alabama Black Belt is:

> A place where more than six of every ten people are black, where doctors and hospitals are so scarce that pregnant women and sick residents must travel up to 30 miles to the nearest clinic . . . A region where there is no local bus ser-vice, where as many as a quarter of all households have no car. A countryside where infant death rates during parts of the 1990s surpassed those in Panama and Uruguay; the percentage of births to teenage mothers was higher than in Uganda and Indonesia.[23]

In Wilcox County in particular, a full 25 percent of all babies are born to teenage girls. The life expectancy of black children growing up in Wilcox is only 69.3 years. This is almost five years shorter than the average statewide life expectancy of seventy-four years, and nearly eight years shorter than the national life expectancy of seventy-seven years. In fact, the life expectancy of individuals born in some Third World countries like Iran, Vietnam, and El Salvador is longer than the life expectancy of black Wilcox residents.[24] At the same time, Wilcox County's unemployment rate stands at 13 percent, one of the highest in the Black Belt. As bad as that is, it is important to realize that nearly 40 percent of Wilcox citizens live in poverty: this is a clear indication that a large number of working poor live in the county alongside those who are impoverished because they are unable to find regular employment.[25] These dismal statistics point to a grim reality: many black residents live in conditions that most Americans, and even many Alabama residents, associ-ate with impoverished, underdeveloped areas in other parts of the world. It is not uncommon to see black neighborhoods in Wilcox County where the houses lack indoor plumbing and the roads are unpaved. In these kinds of con-ditions, hope for the future is in short supply. Predictably, the dropout rate among black students is soaring, and those who stay in school long enough to graduate receive diplomas from a school that is not accredited.

Things are so bad in Wilcox and the other Black Belt counties that, ac-cording to some, the region has become an embarrassment to citizens in other parts of the state who want to present a progressive image to the rest of the world. They desperately want to distance their state from the Old South image represented by Wilcox County that is such an important part of Alabama's past. The desire to shake that Old South image is so strong, according to some, that "most Alabamians are blind to the Black Belt. They complain when Alabama is depicted with Old South stereotypes, with pictures of barefoot children and sharecropper shacks. Politicians and those who live elsewhere in the state[,] people who could help to pull the Black Belt out of its resource-draining decline seldom get far enough off the interstate to see the real problems in Black Belt counties."[26] In view of all these problems, it is not surprising that in the years since the civil rights movement the black out-migration has continued unabated. This movement is actually a continuation of the black out-migration that has been going on since the beginning of the last century, and the impact is stunning: "In 1900 the 12 counties that make up the Vermont-sized soul of Alabama's rural Black Belt contained 21 percent of the state's population, and 36 percent of Alabama's blacks. By 2000 the population in those counties had decreased 42 percent, to a point that only 5 percent of the state's people, and 12 percent of the state's blacks, lived in the region."[27]

In Wilcox County in particular, the black population has registered a steady decline through much of the twentieth century. In 1950, on the eve of the civil rights movement in the South, Wilcox County's total population was 23,476. Of that total 18,558, or 79 percent, were African American. By the next census just as the major campaigns in the movement were about to start, Wilcox County's total population had fallen to 18,739. African Americans numbered 14,598 or 77.9 percent of that total. In the aftermath of the movement by the 1970 census, Wilcox County's population had continued its steady decline. The total numbered only 16,303 that year, and 11,160 of that total or 68 percent were African American. Ten years later in 1980 the county's total population stood at 15,100. Black residents numbered 10,151 or 67.2 percent of the total. By the last decade of the twentieth century, the 1990 census indicated that Wilcox County's total population had shrunk to 13,568. Of that total, 9,353 or 68.9 percent were black. Finally, by 2000 the county's population had sunk to an all-time low of 13,183 of which 9,479 were African American. That black total represented a slight increase over the 1990 figure, and that meant African Americans were 71.9 percent of Wilcox County's total population in 2000. Overall, the county's total population shrank 44 percent from just before the movement in 1950 to the beginning of the twenty-first century in 2000.

It seems that many of those who leave are searching for better opportunities to make a living for themselves and their families. Conversely, there are some who are convinced that "Those who stay there are accustomed to failure. . . . They are surrounded by ignorance, poverty, and low expectations."[28] Today's black high school students at Wilcox Central High School are painfully aware of the limited opportunities that await them if they decide to stay in Wilcox County after they graduate. Andre Saulsberry's honors class at Wilcox Central High School recently expressed their hopes and fears in no uncertain terms. Saulsberry is a young teacher who is a native of Wilcox County. He was born in Coy in 1972, just as the school integration crisis in his county came to a head. After attending elementary school at Tate's Chapel, middle school at Camden Academy, and high school at Wilcox County High, he transferred to the new Wilcox Central High School for his senior year. Upon graduation, Saulsberry enrolled in Langston University in Oklahoma where he majored in English. He later earned a master's degree at the University of West Alabama, and he is currently enrolled in a Ph.D. program at the University of Alabama.

Back in 1990 just as he was about to graduate from high school, Andre Saulsberry, in concert with many of his classmates, swore that he would never come back to Wilcox County to live. However, in 1994, just as he graduated from college, he received news that his mother was gravely ill, and he knew he had to come back home to be with her. He applied for a job teaching English at his alma mater, and he was hired. His homecoming was bittersweet, though, because although he was able to spend a good deal of time with his mother before she died, he has mixed feelings about the kind of treatment he received from county officials, especially those in the school system. He explains, "I had observed that you have to be an outsider in order to be promoted."[29] Despite his misgivings, he quickly settled into his new position as an English teacher at Wilcox Central High School. Before long, the young teacher realized that even though he had not planned to come home, he was actually getting a great deal of pleasure from helping students at his alma mater. At the same time, however, Saulsberry also realized that some of the people in the community, including people he had grown up with, seemed to be suspicious of him and his motives. As he puts it, "I think sometimes when people return, they find themselves being somewhat ostracized. People have the impression that you may think now that you're so much more." Saulsberry further explains that such attitudes are especially hard to understand when they come from people you have known well all your life: "It seems as if sometimes the people who have lived right around you, in your own neighborhood who you may try to do everything you can do to help because you know them, but they still have this sense that you feel that you are more now, and you don't feel that way."[30]

Andre Saulsberry's students agree with their teacher's assessment. They are sure that people who never leave the county are often suspicious of those who leave to further their education. Once they return, they are often in for a rough time. For example, Danita Pettway, a graduating senior who is one of Saulsberry's students and the class valedictorian, plans to become a medical doctor, but she does not plan to return to Wilcox County because, "I don't think I'd be able to benefit from living here, and I don't know if I'd be welcome here." She concludes sadly, "If I was to go to med school and come back with all these degrees and everything, I think I'd get talked about more than appreciated."[31] Another of Saulsberry's students, Marcus McCord, agrees and explains further that many Wilcox residents who have not had the same opportunities are probably suspicious of returning college graduates because they feel uncomfortable in their presence. McCord is convinced that the reason for this discomfort is that those who have never left the county feel they no longer have anything in common with the returning graduates.[32]

At the same time, according to some of Saulsberry's students, recent black college graduates who return to the county might also face a chilly reception from some members of the county's tiny black professional class. For example, Linda Carstarphen, another of Saulsberry's honors students who plans to become a lawyer, lamented, "Here in this county you have black people against black people too." She continues, "If you come back down here with a degree or something, like the black people that's in the higher offices or things like that that need to hire you, they will probably take that white person over you to keep you down."[33]

Andre Saulsberry's honors English class is filled with the best and the brightest at Wilcox Central High School, and their attitudes are quite likely to be very different from those of their classmates. They have big dreams: all want to further their education after high school. Some are interested in becoming medical doctors, others want a career in teaching, a number of them want to major in computer science, there are some who want to major in business and work for a big corporation, still others want to become lawyers. Yet, no matter what their interests are, only one out of a class of nearly twenty students plans on returning to Wilcox County immediately after she finishes her education. It is not that they do not like Wilcox County. On the contrary, a number of them expressed real love and appreciation for the place where they were born. One of the things that many of them find most attractive is the safe atmosphere. For example, Clarice Harris, a slender, lively young woman who dreams of becoming a lawyer, insists, "We don't have a lot of criminals, you know, we [are] sheltered in Wilcox . . . we don't have a lot of criminals, a lot of killing."[34] Valedictorian Danita Pettway insists that in addition to the safety, she also loves the county's natural beauty. She explains, "It's a beautiful place, and if I was the type of person that didn't want to do anything with my life, I'd love to live here." She adds sadly, "It's a wonderful place, it's just not growing."[35]

Yet, as much as they love their county, Saulsberry's students are painfully aware that there is a wider world out there, and they are not being properly prepared for it because of continued segregation in their county. Danita Pettway explains the frustration that many feel: "After a while it's time to get out and meet other people. All my life I went to a school with nothing but black kids. It's 2002 and we're still segregated."[36] Tracey Dees, the only one of Saulsberry's students who plans to return to the county immediately after graduation, says, "When we leave here, all we know is ourselves." Tracey is sure that they are all handicapped because of this. As she puts it, "Naturally, if you don't know anything about someone, you're automatically passing judgment on them, a stereotypical judgment since you don't know how they are. Some people will just say, 'I don't like white people.'" As far as she is concerned, such ignorance contributes to the continued discord in Wilcox County. Tracey advises, "I think someone here needs to take a stand, and say maybe we do need to become more diverse and get to know one another."[37] Clarice Harris succinctly sums it all up: "It shouldn't be like that."[38]

On the other side of town, students at the private all-white Wilcox Academy also have definite ideas about the segregation that defines relations between the races in Wilcox County. As he thought about its continued existence, one student remarked, "It's basically just a tradition that there's no interaction between blacks and whites."[39] Another offered, "It's like an inborn fear that they're going to rob you blind and stab you."[40] As he made this comment, some of his classmates gathered around him giggled uneasily. One of the other students in the group confessed, "I know a few, but they're all older, that helped raise me when I was younger." She concludes, "I have no contact with any below the age of fifty."[41] Clearly, most of these students understood that their county was segregated, but few had ever questioned it. However, one of the students in the group did question the wisdom of maintaining segregated schools. He explained, "I think it would make sense for there to be one school that has the most qualified teachers and that'll offer the best general education for the students." Practical considerations notwithstanding, this student understood that it was highly unlikely that school integration would ever come to Wilcox County because "in Camden . . . it's so inbred that whites go to the white schools, and blacks go to the black schools."[42]

Such white attitudes do not surprise Andre Saulsberry and his students at Wilcox Central High School. They understand how tenaciously their white neighbors support segregation, and the young teacher is convinced that a large part of the reason for the county's economic woes rests squarely on the continuation of this separation. Everyone agrees that there are not nearly enough jobs in the county because they cannot seem to attract any industry into the area, and Saulsberry argues that even though many blame the county's unaccredited public education system or the lack of a transportation infrastructure, these are not the real reasons why companies do not want to locate their operations in Wilcox County. Instead, according to Saulsberry, "They don't want to deal with all this separation."[43]

In the meantime, as many of the county's best and brightest young people continue to leave, some of the same old battles continue to rage. For example, by the last decade of the twentieth century, state representative James Thomas, principal of Wilcox Central High School, became embroiled in a nasty controversy involving charges of sexual harassment, and counter-charges of nepotism. The stage was set when School Superintendent Lester McBride, Odell Tumblin's successor, crossed swords with Thomas. Thomas charges that McBride "forced" him to hire two female employees for "personal reasons." Thomas insists that in a short time he relieved the women of their duties because he realized they were not doing their jobs. The principal goes on to explain, "That was the opportunity for him [McBride] to fire me." At this point, the school board was also drawn into the fray. According to Thomas, "By that time [the 1991–1992 school year], there had been an effort on the part of the school board to remove me from the high school." The controversy came to a head when Superintendent McBride confronted the determined principal in his office at Wilcox Central. McBride informed Thomas that he had been relieved of his duties, and he demanded that the principal leave the premises immediately. Thomas refused. In a defiant tone he declared, "I'm not leaving." The equally determined superintendent replied, "You'll leave one way or the other."[44]

James Thomas did leave that day. He was suspended for six months, but after his suspension he returned to his duties as principal, and he has continued to serve in that capacity ever since. At the same time, he has continued to win reelection to his seat in the state House of Representatives. To this day, there are many who are convinced that it is improper for one person to hold two state jobs simultaneously. Many fear that dividing his attention between two important positions ensures that he will not be able to perform either job effectively. Thomas dismisses his critics by insisting, "I'm a state legislator, and as a result of that, I've done so much for the school system."[45] Despite such reassurances there is an undercurrent of disapproval that seems to surround James Thomas, but his critics have yet to find a way to remove him from either position. In fact, in the

spring of 2002 Thomas managed to win a runoff election in yet another successful bid to hold on to his position in the state legislature.

In the meantime, charges of vote fraud have continued to plague the
county's elections. For example, the headline in the June 6, 1990, *Wilcox
Progressive Era* declared, "Switched or Missing Ballots Cause Anger." The article that followed the dramatic headline explained, "An angry Probate
Judge Jerry Boggan said yesterday that he was asking state and federal authorities to look into how the wrong ballots got into some of yesterday's
boxes." The consequences of these ballot irregularities were quite serious:
voters in one particular district were prevented from casting their votes for
the county commission candidate of their choice. As serious as the problem
of missing ballots was, that June election was plagued by an even more troubling problem: "others offered the view that many older voters had simply
stayed home after hearing reports of early voters being threatened or intimidated at the polls by campaign workers for some of the candidates."[46] Even
though the county's election officials called Washington and Montgomery to
request help from federal and state authorities, by the end of the day, no outside help had arrived.[47]

In the midst of Wilcox County's continued political turmoil, Commissioner Bobby Jo Johnson, the most potent symbol of the county's post–civil
rights movement black leadership, had a change of heart. His wife, Astoria
Johnson, describes the change as little short of miraculous. One day in the
early 1990s, Mrs. Johnson remembers, Bobby Jo sat her down and looked intently at her face as he told her that he had been called to the ministry. Astoria Johnson could not believe her ears. She searched her husband's face for
some sign that he was joking. She found none. Instead, she saw a peaceful expression that smoothed out all the angry lines that had routinely creased his
face. It had always seemed that the lines deepened when he was about to attend a county commission meeting. But now they were gone, and "he was
just as calm."[48] After that announcement, according to Astoria Johnson, her
husband was a changed man. Even when he presided over county commission meetings, "he was not upset. [He] didn't use his Sunday School words."
He even gave up his habits, like betting on dog races.[49]

The new Reverend Bobby Jo Johnson's spiritual rebirth was soon followed
by devastating physical changes. By the mid-1990s his health began to fail. It
seemed that his body that had been so badly mangled more than twenty years
ago when he was defending his country in Vietnam was finally giving out on
him. His kidneys shut down, and he had to have a kidney transplant. A short
time later, he found that much of his physical strength had deserted him, and
he was no longer able to get around on his crutches. After this, Johnson was

forced to rely totally on a wheelchair. His wife of more than twenty years remembers that this was particularly hard for him because before this, "he never
thought of himself as a handicapped person." Within a short time, his ill
health forced Johnson to retire from public office. He died in 1997, and his
death symbolized the end of an era in Wilcox County politics. Bobby Jo Johnson had been a living, breathing transition between the civil rights leadership
of the past and the new confrontational style of the post–civil rights era. But
now he was gone, and following in his wake as a new millennium approached
was an uncertain future. In that uncertain future, it seems that many Wilcox
voters, like voters everywhere, are becoming increasingly disillusioned and
cynical. Charges and countercharges of unintentional errors, deliberate fraud,
and a whole host of other irregularities have continued to plague the county's
elections. In fact, as recently as the June 2002 election, losing candidates
lodged complaints alleging vote fraud.[50]

Many of those who fought so hard in the county's civil rights struggles of
the 1960s and 1970s can only shake their heads sadly as they watch neighbors fight each other over the limited number of political offices and county
positions that are available. Back during the movement these activists had
clearly understood that they represented the forces of good, justice, and tol-
erance. They were fighting the forces of evil, bigotry, and segregation. It had
been as clear as black and white. Now, however, it seems that everything is
painted in shades of gray. The goals are no longer crystal clear; the enemy is
no longer so easily identifiable. Could it be, some wonder, that because their
young people do not know how hard their struggle was, they have no appreciation for how big the struggle is now? For example, Reverend Charley
Pettway insists that because most of the county's younger black residents
know very little about the civil rights struggles of their ancestors, most feel
that they do not have anything to struggle for anymore.[51] Former Wilcox resident and educator Clark Thomas agrees that many young people do not
know how hard the struggle was. Their ignorance scares him, especially when
he recalls how perilous conditions in the movement were. As he thinks about
the extreme danger they faced day after day during those years, a vivid memory fills his head of his 1956 two-tone green Pontiac. It was a huge automobile with shiny chrome bumpers, chrome mirrors, and chrome side molding.
He drove it everywhere during the civil rights movement, and he remembers
how much he needed the reassurance of the big, powerful, eight-cylinder
engine under the hood—and the loaded shotgun that was always under the
driver's seat.[52]

Thus, as Wilcox County enters a new millennium, its citizens are struggling to move beyond the ghost of their racially troubled past, which seems

to hover over their educational troubles, economic deficits, and political problems. Everywhere they look, most see stubborn problems that seem to be insurmountable. Any effective attempt to evaluate Wilcox County's plight must place it within the broader context of regional and national developments. Yet, anyone attempting to construct a critical examination of any part of the rural South quickly runs into a problem: the vast majority of studies of African American communities in recent years have concentrated on urban inner city areas. As one scholar explains,

> By the late 1960s, social scientists had abandoned the critical investigation of rural relations in the predominantly African American plantation counties of the South. When they are examined, there is a tendency to superimpose categories created for the study of northern manufacturing-based cities onto the social and institutional histories of these rural regions.[53]

This urban emphasis in the literature on black communities has important consequences for students of the black rural experience: "What is lost in the process is not only an appreciation of the continuity of plantation-based economic systems and power relations, but also the critique of these relations."[54]

One of the few recent studies of the black rural experience is *Development Arrested: The Blues and Plantation Power in the Mississippi Delta*, by Clyde Woods. Although Woods concentrates his study on the Mississippi Delta, many of his observations are applicable to the Alabama Black Belt. In his examination of the place of plantation agriculture in the nation's economy, Woods insists that although many economists have asserted that unfree labor systems like slavery "are feudal and semifeudal throwbacks that are incompatible with capitalism," more recent analyses have "found capitalist dynamism, adaptability and innovation in plantation regimes."[55] Placing slavery and plantation agriculture squarely in the flow of capitalist development in nineteenth-century America is important for anyone seeking to understand the relationship between labor and capital or black and white in the Alabama Black Belt.

At the same time, a thorough examination of this complicated relationship is essential for anyone seeking to understand the stubborn economic problems that continue to plague black residents in the Alabama Black Belt in general and in Wilcox County in particular, even after the activism of the civil rights movement. Woods argues,

> many of those who proceed from the viewpoint that the plantation South was a noncapitalist semifeudal backwater from 1630 to 1965 would argue that the region needs more unregulated resource and labor exploitation to become fully capitalist. Yet, if we assume industrial capitalism emerged in the plantation

South before it did in the mercantile-oriented North, we can begin to understand how the region's so-called "backwardness" and poverty may actually be the result of too much profit-oriented development.[56]

Thus, Woods concludes that the stubborn poverty that presented such a powerful obstacle to civil rights activists of the 1960s who were trying to help people become empowered is rooted in this long history of "unregulated resource and labor exploitation" on the plantations of the Deep South.

In his study of the founding of the Southern Tenant Farmers' Union, Donald Grubbs also emphasizes the centrality of the plantation system in the Deep South in determining the relationship between labor and capital, and black and white. Furthermore, Grubbs also insists that a whole complex of cultural attitudes grew up around this economic system. As he put it,

> There appear to be two main reasons why the cheap-labor plantation system was so long in yielding to fundamental changes. The first reason was that the cheap-labor system, which was in reality a slave-labor system perpetuated with minor changes after the Civil War, had become an inextricable part of a whole complex of cultural attitudes. These attitudes stereotyped croppers as a good-for-nothing class on whom any systematic help would be wasted, and they underlay the various devices used to keep the tenant class too politically subservient to demand changes. Furthermore, these attitudes upheld the juggling of accounts and the denial of schooling that kept tenants on the plantation.[57]

Grubbs concludes that in addition to the development of these attitudes, there is yet another reason why the plantation labor system that ensnared so many African Americans in Wilcox County and other areas of the Deep South was able to survive for so long after the Civil War. He explains, "The second reason . . . was more simple. Its leaders, making use of their political power, bailed themselves out with government subsidies. This is the story of the cotton program of the Agricultural Adjustment Administration."[58] Thus, Grubbs argues that through the programs of the Agricultural Adjustment Administration in the 1930s, the federal government actually supported the continuation of the planters' exploitation of the descendants of slaves. As he puts it, "Just as surely as the Republicans had allowed the plantation South to survive after a brief post–Civil War interlude of democratic reconstruction, so now [1930s] the Democrats were preserving the planters of the South at the expense of their tenants."[59] Of course, Grubbs is referring to the establishment of the practice of paying government subsidies to planters in exchange for a reduction of their cotton acreage. This helped to accelerate the trend of pushing black sharecroppers off the land.

Even after the economy of the rest of the country began to recover from the Great Depression, the continuation of government subsidies to Deep South planters sealed the fate of Wilcox County's impoverished farm laboring class. As the big white landowners increasingly turned their attention to herding cattle and growing timber, their need for the cheap black labor force that had sustained their ancestors through the antebellum era, through Reconstruction, and into the early years of the twentieth century continued to diminish. Finally, by the civil rights upheavals of the 1960s, Wilcox County planters were easily able to evict troublesome black tenants who were demanding their rights because this cheap black labor was no longer essential to the planters' economic survival. Not surprisingly, the dispossessed black tenants, like their ancestors before them, found that eviction from the land left them with precious few options. It is against this background of diminishing need for their labor in the twentieth century that Wilcox County's African American citizens took on the Herculean task of working to exercise the rights that had been guaranteed to their ancestors some one hundred years ago after the Civil War. Thus, those who marched, picketed, and protested risked everything to assert their rights, and in the years since the movement, some of them have continued to look for some hope for the future of their county.

All of this brings us back to Wilcox County's public schools and the black children who attend them. In Wilcox County, just as in other places all over this country, many are convinced that children hold the key to society's future in the new millennium. Consequently, the proper education of those children is of utmost importance. Wilcox County's public schools are still troubled, and Malcolm Cain, the current Wilcox County school superintendent, has been fighting an uphill battle ever since he was appointed in February of 1999. One of the biggest problems Cain has had to face is the decentralization of the system. In fact, the public schools are so decentralized that, according to Cain, "It was a system in name only." Shortly after being appointed to the superintendent's position, Cain noticed that the principals rarely cooperated with each other. The superintendent recalls, "I made the suggestion that one of the schools use the auditorium of another school, and I mean, I got the funniest looks."[60] Selma civil rights attorney J. L. Chestnut observed a similar attitude in nearby Sumter County. Chestnut explained, "We also had the problem of some black principals who now had blacks over them. These principals had been kings of the hill in their virtually all-black schools. They didn't get a lot of direction from the central office," and they rarely cooperated with each other. According to Chestnut, this lack of cooperation had dire consequences. He insists, "When blacks took over the school board and made the principals more accountable, this didn't sit too well with some of them, and they tried to undermine the board and the black superintendent."[61]

As serious as the decentralization of the system is, it is only one of the problems confronting the county's superintendent. Other problems Cain has had to face are mostly rooted in organizational weakness: it seems that when he took over, there were few written guidelines and procedures for employees of the school system to follow. For an ex-military man like Cain, such a situation is extremely frustrating. For example, there are no written educational requirements for school board members. As a result, the school board has had and continues to have members who have not even graduated from high school. Quite possibly, undereducated black Wilcox residents have elected such people to their school board because they feel they can identify and communicate more easily with them. Regardless of the reason, however, the conclusion is inescapable that the failure to require even minimum educational standards for school board members is bound to have profound consequences for the future of public education in Wilcox County. Cain was also confronted by the lack of a specific pay scale for employees of the system when he first assumed the superintendent's position. He vividly recalls how chaotic things were: "When I first came, I had everybody and their brother coming to me and saying, the board promised me a raise. It was unreal." Invariably, when Cain asked for written confirmation, he was told that there was none. Without an official pay scale to consult or written confirmation from the school board, Cain felt compelled to deny all such requests. Not surprisingly, this decision was quite unpopular. Yet, Malcolm Cain did not have any time to dwell on the impact his decision had on his popularity among black citizens in his new home because he had other issues to tackle. Among the most serious of those issues was the lack of a written code of conduct for students in the system. Cain explains, "In the past, the rules were made up as they go." The amazed superintendent was convinced that this was no way to run a school system. Consequently, he issued a set of rules and regulations and had them compiled in a pamphlet. He was pleased, but a little surprised by the public reaction. According to Cain, "Believe it or not, people read that book. Before they challenge a situation, they'll go look in [it] and they know what the rules are."[62]

Superintendent Cain admits that the Wilcox County system still has problems, but he insists that they are making progress. He points with pride to two recent articles in the *Birmingham News* that profile George W. Watts Elementary School as evidence of that progress. According to that newspaper article, the student body at Watts, which is located in the Pine Apple area of Wilcox

County, is extremely poor: "it is one of a handful of Alabama schools . . . where 100 percent of students qualify for free lunch because their family incomes are well below the federal poverty level."[63] Yet, against this background of economic deprivation, and against all odds, Watts sixth graders achieved impressive test scores on standardized exams recently: "Sixth graders at Watts ranked in the 77th percentile in math and the 82nd percentile in language, compared with other American children."[64] At the end of a follow-up article on Watts Elementary just a few days later, the reporter concluded his article by asking, "But if poor children in the heart of the Black Belt can perform well, shouldn't every public school on Caution or Alert status at least look at what Wilcox County is doing?"[65] Not surprisingly, Superintendent Cain is proud of the achievement of Watts Elementary, but that pride is tempered by his recognition of the system's continuing problems, and also by the reaction of black people in the county. He shakes his head wearily as he admits, "They have a tendency, the majority of the community . . . they always look at the bad things, they don't ever look basically at the progress."[66] Of course it is important to note that with just two exceptions, the schools in the Wilcox County system, including the high school, remain unaccredited.

It all seems so bleak that everywhere they look most can find little reason to hope, and the continued existence of such stubborn problems all around them engenders such a feeling of despair among many of the county's black residents that they seem powerless to resist. Residents of all ages, from children to grandparents, are ensnared in a negative atmosphere that comes from the hopelessness that results from chronic joblessness that ultimately leads to feelings of powerlessness despite the changes ushered in by the civil rights movement of the 1960s. Sociologist William Julius Wilson discusses the development and impact of such negative attitudes among African American populations in areas where work has disappeared. According to Wilson, "work is not simply a way to make a living and support one's family. It also constitutes a framework for daily behavior and patterns of interaction because it imposes discipline and regularities." Predictably, in the absence of "regular employment, life, including family life, becomes less coherent."[67] Wilson goes on to assert that the negative attitudes associated with joblessness are a powerful impediment to the traditional solutions proposed by society, particularly education. As he puts it, "The net effect is that joblessness, as a way of life, takes on a different social meaning. . . . The development of cognitive, linguistic, and other educational and job-related skills necessary for the world of work in the mainstream economy is thereby adversely affected." Wilson concludes, "In such neighborhoods, therefore, teachers become frustrated and do not teach and children do not learn."[68]

While it is important to note that Wilson is examining joblessness among inner city African Americans, it is clear that his description of conditions in that setting is hauntingly familiar to observers of conditions in the Black Belt in general and in Wilcox County in particular. At the same time, any proper analysis must take into consideration the direct link between inner-city conditions and rural realities. According to Donald Grubbs, "a generation later [after the Depression] the sons and daughters of those displaced and dispossessed tenants crowded the ghettoes of Northern cities, and the problem was more acute and visible than ever before."[69] In other words, the problems faced by black urban dwellers are in many ways the same problems that are faced by African Americans in rural areas like Wilcox County. They have just been transported to the city.

Veteran teacher and former Volunteers in Service to America (VISTA) volunteer James Beardsley remarks sadly on the devastating impact of the negative atmosphere in Wilcox County on the self-image of his students. He observes, "Working with the kids that I work with, you hear so much racial hatred of themselves. They make fun of their hair, they make fun of their noses, they make fun of their hips, and there is no counteracting force."[70] As these students mature, it is a short step for them to take from negative feelings about their physical appearance to negative feelings about their ability to influence their own destiny. Sociologist William Wilson asserts that in areas plagued by chronic joblessness like Wilcox County, such negative feelings afflict many of the residents because "[i]nability to influence events and social conditions give rise to feelings of futility and despondency as well as anxiety."[71]

These feelings of powerlessness transcend the generations of Wilcox County's African Americans. Tangled in the web of racial deference patterns of the past, held in thrall by the joblessness and poverty of the present, black Wilcox residents of various ages continue to battle the negative attitudes that have haunted them for generations. Even the seismic social upheavals during the civil rights movement could not shake loose the negative feelings that have been such a prominent part of black life in Wilcox County for generations. Consequently, many continue to suffer in silence, and most rarely complain. In the years immediately following the movement, Reverend Threadgill observed sadly, "people in the black community will tell you they don't have any problems."[72]

In more recent years black Wilcox natives evaluating the position of African Americans in their county are all distressed by this continued black stoic acceptance of the political powerlessness and economic deprivation that have been their reality for so long. For example, black Wilcox native

Bessye Ramsey Neal explains, "Blacks actually accepted that [political powerlessness and economic deprivation] as the way it should be, even after the laws were passed."[73] Like Neal, Reverend Threadgill's son Larry is also convinced that even now many black Wilcox residents do not expect their lives to change. Furthermore, the younger Threadgill is absolutely convinced that white residents do not expect their lives will change either. Thus, it seems that with a few exceptions, both black and white residents of Wilcox County are stuck in the same old patterns and the same old relationships with each other that have existed for generations. From his vantage point as a resident of Atlanta, Georgia, Larry Threadgill shakes his head in wonder as he remarks on life in Wilcox County in the new millennium: "It's like stepping back in time."[74] David Colston Jr., whose father was murdered in front of Antioch Baptist Church in 1966, agrees with Threadgill. He does not think that the "underlying racial beliefs" have changed in Wilcox County. He has no doubt that if those beliefs ever do change, it will be so far in the future that he will not be around to see it.[75] Wilcox judge Jo Celeste Pettway advises that the only way to combat this continued stoic black acceptance is to "start teaching our children that they were born to live in the big house, the white house."[76]

The reason why the low expectations and negative attitudes afflicting African American Wilcox residents have hung on so long cannot be fully understood outside the context of the continued white belief in black inferiority. For example, as late as the mid 1980s, Frank Phillippi, a descendant of an old prominent Wilcox family, insisted, "I don't think there's any such thing as white supremacy, but I think that each race has characteristics. Intellectually, as a whole, I feel sure the Caucasian race is above the Negro race." Phillippi concluded that because of their peculiar [inferior] characteristics, black people are incapable of governing themselves, or anyone else. As he put it, "I don't think black government has shown that they can establish an effective government anywhere in the world."[77] Because of widespread white acceptance of such notions even after the movement, white Wilcox residents continued to expect their black neighbors to observe the same racial etiquette that has defined race relations in their county for generations. *Wilcox Progressive Era* editor Hollis Curl bluntly insisted, "There's a code of behavior between white and niggers."[78] White teacher Tommy Sadler agreed with Curl, and as far as he was concerned, a central feature of that code was strict racial segregation. He explained, "you don't really notice if you live in Camden. There's a code—a separation of the races. It's not inhuman. It's just a practical way of living together."[79] It is important to note that both of these men expressed these views in the early 1970s, right after the movement had come to their county. By 2000, Curl insisted that he had changed, and he added sadly, "There's a lot yet to be done to heal the divisiveness of the past."[80]

Expressing his views in the mid 1980s, white Wilcox farmer Ronnie Simpkins explained that he fervently believed in racial segregation. As he put it, "I'm just trying to tell it like it is. I really think that when Judgment Day comes, the Lord's not going to know what color you are . . . but to keep our community and our standards up like they are, I just basically believe now that we should continue to keep it equal but separate." Although Simpkins claimed to believe that black people are entitled to equal facilities, he also insisted that "they [African Americans] need upgrading."[81] As Simpkins explained his views, his wife, who was sitting next to him, vigorously nodded her head in agreement. When he had finished, Mrs. Simpkins could not resist adding, "The Lord didn't mean for elephants and cats to mix."[82] Although they were expressed at different times, all of these opinions were given by white Wilcox residents after the civil rights movement had changed the laws in their country, their state, and their county.

For many white Wilcox residents, it was a short leap from insisting on strict separation of the races and the observance of antiquated deference patterns to believing that black people did not need or deserve the same things that white people did. The comments of Peyton Burford Jr., a white Wilcox landowner, in the years immediately following the civil rights movement, clearly illustrate this mind-set. Burford explained, "I'm a tenant farmer. That means I supply the house to my people [black people] and as much land as they want." He continued, "I'm trying to get away from the tenant farm, which I realize is outdated. . . . But I don't know what to do about it. I realize that I'm not helping most of my people get ahead, but that's the way they want to live." Without offering any explanation for this assumption, Burford concluded, "My people may not have a full life, but they have it made. They get free wood, and free hunting and fishing and gallivanting. They also get free booze from the bootleggers. They get a good job and all the land they want to raise crops." Burford's belief that tenant farming was a "good job" for his [black] people is particularly telling. It is extremely doubtful that Peyton Burford Jr. would consider tenant farming a good job for a white man, but in his estimation it was good for his [black] people because whenever he observed them, they were "just as happy as a lark, couldn't care less."[83] Speaking in the mid-1980s, Virginia Phillippi, the wife of Frank Phillippi, was convinced that black people really did not deserve the same things as white people because they were not willing to work for them. As she put it, "they [black people] don't really work very hard at it. They demand to be given these powers, or these privileges but once they get them, they don't do anything; they don't even do anything for their own race. They don't want to work for it, they just want to demand it and they don't want to improve anything once they get it." She concluded adamantly, "they improve nothing."[84]

Clearly, the sentiments expressed by many white Wilcox residents make it abundantly clear that they feel absolutely no responsibility for the plight of their black neighbors. It is against this background of callous white disregard that the twin evils of poverty and powerlessness continue to hold many of the black residents of Wilcox County firmly in their grip. Things are so bad that many are left wondering if there is anything that can be done to alter this grim reality. In fact, the new millennium has ushered in a new initiative by the state of Alabama. Recognizing that the state's Black Belt counties present unique developmental challenges, the Alabama legislature voted to create a Black Belt Infrastructure Joint Legislative Committee. The group, which held its first organizational meeting on March 2, 2000, was created to "study all facets of infrastructure needs in the Black Belt counties of Alabama; how best to meet those needs; and the appropriate types of infrastructure in the Black Belt to encourage and facilitate industrial development."[85] The committee quickly identified the problems: "The largely rural counties of the region have higher than average concentrations of African-American populations, and are facing declining populations and loss of jobs."

However, while the problems are obvious, the solutions are not, and the task force proposed a number of possible remedies. First of all, because task force members are convinced that the underdevelopment of the region is directly linked to an inadequate road system, they have proposed that all of U.S. 80, and parts of U.S. 82 and U.S. 43, should be upgraded. Only one of these highways, U.S. 43, goes through Wilcox County, and the impact of upgrading this one road on the county's catastrophic economic problems is questionable. In fact, task force members admit that "Alabama's Black Belt counties of Bullock, Barbour, Russell, Montgomery, Lowndes, Dallas, Marengo, Sumter, Hale, Greene, and Pickens would benefit most from the proposed highway link."[86] Their discussion on road improvements does not even mention Wilcox County. The task force goes on to recommend the establishment of regional industrial parks in Demopolis, Selma, Montgomery, and Tuskegee. None of these facilities would be located in Wilcox County. The other recommendations of the committee include the establishment of a "state-of-the-art" regional air cargo facility in Montgomery, and full utilization of tourism opportunities. The impact of the Montgomery air cargo facility on Wilcox County's economy is questionable, and the recommendation on tourism opportunities does not even mention Wilcox County.

Instead, committee members specify that "the population centers along the [Selma to Montgomery National Historic] Trail are rich in African American cultural heritage which, coupled with the special place in history that towns like Tuskegee, Uniontown and Demopolis [hold] could be woven into a theme attraction."[87] None of these towns is located in Wilcox County.

The six-page report by the legislative committee only specifically mentions Wilcox County one time. That reference is contained in a committee recommendation that the region should attempt to lure more industry by publicizing its rich lignite deposits. The committee reasoned that the existence of these fuel deposits could help to lure industry to the area. "In particular," the committee declared, "incentives should be provided for Alabama Power Company to construct mine-mouth power plants within the Alabama and Tombigbee rivers region of west Alabama and utilize lignite for electricity generation."[88] The report continues, "As the Alabama Geological Survey has pointed out in its reports, Alabama's large near-surface lignite deposits in Sumter, Choctaw, Marengo, Wilcox, Crenshaw, Coffee, and Pike Counties have the greatest potential for development."[89] Thus, although the Black Belt Infrastructure Joint Legislative Committee has devised a number of plans for development in certain Black Belt areas, it seems that there is no part of Wilcox County that is an integral part of the plan.

At the same time, there are others outside of state government who are interested in helping the people of Wilcox County. One of those is Winifred Green, a white civil rights activist who first became acquainted with the plight of the county's residents during the struggles of the 1960s. Ever since that time, the searing images of black courage in the face of grinding poverty and determined white resistance have haunted Green. Thus, when she and other women activists established the Southern Rural Black Women's Initiative in 2002, women in Wilcox County were included on the list of those who desperately needed help. In addition to Wilcox, the group targeted seventy-three other counties in the Black Belt and the Mississippi Delta. After meeting with women in all of these counties, those guiding the Rural Black Women's Initiative formulated a "Human Rights Agenda for Women in the Rural South."[90] They also began work on their five-year plan, which was designed "to promote women's economic and social independence and eradicate the persistent burden of poverty on women. The plan will address structural causes of poverty through changes in economic, social and political structures and by ensuring access to education, training, technical assistance, resources and public services as vital ingredients to increased opportunity."[91] Because the initiative has just begun, it will be some time before it will be possible to gauge the program's effectiveness.

In the meantime, just recently a new congressman was elected to represent the Alabama seventh district, which includes Wilcox and the other Black Belt Counties along with parts of Birmingham and Tuscaloosa. The new congressman is Artur Davis. Davis is a black thirty-four-year-old native of Montgomery. After graduating from Montgomery's Jefferson Davis High School, Davis went on to earn his undergraduate degree and his law degree from Harvard University. The recent campaign for the congressional seat in the Alabama seventh district was particularly nasty. Davis's opponent, four-term incumbent Earl Hilliard, tried to play the race card, even though his opponent was black. Congressman Davis explains, "He [Hilliard] said that the Ivy League schools were being used as recruitment tools for anti-black black candidates. His rationale was that the kind of blacks that go to Ivy League schools are predisposed to be brainwashed; to be turned against the black establishment." Davis continued, "His other analysis was that we had carried white areas and we had carried black areas where people worked for corporate America, and that they had been brainwashed to vote for candidates like me."[92] Despite Hilliard's charges, Davis ran well enough to force the incumbent into a runoff, and when the votes were counted afterward, Davis emerged victorious. Predictably, he ran strong in the urban areas, but he also ran well in some of the Black Belt counties. Yet, he ran very poorly in Wilcox county: he only received 34 percent of the vote. Davis is not surprised at his poor showing in Wilcox because, he charges, "there are always contested races there [Wilcox County], but the same group of people, it seems, have been in power for the last generation or so in Wilcox County, and newer candidates who come along have by and large not just been defeated, but discredited."[93]

Regardless of their feelings about their new congressman, however, Davis is ready to step directly into the eye of the storm as he prepares to tackle the stubborn problems confronting his new constituents. He has no doubt that race matters in Wilcox County. As he puts it, "everything is so racialized, everything is so divisive." Davis is convinced, however, that his own particular philosophy will enable him to deal effectively with such a supercharged racial atmosphere. As he states,

> If you are historically aware of the civil rights movement, if you are historically aware of the legacy of racism, it certainly affects the way you view the world. I think you can respond in one of two ways. One way is to respond with a very negative sense of pessimism and resentment toward outsiders. Another way is to . . . appreciate the progress we've made as a country and a community, and to realize the need to continue to move forward, the need to continue to strive, and I think I was from the latter category. . . . I was motivated by the history of the region.[94]

Davis has absolutely no doubt that he has a big job ahead of him, because in addition to the devastating problems of the Black Belt counties he represents, the congressman will also be faced with a different set of issues in the urban areas of Birmingham and Tuscaloosa that he also represents. He explains, "As the rest of the state has moved forward economically, you've seen this split. Fifty years ago the Black Belt was not dramatically distinct from much of the rest of Alabama. Today it is." Yet, in addition to those Black Belt counties, the congressman also represents some of the most affluent areas of the state. According to Davis, "The Seventh District actually is one of the three most disparate income districts in the entire country in terms of income disparity between rich and poor because there are some enclaves in Birmingham and the Forest Park area that are within District Seven that are some of the most affluent parts of the state of Alabama."[95] Since taking the oath of office in January of 2003, Davis has been obliged to find ways to balance the interests of his constituents who are affluent with those who are desperately poor. The residents of Wilcox County can only wait and hope.

And so the discussion continues in the halls of government and in private groups about how best to help Wilcox County out of the downward spiral of economic, demographic, and spiritual decay. It is important to consider this discussion against the broader backdrop of American concerns about race in the new millennium. In fact, African American communities all over this country are facing joblessness, stubborn poverty, undereducation, and a teenage pregnancy rate that is out of control. As far as some are concerned, these problems are a direct result of the economic exploitation suffered by earlier generations of African Americans during the institution of slavery when their labor and their lives were stolen from them. Wilcox County judge Jo Celeste Pettway bluntly insists, "The reason it [Wilcox County] was built [was] off labor; free labor. If we [black people] were paid for that labor, we probably would not be in the position we're in now."[96] In light of this historical reality, there are some increasingly shrill voices being raised in support of reparations. Proponents argue that the only way African Americans can ever flourish is if the federal government pays its long overdue debt to the descendants of American slaves.

The reparations argument has been raging for some time. Just a year after Dr. Martin Luther King Jr. was assassinated in 1968, James Forman of the Student Nonviolent Coordinating Committee delivered a "black manifesto" demanding reparations for African Americans. The occasion was a conference on National Black Economic Development sponsored by the Interreligious Foundation for Community Organization, an interdenominational Protestant organization. Forman explains why black demands for reparations were particularly appropriate within this religious atmosphere: "Since the conference was being staged by 'Christians,' we felt it was the right occasion to demand reparations from the Christian churches for the centuries of exploitation and oppression which they had inflicted on black people around the world." Forman continues, "We saw it as a politically correct step, for the concept of reparations reflected the need to adjust past wrongs—to compensate for the enslavement of black people by Christians and their subsequent exploitation by Christians and Jews in the United States."[97]

Thus, on May 4, 1969, James Forman was ready to deliver his black manifesto. He describes the feelings he had that Sunday morning with passionate eloquence.

> I was more than angry as I walked into the nave of Riverside Church and stood behind the pastor, waiting to announce that the Black Manifesto demanded five hundred million dollars in reparations from the racist white "Christian" churches and the Jewish synagogues. I felt my action as one more rebellion against the vast system of controls over black people and their minds. . . . For years I had been fighting many of these control mechanisms—the educational system, the segregated lunch counters, denial of the right to vote, the court system, the racist Democratic Party and its conventions.[98]

No action was ever taken on the manifesto, but it did spark a good deal of discussion when it was issued against the backdrop of Dr. King's assassination, a long string of urban riots including Watts in 1965 and Detroit in 1967, and the militant impatience of a Black Power movement that included cultural black nationalism and political black nationalism. Most who heard the demand for reparations during this era were convinced that it came directly out of the Black Power movement. However, although the Black Power setting of the late 1960s undoubtedly had some impact on the reparations arguments, it is important to note that the question of payments to ex-slaves and their descendants has had a long and emotional history, stretching all the way back to the chaotic but hopeful period when slavery was ending and everyone, both black and white, wondered what would come next. In a few select cases ex-Confederate plantations were confiscated and a fortunate few ex-slave families were granted small parcels of land. For the most part, though, the slaves were freed with nothing. For some time, there was talk circulating in Congress about granting each ex-slave family forty acres and a mule, but of course, nothing ever came of it.

Yet, even though most did not receive any material possessions with their freedom, many ex-slaves continued to feel that they were entitled to some form of compensation for all that had been taken from them. For some time, many tried to hang on to the hope that those who had freed them would make their freedom meaningful by compensating them for labor that had been stolen from them. Through the end of the nineteenth century when it finally became clear that freedom from slavery was all they would get, the freedmen, who remained mostly rural and southern, scrimped, saved, and sacrificed to acquire the one thing that would finally allow them to become truly free: their own piece of land. Miraculously, by the end of the first decade of the twentieth century, African American Southerners had managed to acquire a total of fifteen million acres of land.[99] Just a few years later, by 1914–1915, the beginning of a decades-long crisis in southern agriculture was punctuated by falling prices, and boll weevil infestations had a devastating impact on black landowners. Because many had only been able to acquire land and plant their crops by using credit, they soon found themselves in an extremely vulnerable position. So many were forced to default on loans that the number of acres owned by African Americans steadily declined in every succeeding decade of the twentieth century from the fifteen million acre peak in 1910. Just as this crisis in black landownership was starting, Cornelius J. Jones filed suit in an attempt to recover reparations for the ex-slaves and their heirs. Jones reasoned that the federal government had benefited directly from slave labor because they had collected taxes on the raw cotton produced by slave labor in the South. Jones calculated that the value of the debt the United States owed the ex-slaves was sixty-eight million dollars, and in 1915, he filed suit against the United States Department of the Treasury.[100] A federal appeals court dismissed the suit. The court did not rule on the allegations in the suit. Instead, the court held that Jones could not sue the federal government without permission.[101]

In more recent years, in 1993 Congressman John Conyers, a Democrat representing a district in Detroit, Michigan, introduced a bill to

> acknowledge the fundamental injustice, cruelty, brutality, and inhumanity of slavery in the United States and the 13 American colonies between 1619 and 1865 and to establish a commission to examine the institution of slavery in the United States and the 13 American colonies, subsequent de jure and defacto racial and economic discrimination against African Americans, and the impact of these forces on living African Americans, to make recommendations to the Congress on appropriate remedies.[102]

Far from the seat of power in Washington, D.C., African Americans in Wilcox County look around them at the grinding poverty and low expectations that circumscribe so many black lives, and they are sure they already know the impact of slavery and segregation. They do not need a congressional commission to tell them when the evidence is all around them. Even a cursory examination of the welfare rolls in the county reveals the names of African Americans who can trace their ancestry in an unbroken line all the way back through sharecropping and debt peonage to slavery. Likewise, many of the largest white landowners in the county who still live in relative ease can trace their ancestry in an unbroken line all the way back to the county's leading slaveholding families. Obviously, white Wilcox residents who exploited black labor first during slavery, and then later during sharecropping, tenant farming, and debt peonage, all the way up through the civil rights era were able to amass enough wealth to pass on to their descendants. Conversely, the black people who were exploited were left with only indebtedness and hopelessness to pass on to their descendants. In such an atmosphere, the argument for reparations resonates with a compelling urgency.

Despite the power of the arguments, however, most black residents in Wilcox County are under no illusion that they will receive any just compensation after all these years. In the meantime, as their county continues to decline, black and white, rich and poor, continue to struggle to live with each other. Even though their daily struggles are clearly defined by the ghosts of slavery, Jim Crow, and continued economic exploitation, most do not dwell on these cruel realities. However, many are still haunted by ghosts from the more recent past. During Wilcox County's civil rights movement, African Americans who had the temerity to challenge the reign of Jim Crow often faced violent opposition from white people they had known all their lives. By the 1970s after movement activities had resulted in some superficial changes to the county's racial order, black and white residents had to find a way to relate to each other once again.

It was inevitable that as they tried to fashion a new relationship between the races, those who had tried the hardest to make the changes would have to confront those who had tried to stop them. Predictably, there have been many awkward moments as activists and segregationists have had to face each other day after day, and in a county with a population of only 13,000, it is inevitable that these face-to-face meetings will happen on a regular basis. In one encounter after another, activists find themselves wondering, Do they remember? For example, Sheryl Threadgill regularly sees one of the main bullies who brutalized her day after day as she attempted to integrate Wilcox County High School. Of course, Sheryl is all grown up now, but sometimes when she encounters her tormentor from so long ago, it almost seems as if no time has passed at all. Her conscious mind understands that in front of her is the smiling white face of a mature man, but behind the smile and the cordial greeting Sheryl can almost see the blazing eyes and the lips twisted into a snarl on the face of the skinny teenager who tormented her so many years ago. Their encounters are often a bit awkward. Sheryl explains,

> I think in his own way, whenever he sees me, he'll always have something complimentary to say, and I kind of think that's his way—he can't really come out and say he's sorry—but, he's always got something really nice to say to me.[103]

Sheryl smiles through the compliments, but scrutinizes his face very carefully to see if she can find any sign that he remembers.

Similarly, Brenda Bussey Carson, one of the main student leaders in the school desegregation struggle, sees people who tormented her during the movement. In particular, she recalls that when she attempted to present a letter of grievances to Reg Albritton, the probate judge at the time, his secretary, Annie Bailey, "was so ugly to black people." Years later, however, any time Brenda has contact with her, Bailey is "just as nice as she could be." As Brenda looks in the former secretary's face, and the years seem to melt away, she thinks sadly, "I just wonder, do you remember, do you remember, DO YOU REMEMBER?"[104] Carson also encounters others who fought the changes, and she explains, "It's amazing then, you see some of the same people now. [For example, a] guy that works for the telephone company. He tried to run over us one day [during the demonstrations]." When she sees him, Carson can only shake her head sadly and ask that painful question once again: "Do they remember?"[105] Yet, regardless of what white opponents of Wilcox County's civil rights movement think, African Americans who were in the movement remember, and every time a chance encounter with one of their white neighbors brings those memories of the movement back, the old wounds are opened up all over again.

It is important to note that not all the painful memories of the movement years are associated with white opposition. On the contrary, those who were willing to sacrifice and take risks often have vivid memories of their black neighbors who refused to support their efforts. Ironically, the opportunities for African Americans that resulted from the county's civil rights movement are equally available to African Americans who worked in the movement, and those who did not. Thus, every time they encounter a black resident who has benefited from the movement, but who refused to support it, the county's black activists cannot help but wonder, "Do they remember?" At the same time, there are some black Wilcox residents who also feel betrayed by some of the outside civil rights workers who came into their county and raised their hopes. For example, Joe and Marie Anderson still feel that SCLC betrayed them. The Andersons recalled that as the demonstrations heated up in their county and SCLC began sending personnel in, they offered to house some of the organization's field staff. It was not easy, because the house they lived in at the time was small. They moved their own children out into the living room so that two young men from SCLC could sleep in the bedroom. The Andersons knew that housing civil rights workers was dangerous business, but they were willing to take the risk. Furthermore, like so many of their black neighbors, the Andersons sometimes had to struggle to make ends meet, and having two more mouths to feed was not going to be easy, but they did expect at least a little help from SCLC. Joe Anderson explains, "We volunteered to take them [SCLC workers]. They [SCLC] were supposed to have paid us . . . but they didn't give us nary a dime. . . . We did the best we could to feed them and to wash their clothes with the little money we had, cause they never did give us anything to help."[106] Under such circumstances, it has been difficult all these years for the Andersons to feel that their sacrifice was really appreciated. Long ago they realized that SCLC would never pay them. Yet, they cannot help but wonder, "Do they remember?"

Thus, as Wilcox County faces an uncertain future in a new millennium, the ghosts of the past continue to haunt the residents. There are times when it seems like they will never be free of these ghosts. In the meantime, the "myth" of the New South continues to gather strength from the existence of cosmopolitan cities like Atlanta and Charlotte, from the inclusion of its politicians in high visibility national politics, and from the relocation to the region of businesses and industries with multinational links. But none of this has changed anything in areas like Wilcox County: it remains isolated and virtually ignored. In the atmosphere of frenzied progress in some areas of the New South, many civic leaders comfort themselves with the belief that the civil rights movement exorcized all the racial demons from their past a generation ago, and they are now free to concentrate on a future of social progress and economic development. After all, many reason, Wilcox County and other areas like it are only old relics of a distant past kept alive by Hollywood movies and romance novels. Yet, for the poor black people who live there, the struggle to realize the promises made by the civil rights movement over a generation ago continues. Ironically, Wilcox County's physical isolation makes it that much easier for the rest of the South and the nation to ignore the dramatic struggle still going on there: it is far from any main interstate highway and accessible only by two-lane county roads. Despite its isolation, however, the rest of the South and the rest of the country need to heed the difficult lessons of race and economics inherent in the county's plight, because Wilcox County and other southern rural areas like it are living links to a national past of black economic exploitation and vicious racial discrimination. In such an environment it is possible to gauge with frightening clarity the devastating impact of our long history of racial victimization on the descendants of the victims. As America moves into the new millennium, it is imperative that national policy makers begin to come to grips with the reality of these links between past exploitation that resulted in an incredible maldistribution of wealth and present degradation of the victims of this process. The lessons the county has to teach are too valuable; the consequences that we will suffer if we refuse to heed these lessons are too serious for us to let the plight of Wilcox County remain in the shadow of Selma.

~

Notes

Preface

1. Tamara Lipper, "Africa, Alternative Motive, Maybe?" *Newsweek*, July 21, 2003.
2. Lipper, "Africa."

Chapter 1

1. James Benson Sellers, *Slavery in Alabama* (University, Alabama: University of Alabama Press, 1950).
2. Ouida Starr Woodson, *Within the Bend: Stories of Wilcox County*, Book II (n.p.: 1989), 1. In the Wilcox County Public Library, Camden, Alabama.
3. Sellers, *Slavery in Alabama*, 31.
4. Tootie Slade, "History of Wilcox County," 1944, 15. Typescript in the Wilcox County Library, Camden, Alabama.
5. Slade, "History of Wilcox County," 9.
6. Slade, "History of Wilcox County," 3.
7. Sellers, *Slavery in Alabama*, 67.
8. Sellers, *Slavery in Alabama*, 67.
9. Sellers, *Slavery in Alabama*, 113.
10. Sellers, *Slavery in Alabama*, 33.
11. George Raiwick, ed., *The American Slave: A Composite Autobiography*, Vol. 4 (Westport, Conn.: Greenwood, 1972), 149.
12. Raiwick, *The American Slave*, Vol. 4, 159.
13. Donald Stone, *Fallen Prince—William James Edwards, Black Education and the Quest for Afro-American Nationality* (Snow Hill, Ala.: Snow Hill Press, 1990), 188.
14. Raiwick, *The American Slave*, Vol. 4, 205.
15. Raiwick, *The American Slave*, Vol. 4, 205.
16. Raiwick, *The American Slave*, Vol. 6, 42.
17. Sellers, *Slavery in Alabama*, 245.

18. Sellers, *Slavery in Alabama*, 248.

19. Slade, "History of Wilcox County," 6.

20. Raiwick, *The American Slave*, Vol. 6, 341.

21. Raiwick, *The American Slave*, Vol. 4, 209.

22. Walter Fleming, *Civil War and Reconstruction in Alabama* (New York: Columbia University Press, 1905), 714–15.

23. Peter Kolchin, *First Freedom: The Responses of Alabama's Blacks to Emancipation and Reconstruction* (Westport, Conn.: Greenwood, 1972), 15.

24. Department of Interior, Census Office, *Statistics of the Population of the United States at the Tenth Census, June 1, 1880*, Vol. 1. (Washington, D.C.: Government Printing Office, 1883), 380.

25. Kolchin, *First Freedom*, 22.

26. *Tenth Census, June 1, 1880*, 380.

27. Kolchin, *First Freedom*, 17.

28. Kolchin, *First Freedom*, 34.

29. Horace Mann Bond, *Negro Education in Alabama: A Study in Cotton and Steel* (New York: Atheneum, 1969), 25.

30. Bond, *Negro Education in Alabama*, 24.

31. Woodson, *Within the Bend*, Book IV, 25.

32. William Rogers, Robert Ward, Leah Atkins, and Wayne Flynt, *Alabama, the History of a Deep South State* (Tuscaloosa: University of Alabama Press, 1994), 263.

33. Woodson, *Within the Bend*, Book IV, 38.

34. Quoted in Clinton McCarty, *The Reins of Power, Racial Change, and Challenge in a Southern County* (Tallahassee, Fla.: Sentry Press, 1999), 68.

35. McCarty, *The Reins of Power*, 55, 60.

36. McCarty, *The Reins of Power*, 60.

37. Viola Goode Liddell, *A Place of Springs* (University: University of Alabama Press, 1979), 52.

38. Rayford Logan, *The Betrayal of the Negro—From Rutherford B. Hayes to Woodrow Wilson* (New York: DeCapo Press, 1997), 15.

39. Logan, *The Betrayal of the Negro*, 79.

40. Logan, *The Betrayal of the Negro*, 11.

41. Logan, *The Betrayal of the Negro*, 112.

42. McCarty, *The Reins of Power*, 69.

43. Dan T. Carter, *The Politics of Rage; George Wallace, the Origins of the New Conservatism* (Baton Rouge: Louisiana State University Press, 1995), 38. See also Sheldon Hackney, *Populism to Progressivism in Alabama* (Princeton, N.J.: Princeton University Press, 1969).

44. Carter, *The Politics of Rage*, 39.

45. Carter, *The Politics of Rage*, 39.

46. Carter, *The Politics of Rage*, 40.

47. Bond, *Negro Education in Alabama*, 170.

48. Bond, *Negro Education in Alabama*, 172.

49. Leon Litwack, *Trouble in Mind: Black Southerners in the Age of Jim Crow* (New York: Vintage, 1998), 218.

50. Liddell, *A Place of Springs*, 72.

51. Hollis Curl, interview by author, March 6, 2000, Camden, Alabama.

52. Curl interview.

53. McCarty, *The Reins of Power*, 112.

54. Melton McLaurin, *Separate Pasts: Growing up White in the Segregated South* (Athens: University of Georgia Press, 1987), 14

55. Lawrence Parrish, interview by author, October 18, 1999, Camden, Alabama.

56. William J. Edwards, *Twenty-Five Years in the Black Belt* (Boston: Cornhill Company, 1918), 69.

57. Edwards, *Twenty-Five Years in the Black Belt*, 50.

58. Edwards, *Twenty-Five Years in the Black Belt*, 50.

59. Alice Walker, *The Third Life of Grange Copeland* (New York: Harcourt Brace Jovanovich, 1970), 140.

60. Nellie Williams Abner, interview by author, August 15, 1999, Washington, D.C.

61. Abner interview.

62. Marguerite Wilson Griggs, interview by author, May 12, 1999, Detroit, Michigan.

63. Kayte Marsh Fearn, interview by author, August 15, 1999, Washington, D.C.

64. Lucy and James Ephraim, interview by author, June 16, 1999, Camden, Alabama.

65. Ephraim interview.

66. Ephraim interview.

67. Joseph and Marie Anderson, interview by author, October 17, 1999, Camden, Alabama.

68. Abner interview.

69. Abner interview.

70. Clinton Marsh, interview by author, July 3, 1999, Atlanta, Georgia.

71. Marsh interview.

72. Abner interview.

73. Ephraim interview.

74. Parrish interview.

75. Abner interview.

76. Anderson interview.

77. Letter from Eliza B. Wallace to "my dear young friends," April 25, 1893, Wallace Letter Book, Knoxville College Archives, Knoxville, Tennessee.

78. Wallace letter.

79. *Aurora*, March 1897.

80. Morton Rubin, *Plantation County* (Chapel Hill: University of North Carolina Press, 1951), 27.

81. Anderson interview.

82. Ruby Abercrombie, interview by author, November 1, 1999, Detroit, Michigan.

83. Abercrombie interview.

84. Wallace letter.

85. *Aurora*, March 1897.

86. Edwards, *Twenty-Five Years in the Black Belt*, 49.

87. *Aurora*, March 1897.

88. *Aurora*, April 2, 1900.

89. *Aurora*, April 2, 1900.

90. *Aurora*, April 2, 1900

91. Pete Daniel, *The Shadow of Slavery: Peonage in the South, 1901–1969* (Urbana: University of Illinois Press, 1972), 24.

92. Daniel, *The Shadow of Slavery*, 22.

93. Daniel, *The Shadow of Slavery*, 25.

94. Daniel, *The Shadow of Slavery*, 58.

95. Daniel, *The Shadow of Slavery*, 66.

96. Daniel, *The Shadow of Slavery*, 67.

97. Daniel, *The Shadow of Slavery*, 67.

98. Daniel, *The Shadow of Slavery*, 68.

99. Daniel, *The Shadow of Slavery*, 77.

100. Daniel, *The Shadow of Slavery*, 81.

101. Abercrombie interview.

102. Edwards, *Twenty-Five Years in the Black Belt*, 31.

103. Abner interview.

104. John Hope Franklin and Alfred Moss Jr., *From Slavery to Freedom—A History of African Americans*, 8th ed. (Boston: McGraw-Hill, 2000), 340.

105. McCarty, *The Reins of Power*, 110.

106. McCarty, *The Reins of Power*, 110.

107. Franklin and Moss, *From Slavery to Freedom*, 340.

108. Franklin and Moss, *From Slavery to Freedom*, 340.

109. McCarty, *The Reins of Power*, 109.

110. McCarty, *The Reins of Power*, 92.

111. McCarty, *The Reins of Power*, 107.

Chapter 2

1. V. P. Franklin, *Black Self-Determination: A Cultural History of the Faith of the Fathers* (Westport, Conn.: Lawrence Hill & Company, 1984), 146.

2. Booker T. Washington, *Up from Slavery* (New York: Doubleday, 1900), included in *Three Negro Classics*, ed. James W. Johnson (New York: Avon, 1965), 44.

3. Robert Sherer, *Subordination or Liberation: Black Education in Nineteenth Century Alabama* (University: University of Alabama Press, 1977), 2.

4. Franklin, *Black Self-Determination*, 161.

5. Sherer, *Subordination or Liberation*, 1.

6. Bond, *Negro Education in Alabama*, 111.

7. Bond, *Negro Education in Alabama*, 113.

8. Sherer, *Subordination or Liberation*, 2.

9. Sherer, *Subordination or Liberation*, 5.

10. Bond, *Negro Education in Alabama*, 113.

11. James D. Anderson, *The Education of Blacks in the South, 1860–1935* (Chapel Hill: University of North Carolina Press, 1988), 26.

12. C. Vann Woodward, *Origins of the New South, 1877–1913* (Baton Rouge: Louisiana State University Press, 1951), 63.

13. Bond, *Negro Education in Alabama*, 142.

14. Franklin, *Black Self-Determination*, 173.

15. Lawrence Cremin, *The Transformation of the School* (New York: Knopf, 1961), 20.

16. Cremin, *The Transformation of the School*, 20.

17. Cremin, *The Transformation of the School*, 85.

18. Cremin, *The Transformation of the School*, 22.

19. Donald Spivey, *Schooling for the New Slavery* (Westport, Conn.: Greenwood, 1978), ix.

20. John White, *Black Leadership in America: From Booker T. Washington to Jesse Jackson* (New York: Longman, 1985), 30.

21. Eric J. Sundquist, ed. *The Oxford W. E. B. Du Bois Reader* (New York: Oxford University Press, 1996), 356.

22. Donald Stone, *Fallen Prince—William James Edwards, Black Education and the Quest for Afro-American Nationality* (Snow Hill, Ala.: Snow Hill Press, 1990), 70.

23. William J. Edwards, *Twenty-Five Years in the Black Belt* (Boston: Cornhill Company, 1918), 36.

24. Edwards, *Twenty-Five Years in the Black Belt*, 36.

25. Stone, *Fallen Prince*, 166.

26. Stone, *Fallen Prince*, 168.

27. Stone, *Fallen Prince*, 89–90.

28. Stone, *Fallen Prince*, 90–91.

29. Stone, *Fallen Prince*, 128–29.

30. Stone, *Fallen Prince*, 167.

31. Bond, *Negro Education in Alabama*, 162.

32. Bond, *Negro Education in Alabama*, 160–61.

33. Bond, *Negro Education in Alabama*, 162.

34. Robert Booker, "Before There Was Light—How Knoxville College Came to Be, 1863–1879," Typescript in the Knoxville College Archives, Knoxville, Tennessee, 21.

35. Booker, "Before There Was Light," 17.

36. *The Women's Missionary Magazine of the United Presbyterian Church* Vol. II, No. 8 (March 1898): 17, in the Knoxville College Archives, Knoxville, Tennessee.

37. Quoted in a letter to "my dear young friends" from Eliza B. Wallace, Knoxville College, Knoxville, Tennessee, April 25, 1893, Wallace Letter Book, Knoxville College Archives, Knoxville, Tennessee.

38. Bond, *Negro Education in Alabama*, 111.

39. Bond, *Negro Education in Alabama*, 102.

40. Bond, *Negro Education in Alabama*, 114.

41. Bond, *Negro Education in Alabama*, 114.

42. J. S. McCulloch to J. W. Witherspoon, November 26, 1890, McCulloch Letter Book, Knoxville College Archives, Knoxville, Tennessee.

43. *Aurora*, April 1894.

44. Sophia Cox Johnson, *Beginnings in the Black Belt* (n.p., 1940), pamphlet in the Knoxville College Archives, Knoxville, Tennessee.

45. *Aurora*, October 1893.

46. J. S. McCulloch to J. W. Witherspoon, July 31, 1889, McCulloch Letter Book, Knoxville College Archives, Knoxville, Tennessee.

47. Johnson, *Beginnings in the Black Belt*, 24.

48. *Historical Sketch of the Freedmen's Missions of the United Presbyterian Church, 1862–1904* (Knoxville, Tenn.: Printing Department of Knoxville College), 50–51.

49. *Historical Sketch of the Freedmen's Missions*, 49.

50. J. S. McCulloch to J. W. Witherspoon, June 24, 1890, Knoxville College Archives, Knoxville, Tennessee.

51. *Historical Sketch of the Freedmen's Missions*, 53.

52. *Historical Sketch of the Freedmen's Missions*, 52.

53. Ella Earls Cotton, *A Spark for My People* (New York: Exposition Free Press, 1954), 212, Presbyterian Historical Society Archives, Philadelphia, Pennsylvania.

54. Johnson, *Beginnings in the Black Belt*, 27–28.

55. *Aurora*, October 1893.

56. *Aurora*, April 2, 1900.

57. *Historical Sketch of the Freedmen's Missions*, 60.

58. *Historical Sketch of the Freedmen's Missions*, 60.

59. *Historical Sketch of the Freedmen's Missions*, 60.

60. *Historical Sketch of the Freedmen's Missions*, 58.

61. *Aurora*, March 1897.

62. *Aurora*, March 1897.

63. *Aurora*, March 1897.

64. *Our Mission to the Colored People of the South*, published by the Board of Freedmen's Missions of the United Presbyterian Church, 1912, 14, Knoxville College Archives, Knoxville, Tennessee.

65. A History of the United Presbyterians of Wilcox County, Inc., typescript in the papers of Reverend Benjamin Thompson, Camden, Alabama.

66. Cotton, *A Spark for My People*, 210–11.

67. Cotton, *A Spark for My People*, 210.

68. Cotton, *A Spark for My People*, 241.

69. Cotton, *A Spark for My People*, 248.

70. A History of the United Presbyterians of Wilcox County.

71. *Our Southern Missions*, published by the Board of Missions of the United Presbyterian Church, 1913, 13, Record Group 46, Box 1, Series 1, Folder 2, Presbyterian Historical Society Archives, Philadelphia, Pennsylvania.

72. August Meier, *Negro Thought in America, 1880–1915: Racial Ideologies in the Age of Booker T. Washington* (Ann Arbor: University of Michigan Press, 1971), 44.

73. J. S. McCulloch to J. W. Witherspoon, Knoxville, Tennessee, April 30, 1890, McCulloch Letter Book, Knoxville College Archives, Knoxville, Tennessee.

74. J. S. McCulloch to J. W. Witherspoon, Knoxville, Tennessee, April 30, 1890.

75. Cotton, *A Spark for My People*, 241.

76. Cotton, *A Spark for My People*, 241.

77. *The United Presbyterian*, March 2, 1905, 11, Presbyterian Historical Society Archives, Philadelphia, Pennsylvania.

78. *Historical Sketch of the Freedmen's Missions*, 48.

79. *Historical Sketch of the Freedmen's Missions*, 48, 49.

80. Emma Stokes, interview by author, May 20, 1978, Knoxville, Tennessee.

81. Stokes interview.

82. Stokes interview.

83. Cotton, *A Spark for My People*, 213.

84. *The United Presbyterian*, December 27, 1923.

85. Cotton, *A Spark for My People*, 213.

86. Cotton, *A Spark for My People*, 262.

87. *The United Presbyterian*, June 6, 1935.

88. William Green Wilson, *Rhymes and Sketches from the Cabin Fireside* (Birmingham: Wheaten Printing Company, 1931), 50–51.

89. Edwards, *Twenty-Five Years in the Black Belt*, 125–26.

90. Cotton, *A Spark for My People*, 263.

91. Cotton, *A Spark for My People*, 213.

92. *The United Presbyterian*, December 27, 1923, 12.

93. *Historical Sketch of the Freedmen's Missions*, 46.

94. Cotton, *A Spark for My People*, 230.

95. Kayte Marsh Fearn, interview by author, August 15, 1999, Washington, D.C.

96. Lucy and James Ephraim, interview by author, June 16, 1999, Camden, Alabama.

97. Clinton Marsh, interview by author, July 3, 1999, Atlanta, Georgia.

98. Fearn interview.

Chapter 3

1. Glen Nolen Sisk, "Alabama Black Belt: A Social History, 1875–1917," Ph.D. dissertation, Duke University, 1951, 456.

2. Sisk, "Alabama Black Belt," 456.

3. Sisk, "Alabama Black Belt," 458.

4. Sisk, "Alabama Black Belt," 458–59.

5. *Wilcox Progressive Era*, April 6, 1916.

6. *Wilcox Progressive Era*, June 26, 1924.

7. *Wilcox Progressive Era*, June 26, 1924.

8. *Wilcox Progressive Era*, June 26, 1924.

9. Sisk, "Alabama Black Belt," 448.

10. *Wilcox Progressive Era*, October 29, 1925.

11. Raymond Wolters, *Negroes and the Great Depression: The Problem of Economic Recovery* (Westport, Conn.: Greenwood, 1970), 4.

12. Wolters, *Negroes and the Great Depression*, 5.

13. Wolters, *Negroes and the Great Depression*, 9.

14. Clinton McCarty, *The Reins of Power, Racial Change, and Challenge in a Southern County* (Tallahassee, Fla.: Sentry Press, 1999), 114.

15. Wolters, *Negroes and the Great Depression*, 9.

16. Wolters, *Negroes and the Great Depression*, 10.

17. Donald Grubbs, *Cry from the Cotton: The Southern Tenant Farmers Union and the New Deal* (Chapel Hill: University of North Carolina Press, 1971), 18–19.

18. McCarty, *The Reins of Power*, 115.

19. Grubbs, *Cry from the Cotton*, 42.

20. Grubbs, *Cry from the Cotton*, preface.

21. Wolters, *Negroes and the Great Depression*, 8.

22. Renwick Kennedy, "Life at Gee's Bend," *Christian Century*, September 1, 1937, 1072.

23. Kennedy, "Life at Gee's Bend," 1072.

24. John Temple Graves II, "The Big World at Last Reaches Gee's Bend," *The New York Times Magazine*, August 22, 1937, 12.

25. Graves, "The Big World at Last Reaches Gee's Bend," 12.

26. Report of the U. S. Department of Agriculture, Farm Security Administration, September 16, 1939, 13, Gee's Bend Files, Box 82, Folder AL- 51000-900, the National Archives, College Park, Maryland.

27. E. S. Morgan, regional director, to Dr. W. W. Alexander, administrator, FSA, Washington D.C., September 28, 1939 in Box 84, Folder AD-AL-31 060, Records of the Farm Security Administration, Gee's Bend, National Archives, College Park, Maryland.

28. Giles A. Hubert, agricultural economist at Fisk University, to Ernest S. Morgan, regional director, FSA, Montgomery, Alabama, April 9, 1940, FSA Record, Gee's Bend, Box 82, Folder AL-51 000-900, the National Archives, College Park, Maryland.

29. Kennedy, "Life at Gee's Bend," 1072.

30. Kennedy, "Life at Gee's Bend," 1072.

31. *From Fields of Promise*, PBS Video, narrated by Ossie Davis and John O'Neal, produced by Auburn Television, Auburn University, Auburn, Alabama.

32. *From Fields of Promise*.

33. *From Fields of Promise*.

34. *From Fields of Promise*.

35. *From Fields of Promise*.

36. *From Fields of Promise*.

37. *From Fields of Promise*.

38. *From Fields of Promise*.

39. *From Fields of Promise*.

40. *From Fields of Promise*.

41. *From Fields of Promise*.

42. *From Fields of Promise*.

43. Narrative Report Covering the Economic, Educational, Social and Community Progress for the Gee's Bend Project for the Year 1938, p. 1, FSA Records, Box 82, Folder AL-51-000-900, National Archives, College Park, Maryland.

44. Narrative Report, 2.

45. Narrative Report, 2.

46. Narrative Report, 2.

47. Report of Gee's Bend Farm School by Robert Pierce, principal, in FSA Records, Gee's Bend File, Box 82, Folder RP-900, National Archives, College Park, Maryland.

48. Report of Gee's Bend Farm School.

49. Report of Gee's Bend Farm School.

50. Kennedy, "Life at Gee's Bend," 1073.

51. Kennedy, "Life at Gee's Bend," 1073.

52. Report on the Gee's Bend Cooperative and Its Medical Care Costs for 1938–39 by Dr. J. Paul Jones, Camden, Alabama, and Dr. R. E. Dixon, Alberta, Alabama, in FSA Records, Box 82 Folder RP-900, 1. National Archives, College Park, Maryland.

53. Report on the Gee's Bend Cooperative, 1.

54. Report on the Gee's Bend Cooperative, 1.

55. *From Fields of Promise.*

56. *From Fields of Promise.*

57. *From Fields of Promise.*

58. *From Fields of Promise.*

59. *From Fields of Promise.*

60. Christmas Message to Parents and Workers on the Gee's Bend Project from R. R. Pierce, Principal, Gee's Bend School, n.d., FSA Records, Gee's Bend Records, Box 82, Folder RP-900, the National Archives, College Park, Maryland.

61. F. D. Tattun to R. W. Hudgens, assistant administrator, FSA, Washington, D.C., 11 July 1939, FSA Records, Gee's Bend Project General Information, Box 84, Folder AD-AL-31,060, National Archives, College Park, Maryland.

62. Hattie Irene Steele, interview by author, August 19, 2000, Mobile, Alabama.

63. Steele interview.

64. Steele interview.

65. Edna Bonner Rhodes, interview by author, August 19, 2000, Mobile, Alabama.

66. Rhodes interview.

67. Rhodes interview.

68. Franklin and Moss, 434.

69. Kayte Marsh Fearn telephone interview by author, September 10, 2000.

70. Fearn interview.

71. Fearn interview.

72. Fearn interview.

73. Mabel Walker Thornton, interview by author, August 19, 2000, Mobile, Alabama.

74. Thornton interview.

75. Rhodes interview.

76. *Wilcox Progressive Era*, June 4, 1931.

77. Jack Bonham, interview by author, August 19, 2000, Mobile, Alabama.

78. Bonham interview.

79. Bonham interview.

80. Paul Washington, interview by author, May 11, 1999, Detroit, Michigan.

81. Rhodes interview.

82. Washington interview.

83. Rubin, *Plantation County*, 101.

84. Gwendolyn Bonham, interview by author, June 16, 1999, Camden, Alabama.

85. Washington interview.

86. Nellie Williams Abner, interview by author, August 15, 1999, Washington, D.C.

87. Abner interview.

88. Robin Kelley, *Hammer and Hoe: Alabama Communists during the Great Depression* (Chapel Hill: University of North Carolina Press, 1990), 17.

89. Kelley, *Hammer and Hoe*, 38.

90. Kelley, *Hammer and Hoe*, 38.

91. Angelo Herndon, *Let Me Live* (New York: Arno Press and the *New York Times*, 1969), 130.

92. Herndon, *Let Me Live*, 135.

93. Herndon, *Let Me Live*, 131–32.

94. Herndon, *Let Me Live*, 132.

95. Herndon, *Let Me Live*, 134.

96. Herndon, *Let Me Live*, 135.

97. Herndon, *Let Me Live*, 137.

98. Herndon, *Let Me Live*, 137.

99. Patricia Sullivan, *Days of Hope: Race and Democracy in the New Deal Era* (Chapel Hill: University of North Carolina Press, 1996), 60.

100. Sullivan, *Days of Hope*, 60.

101. Sullivan, *Days of Hope*, 56.

102. Sullivan, *Days of Hope*, 91.

103. Sullivan, *Days of Hope*, 92.

Chapter 4

1. Sullivan, *Days of Hope*, 5.

2. Sullivan, *Days of Hope*, 99.

3. Sullivan, *Days of Hope*, 100.

4. Sullivan, *Days of Hope*, 100.

5. Sullivan, *Days of Hope*, 99.

6. Sullivan, *Days of Hope*, 99.

7. Sullivan, *Days of Hope*, 99.

8. Sullivan, *Days of Hope*, 94.

9. Sullivan, *Days of Hope*, 93.

10. Sullivan, *Days of Hope*, 91.

11. Sullivan, *Days of Hope*, 91.

12. McCarty, *The Reins of Power*, 122.

13. Gwendolyn Bonham, interview by author, August 19, 2000, Mobile, Alabama.

14. Ruth Bonner Collins, interview by author, August 19, 2000, Mobile, Alabama.

15. S. C. Collier, interview by author, June 17, 1999, Camden, Alabama.

16. Liddell, *A Place of Springs*, 166.

17. Liddell, *A Place of Springs*, 167.

18. Liddell, *A Place of Springs*, 104.

19. *From Fields of Promise*.

20. Paul Washington, interview by author, 11 May 1999, Detroit, Michigan.

21. Collins interview.

22. Collins interview.

23. Collins interview.

24. Mabel Walker Thornton, interview by author, August 19, 2000, Mobile, Alabama.

25. Thornton interview.

26. Thornton interview.

27. Thornton interview.

28. Thornton interview.

29. Thornton interview.

30. Steven F. Lawson, *Running for Freedom: Civil Rights and Black Politics in America since 1941* (New York: McGraw-Hill, 1991), 21.

31. Monroe Pettway, interview by author, May 23, 2001, Gee's Bend Alabama.

32. Lawson, *Running for Freedom*, 16.

33. Lawson, *Running for Freedom*, 19.

34. Lawson, *Running for Freedom*, 19.

35. Sullivan, *Days of Hope*, 197.

36. Hattie Irene Steele, interview by author, August 19, 2000, Mobile, Alabama; Nancie Thomas, interview by author, May 19, 2001, Mobile, Alabama.

37. Sullivan, *Days of Hope*, 202-203.

38. Lawson, *Running for Freedom*, 22.

39. Lawson, *Running for Freedom*, 33.

40. Quoted from "To Secure These Rights: The Report of the President's Committee on Civil Rights, 1947," in Leslie Fishel Jr. and Benjamin Quarles, *The Negro American: A Documentary History* (Glenview, Ill.: Scott Foresman, 1967), 482.

41. Lawson, *Running for Freedom*, 34.

42. Lawson, *Running for Freedom*, 35.

43. Lawson, *Running for Freedom*, 35.

44. *Wilcox Progressive Era*, February 12, 1948.

45. Cabell Phillips, "Camden, Alabama: A Case Study," *New York Times Magazine*, August 28, 1949, 52.

46. Phillips, "Camden, Alabama," 53.

47. Thornton interview.

48. Thornton interview.

49. Thornton interview.

50. Thornton interview.

51. Thornton interview.

52. Thornton interview

53. Phillips, "Camden, Alabama," 53.

54. Phillips, "Camden, Alabama," 52.

55. Phillips, "Camden, Alabama," 52.

56. Phillips, "Camden, Alabama," 52

57. Phillips, "Camden, Alabama," 53.

58. Steve Lawson and Charles Payne, *Debating the Civil Rights Movement* (Lanham, Md.: Rowman and Littlefield, 1998), 15.

59. Lawson and Payne, *Debating the Civil Rights Movement*, 15.

60. Lawson and Payne, *Debating the Civil Rights Movement*, 16.

61. Rubin, *Plantation County*, 95.

62. Rubin, *Plantation County*, 90.

63. Rubin, *Plantation County*, 93.

64. Liddell, *A Place of Springs*, 108.

65. Horace Young, interview by author, August 19, 2000, Mobile, Alabama.

66. Charles S. Johnson, *Backgrounds to Patterns of Negro Segregation* (New York: Thomas Y. Crowell Company, 1943), 124.

67. Johnson, *Backgrounds*, 125.

68. Johnson, *Backgrounds*, 125.

69. Johnson, *Backgrounds*, 125.

70. Matthew Wilmer, interview by author, June 25, 2000, Philadelphia, Pennsylvania.

71. Matthew Wilmer, interview.

72. Gertrude Wilmer, interview by author, June 25, 2000, Philadelphia, Pennsylvania.

73. Geraldine Pettway White, interview by author, November 3, 2001, Knoxville, Tennessee.

74. White interview.

75. Bessye Ramsey Neal, interview by author, August 15, 1999, Washington, D.C.

76. Larry Nettles, interview by author, May 12, 2001, Findlay, Ohio.

77. Liddell, *A Place of Springs*, 107.

78. Lawson and Payne, *Debating the Civil Rights Movement*, 56–57.

79. Bonham, interview.

80. Neil McMillan, *The Citizens' Councils: Organized Resistance to the Second Reconstruction, 1954–64* (Urbana: University of Illinois Press, 1971), 17.

81. Numan Bartley, *The Rise of Massive Resistance: Race and Politics in the South during the 1950s* (Baton Rouge: Louisiana State University Press, 1997), 84.

82. Bartley, *The Rise of Massive Resistance*, 85.

83. *Wilcox Progressive Era*, August 23, 1956.

84. *Wilcox Progressive Era*, August 23, 1956.

85. McMillan, *The Citizens' Councils*, 222.

86. *Wilcox Progressive Era*, August 23, 1956.

87. James Foster Reese, interview by author, July 3, 1999, Atlanta, Georgia.

88. Clifford Crowder, interview by author, August 16, 1999, Washington, D.C.

89. Reese interview.

90. Reese interview.

91. Reese interview.

92. Reese interview.

93. Reese interview.

94. Gertrude Wilmer interview.

95. Liddell, *A Place of Springs*, 108.

Chapter 5

1. White interview.

2. Tydie D. Pettway, interview by author, October 20, 2001, Gee's Bend, Alabama.

3. Lonnie Brown interview by author, May 23, 2001, Gee's Bend, Alabama.

4. Brown interview.

5. Brown interview.

6. Brown interview.

7. Brown interview.

8. Brown interview.

9. Monroe Pettway interview.

10. Brown interview.

11. Bernard Lafayette, interview by author, April 1, 2000, Atlanta, Georgia.

12. Brown interview.

13. Lafayette interview.

14. Lafayette interview.

15. Lafayette interview. See also "Officials Attempt Legal Circumvention," in *The Student Voice* Vol. 6, No. 1 (March 26, 1965): 4.

16. Lafayette interview.

17. Lafayette interview.

18. Lafayette interview.

19. Lafayette interview.

20. Lafayette interview.

21. *Wilcox Progressive Era*, clipping, n.d. The Miscellaneous Clipping Files, Wilcox County, Alabama. Birmingham Public Library, Birmingham, Alabama.

22. Lafayette interview.

23. Tydie D. Pettway interview.

24. Tydie D. Pettway interview.

25. Andrew Manis, *A Fire You Can't Put Out: The Civil Rights Life of Birmingham's Reverend Fred Shuttlesworth* (Tuscaloosa: University of Alabama Press, 1999), 17.

26. Manis, *A Fire You Can't Put Out*, 17.

27. Manis, *A Fire You Can't Put Out*, 18.

28. Paulette Pettway, interview by author, October 20, 2001, Gee's Bend, Alabama.

29. Lafayette interview.

30. David Halberstam, *The Children* (New York: Random House, 1998), 425.

31. Halberstam, *The Children*, 426–27.

32. Halberstam, *The Children*, 429.

33. S. Jonathan Bass, *Blessed Are the Peacemakers: Martin Luther King, Jr., Eight White Religious Leaders, and the "Letter from Birmingham Jail"* (Baton Rouge: Louisiana State University Press, 2001), 95.

34. Bass, *Blessed Are the Peacemakers*, 181.

35. Worth Long, interview by author, July 9, 2000, Atlanta, Georgia.

36. Long interview.

37. Long interview.

38. Long interview.

39. John Blassingame, *The Slave Community* (New York: Oxford University Press, 1979), 47–48, 284–86.

40. Paulette Pettway interview.

41. Tydie D. Pettway interview.

42. Long interview.

43. Andrew Young, *An Easy Burden: The Civil Rights Movement and the Transformation of America* (New York: HarperCollins, 1996), 144.

44. Young, *An Easy Burden*, 143.

45. Adam Fairclough, *To Redeem the Soul of America: The Southern Christian Leadership Conference and Martin Luther King, Jr.* (Athens: University of Georgia Press, 1987), 147.

46. Fairclough, *To Redeem the Soul of America*, 147.

47. Fairclough, *To Redeem the Soul of America*, 148.

48. McCarty, *The Reins of Power*, 142.

49. Brown interview.

50. McCarty, *The Reins of Power*, 142.

51. Brown interview.

52. Brown interview.

53. McCarty, *The Reins of Power*, 143.

54. Brown interview.

55. Liddell, *A Place of Springs*, 109.

56. James Foster Reese, interview by author, July 3, 1999, Atlanta, Georgia.

57. Reese interview.

58. Sheryl Threadgill, interview by author, October 17, 1999, Camden, Alabama.

59. *The Student Voice* Vol. 5, No. 11 (May 19, 1964): 4.

60. *Wilcox Progressive Era*, June 15, 1961.

61. *Wilcox Progressive Era*, July 26, 1962.

62. C. T. Vivian, interview by author, July 9, 2000, Atlanta, Georgia.

63. Paulette Pettway interview.

64. *Birmingham News*, March 2, 1965; Priscilla Charley Washington interview by author, October 31, 1999, Detroit, Michigan.

65. *Birmingham News*, March 2, 1965.

66. *Birmingham News*, March 2, 1965.

67. *Mobile Register*, March 4, 1965.

68. *Birmingham News*, March 5, 1965.

69. *Birmingham News*, March 5, 1965.

70. Monroe Pettway interview.

71. Monroe Pettway interview.

72. Patricia Kemmons Pettway, interview by author, October 17, 1999, Camden, Alabama.

73. Reverend Charlie Pettway, interview by author, October 17, 1999, Camden, Alabama.

74. Report on Wilcox County by Gerald Olivari to SNCC office, May 18, 1965 in the Student Nonviolent Coordinating Committee Papers, Reel 17, Frame 43.

75. Report on Wilcox County by Gerald Olivari.

76. Edith Ervin Brooks, interview by author, August 20, 2001, Annemanie, Alabama.

77. Lawrence Parrish, interview by author, October 18, 1999, Camden, Alabama.

78. Parrish interview.

79. Priscilla Washington interview.

80. Lucy and James Ephraim, interview by author, June 16, 1999, Camden, Alabama.

81. Patricia Kemmons Pettway interview.

82. Alicia Parrish Foster, interview by author, October 21, 2001, Camden, Alabama.

83. Liddell, *A Place of Springs*, 115.

84. Patricia Kemmons Pettway interview.

85. *Mobile Register*, August 17, 1965.

86. *Mobile Register*, August 19, 1965.

87. *Mobile Register*, August 19, 1965.

88. *Wilcox Progressive Era*, September 2, 1965.

89. Report on Wilcox County by Gerald Olivari.

90. *Proposal from the Student Nonviolent Coordinating Committee for an Alabama Voter Education Project*, in the Papers of the SNCC, Reel 37, Frame 247.

91. *Proposal from the Student Nonviolent Coordinating Committee.*

92. Lizzie Miller Affidavit, December 16, 1965, SCLC Papers, Wilcox County Project, Box 148, Folder 17, Martin Luther King Jr. Center for Nonviolent Social Change, Atlanta, Georgia.

93. Lizzie Miller Affidavit.

94. Mary Charley Affidavit, December 29, 1965, SCLC Papers, Wilcox County Project, Box 148, Folder 17.

95. Leathia Foster Affidavit, November 19, 1965, SCLC Papers, Wilcox County Project, Box 148, Folder 17.

96. *Mobile Register*, August 19, 1965.

97. *Report of an Investigation—Wilcox County, Alabama—A Study of Social, Economic, and Educational Bankruptcy*, National Education Association Commission on Professional Rights and Responsibilities, June 1967, 25.

98. Lawrence Parrish interview.

99. Alicia Parrish Foster interview.

100 Foster interview.

101. Foster interview.

102. Letter from John Golden to the SNCC office in the papers of the SNCC, Reel 19, Series 76.

103. Letter from John Golden.

104. *Report of an Investigation*, 30.

105. Sheryl Threadgill interview.

106. Larry Threadgill, interview by author, May 6, 2001, Atlanta, Georgia.

107. Larry Threadgill interview.

108. Sheryl Threadgill interview.

109. Larry Threadgill interview.

110. Willie Ozzie Threadgill, interview by author, August 20, 2001, Annemanie, Alabama.

111. Willie Ozzie Threadgill interview.

112. Thomas Threadgill quoted in *First Tuesday: A Comparison of Camden, Alabama, and Belfast, Northern Ireland*. Produced by the BBC.

113. *Wilcox Progressive Era*, October 20, 1982.

114. Thomas Threadgill quoted in *First Tuesday*.

115. Sheryl Threadgill interview.

116. Ephraim interview.

117. *Jet Magazine*, February 10, 1966.

118. Larry Threadgill interview.

Chapter 6

1. David Colston, interview by author, May 22, 2001, Camden, Alabama.

2. Colston interview.

3. Colston interview.

4. Colston interview.

5. Alicia Foster Parrish, interview by author, October 21, 2001, Camden, Alabama.

6. Patricia Kemmons Pettway interview.

7. Bob Adelman, *Down Home* (New York: McGraw-Hill, 1972), 83.

8. Foster interview.

9. Foster interview.

10. Report by Gerald Olivari to the SNCC office, May 18, 1965, Student Nonviolent Coordinating Committee Papers, Reel 17, Frame 43.

11. Report by Gerald Olivari.

12. Lucy and James Ephraim, interview by author, October 17, 1999, Camden Alabama.

13. Ephraim interview.

14. Edith Ervin Brooks, interview by author, August 20, 2001, Annemanie, Alabama.

15. Brooks interview.

16. Jack Bloom, *Class, Race, and the Civil Rights Movement* (Bloomington: Indiana University Press, 1987), 155.

17. *Report of an Investigation—Wilcox County, Alabama—A Study of Social, Economic, and Educational Bankruptcy*, National Education Association Commission on Professional Rights and Responsibilities, June 1967, 25, 31.

18. Appendices to plaintiff's trial brief in *United States v. Wilcox County Board of Education*, Civil Action 3934-65, U.S. District Court, Southern District of Alabama. Quoted in National Education Association Report, 34.

19. National Education Association Report, 42.

20. National Education Association Report, 45.
21. National Education Association Report, 45.
22. Larry Nettles, interview by author, May 12, 2001, Findlay, Ohio.
23. Brenda Bussey Carson, interview by author, October 18, 1999, Camden, Alabama.
24. James Ephraim Jr., interview by author, November 6, 2000, Detroit, Michigan.
25. James Ephraim Jr., interview.
26. National Education Association Report, 17.
27. Paulette Pettway interview.
28. Paulette Pettway interview.
29. National Education Association Report, 19.
30. National Education Association Report, 54.
31. National Education Association Report, 54.
32. National Education Association Report, 19.
33. United States of America, *Appellant v. Wilcox County Board of Education, et al.*, Appellees No. 23982, United States Court of Appeals for the Fifth Circuit, 366 F. 2d 769; 1966 U.S. App. LEXIS 5073.
34. National Education Association Report, 20.
35. Sheryl Threadgill, interview by author, October 17, 1999, Camden, Alabama.
36. Sheryl Threadgill interview; National Education Association Report, 55.
37. Sheryl Threadgill interview.
38. Sheryl Threadgill interview; National Education Association Report, 55.
39. Sheryl Threadgill interview.
40. Adelman, *Down Home*, 159.
41. National Education Association Report, 55.
42. National Education Association Report, 55.
43. Sheryl Threadgill interview.
44. National Education Association Report, 55.
45. National Education Association Report, 57.
46. Adelman, *Down Home*, 84.
47. Adelman, *Down Home*, 84.
48. Larry Nettles interview.
49. Larry Nettles interview.
50. Larry Nettles interview.
51. Larry Nettles interview.
52. Larry Nettles interview.
53. Larry Nettles interview.
54. Larry Nettles interview.
55. Larry Nettles interview.
56. Larry Nettles interview.
57. Mattie Nettles, interview by author, October 17, 1999, Camden, Alabama.
58. Mattie Nettles interview.
59. Mattie Nettles interview.
60. Mattie Nettles interview.
61. Mattie Nettles to C. C. McKelvey, principal, September 28, 1967, Camden, Alabama, in the papers of Loretta Nettles Gordon, Cincinnati, Ohio.
62. Larry Nettles interview.
63. Larry Nettles interview.
64. Larry Nettles interview.
65. Larry Nettles interview.
66. Larry Nettles interview.
67. National Education Association Report, 57.
68. National Education Association Report, 67.

69. James Beardsley, interview by author, March 4, 2000, Boykin, Alabama.
70. McCarty, *The Reins of Power,* 170.
71. McCarty, *The Reins of Power,* 170.
72. McCarty, *The Reins of Power,* 171.
73. McCarty, *The Reins of Power,* 171.
74. *Wilcox Progressive Era,* May 20, 1971.
75. McCarty, *The Reins of Power,* 174.
76. Adelman, *Down Home,* p. 48
77. McCarty, *The Reins of Power,* 177.
78. McCarty, *The Reins of Power,* 175–76.
79. McCarty, *The Reins of Power,* 175.
80. Carson interview.
81. Carson interview.
82. Larry Threadgill, interview by author, May 6, 2001, Atlanta, Georgia.
83. Carson interview.
84. Carson interview.
85. Carson interview, and Larry Threadgill interview.
86. *Wilcox Progressive Era,* September 9, 1971.
87. *Wilcox Progressive Era,* September 9, 1971.
88. *Wilcox Progressive Era,* September 9, 1971.
89. *Wilcox Progressive Era,* September 9, 1971.
90. James Beardsley interview.
91. McCarty, *The Reins of Power,* 150.
92. McCarty, *The Reins of Power,* 150.
93. Larry Threadgill interview, and Carson interview.
94. *Wilcox Progressive Era,* September 9, 1971.
95. Larry Threadgill interview.
96. Carson interview.
97. Carson interview.
98. Carson interview.
99. Carson interview.
100. Carson interview.
101. Larry Threadgill interview.
102. Carson interview.
103. *Wilcox Progressive Era,* September 16, 1971.
104. *Wilcox Progressive Era,* September 16, 1971.
105. *Wilcox Progressive Era,* September 16, 1971
106. McCarty, *The Reins of Power,* 176–77.
107. McCarty, *The Reins of Power,* 181.
108. McCarty, *The Reins of Power,* 181.
109. *Wilcox Progressive Era,* October 3, 1971.
110. Carson interview.
111. *Wilcox Progressive Era,* October 14, 1971.
112. *Wilcox Progressive Era,* October 14, 1971.
113. *Wilcox Progressive Era,* October 14, 1971.
114. *Wilcox Progressive Era,* October 14, 1971.
115. *Wilcox Progressive Era,* October 14, 1971.
116. *Wilcox Progressive Era,* October 14, 1971.
117. *Wilcox Progressive Era,* October 28, 1971.
118. *Wilcox Progressive Era,* October 28, 1971.
119. *Wilcox Progressive Era,* October 28, 1971.

120. *Wilcox Progressive Era*, October 28, 1971.
121. Adelman, *Down Home*, 83.
122. Carson interview.
123. Carson interview.
124. Carson interview.
125. *Wilcox Progressive Era*, November 25, 1971; Larry Threadgill interview.
126. Carson interview.
127. Larry Threadgill interview.
128. *Wilcox Progressive Era*, March 9, 1972; quoted in McCarty, *The Reins of Power*, 198.

Chapter 7

1. Larry Threadgill, interview by author, May 6, 2001, Atlanta, Georgia.
2. *Wilcox Progressive Era*, August 24, 1972; see also McCarty, *The Reins of Power*, 202.
3. *Wilcox Progressive Era*, September 7, 1972; see also McCarty, *The Reins of Power*, 202.
4. Quoted from Memorandum of the United States filed with the U.S. District Court, Mobile, November 13, 1972, 44–45; quoted in McCarty, *The Reins of Power*, 203.
5. James A. Henretta, David Brody, and Lynn Dumenil, *America—A Concise History*, 2nd ed. (New York: Bedford/ St. Martin's, 2002), 875.
6. Henretta, Brody, and Dumenil, *America*, 875.
7. McCarty, *The Reins of Power*, 200.
8. McCarty, *The Reins of Power*, 201.
9. McCarty, *The Reins of Power*, 201.
10. McCarty, *The Reins of Power*, 204; see also *Wilcox Progressive Era*, April 5, 1973.
11. McCarty, *The Reins of Power*, 204.
12. James Beardsley, interview by author, March 4, 2000, Boykin, Alabama.
13. U.S. Court of Appeals for the Fifth Circuit; 494F .2d 575; 2 May 1974 U.S. App. LEXIS 8862; United States of America, *Plaintiff-Appellant, William P. Thompson et al., Intervenors-Appellants, Patsie Primm, as next friend of Bobbie Lewis Knight, et al., Intervenors, v. Wilcox County Board of Education et al., Defendants-Appellees*, 4.
14. U.S. Court of Appeals for the Fifth Circuit, 5.
15. U.S. Court of Appeals for the Fifth Circuit, 7.
16. *Report of an Investigation—Wilcox County, Alabama—A Study of Social, Economic, and Educational Bankruptcy*, National Education Association Commission on Professional Rights and Responsibilities, June 1967, 25, 66.
17. National Education Association Report, 66.
18. United States of America, by Nicholas de B. Katzenbach, attorney general, *Plaintiff, v. Wilcox County Board of Education et. Al.*, Defendants, Civ. A. No. 3934-65-H; U.S. District Court for the Southern District of Alabama, Southern Division; 382F. Supp, 1080; 12 July 1974 U.S. Dist. LEXIS 7629, 3.
19. U.S. Court of Appeals for the Fifth Circuit, 6.
20. U.S. District Court, No. 3934-65-H, July 12, 1974, 3.
21. U.S. Court of Appeals for the Fifth Circuit, 6.
22. U.S. Court of Appeals for the Fifth Circuit, 6.
23. U.S. Court of Appeals for the Fifth Circuit, 6.
24. U.S. Court of Appeals for the Fifth Circuit, 3.
25. U.S. Court of Appeals for the Fifth Circuit, 1.
26. U.S. Court of Appeals for the Fifth Circuit, 8.
27. McCarty, *The Reins of Power*, 219.
28. Hannah Bell Ramsey, interview by author, June 19, 2001, Washington, D.C.

29. Ramsey interview.
30. Ramsey interview.
31. S. C. Collier, interview by author, 17 June 1999, Camden, Alabama.
32. Clark Thomas, interview by author, June 12, 2001, Birmingham, Alabama.
33. Ralph Ervin, interview by author, October 18, 1999, Camden, Alabama.
34. Ervin interview.
35. Adelman, *Down Home*, 143.
36. Adelman, *Down Home*, 143.
37. Larry Threadgill interview.
38. Reverend Charley Pettway interview.
39. Adelman, *Down Home*, 157.
40. Adelman, *Down Home*, 132.
41. Adelman, *Down Home*, 92.
42. Adelman, *Down Home*, 144.
43. Reverend Lonnie Brown, interview by author, March 31, 2002, Alberta, Alabama.
44. Brown interview.
45. Brown interview.
46. James Thomas, interview by author, April 1, 2002, Camden, Alabama.
47. Thomas interview.
48. Thomas interview.
49. Brown interview.
50. *Wilcox Progressive Era*, May 2, 1974.
51. *Wilcox Progressive Era*, May 2, 1974.
52. *Wilcox Progressive Era*, May 2, 1974.
53. *Wilcox Progressive Era*, November 7, 1974.
54. J. L. Chestnut Jr. and Julia Cass, *Black in Selma—The Uncommon Life of J. L. Chestnut* (New York: Farrar, Straus & Giroux, 1990), 124.
55. Chestnut and Cass, *Black in Selma*, 124.
56. Chestnut and Cass, *Black in Selma*, 124.
57. Astoria Johnson, interview by author, April 1, 2002, Kimbro, Alabama.
58. Johnson interview.
59. Johnson interview.
60. Johnson interview.
61. Johnson interview.
62. Ervin interview.
63. Prince Arnold, interview by author, October 18, 1999, Camden, Alabama.
64. Arnold interview.
65. Arnold interview.
66. Arnold interview.
67. Arnold interview.
68. Arnold interview.
69. Ervin interview.
70. Arnold interview.
71. Arnold interview.
72. Ervin interview.
73. Ervin interview.
74. Ervin interview.
75. Ervin interview.
76. *Wilcox Progressive Era*, January 21, 1981.
77. *Wilcox Progressive Era*, January 21, 1981.
78. Johnson interview.
79. Johnson interview.

80. Johnson interview.
81. Johnson interview.
82. *Wilcox Progressive Era*, August 30, 1989.
83. *Wilcox Progressive Era*, August 30, 1989.
84. *Wilcox Progressive Era*, August 30, 1989.
85. *Wilcox Progressive Era*, August 30, 1989.
86. *Wilcox Progressive Era*, September 13, 1989.
87. *Wilcox Progressive Era*, September 13, 1989.
88. *Wilcox Progressive Era*, September 13, 1989.
89. Johnson interview.
90. Johnson interview.
91. *Wilcox Progressive Era*, September 13, 1989.
92. Chestnut and Cass, *Black in Selma*, 326.
93. Chestnut and Cass, *Black in Selma*, 327.
94. Chestnut and Cass, *Black in Selma*, 327.
95. Chestnut and Cass, *Black in Selma*, 328.
96. Brown interview.
97. Brown interview.
98. James Thomas interview.
99. Brown interview.
100. Thomas interview.
101. Brown interview.
102. Brown interview.
103. James Thomas interview.
104. *Wilcox Progressive Era*, October 5, 1983.
105. *Wilcox Progressive Era*, October 5, 1983.
106. *Wilcox Progressive Era*, October 12, 1983.
107. *Wilcox Progressive Era*, November 7, 1984.
108. Brown interview.
109. James Thomas interview.
110. James Thomas interview.
111. James Thomas interview.
112. Brown interview.
113. Brown interview.
114. Brown interview.
115. Brown interview.
116. Brown interview.
117. Brown interview.
118. Brown interview.
119. *Wilcox Progressive Era*, May 10, 1989.
120. *Wilcox Progressive Era*, May 10, 1989.
121. *Wilcox Progressive Era*, May 10, 1989.
122. *Wilcox Progressive Era*, May 10, 1989.
123. *Wilcox Progressive Era*, May 10, 1989.
124. *Wilcox Progressive Era*, June 7, 1989.
125. *Wilcox Progressive Era*, June 7, 1989.
126. *Wilcox Progressive Era*, July 4, 1990.
127. *Wilcox Progressive Era*, July 4, 1990.
128. *Wilcox Progressive Era*, October 1, 1980.
129. *Wilcox Progressive Era*, October 22, 1980.
130. *Wilcox Progressive Era*, September 10, 1980.
131. *Wilcox Progressive Era*, May 6, 1981.

132. *Wilcox Progressive Era*, May 6, 1981.
133. *Wilcox Progressive Era*, October 28, 1981.
134. *Wilcox Progressive Era*, October 28, 1981.
135. *Wilcox Progressive Era*, September 15, 1982.
136. *Wilcox Progressive Era*, September 15, 1982.
137. *Wilcox Progressive Era*, September 22, 1982.
138. *Wilcox Progressive Era*, September 22, 1982.
139. *Wilcox Progressive Era*, October 20, 1982.
140. Larry Threadgill interview.
141. Larry Threadgill interview.
142. Jessie Pettway, interview by author, May 23, 2001, Gee's Bend, Alabama.
143. Ramsey interview.
144. Thomas interview.
145. Long interview.
146. Brown interview.
147. John White, *Black Leadership, From Booker T. Washington to Jesse Jackson* (New York: Longman, 1990), 2.
148. White, *Black Leadership*, 192.
149. John Cell, *The Highest Stage of White Supremacy—The Origins of Segregation in South Africa and the American South* (Cambridge: Cambridge University Press, 1982), 252.
150. Quoted in White, *Black Leadership*, 2–3.
151. Manning Marable, *Black Leadership—Four Great American Leaders and the Struggle for Civil Rights* (New York: Penguin, 1999), xiii.
152. Marable, *Black Leadership*, xiii.
153. Sheryl Threadgill interview.
154. Marable, *Black Leadership*, 146.
155. White, *Black Leadership*, 2.
156. White, *Black Leadership*, 1.
157. Marble, *Black Leadership*, xv.

Chapter 8

1. Paul Washington, interview by author, May 11, 1999, Detroit, Michigan.
2. Clifford Crowder, interview by author, August 16, 1999, Washington, D.C.
3. Chestnut and Cass, *Black in Selma*, 350.
4. Chestnut and Cass, *Black in Selma*, 350.
5. Chestnut and Cass, *Black in Selma*, 356
6. Chestnut and Cass, *Black in Selma*, 356.
7. Chestnut and Cass, *Black in Selma*, 357.
8. Paulette Pettway, interview by author, October 20, 2001, Gee's Bend, Alabama.
9. Lawrence Parrish, interview by author, October 18, 1999, Camden, Alabama.
10. Lucy and James Ephraim, interview by author, June 16, 1999, Camden, Alabama.
11. Gwendolyn Bonham, interview by author, June 16, 1999, Camden, Alabama.
12. David Colston, interview by author, May 22, 2001, Camden, Alabama.
13. Crowder interview.
14. Mabel Walker Thornton, interview by author, August 19, 2000, Mobile, Alabama.
15. Tydie D. Pettway, interview by author, October 20, 2001, Gee's Bend, Alabama.
16. Colston interview.
17. Matthew Wilmer, interview by author, June 25, 2000, Philadelphia, Pennsylvania.
18. Chestnut and Cass, *Black in Selma*, 328.

19. Chestnut and Cass, *Black in Selma*, 328.

20. Wilmer interview.

21. Priscilla Washington interview.

22. Artur Davis, interview by author, August 30, 2002, Birmingham, Alabama.

23. *Birmingham News*, May 12, 2002.

24. *Birmingham News*, May 12, 2002.

25. Davis interview.

26. *Birmingham News*, May 12, 2002.

27. *Birmingham News*, May 12, 2002.

28. *Birmingham News*, May 12, 2002.

29. Andre Saulsberry, interview by author, April 1, 2002, Camden, Alabama.

30. Saulsberry interview.

31. Andre Saulsberry's Honors English Class, interview by author, Wilcox Central High School, April 1, 2002, Camden, Alabama.

32. Honors English Class interview.

33. Honors English Class interview.

34. Honors English Class interview.

35. Honors English Class interview.

36. Honors English Class interview.

37. Honors English Class interview.

38. Honors English Class interview.

39. *First Tuesday: A Comparison of Camden, Alabama, and Belfast, Northern Ireland.* Produced by the BBC.

40. *First Tuesday.*

41. *First Tuesday.*

42. *First Tuesday.*

43. Saulsberry interview.

44. James Thomas, interview by author, April 1, 2002, Camden, Alabama.

45. Thomas interview.

46. *Wilcox Progressive Era*, June 6, 1990.

47. *Wilcox Progressive Era*, June 6, 1990.

48. Astoria Johnson, interview by author, April 1, 2002, Kimbro, Alabama.

49. Johnson interview.

50. Sheryl Threadgill, interview by author, October 17, 1999, Camden, Alabama.

51. Reverend Charlie Pettway, interview by author, October 17, 1999, Camden, Alabama.

52. Clark Thomas, interview by author, Birmingham, Alabama, June 12, 2001.

53. Clyde Woods, *Development Arrested: The Blues and Plantation Power in the Mississippi Delta* (New York: Verso, 1998), 4.

54. Woods, *Development Arrested*, 4.

55. Woods, *Development Arrested*, 6.

56. Woods, *Development Arrested*, 7.

57. Grubbs, *Cry from the Cotton*, 15.

58. Grubbs, *Cry from the Cotton*, 16.

59. Grubbs, *Cry from the Cotton*, 26.

60. Malcolm Cain, interview by author, April 1, 2002, Camden, Alabama.

61. Chestnut and Cass, *Black in Selma*, 330.

62. Cain interview.

63. *Birmingham News*, February 7, 2002.

64. *Birmingham News*, February 7, 2002.

65. *Birmingham News*, February 11, 2002.

66. Cain interview.

67. William Julius Wilson, *When Work Disappears: The World of the New Urban Poor* (New York: Knopf, 1996), 73.

68. William Julius Wilson, *The Truly Disadvantaged: The Inner City, The Underclass, and Public Policy* (Chicago: University of Chicago Press, 1987), 57.

69. Grubbs, *Cry from the Cotton*, 26.

70. James Beardsley, interview by author, March 4, 2000, Boykin, Alabama.

71. Wilson, *When Work Disappears*, 75.

72. Adelman, *Down Home*, 158.

73. Bessye Ramsey Neal, interview by author, August 15, 1999, Washington, D.C.

74. Larry Threadgill, interview by author, May 6, 2001, Atlanta, Georgia.

75. Colston interview.

76. *First Tuesday*.

77. *First Tuesday*.

78. Adelman, *Down Home*, 79.

79. Adelman, *Down Home*, 86.

80. *60 Minutes II*, "The Gee's Bend Ferry Project." Vicki Mabry reporting.

81. *First Tuesday*.

82. *First Tuesday*.

83. Adelman, *Down Home*, 100.

84. *First Tuesday*.

85. Alabama State Legislature, Report of the Black Belt Infrastructure Joint Legislative Committee for the Year 2000, authorized by HJR44, 1.

86. Report of the Black Belt Infrastructure Joint Legislative Committee, 3.

87. Report of the Black Belt Infrastructure Joint Legislative Committee, 5.

88. Report of the Black Belt Infrastructure Joint Legislative Committee, 4.

89. Report of the Black Belt Infrastructure Joint Legislative Committee, 4.

90. Southern Rural Black Women's Initiative for Economic and Social Justice; Briefing Summary for the Trustees of the Ford Foundation, March 27, 2002, 4.

91. Southern Rural Black Women's Initiative, 4.

92. Davis interview.

93. Davis interview.

94. Davis interview.

95. Davis interview.

96. *First Tuesday*.

97. James Forman, *The Making of Black Revolutionaries* (Washington, D.C.: Open Hand Publishing, Inc., 1985), 545.

98. Forman, *The Making of Black Revolutionaries*, 547.

99. Marable, *Black Leadership*, 18.

100. Randall Robinson, *The Debt: What America Owes to Blacks* (New York: Penguin Putnam, 2001), 206.

101. Robinson, *The Debt*, 207.

102. Robinson, *The Debt*, 201.

103. Sheryl Threadgill interview.

104. Brenda Bussey Carson, interview by author, October 18, 1999, Camden, Alabama.

105. Carson interview.

106. Joseph and Marie Anderson, interview by author, October 17, 1999, Camden, Alabama.

Index

AAA. *See* Agricultural Adjustment
  Administration
Abbot, Robert, 32
Abercrombie, Ruby, 26, 29–30
Abner, Nellie Williams, 18, 21, 23, 31,
  93–94
accreditation issues, 55, 240, 270
African Americans: and carpetbaggers,
  11; categories of, ix–x; out-migration
  of, 31–33; population, in Wilcox
  County, xvi, 8, 32, 173, 289; during
  Reconstruction, 9–13; self-image of,
  17, 59–61; views of, 9, 79
Agricultural Adjustment Act, 70–72
Agricultural Adjustment
  Administration (AAA), 71, 297
Alabama: constitutional convention,
  14–15; creation of, 1; educational
  system, 37–38
Alabama Democratic Conference, 250
Alabama Voter Education Project, 152
Albany, GA, 150
Albert, Cleve, 109, 114–15
Albritton, F. Reg: and County
  Commission, 258; and elections,

272–73; and schools, 215, 223; as
  sheriff, 225, 227; and voter
  registration efforts, 164
Allen, Walter, 227
Anderson, Joseph, 20, 24, 26, 311–12
Anderson, Marie, 311–12
Ann, 5
Antioch Baptist Church: and
  integration of schools, 196, 198–99,
  204–5, 225–26; and voter
  registration efforts, 163, 184–85
Arlington Mission School, 56
Arnold, Cato, 7
Arnold, Prince, 253–56, 261, 272
Arter, John T., 56

Bailey, Alonzo, 29
Bailey, Annie, 311
Bailey v. Alabama, 29
Baker, Ray Stannard, 29
Baldwin, James, 276–77
Bartley, Numan, 127–28
Beals, Melba Patillo, 205
Beardsley, James, 211, 238, 301
Bennett, Fred, 68–69

Bethune, Mary McCleod, 86
Billingsley, Orzell, 250
Birmingham, AL: civil rights campaign in, 150–51; SCHW conference at, 99–100
Birth of a Nation, 89–90
Black Belt counties, 1
Black Belt Improvement Society, 43
Black Belt Infrastructure Joint Legislative Committee, 304–5
Black Power movement, 216, 280, 308
Blair, Henry, 38
Blair Bill, 38–39
Bloody Sunday, 165
Boggan, Jerry, 294
boll weevil, 67–69
Bond, Julian, 151–52
Bonham, Gwendolyn Bridges, 93, 102, 286
Bonham, Jack, 90–91, 275
Bonner, Miller, 113
Bowen, Jennie, 5
boycotts: economic, 94, 127, 224; student, 167–69, 172–73, 189–90, 214–33
Boykin High School, 153
Bradford, Ira, 270
Brooks, Edith Ervin, 167–68, 193
Brown, Lonnie: background of, 135–37; and politics, 246–48; and schools, 263–64, 266–69, 275; and voter registration efforts, 138–39, 154, 156–59
Brownell, Herbert, 120
Brown v. Board of Education, 126–27
Burford, Peyton, Jr., 303

Cain, Malcolm, 298–300
Calhoun, Walter J., 246
Camden (town), xiv, 2
Camden Academy: campus of, 18–19; card class, 85; Carson on, 220; conditions at, 224; cost of civil rights

movement to, xviii, 124, 180–81; establishment of, 53–55; extracurricular activities at, 106–7; financial issues at, 57–58; fund-raising activities at, 87–88; King at, 163; school song, 54–55; and student boycott, 167–70, 214–33; Wilson and, xiv
Camden Theatre, 89
Camp Camden, 230–31
Canton Bend Mission School, 55, 58
Carmichael, James, 4–5
carpetbaggers, 10–11
cars, owned by African Americans, 121–22
Carson, Brenda Bussey, 215, 311; background of, 219–21; and leadership, 279–80; on segregation, 195; and student boycott, 224–25, 229, 231–32
Carstarphen, Linda, 291
Carter, Cato, 5
Cawthorn, Archibald, 5
Cell, John, 276
Charley, Mary, 176
Chestnut, J. L., 250, 262, 272, 285, 287, 298–99
CIO. *See* Congress of Industrial Organizations
citizenship classes, 155, 166
civil rights activists, xvii; costs to, 179; courage of, 139, 166–67, 173; reputation of, 159, 166, 173, 192–93, 220; working with, 279
Civil Rights Act of 1957, 120
Civil Rights Commission, 131–32, 161–62
civil rights movement: aftermath of, 235–81; cost of, xvii–xviii, 176; integration of schools, 187–233; voter registration efforts, 135–86
Civil War, 6; aftermath of, 7–8, 12–13
Clanton, James H., 47

Clark, Jim, 143–44, 163
class conflict: among African
    Americans, 190–93; among whites,
    213–14. *See also* middle class,
    African-American
classical education, 40–42, 65
Cloud, Peter, 49, 57
Collier, S. C., 102, 242
Collins, Ruth Bonner, 102, 105–6, 108,
    110
Colston, David, Jr., 187–88, 286, 302
Colston, David, Sr., 184–86
Communist Party, 94–97
Compromise of 1820, 1
Congress of Industrial Organizations
    (CIO), 100–101
Connor, Eugene "Bull," 100, 150–151
Conyers, John, 309
Cook, Jo, 6
Cooper, Roland, 249
Cooper, Rudolph, 190
cotton: boll weevil and, 67–69; market
    for, 71; production of, 2
Cotton, Ella Earls, 51, 55–56, 58,
    60–61, 63–64
Cotton, J. N., 69
country life, education for, 39–40
Coy, student from, 204–6, 210
Crow, Harold, 260
Crowder, Clifford, 133, 284, 286
Curl, Hollis, 16, 271, 302–3

Dallas County Voters League, 143
Davis, Artur, 287–88, 306–7
Dees, D. F., 227
Dees, Tracey, 292
Democratic Party, 97, 113, 249; in
    nineteenth century, 9–10, 13
despair: contemporary, 300–302; after
    movement, 273–74; sharecropping
    and, 28
Diamond, Dion, 142
Dixiecrats, 113–14

Dixon, R. E., 80
Doar, John, 157
Dox, Peter, 36–37
DuBois, W. E. B., 40
Dunn, G. W., 2

economic issues: Abner on, 94; activism
    and, 172; current status, 286–88,
    296–97; and education, 265–66,
    268–70, 275; evictions, 175–77;
    Great Depression, 67–98; and
    violence, 148; White and, 123–24.
    See also poverty
Edmund Pettus Bridge, xv, 165
education, xvi; for country life, 39–40;
    current status of, 290–93, 298–300;
    Depression and, 83–84; desire for,
    35–36; expenditures on, county,
    43–45; funding, attendance statistics
    and, 240–41; in Gee's Bend, 78–79;
    industrial versus liberal, 40–43; after
    integration, 236–44; integration of
    schools, xviii, 126, 187–233, 239–40;
    missionaries and, 35–66; after
    movement, 263–70; ninteenth-
    century reform movement for, 39;
    organizational issues in, 38, 298–300;
    sharecropping and, 26; student
    boycotts, 167–69; white attitude
    toward, 37
Edwards, Jack, 175
Edwards, William, 247
Edwards, William J.: on African-
    American self-esteem, 17; on
    curriculum debate, 40–41, 43; on
    housing, 27; on racial justice, 62–63;
    on Saturday junkets, 30
Eggleston, Ralph, 167–69
Eisenhower, Dwight D., 120, 202
Englehardt, Sam, 128–29
Ephraim, James, Jr., 170–71, 195
Ephraim, James, Sr., 20, 26, 171–72,
    192–93, 263

Ephraim, Lucy, 19–20, 23, 64, 192–93, 286
Ervin, Ferdinand S., 193, 243
Ervin, Ralph, 254, 256–57
extracurricular activities: at Camden Academy, 106–7; Nettles on, 207

Farm Security Administration (FSA), and Gee's Bend, xvii, 74, 78–79
fear, African-American, 23–24; Collins on, 105; Herndon on, 95–96; Threadgill on, 200–201
Fearn, Kayte Marsh, 19, 64, 86–87
federal government: African Americans and, 114; and agriculture, 71, 297–98; Civil Rights Act, 120; Civil Rights Commission, 131–32, 161–62; criticism of, 83; and Gee's Bend, xvii; Hayes and, 12; and integration of schools, 197, 216–17; New Deal, 70–72, 77–83, 99–100; resentment of, 81; and voter registration inquiries, 161–62, 174
Fendley, George, 213–14
ferry service, to Gee's Bend, xvii, 73
First Reconstruction Act, 9
Fish, Hamilton, 94
Fitch, Elijah, 37
Forman, James, 142–43, 307–8
Foster, Alicia Parrish, 172, 177–78, 189
Foster, Leathia, 176–77
Franklin, Vincent P., 35–36
fraud, electoral, 246–48, 270–72, 294
Freedmen's Bureau, 37
Freedom Rides, 142
Freedom Summer, 162
FSA. See Farm Security Administration

Gaines, Lloyd, 101
Gaye, Marvin, 216
Gee, Joseph, 74
Gee's Bend, xvii; culture of, 73–74, 145–46, 153; current status of,
285–86; formation of, 74–76; Great Depression and, 67–98; isolation of, 73; and repossession, 76–77, 137; and voter registration efforts, 137–41, 153
generational conflict, 170–72
George W. Watts Elementary School, 299–300
Giffen, J. Kelley, 60
Gildersleeve, James, 143–45, 158
Gilmore, Wyman, 285
Golden, John, 179
Gomillion, C. G., 250
Gordon, Albert, 170, 217–18, 238
Gordon, Donna, 201
Grady, Henry, 15
Graves, John, 74
Great Depression, 67–98
Great Migration, 31–33
Great Society, 194
Green, Winifred, 305
Griffith, D. W., 89–90
Griggs, Marguerite Wilson, 18–19
Grubbs, Donald, 72, 297, 301
guns: King on, 186; Lafayette and, 144–45, 148

Hale, Percy Luke, 257
Hall, Peter, 250
Hand, W. Brevard, 239–40, 271
Hanson, Bill, 142
Harrell, Daniel, 154–56, 167
Harris, Clarice, 291–92
Hayes, Rutherford B., 12
health issues: current status, 288; in Gee's Bend, 78–81; Robinson Memorial Hospital, 51; segregation and, 195; sharecropping and, 27; slavery and, 4
Henderson, Bain, 284–85
Henderson, Dale, 213
Henderson, Fred, 128
Henderson, J. Bruce, 128–29

Henderson, Sarah, 176
Henderson, William, 10–11; and
    Wallace, 24, 45–48; white
    supremacists and, 50–51
Herndon, Angelo, 95–97
Hicks, Helen, 172
Hill, Lister, 165
Hill, Nathaniel, 181
Hilliard, Earl, 306
Hobbs, James E., 159, 161, 220, 224;
    and student boycott, 168–69,
    189–90, 214–15, 218, 229–30
Hobbs, Martha, 5
Holtzclaw, W. H. T., 14
Hoover, Herbert, 70
housing, sharecropping and, 26–27
Houston, Charles Hamilton, 98, 101
Hoyt, A. J., 28
Huckabee, Kathy, 260
Hughes, Charles Evans, 29

industrial education, 40–42
integration of schools, 187–233; *Brown
    v. Board of Education* and, 126; cost
    of, xviii; methods of, 239–40
Interreligious Foundation for
    Community Organization, 307
Irby, Donnie, 246
Ivey, B. N., 78, 81–82

Jackson, Jimmie Lee, 164
Jeffersonian Democrats, 14
Jenkins, Lummie: and African-
    American vote, 246; and band,
    22–23; and Brown, 158–59; and
    integration of schools, 169, 196,
    206–7; and Johnson, 251–52; and
    King, 163; and Reaves, 187;
    reputation of, 31, 143–44; and voter
    registration efforts, 164–66
John, 5
Johns, Major, 155
Johnson, Andrew, 9

Johnson, Astoria Mason, 252–53,
    258–61, 294
Johnson, Bobby Jo, 250–55, 257–61,
    263, 280, 294–95
Johnson, C. H., 60–61, 63
Johnson, Charles S., 74, 122
Johnson, Lyndon B., xv, 165, 173, 194
Johnson, Roy, 272
Johnson, Tillie, 50
Jones, Cornelius J., 309
Jones, J. Paul, 80–81
Jones, William, 168–69

Katzenbach, Nicholas, 174
Kelly, Guy: background of, 217; and
    civil rights movement, 242–43; and
    integration, 236–38; and student
    boycott, 214, 217–18, 223–24,
    228–30
Kemmons, principal, 170–71
Kennedy, John F., 142, 194
Kennedy, Renwick, 73
Kimbro, Essie Mae, 102
King, Martin Luther, Jr.: and Alabama,
    163; assassination of, 209–10; and
    Birmingham, 150–51; in Camden,
    163; on nonviolence, 185–86; and
    Selma-to-Montgomery march, xv
Knoxville College, 45, 58–59

Lafayette, Bernard: attack on, 149–50;
    background of, 141–42; and voter
    registration efforts, 138–46, 148
law enforcement, African Americans
    in, 283–84
lawyers, African-American, reputation
    of, 101
leadership, African-American, 272–73,
    275–81
Lewis, John, 164
Lewis, Rufus, 143–44, 250
Lewis, Walter, 94
liberal education, 40–42, 65

Liddell, Viola Goode: on cars, 121; on change, 134; on civil rights activists, 159; on integration, 126; on race relations, 15, 102–3; on student boycotts, 173
lignite, 305
Logan, Rayford, 12
Long, Worth, 151–53, 274
Louis, Joe, 88–89
Lowe, Bruce, 213
Luker, Clinton, 225, 227

Macintosh, storekeeper, 91
malaria, 80–81
Malcolm X, 191–92
Manis, Andrew, 148
Marable, Manning, 277–78
Marsh, Clinton, 21–23
Marsh, T. P., Jr., 21
Marsh, T. P., Sr., 21–23, 86–87, 112
Martin, Jonah, 91–93
Martin, Louis, 250
Martin, William, 104–5
Mason, Henrietta, 48
Masonic Hall, Wilcox, 2
May Day celebrations, 106–7
McBride, Lester, 293–94
McCarthy, Charles, 246
McCarty, Clinton, 16
McCord, Marcus, 291
McCulloch, J. S., 45, 48, 57–58
McDew, Chuck, 142
McDuffie, Emmanuel, 17
McKelvey, C. C., 209
McLaurin, Melton, 16–17
McLeod, Donnie, 260
middle class, African-American, ix–x; conditions of, xiv; costs of movement and, 177; and education, 54; Lafayette on, 145–46; and leadership, 278; Long on, 154; and movement, 188–89; and politics, 274; and SCLC-SNCC split, 192; sheltering of

children, 17–20, 105, 190–91; and student boycott, 228; Threadgill on, 190; and voting rights, 112
Midway Mission School, 53
Miller, Lizzie, 176
Miller's Ferry Mission School, 48–52
Minerva, 16
Mingo, Eddie, 275
missionaries, 35–66; and racism, 60–61; reputation of, 52, 63–64; treatment of, 37
Missouri ex rel Gaines v. Canada, 101
Mitchell, Bonnie, 202
Moody, Louise, 222
moral instruction: at Camden Academy, 88; and Knoxville College, 59; SNCC and, 192–93
Morehouse College, 183, 235
Morgan, John Tyler, 38
Moses, Bob, 142
mothers' meeting, Miller's Ferry School, 52
movie theaters, 89–90, 123

Nancy, 5
National Association for the Advancement of Colored People (NAACP), 72–73, 98, 101, 111, 113; Wilcox County chapter, 111–12
National Democratic Party of Alabama (NDPA), 249–50
National Education Association (NEA), 194, 201, 211, 239
National Youth Administration (NYA), 86
Neal, Bessye Ramsey, 125, 302
Nettles, Larry, 125–26, 195; and integration of schools, 204–11
Nettles, Mattie, 204, 206–10; background of, 207–8
Nettles, Pat, 245
New Deal, 70–72; consequences of, 99–100; and Gee's Bend, 77–83

New Frontier, 194
Newman, 5
Nixon, Richard M., 236–37
nonviolence, 185–86; Lafayette and,
144–45, 148
NYA. *See* National Youth
Administration

Olivari, Gerald, 167, 175, 192
Olympics, 114–19
out-migration, African-American,
31–33, 86–87; boll weevil and,
68–69; current status of, 289

Pan-Africanism, 153
Parrish, Lawrence, 23, 177–79, 286;
background of, 189–90; and student
boycott, 169, 218
"A Parting Word" (Wilson), 62
Patterson, Robert, 127
Patton, R. M., 9
peonage, 28–30
Peoples, A. C., 86, 106, 115–16, 118
Perryman, James, 246
Pettway (family), 146–48, 279
Pettway, Charles, 166, 245, 295
Pettway, Danita, 291–92
Pettway, Eddie, 135
Pettway, Jessie Monroe, 274
Pettway, Jo Celeste, 302, 307
Pettway, Mark, 74
Pettway, Monroe, 110, 279; and
integration of schools, 196; and
voter registration efforts, 137–38,
140–41, 146, 165–66
Pettway, Pat Kemmons, 166, 170–71,
190
Pettway, Paulette, 286; on integration
of schools, 196–97; on voter
registration efforts, 146–47, 154,
163
Pettway, Roman, Jr., 197
Pettway, Tydie D., 135, 146, 154, 286

Phillippi, Frank, 302
Phillippi, Virginia, 303–4
Phillips, Cabell, 119–20
Pierce, Robert, 79, 82–83
Pine Hill Consolidated School, 222,
228, 236
Pitts, McLean, 212
planned community, in Gee's Bend,
77–83
plantations, 1–33
Pleasant Grove Baptist Church, 163
Plessy, Homer, 12–13
Plessy v. Ferguson, 12–13
political issues: after Civil War, 11–13;
current status of, 306–7;
expectations versus reality, 261–62;
after movement, 244–63, 270–81;
redistricting, 161
Pompey, William, 260–61, 270
Populism, 14
Possum Bend, 90–91
poverty, xvi; Carson on, 220; current
status of, 288; Foster on, 191; lack of
study of, ix–x; New Deal and, 70–72,
77–83, 99–100; and violence, 148;
after World War II, 125–26
Prairie Bluff Mission, 48
Prairie Mission School, 53
Presbyterian Church: and education,
xvi, 35–66; and sharecropping,
27–28; and voter registration efforts,
159–60
President's Committee on Civil Rights,
112
principals: dissension among, 298–99;
and student boycott, 229–30
Pritchett, landowner, 29–30
Pritchett, Laurie, 150
punishment: familial, 147–48; of slaves,
4–5. *See also* violence

race relations: Liddell on, 15, 102–3;
after Reconstruction, 15–17

racial etiquette: Bonham on, 90;
current status of, 302–3; education
and, 36; elements of, 121; Johnson
and, 252; missionaries and, 63;
Parrish and, 178–79; after
Reconstruction, 17; and voter
intimidation, 245; World War II
and, 103, 120–23
racial uplift, 56, 58–59
racism: coping strategies for, 61;
Crowder on, 286; persistence of,
xviii–xix, 302–4; Ramsey on, 274;
teachers and, 60–61
Radical Republicans, 9–10, 13
Ramsey, Hannah Bell, 241–42, 274
Randolph, A. Philip, 113
Ratcliffe, Irby, 227
Ray, Dolores, 203
Reaves, James T., 185, 187
Reconstruction, 8–13; aftermath of,
14–20
Reese, James Foster, 129–33, 159–61
religion: and education, 54, 269–70;
Johnson and, 294–95; and
leadership, 277–78; and reparations,
307–8; Threadgill and, 183–84; and
voter registration efforts, 139, 148
reparations, 307–9
Republican Party, 120
resentment, African-American: lack of
acknowledgement of, 191; Liddell
on, 103; of New Deal, 81; after
Reconstruction, 17, 20–21; slavery
and, 5
resistance, African-American: Nettles
and, 208–9; after Reconstruction,
20–24; slavery and, 5; Young and,
81–82
Rhodes, Edna Bonner, 84–86, 89, 92
Robinson, James, 246
Robinson Memorial Hospital, 51
Rogers, Robert, 272
Roosevelt, Eleanor, 100

Roosevelt, Franklin Delano, 70–72, 97
Rubin, Morton, 25–26, 120–21
rural African Americans: current status
of, 283–313; development of
sharecropping and, 24–31; lack of
study of, ix–x, 296–97; and voter
registration efforts, 141

Sadler, Tommy, 302
Saturday junkets, 30–31
Saulsberry, Andre, 290
Saunders, landowner, 47
Schmeling, Max, 88
SCHW. See Southern Conference for
Human Welfare
SCLC. See Southern Christian
Leadership Conference
Scott, Erskine, 199
segregation: Bonner and, 113; current
status of, 302–4; Ephraim on, 286;
in-school, 202–3; Pettway on, 292;
after Reconstruction, 17; SCHW
conference and, 99–100; views of,
119; during World War II, 103–104
self-help, African-American, 56–57,
87–88, 153
Selma, AL, xiv; Lafayette and, 142–43;
and voter registration efforts, 162–63
Selma-to-Montgomery march, xv, 165
Seward, Herbert, 110
sexism, Walker and, 117
Shamburg, Annie, 80
sharecroppers, xvi; evictions of, 175–77,
245; protest by, 94–95
sharecropping: development of, 24–31;
subsidies and, 71–72
sheriff, office of, importance of, 143–44,
253–54
Sherrod, Charles, 142
Shores, Arthur, 98, 250
Shuttlesworth, Fred, 148, 150
Simpkins, Ronnie, 303
Simpson, Ransom O., 42

Sixteenth Street Baptist Church
bombing, 151–52
slavery, 1–33; conditions of, 3–4;
Threadgill on, 182–83
Smith, E. K., 25, 27, 53–54
Smith, Frank, 242–43, 263
Smith, Nora, 107–10, 114–19
Smith v. Allwright, 111
SNCC. See Student Nonviolent
Coordinating Committee
Snow Hill Institute, 40–43
social issues: current status of, 300–301.
See also class conflict; racial etiquette
Southern Association of Colleges and
Secondary Schools, 55
Southern Christian Leadership
Conference (SCLC), xv; in Albany,
GA, 150; leadership style of, 279;
and local supporters, 311–12; split
with SNCC, 167, 191–92; and
student boycotts, 170
Southern Conference for Human
Welfare (SCHW), 99–100, 111–12
Southern Rural Black Women's
Initiative, 305
Sparkman, John, 111, 165
sports, 65; Joe Louis, 88–89; women's
track and field, 107–10, 114–19
States' Rights Party, 113–14
Steele, Hattie Irene, 83–84, 112
Stokes, Emma, 59
Student Nonviolent Coordinating
Committee (SNCC), 138; Alabama
Voter Education Project, 152;
leadership style of, 279; split with
SCLC, 167, 191–92; and student
boycotts, 170
students: boycotts by, 167–69, 172–73,
189–90, 214–33; of Camden
Academy, 54–55; on future, 290–93;
after integration, 241–42; and
leadership, 279–80; position of,
194–96

suffrage: in nineteenth century, 9;
preparation for, 64–65; after
Reconstruction, 14–20. See also voter
registration efforts
Sumner, Charles, 11–12

Tait, James A., 4
Tattun, F. D., 83
teachers: and civil rights activists, 154;
after Civil War, 46–47; costs to, 189,
228–29, 242–44; and integration of
schools, 202, 205–6, 211; racism
and, 60–61; reinstatement of, 241;
reorganization of, 267–68; and
student boycott, 169–70, 189–90,
217, 228–29; white resistance and,
177
Tennessee State University, 109
Thomas, Clark, 242, 295
Thomas, James, 247–48, 264–67, 269,
274, 293–94
Thomas, K. P., 263
Thomas, Nancy, 112
Thompson, Benjamin, 263
Thornton, Mabel Walker, 88, 106–10,
114–19, 286
Threadgill, Larry, 172, 181–82, 245,
302; background of, 218–19; later
career of, 235; and leadership,
279–80; and politics, 272–73; and
student boycott, 218, 221–22,
224–26, 231–32
Threadgill, Obediah, 182–83
Threadgill, Sheryl, 160, 310–11; and
integration of schools, 198–204; on
Thomas, 277–78
Threadgill, Thomas, 235, 273;
background of, 182–84; and Colston,
185–86; on despair, 301; and
integration of schools, 198–99, 201,
203–4; and leadership, 277–78; and
politics, 272–73; and Reese, 160–61;
and student boycott, 215, 218, 222,

229; on unsupportive teachers, 190; on voter intimidation, 244; and Washington, 170; white resistance and, 180–82

Threadgill, Willie, 182

Thurmond, Strom, 113

Tom, 5

Truman, Harry S, 112–14

Tumblin, Odell, 265–67, 269–70

Tuskegee University, 108–9

underclass, African-American, x

unemployment, current status of, 300–301

Union soldiers, reactions to, 6–7

United Daughters of the Confederacy, 33

United Nations, 113

University of Missouri, 101

Vandergraff, A. S., 75–76

Vandergraff, Hargrove, 76

veterans, African-American, 110–11; attacks on, 112; and voter registration efforts, 137, 166, 183, 187

violence: Colston murder, 184–86; defensive strategies for, 204; in Depression, 90–94; familial, 147–48; and integration of schools, 200–201, 225; Miller's Ferry Mission School arson, 49–50; Pettway on, 197; and political change, 260–61; Sixteenth Street Baptist Church bombing, 151–52; on veterans, 112; and voter registration efforts, 149–50, 157–58, 160; during World War II, 104–5. *See also* punishment

Vivan, C. T., 162

vocational education, 40–42

Volunteers in Service to America (VISTA), 211

voter registration efforts, xvi, 135–86; aftermath of, 244–45; inquiries into, 161–62; Reese and, 129–33; statistics on, 177; after World War II, 111

voter reidentification ordinance, 271

Voting Rights Act, xviii, 173; effects of, 173–77

Walker, Alice, 17

Walker, Juanita, 114–16, 118

Wallace, Eliza B.: background of, 46; and Bible School, 58; and education, 45–48; and living conditions, 24–27

Wallace, George, xv, 156

Wallace, Henry A., 70–71

Ward, Morris, 238–39

Washington, Booker T., 29, 35, 40

Washington, Harold, 278

Washington, Paul, 91, 93, 104–5, 284

Washington, Priscilla Charley, 170, 287

WCCPL. *See* Wilcox County Civic and Progressive League

White, Geraldine Pettway, 123–24, 135

White, John, 276, 278

White Citizens' Council, 127–28

whites: and African-American political officials, 257; beliefs of, 119; and carpetbaggers, 10–11; and education, 37; insecurity of, 6–7, 120–21, 123–24, 133; and New Deal, 71–72; and out-migration, 69–70; as teachers, 47; and Truman, 112; withdrawal from public school system, 212–14, 232–33, 236

white supremacist activity: Brown on, 248; after *Brown v. Board of Education*, 126; after civil rights movement, xvii–xviii; Colston on, 188; control mechanisms of, 4–6; in Depression, 90–94; Ephraim on, 171; and integration of schools, 197–98, 206–7, 213, 223–24; and King, 209–10; and missionary education,

36, 49–50, 60–61, 63; and political change, 245–49, 258–61; after Reconstruction, 14–20, 25–26; Saulsberry on, 292–93; and sharecropping, 29–30; Sixteenth Street Baptist Church bombing, 151–52; after slavery, 7–9; Threadgill on, 222; and voter registration efforts, 139, 156–58, 173–77, 179–80, 184–86; after World War II, 127–29
Wickersham, M. D., 28
Wilcox Academy, 212–14, 292
Wilcox Central High School, 267, 269–70
Wilcox County, AL, x, xv; county commission, 257–58, 261–62; current status of, 283–313; demographics of, xvi, 8, 32, 173, 271, 289; early history of, 1–33; future of, 304–5; isolation of, xix; landscape of, 2–3; reputation of, 143–44, 152–53; returning to, 291; World War II and, 99–134
Wilcox County Board of Education, 197–98
Wilcox County Civic and Progressive League (WCCPL), 137–38, 145
Wilcox County Courthouse, 6, 30–31, 130–33, 140–41, 284
Wilcox County Democratic Executive Committee, 13
Wilcox County High School, 195, 198–99, 217–18, 236

Wilcox County Teachers Association, 194, 211
Wilcox Education Foundation, 212–13
Williams, Ebbie, 170
Wilmer, Gertrude, 123, 133
Wilmer, Matthew, 123, 286–87
Wilson, Gertrude, 88
Wilson, William Garrette, 64
Wilson, William Green, xiii–xiv; and band, 21; and Camden Academy, 54, 61; and fund-raising activities, 87–88
Wilson, William Julius, 300–301
women: and cars, 122; current status of, 305; mothers' meeting, 52; salaries of, 58; and voter registration efforts, 139; work of, 147
Women's General Missionary Society, 53
Woods, Clyde, 296–97
Woodward, Isaac, 112
World War I, 62–63
World War II, 99–134

Yellow Front Store, 133
"You'll Git Dar after While" (Wilson), xiii–xiv
Young, Andrew, 155–56, 163
Young, Horace, 121–22
Young, Johnnie, 170, 220
Yount, Earl Lee, 81–82
youth. See students

Zellner, Bob, 142

~

About the Author

Cynthia Griggs Fleming is associate professor of history at the University of Tennessee, Knoxville. She has written extensively on the civil rights movement of the 1960s and is the author of *Soon We Will Not Cry: The Liberation of Ruby Doris Smith Robinson.*